PENSIONS POCKET BOOK
2012

GW00493845

ECONOMIC AND FINANCIAL PUBLISHING
IN ASSOCIATION WITH

PENSIONS POCKET BOOK
2012 EDITION

© Copyright and database rights:
  Economic and Financial Publishing Ltd 2011, 2012

All rights reserved. This publication is protected by copyright. No part of it may be reproduced, stored in a retrieval system, or transmitted, in any form or by any means, electronic, mechanical, photocopying, recording or otherwise, without the prior permission of the publishers and copyright owners.

ISBN: 978-0-9567104-1-3

Produced and published by:

  Economic and Financial Publishing Ltd ● 1, Ivory Square
    ● Plantation Wharf ● London SW11 3UF ● United Kingdom
      Tel: (020) 7326 8350 ● Fax: (020) 7326 8351

Comments and suggestions for future editions of this pocket book are welcomed. Please contact: Editor, Pensions Pocket Book, Economic and Financial Publishing Ltd at the above address.

Whilst every effort has been made in the preparation of this book to ensure accuracy of the statistical and other contents, the publishers and data suppliers cannot accept any liability in respect of errors or omissions or for any losses or consequential losses arising from such errors or omissions. Readers will appreciate that the data contents are only as up-to-date as their availability and compilation, and printing schedules, will allow and are subject to change during the natural course of events.

Printed and bound in Great Britain by MPG Biddles Ltd
www.mpg-biddles.co.uk

NOTES

(i)   Symbols used:
      '–' *or* 'n/a' = data not available or not available on a comparable basis.
(ii) Constituent figures in the tables may not add up to the totals, due to rounding.
(iii) For full definitions readers are referred to the sources given at the foot of the tables.
(iv) Some topics are mentioned in more than one place but the information is not necessarily from the same source. Any differences are likely to be due to difference in definition, method of calculation or periods covered.

ACKNOWLEDGEMENTS

The publishers would like to thank all those who have contributed to this compilation of pensions data, in particular Aon Hewitt – co-producers of the book – whose contribution and support have been invaluable.

Other contributors, including government departments, whose help is gratefully acknowledged, include:

AP Information Services, a trading name of
Waterlow Legal & Regulatory Ltd

Association of Consulting Actuaries

Barclays Capital

BNY Mellon Asset Servicing

Financial Services Authority (FSA)

General Register Office for Scotland

International Monetary Fund

International Social Security Association

The National Association of Pension Funds Ltd

Northern Ireland Statistics and Research Agency

Office for National Statistics (ONS)

Organization for Economic Cooperation and Development

The Pension Protection Fund

The Pensions Management Institute

The Pensions Regulator

Population Research Bureau

TradingEconomics.com

US Social Security Administration

The World Bank

AON HEWITT

Aon Hewitt is the global leader in human resource consulting and outsourcing solutions. The company partners with organisations to solve their most complex benefits, talent and related financial challenges, and improve business performance. Aon Hewitt designs, implements, communicates and administers a wide range of human capital, retirement, investment management, health care, compensation and talent management strategies. With more than 29,000 professionals in 90 countries, Aon Hewitt makes the world a better place to work for clients and their employees. For more information on Aon Hewitt, please visit *www.aon.com*.

ECONOMIC AND FINANCIAL PUBLISHING LIMITED

Economic and Financial Publishing Ltd, formerly known as NTC Publications, is a specialist provider of information to pensions professionals and economists working in industry, government and public bodies, education and research institutions.

FOREWORD

In my Foreword to last year's *Pocket Book* I questioned whether there had ever been a year with so much change anticipated. Over the last twelve months many of the anticipated changes have taken place and others will come into effect in 2012. The pace of change for pension schemes, and their trustees, sponsors and advisers, remains unrelenting.

The introduction of the Consumer Prices Index as the default measure of inflation for pension indexation has had a varied impact on private sector schemes and their members: in some cases there has been a significant reduction in pension expectations (in relation to past and future benefits); in other cases pensions are unaffected unless specific action is taken for future service. We estimate the overall financial impact on the past service liabilities of private sector schemes could amount to around £50bn but this is not evenly spread: around one in five schemes were not affected by the change; a similar proportion were impacted both in deferment and in payment. The legislative changes resulted in a 'scheme rule lottery' in which some members were losers and some sponsors were winners.

All registered schemes have been affected by significant tax changes that lowered the amount of benefit that could be earned without being subject to a tax penalty. In some cases the additional tax payable by individual members could be huge, so schemes must set up completely new procedures to pay tax for members and adjust benefits accordingly. Complex disguised remuneration provisions have been introduced, imposing additional tax on some non-registered pension schemes. The tax legislation has also been made more flexible, allowing retirement to be deferred beyond age 75 and permitting funds to be taken in lump sum form once an individual has secured a certain amount of pension.

The final requirements for automatic enrolment are now almost in place and larger employers will be required to fulfil their obligations from 2012. Complying with the requirements will be a huge exercise in many cases and one where the devil will be in the detail. Where employers have a significant number of employees who are not currently pension scheme members the additional costs could be considerable.

It is far from clear that automatic enrolment will result in adequate levels of pension provision for future generations. The minimum level of contribution is relatively low. The Government is undertaking a fundamental review of state pensions, considering a move to a single state pension with perhaps an end to contracting out. A simpler state system will at least make it easier for individuals to assess how much they need to save for their retirement.

All this change is taking place in the context of general uncertainty over prospects for the wider global economy. The appetite for schemes to manage liabilities, in an affordable and controlled way, continues to grow. Employers and trustees are thinking increasingly about the long-term objectives for their schemes, and how to reach those objectives.

Coupled with these major changes are the smaller changes regularly being introduced by new legislation, legal cases and guidance, meaning that trustees and employers need to focus continually on being aware of their duties and meeting the requirements.

As you would expect, this year's *Pocket Book* reflects all the latest developments. I am sure you will find it as useful as previous editions.

Andy Cox
UK & Ireland CEO, Aon Hewitt

CONTENTS

Section 5: UK SOCIAL SECURITY BENEFITS AND TAX RATES (continued)

Section 6: CONTRACTING OUT

Section 7: SCHEME DESIGN AND BENEFITS

Section 8: DEFINED CONTRIBUTION PENSION SCHEMES

Section 12: THE PENSIONS REGULATORY SYSTEM

Section 13: PENSIONS TAXATION – REGISTERED PENSION SCHEMES   87

Section 14: EMPLOYER-FINANCED RETIREMENT BENEFIT SCHEMES

Section 15: LEAVING SERVICE BENEFITS

Section 28: PENSION COSTS IN COMPANY ACCOUNTS (continued)

Section 29: FINANCIAL SERVICES LEGISLATION AND PENSION SCHEMES

Section 30: RECENT DEVELOPMENTS

Section 31: EMERGING DEVELOPMENTS

Section 32: SIGNIFICANT PENSION DATES

Section 32: SIGNIFICANT PENSION DATES (continued)

Section 33: UK PENSIONS CASE LAW

Section 34: INTERNATIONAL

High Level Overview:
  Economy and Government; Labour Relations; Cost of Employment;
  Employment Terms and Conditions; Social Security and other
  Required Benefits; Healthcare System; Taxation of Compensation and
  Benefits; Recent Developments,
for the following countries:

APPENDICES

It takes skill to produce a perfect rose

It also takes skill and constant care to achieve your investment objectives.

Managing investments is becoming increasingly demanding. Added complexity means trustees need dedicated investment expertise to deliver improved fund performance.

The good news is that, within clearly defined parameters that you set, our specialists can make and implement day-to-day investment decisions. They exercise their skill and care every day.

Schemes are using our expertise to deliver their investment objectives within a risk-controlled framework.

To find out how you could benefit from our Delegated Consulting Services call 0800 279 5588 or email enquiries@aonhewitt.com

www.aonhewitt.co.uk/delegatedconsulting

Hewitt Risk Management Services Limited is authorised and regulated by the Financial Services Authority. Registered in England and Wales. Registered No: 5913159. Registered Office: 8 Devonshire Square, London EC2M 4PL.

ECONOMICS

THE INTERNAL AND EXTERNAL VALUE OF THE POUND: 1981–2011

	General Index of UK Retail Prices (2000 = 100)		Purchasing power of the £[2] (2000 = 100)	Exchange Rates[1] (Foreign Currency per £ sterling)		
	Index	Yr-on-Yr % Change		US$	Yen	Euro[3]
1981	43.9	11.9	227.7	2.025	444.6	1.785
1982	47.7	8.6	209.7	1.749	435.2	1.767
1983	49.9	4.6	200.5	1.516	359.9	1.706
1984	52.4	5.0	191.0	1.336	316.8	1.697
1985	55.6	6.1	180.0	1.298	307.1	1.710
1986	57.4	3.4	174.1	1.467	246.8	1.482
1987	59.8	4.1	167.1	1.639	236.5	1.404
1988	62.8	4.9	159.3	1.780	228.0	1.499
1989	67.7	7.8	147.8	1.638	225.7	1.469
1990	74.1	9.5	135.0	1.786	257.4	1.373
1991	78.4	5.9	127.5	1.769	237.6	1.400
1992	81.3	3.7	123.0	1.767	223.7	1.333
1993	82.6	1.6	121.0	1.502	166.7	1.262
1994	84.6	2.5	118.2	1.533	156.4	1.272
1995	87.6	3.4	114.2	1.578	148.4	1.191
1996	89.7	2.4	111.5	1.562	170.0	1.210
1997	92.5	3.1	108.1	1.638	198.1	1.449
1998	95.7	3.4	104.5	1.657	216.7	1.489
1999	97.1	1.5	103.0	1.618	184.0	1.519
2000	100.0	3.0	100.0	1.516	163.4	1.642
2001	101.8	1.8	98.3	1.440	174.9	1.609
2002	103.5	1.7	96.6	1.503	187.8	1.591
2003	106.5	2.9	93.9	1.634	189.3	1.445
2004	109.6	3.0	91.2	1.832	198.1	1.474
2005	112.7	2.8	88.7	1.820	200.1	1.463
2006	116.3	3.2	86.0	1.843	214.3	1.467
2007	121.3	4.3	82.4	2.002	235.6	1.462
2008	126.1	4.0	79.3	1.854	192.3	1.258
2009	125.5	-0.5	79.7	1.565	146.2	1.123
2010	131.3	4.6	76.2	1.546	135.6	1.166
2011[1,4]	137.5	4.7	72.7	1.614	130.0	1.148

Notes: [1] Average values over each period. [2] Movements in the purchasing power of the pound are based on movements in the RPI. [3] Prior to January 1999, a synthetic euro has been calculated by geometrically averaging the bilateral exchange rates of the 11 eurozone countries using 'internal weights' based on each country's share of extra-eurozone trade. [4] As to September 2011.

Sources: *Financial Statistics*, National Statistics, © National Statistics website: *www.statistics.gov.uk* Crown copyright material is reproduced with the permission of the Controller of TSO; E&FP.

UK MAIN ECONOMIC INDICATORS, 2004–2010

		2004	2005	2006	2007	2008	2009	2010
Gross Domestic Product[1]								
at current prices	£billion	1,202.4	1,254.3	1,328.6	1,405.8	1,433.9	1,393.9	1,458.5
	% change	5.5	4.3	5.9	5.8	2.0	−2.8	4.6
at 2008 prices	£billion	1,337.8	1,365.7	1,401.3	1,449.9	1,433.9	1,371.2	1,395.3
	% change	3.0	2.1	2.6	3.5	−1.1	−4.4	1.8
Gross Domestic Product per capita[1]								
at current prices	£	20,092	20,823	21,930	23,051	23,354	22,557	23,424
	% change	5.0	3.6	5.3	5.1	1.3	−3.4	3.8
at 2008 prices	£	22,355	22,673	23,130	23,774	23,354	22,190	22,410
	% change	2.5	1.4	2.0	2.8	−1.8	−5.0	1.0
Household Final Consumption Expenditure								
at current prices	£billion	749.6	784.1	819.2	862.2	878.0	858.2	900.2
	% change	4.9	4.6	4.5	5.3	1.8	−2.3	4.9
at 2008 prices	£billion	832.7	851.3	867.1	890.9	878.0	847.0	855.3
	% change	3.1	2.2	1.8	2.7	−1.4	−3.5	1.0
Retail Sales Volume	Index	91.6	92.7	95.9	99.0	100.0	100.6	100.3
(2008 = 100)	% change	5.7	1.2	3.5	3.2	1.0	0.6	−0.3
Consumer Prices	Index	86.9	89.4	92.2	96.2	100.0	99.5	104.1
(2008 = 100)	% change	3.0	2.8	3.2	4.3	4.0	−0.5	4.6
Population (Mid-year Est.)	Million	59.8	60.2	60.6	61.0	61.4	61.8	62.3
Average Earnings	Index	84.1	88.0	92.1	96.5	100.0	99.9	102.2
(2008 = 100)	% change	4.3	4.6	4.7	4.8	3.6	−0.1	2.3
Industrial Production	Index	104.3	103.1	103.1	103.2	100.0	89.9	91.9
(2008 = 100)	% change	1.0	−1.2	0.0	0.1	−3.1	−10.1	2.2
Unemployment Rate[2]	%	2.7	2.7	2.9	2.7	2.8	4.7	4.7
Interest Rate (Bank Rate)[3]	%	4.38	4.65	4.64	5.51	4.69	0.64	0.50
Gross Fixed Capital Formation								
at 2008 prices	£billion	230.6	234.6	246.5	259.4	240.4	204.6	205.2
	% change	4.3	1.7	5.0	5.2	−7.3	−14.9	0.3
Gross Trading Profits[4]								
UK Continental Shelf companies								
at current prices	£billion	16.0	19.3	22.4	23.3	27.9	21.3	32.9
	% change	4.6	20.4	15.8	4.3	19.5	−23.7	54.9
Other companies								
at current prices	£billion	188.1	192.8	209.1	220.3	209.9	196.1	199.0
	% change	9.3	2.5	8.4	5.4	−4.7	−6.6	1.5
at 2008 prices	£billion	216.4	215.7	226.8	229.0	209.9	197.1	191.1
	% change	6.2	−0.3	5.1	1.0	−8.4	−6.1	−3.0
Balance of Payments								
at current prices	£billion	−24.9	−32.8	−44.9	−36.5	−23.8	−20.3	−36.7

Notes: [1] Gross Domestic Product at market prices, seasonally adjusted. [2] Unemployment rate is the claimant count, seasonally adjusted. Workforce jobs comprise employee jobs, self-employed jobs, HM forces and participants in work-related government supported training. [3] London clearing banks' base rate. [4] Private non-financial corporations.

Sources: Mid-2010 population estimates, Economic & Labour Market Review, Financial Statistics and *Consumer Trends,* National Statistics © Crown Copyright 2011; E&FP.

RETAIL PRICES INDEX (RPI)

Index based on January 1987 = 100

	Jan.	Feb.	Mar.	Apr.	May	Jun.	Jul.	Aug.	Sep.	Oct.	Nov.	Dec.
2006	193.4	194.2	195.0	196.5	197.7	198.5	198.5	199.2	200.1	200.4	201.1	202.7
2007	201.6	203.1	204.4	205.4	206.2	207.3	206.1	207.3	208.0	208.9	209.7	210.9
2008	209.8	211.4	212.1	214.0	215.1	216.8	216.5	217.2	218.4	217.7	216.0	212.9
2009	210.1	211.4	211.3	211.5	212.8	213.4	213.4	214.4	215.3	216.0	216.6	218.0
2010	217.9	219.2	220.7	222.8	223.6	224.1	223.6	224.5	225.3	225.8	226.8	228.4
2011	229.0	231.3	232.5	234.4	235.5	235.2	234.7	236.1	237.9	238.0		

Source: E&FP, compiled from government information.

RPI INFLATION

Percentage increase in the Retail Prices Index over previous 12 months

	Jan. %	Feb. %	Mar. %	Apr. %	May %	Jun. %	Jul. %	Aug. %	Sep. %	Oct. %	Nov. %	Dec. %
2006	2.4	2.4	2.4	2.6	3.0	3.3	3.3	3.4	3.6	3.7	3.9	4.4
2007	4.2	4.6	4.8	4.5	4.3	4.4	3.8	4.1	3.9	4.2	4.3	4.0
2008	4.1	4.1	3.8	4.2	4.3	4.6	5.0	4.8	5.0	4.2	3.0	0.9
2009	0.1	0.0	−0.4	−1.2	−1.1	−1.6	−1.4	−1.3	−1.4	−0.8	0.3	2.4
2010	3.7	3.7	4.4	5.3	5.1	5.0	4.8	4.7	4.6	4.5	4.7	4.8
2011	5.1	5.5	5.3	5.2	5.2	5.0	5.0	5.2	5.6	5.4		

Source: E&FP, compiled from government information.

CONSUMER PRICES INDEX (CPI)

Index based on June 2005 = 100

	Jan.	Feb.	Mar.	Apr.	May	Jun.	Jul.	Aug.	Sep.	Oct.	Nov.	Dec.
2006	100.5	100.9	101.1	101.7	102.2	102.5	102.5	102.9	103.0	103.2	103.4	104.0
2007	103.2	103.7	104.2	104.5	104.8	105.0	104.4	104.7	104.8	105.3	105.6	106.2
2008	105.5	106.3	106.7	107.6	108.3	109.0	109.0	109.7	110.3	110.0	109.9	109.5
2009	108.7	109.6	109.8	110.1	110.7	111.0	111.0	111.4	111.5	111.7	112.0	112.6
2010	112.4	112.9	113.5	114.2	114.4	114.6	114.3	114.9	114.9	115.2	115.6	116.8
2011	116.9	117.8	118.1	119.3	119.5	119.4	119.4	120.1	120.9	121.0		

Source: E&FP, compiled from government information.

CPI INFLATION

Percentage increase in the Consumer Prices Index over previous 12 months

	Jan. %	Feb. %	Mar. %	Apr. %	May %	Jun. %	Jul. %	Aug. %	Sep. %	Oct. %	Nov. %	Dec. %
2006	1.9	2.0	1.8	2.0	2.2	2.5	2.4	2.5	2.4	2.4	2.7	3.0
2007	2.7	2.8	3.1	2.8	2.5	2.4	1.9	1.8	1.8	2.1	2.1	2.1
2008	2.2	2.5	2.5	3.0	3.3	3.8	4.4	4.7	5.2	4.5	4.1	3.1
2009	3.0	3.2	2.9	2.3	2.2	1.8	1.8	1.6	1.1	1.5	1.9	2.9
2010	3.5	3.0	3.4	3.7	3.4	3.2	3.1	3.1	3.1	3.2	3.3	3.7
2011	4.0	4.4	4.0	4.5	4.5	4.2	4.4	4.5	5.2	5.0		

Source: E&FP, compiled from government information.

TRENDS IN AVERAGE EARNINGS PER PERSON
PER WEEK AND THE HOUSEHOLDS' SAVINGS RATIO

	at Current Prices		at Constant 2010 Prices		Households' Savings Ratio (%)
	Average Earnings (£pw)	Annual Change (%)	Average Earnings (£pw)	Annual Change (%)	
1970	29.02	10.2	349.94	3.5	6.6
1971	31.43	8.3	347.12	−0.8	5.0
1972	34.26	9.0	352.05	1.4	7.3
1973	37.38	9.1	351.98	0.0	8.2
1974	44.74	19.7	363.37	3.2	8.4
1975	59.04	32.0	386.54	6.4	9.2
1976	64.81	9.8	363.70	−5.9	8.7
1977	70.62	9.0	342.07	−5.9	7.6
1978	79.69	12.8	356.57	4.2	9.4
1979	92.00	15.4	362.97	1.8	10.9
1980	111.15	20.8	371.76	2.4	12.3
1981	125.35	12.8	374.75	0.8	12.0
1982	137.15	9.4	377.56	0.8	10.8
1983	148.77	8.5	391.50	3.7	9.0
1984	157.67	6.0	395.31	1.0	10.2
1985	171.00	8.5	404.15	2.2	9.7
1986	184.80	8.1	422.32	4.5	8.1
1987	198.90	7.6	436.47	3.4	5.4
1988	218.70	10.0	457.47	4.8	3.9
1989	239.80	9.6	465.31	1.7	5.7
1990	263.20	9.8	466.52	0.3	8.1
1991	284.70	8.2	476.72	2.2	10.3
1992	304.80	7.1	492.02	3.2	11.7
1993	317.30	4.1	504.30	2.5	10.8
1994	326.10	2.8	505.76	0.3	9.3
1995	337.60	3.5	506.33	0.1	10.3
1996	351.50	4.1	514.58	1.6	9.4
1997	367.60	4.6	521.80	1.4	9.5
1998	392.50	6.8	538.73	3.2	7.4
1999	407.80	3.9	551.16	2.3	5.2
2000	425.10	4.2	558.20	1.3	4.7
2001	449.70	5.8	579.94	3.9	6.1
2002	472.10	5.0	599.04	3.3	4.8
2003	487.10	3.2	600.57	0.3	5.0
2004	498.20	2.3	596.62	−0.7	3.6
2005	516.40	3.7	601.43	0.8	3.7
2006	534.90	3.6	603.62	0.4	3.1
2007	550.30	2.9	595.56	−1.3	2.7
2008	575.60	4.6	599.02	0.6	3.1
2009	587.20	2.0	614.37	2.6	7.8
2010	598.30	1.9	598.30	−2.6	7.5

Notes: **Constant 2010 Prices**: Deflated by the Retail Prices Index (2010 = 100). **Earnings**: Wages and salaries of those in employment, excluding those whose pay is affected by absence. Pre-1971 data are derived from average salaries/unit of output; later data from the earnings index of all adults in employment. **Households' Savings Ratio**: Households' saving as % Total Resources; the latter is the sum of Gross Household Disposable Income and the Adjustment for the net equity of the households in pension funds.

Sources: *ASHE* and *Financial Statistics*, National Statistics, © Crown Copyright 2011; E&FP.

DEMOGRAPHIC & EMPLOYMENT DATA

POPULATION DATA, MID-2010

By Nation Thousands

	Total	Males	Females
England	52,234	25,758	26,476
Wales	3,006	1,471	1,536
Scotland	5,222	2,530	2,692
Great Britain	**60,463**	**29,759**	**30,704**
Northern Ireland	1,799	884	915
United Kingdom	**62,262**	**30,643**	**31,619**

By Sex and Age, UK

	Total		Males		Females	
Age	'000s	%	'000s	%	'000s	%
0–4	3,858	6.2	1,977	3.2	1,881	3.0
5–9	3,446	5.5	1,762	2.8	1,685	2.7
10–14	3,567	5.7	1,825	2.9	1,742	2.8
15–19	3,912	6.3	2,013	3.2	1,899	3.0
20–24	4,310	6.9	2,213	3.6	2,097	3.4
25–29	4,250	6.8	2,169	3.5	2,081	3.3
30–34	3,891	6.3	1,960	3.1	1,932	3.1
35–39	4,202	6.7	2,085	3.3	2,117	3.4
40–44	4,632	7.4	2,293	3.7	2,339	3.8
45–49	4,566	7.3	2,250	3.6	2,316	3.7
50–54	3,981	6.4	1,965	3.2	2,016	3.2
55–59	3,578	5.7	1,759	2.8	1,820	2.9
60–64	3,764	6.0	1,840	3.0	1,924	3.1
65–69	2,932	4.7	1,412	2.3	1,520	2.4
70–74	2,468	4.0	1,160	1.9	1,307	2.1
75–79	2,002	3.2	894	1.4	1,108	1.8
80–84	1,493	2.4	607	1.0	886	1.4
85–89	935	1.5	326	0.5	609	1.0
90+	476	0.8	134	0.2	342	0.5
Total	**62,262**	**100.0**	**30,643**	**49.2**	**31,619**	**50.8**

Population Projections, UK Thousands

		Projections			
	2010 (2010 base)	2015	2020	2025	2030
0–14	10,872	11,497	12,231	12,455	12,279
15–44	25,197	25,164	25,354	26,230	26,917
45–64	15,889	16,463	16,922	16,809	16,681
65–74	5,399	6,264	6,574	6,631	7,465
75+	4,905	5,388	6,093	7,279	8,051
Total	**62,262**	**64,776**	**67,173**	**69,404**	**71,392**

Sources: *Mid-2010 Population Estimates*, National Statistics © Crown Copyright 2011; General Register Office for Scotland; Northern Ireland Statistics and Research Agency; Government Actuary's Department.

EXPECTATIONS OF LIFE

Age x	Males Expectation	Females Expectation	Age x	Males Expectation	Females Expectation
0	78.31	82.33			
1	77.71	81.68	51	29.69	32.92
2	76.74	80.70	52	28.80	32.00
3	75.75	79.71	53	27.92	31.09
4	74.76	78.73	54	27.04	30.18
5	73.77	77.74	55	26.17	29.28
6	72.78	76.74	56	25.31	28.38
7	71.78	75.75	57	24.46	27.49
8	70.79	74.76	58	23.62	26.60
9	69.80	73.76	59	22.78	25.72
10	68.81	72.77	60	21.96	24.85
11	67.81	71.78	61	21.14	23.98
12	66.82	70.78	62	20.33	23.12
13	65.83	69.79	63	19.53	22.27
14	64.83	68.80	64	18.74	21.42
15	63.84	67.80	65	17.97	20.59
16	62.86	66.81	66	17.21	19.76
17	61.87	65.83	67	16.46	18.94
18	60.90	64.84	68	15.72	18.13
19	59.93	63.85	69	15.00	17.33
20	58.96	62.87	70	14.30	16.54
21	58.00	61.88	71	13.60	15.77
22	57.03	60.90	72	12.92	15.01
23	56.07	59.91	73	12.26	14.25
24	55.10	58.93	74	11.62	13.52
25	54.13	57.94	75	10.98	12.80
26	53.17	56.96	76	10.37	12.10
27	52.20	55.97	77	9.78	11.41
28	51.24	54.99	78	9.21	10.75
29	50.28	54.01	79	8.66	10.11
30	49.31	53.03	80	8.14	9.49
31	48.36	52.05	81	7.64	8.90
32	47.40	51.07	82	7.17	8.33
33	46.44	50.10	83	6.72	7.78
34	45.49	49.12	84	6.29	7.26
35	44.54	48.15	85	5.90	6.77
36	43.59	47.18	86	5.54	6.30
37	42.64	46.21	87	5.21	5.86
38	41.69	45.24	88	4.90	5.44
39	40.75	44.27	89	4.62	5.06
40	39.81	43.31	90	4.31	4.68
41	38.87	42.35	91	4.02	4.33
42	37.94	41.39	92	3.71	3.99
43	37.01	40.44	93	3.45	3.70
44	36.08	39.48	94	3.21	3.43
45	35.15	38.54	95	3.01	3.19
46	34.23	37.59	96	2.83	2.98
47	33.31	36.65	97	2.68	2.78
48	32.40	35.71	98	2.55	2.59
49	31.49	34.77	99	2.43	2.42
50	30.59	33.84	100	2.30	2.25

Note: The table shows the average expectation of life at various ages, that is, if a person experienced the age-specific mortality rates of England and Wales in the years 2008 to 2010 throughout their life. The table makes no allowance for future improvements in mortality.

Source: Office for National Statistics © Crown Copyright 2011.

WORKING POPULATION – UNITED KINGDOM

	June 1991		June 2010		June 2011	
	'000s	%	'000s	%	'000s	%
Employees in employment:						
– Male	11,596	41.0	12,662	41.2	12,727	41.3
– Female	10,624	37.6	12,281	40.0	12,292	39.9
All employees	22,221	78.6	24,943	81.2	25,019	81.2
Self-employed persons	3,143	11.1	3,972	12.9	3,973	12.9
HM Forces	297	1.0	198	0.6	193	0.6
Government-supported trainees	353	1.2	134	0.4	90	0.3
Total employed labour force	26,014	92.0	29,246	95.2	29,274	95.0
Claimant unemployment	2,274	8.0	1,465	4.8	1,527	5.0
Total	28,288	100.0	30,711	100.0	30,801	100.0
Index (June 1991=100)	100.0		108.6		108.9	

Notes: [1] Seasonally adjusted.

[2] Totals might differ from sum of preceding figures owing to rounding.

Source: *Labour Market Statistics*, Office for National Statistics © Crown Copyright 2011.

UK EMPLOYMENT AND UNEMPLOYMENT

	Total Workers '000s	Employed Labour Force '000s	Employees in Employment '000s	Claimant unemployment	
				'000s	% of Working Population
1991	28,584	26,162	22,404	2,268	7.9
1992	28,454	25,540	21,634	2,742	9.6
1993	28,180	25,303	21,405	2,877	10.0
1994	28,103	25,504	21,528	2,599	9.2
1995	28,108	25,818	21,865	2,290	8.1
1996	28,147	26,060	22,197	2,087	8.1
1997	28,111	26,526	22,743	1,585	5.6
1998	28,143	26,795	23,182	1,348	4.8
1999	28,416	27,168	23,603	1,248	4.4
2000	28,572	27,484	23,975	1,088	3.8
2001	28,680	27,710	24,184	970	3.4
2002	28,867	27,920	24,385	947	3.3
2003	29,115	28,182	24,424	933	3.2
2004	29,333	28,480	24,642	853	2.9
2005	29,632	28,770	24,924	862	2.9
2006	29,970	29,025	25,095	945	3.2
2007	30,093	29,228	25,212	865	2.9
2008	30,346	29,440	25,408	906	3.0
2009	30,488	28,960	24,924	1,528	5.0
2010	30,532	29,035	24,852	1,497	4.9
2011 Jul–Sep	30,647	29,069	24,788	1,578	5.1

Source: *Labour Market Statistics*, Office for National Statistics © Crown Copyright 2011.

ANALYSIS BY INDUSTRY
OF WORKFORCE JOBS – UNITED KINGDOM

Seasonally adjusted

	June 2001		June 2011	
	'000s	%	'000s	%
Agriculture, forestry & fishing	376	1.3	434	1.4
Mining & quarrying	76	0.3	58	0.2
Manufacturing	3,873	12.9	2,534	8.1
Electricity, gas, steam & air conditioning supply	101	0.3	138	0.4
Water supply, sewerage, waste & remediation activities	169	0.6	173	0.6
Construction	1,945	6.5	2,093	6.7
Wholesale & retail trade; repair of motor vehicles and motorcycles	4,969	16.6	4,760	15.3
Transport & storage	1,413	4.7	1,493	4.8
Accommodation & food service activities	1,801	6.0	1,953	6.3
Information & communication	1,174	3.9	1,174	3.8
Financial & insurance activities	1,156	3.9	1,125	3.6
Real estate activities	295	1.0	414	1.3
Professional scientific & technical activities	1,803	6.0	2,402	7.7
Administrative & support service activities	2,131	7.1	2,311	7.4
Public administration & defence; compulsory social security	1,653	5.5	1,657	5.3
Education	2,238	7.5	2,657	8.5
Human health & social work activities	3,130	10.5	4,080	13.1
Arts, entertainment & recreation	758	2.5	888	2.8
Other service activities	861	2.9	819	2.6
All industries & services	29,920	100.0	31,160	100.0

Note: Employer surveys now measure 'jobs' rather than 'people'.

Source: *Labour Market Statistics*, Office for National Statistics © Crown Copyright 2011.

INVESTMENT DATA

UK ANNUAL INFLATION

UK INVESTMENT YIELDS AND INFLATION

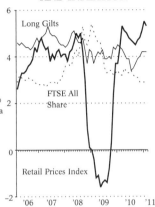

UK INTEREST RATES AND INFLATION

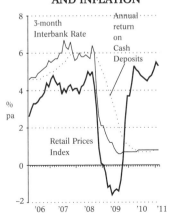

Notes:

[1] Base for Retail Prices Index (RPI) is 1987, and base for Average Weekly Earnings index (AWE) is 2000.

[2] Index for Long Gilts is based on all issues with a term of 15 years.

[3] 3-month Interbank Rate shown is the mid-rate.

Sources:

RPI and AWE data derived from information published by Office for National Statistics. AWE figures are based on the 2007 Standard Industrial Classification (SIC 2007). All other figures collated by Aon Hewitt.

UK INVESTMENT HISTORY (1)

One year returns to end of:	Annual Increase:[1]			Corresponding Annual Rate of Return on Investments:				
	RPI[2] %	CPI[3] %	AWE[4] %	Cash Deposits %	Long Gilts %	Index- linked Gilts %	U.K. Equities %	Median Fund[5] %
2001	0.7	1.1	3.1	5.0	−0.9	−0.5	−13.3	−9.7
2002	2.9	1.7	2.3	4.0	9.9	8.2	−22.7	−15.5
2003	2.8	1.3	3.8	3.7	1.2	6.6	20.9	16.9
2004	3.5	1.7	4.2	4.6	8.4	8.5	12.8	10.5
2005	2.2	1.9	4.4	4.7	11.0	9.0	22.0	19.2
2006	4.4	3.0	5.8	4.8	0.0	2.9	16.8	9.3
2007	4.0	2.1	3.4	6.0	2.7	8.5	5.3	6.0
2008	0.9	3.1	2.5	5.5	13.7	3.7	−29.9	−15.6
2009	2.4	2.9	0.7	1.2	−4.8	6.5	30.1	16.0
2010	4.8	3.7	1.3	0.7	8.8	8.9	14.5	12.2

Length of period:	*Average annual increases and rates of return for different periods to end of 2010:*							
10 years	2.9	2.2	3.1	4.0	4.8	6.2	3.7	4.4
9 years	3.1	2.4	3.1	3.9	5.5	6.9	5.7	5.9
8 years	3.1	2.4	3.2	3.9	4.9	6.8	10.0	8.8
7 years	3.2	2.6	3.2	3.9	5.5	6.8	8.5	7.6
6 years	3.1	2.8	3.0	3.8	5.0	6.5	7.8	7.2
5 years	3.3	2.9	2.7	3.6	3.9	6.0	5.1	5.0
4 years	3.0	2.9	2.0	3.3	4.8	6.9	2.4	3.8
3 years	2.7	3.2	1.5	2.5	5.6	6.3	1.4	3.3
2 years	3.6	3.3	1.0	1.0	1.7	7.7	22.1	14.4

Notes: [1] The increase shown is measured over the calendar year(s) from December to December.

[2] Retail Prices Index, all items.   [3] Consumer Prices Index, all items.

[4] Average Weekly Earnings, whole economy, not seasonally adjusted, including bonus and arrears. AWE figures are based on the 2007 Standard Industrial Classification (SIC 2007).

[5] The median fund represents the total return, as at 31 December, achieved by all pension funds participating in BNY Mellon Asset Servicing's UK Pension Fund Universe.

Source: Annual increases in indices and annual rates of return collated, and averages calculated, by Aon Hewitt.

UK INVESTMENT HISTORY (2)

Historic Yields and Returns (% p.a.)

5 Years to end of:	Retail Prices Index	UK Assets: Real Rates of Return		
		Equities	Government Bonds	Treasury Bills
1965	3.5	1.5	0.3	1.1
1970	4.6	5.0	–3.1	2.0
1975	13.0	–4.6	–7.7	–4.7
1980	14.4	5.6	1.5	–1.5
1985	7.2	16.7	9.0	4.7
1990	5.9	6.9	3.1	5.8
1995	3.4	13.0	10.5	4.6
2000	2.7	10.7	8.2	3.7
2005	2.4	–0.3	3.1	2.1
2010	3.1	1.5	1.8	0.1
10 Years to end of:				
1965	–	7.3	–1.0	–
1970	4.1	3.3	–1.4	1.6
1975	8.7	0.1	–5.4	–1.4
1980	13.7	0.4	–3.2	–3.1
1985	10.7	11.0	5.2	1.5
1990	6.6	11.7	6.0	5.2
1995	4.7	9.9	6.8	5.2
2000	3.0	11.8	9.4	4.2
2005	2.6	5.0	5.6	2.9
2010	2.8	0.6	2.4	1.1

Sources: Office for National Statistics and Barclays Capital Equity Gilt Study 2010.

UK INVESTMENT RETURNS AND INFLATION

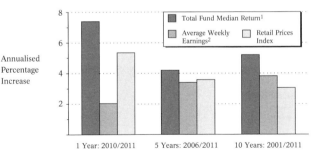

Notes:

[1] The median fund return represents the median return achieved by all pension funds participating in BNY Mellon Asset Servicing's UK Pension Fund Universe.

[2] Average Weekly Earnings data: whole economy, not seasonally adjusted, including bonus and arrears. AWE figures are based on the 2007 Standard Industrial Classification (SIC 2007).

Returns shown are to March 2011.

Sources: BNY Mellon Asset Servicing pension fund information service, data to 31 March 2011. Aon Hewitt, compiled from government information.

INDEX RETURNS FOR YEARS TO 31 MARCH

	2002 %	2003 %	2004 %	2005 %	2006 %	2007 %	2008 %	2009 %	2010 %	2011 %
FTSE All-Share	-3.2	-29.8	31.0	15.6	28.0	11.1	-7.7	-29.3	52.3	8.7
FTSE-AW All-World excl. UK	-3.4	-31.4	25.4	7.3	31.9	2.4	-1.0	-19.8	47.8	8.3
CAPS Consensus Overseas (incl. Emerging Mkts)	-6.0	-30.2	35.2	10.7	36.3	5.5	0.1	-22.6	49.8	8.3
FTSE-AW USA	-0.6	-32.4	15.9	3.8	23.0	-1.0	-6.2	-13.4	41.8	9.2
FTSE W Europe excl. UK	-7.4	-34.4	36.4	18.2	35.5	12.0	2.4	-31.4	48.0	7.0
FTSE-AW Japan	-20.8	-25.6	46.4	-4.3	48.1	-10.0	-15.5	-10.8	29.5	-4.2
FTSE-AW Dev. Asia Pacific excl. Japan	5.8	-19.1	33.4	18.5	33.8	**19.9**	8.6	-22.4	69.1	**14.0**
incl. Japan	-15.1	-23.7	42.5	1.9	44.0	-2.0	-7.6	-15.3	44.4	4.5
FTSE-AW Canada	3.1	-19.6	31.8	**20.0**	47.5	0.6	17.3	-22.1	61.8	13.3
MSCI Emerging Markets Free	**14.6**	-28.6	**56.2**	13.4	**60.6**	6.7	**19.7**	-26.6	**71.1**	12.1
FTSE Actuaries All Stocks Gilts	1.6	11.3	2.3	5.0	7.4	0.6	7.6	10.3	0.8	5.2
ILG[1] (All Stocks)	3.3	10.4	6.2	5.4	8.4	3.0	13.1	-1.3	10.3	6.5
ML Sterling Non-gilt	5.4	10.9	5.0	6.4	7.8	1.2	-0.8	-5.9	21.7	5.3
JP Morgan Traded WXUK	0.3	**12.5**	-2.8	2.3	3.7	-5.1	19.1	**36.7**	0.0	2.1
CAPS UK Cash	4.4	3.7	3.5	4.5	4.5	4.8	5.6	3.6	0.4	0.4
CAPS Property	4.4	7.1	9.3	18.4	21.9	17.6	-11.3	-27.4	6.5	7.3
CAPS Discretionary excl. Property	-2.7	-23.0	26.2	12.2	27.3	7.4	-2.2	-19.2	40.1	7.7
CAPS Discretionary incl. Property	-2.5	-22.2	25.6	12.2	27.2	7.6	-2.2	-19.2	39.9	7.7
RPI	1.3	3.1	2.6	3.2	2.4	4.8	3.8	-0.4	4.4	5.3
AWE[2]	2.5	4.7	3.8	4.3	6.2	4.6	4.8	-1.1	6.6	2.1
CPI	1.5	1.5	1.1	1.9	1.8	3.1	2.5	2.9	3.4	4.0

Notes: [1] UK index-linked gilts.

[2] AWE figures are based on the 2007 Standard Industrial Classification (SIC 2007).

This table highlights (in **bold**) the best index in each year. Increases in the Retail Prices Index, Average Weekly Earnings and the Consumer Prices Index are also shown for comparison *(see previous tables for details)*.

Sources: BNY Mellon Asset Servicing's Index Returns to 31 March 2011, and Office for National Statistics.

INDEX RETURNS OVER CUMULATIVE PERIODS ENDING 31 MARCH 2011

Annualised Returns	Last 12 Months %	Last 3 Years %	Last 5 Years %	Last 10 Years %
UK Equities	8.7	5.4	3.7	4.7
UK Smaller Companies	**14.5**	4.9	0.4	3.7
Overseas Equities	8.3	8.7	5.4	4.4
North American	9.5	10.5	4.9	2.7
European (excl. UK)	7.0	2.8	4.5	5.2
Pan-European	7.4	3.9	4.5	5.2
Japanese	–4.2	3.4	–3.4	0.3
Pacific Basin (excl. Japan)	14.0	**14.4**	**14.3**	13.4
Emerging Markets	12.4	12.4	12.8	**15.7**
UK Bonds (Standard)	5.2	5.3	4.8	5.1
UK Bonds (Long Term)	6.9	5.1	3.8	4.9
International Bonds	2.1	11.8	9.6	–
Index-linked Gilts	6.5	5.0	6.2	6.5
Sterling Cash	0.4	1.6	3.0	3.6
Property Assets	7.3	–6.0	–2.8	4.3

Note: The best performing sector over each period is highlighted in **bold** typeface. Returns calculated on a net-of-fees basis.

Source: BNY Mellon Asset Servicing.

PENSION FUND INVESTMENT PERFORMANCE FOR YEARS TO 31 MARCH

Table 1: Total Fund
Per cent

	9th Decile	Lower Quartile	Median	Upper Quartile	1st Decile
2001/02	–3.6	–2.4	–1.5	–0.5	0.6
2002/03	–26.2	–23.1	–20.9	–16.2	–10.1
2003/04	16.0	20.0	23.3	25.7	28.1
2004/05	8.6	9.6	10.6	11.7	13.0
2005/06	18.1	20.3	23.1	25.4	28.1
2006/07	3.1	4.3	5.7	6.8	8.1
2007/08	–5.0	–3.1	–1.5	0.6	3.1
2008/09	–21.9	–19.3	–15.8	–11.8	–7.1
2009/10	18.9	25.9	30.5	34.7	39.5
2010/11	6.4	7.0	7.4	8.6	9.9

Table 2: Total Fund excluding Property
Per cent

	9th Decile	Lower Quartile	Median	Upper Quartile	1st Decile
2001/02	–3.6	–2.6	–1.6	–0.6	0.4
2002/03	–26.6	–23.7	–21.4	–16.8	–10.4
2003/04	16.0	20.1	23.6	26.0	28.5
2004/05	8.6	9.5	10.5	11.6	12.9
2005/06	18.0	20.3	23.1	25.5	28.1
2006/07	3.0	4.0	5.4	6.6	7.7
2007/08	–4.7	–2.8	–1.2	0.7	3.9
2008/09	–21.8	–19.3	–15.6	–11.2	–6.6
2009/10	18.9	26.6	31.5	35.7	40.5
2010/11	6.2	6.9	7.4	8.7	9.8

(Continued overleaf)

Table 3: UK Equities

Per cent

	9th Decile	Lower Quartile	Median	Upper Quartile	1st Decile
2001/02	−5.0	−3.5	−2.4	−1.3	0.2
2002/03	−31.5	−30.6	−29.8	−29.0	−28.3
2003/04	28.9	30.3	31.5	33.3	35.2
2004/05	13.6	14.5	15.2	15.8	17.2
2005/06	24.6	26.2	27.8	29.3	31.1
2006/07	8.4	9.7	11.1	11.9	13.3
2007/08	−12.1	−9.2	−7.8	−6.2	−2.8
2008/09	−33.7	−30.3	−29.1	−27.2	−23.7
2009/10	47.6	50.2	52.8	53.5	56.3
2010/11	5.0	8.2	8.9	10.3	12.6

Table 4: Overseas Equities

Per cent

	9th Decile	Lower Quartile	Median	Upper Quartile	1st Decile
2001/02	−6.9	−5.6	−4.5	−3.1	−1.5
2002/03	−32.8	−31.9	−30.9	−29.7	−28.5
2003/04	26.6	29.6	32.0	33.9	35.9
2004/05	6.0	7.9	9.4	10.6	12.2
2005/06	31.0	33.0	35.0	37.5	39.9
2006/07	0.1	1.8	3.6	5.5	8.4
2007/08	−8.0	−5.6	−3.3	−0.9	2.1
2008/09	−33.5	−28.0	−22.3	−19.7	−17.7
2009/10	40.2	44.6	47.3	49.6	52.7
2010/11	4.5	6.8	8.1	9.3	11.1

Table 5: US Equities

Per cent

	9th Decile	Lower Quartile	Median	Upper Quartile	1st Decile
2001/02	−5.8	−4.7	−2.8	−0.6	3.2
2002/03	−39.1	−34.4	−32.4	−30.8	−29.9
2003/04	12.6	13.4	15.8	16.6	22.2
2004/05	−3.1	3.3	4.2	5.8	9.3
2005/06	19.6	21.8	23.5	26.2	30.1
2006/07	−7.4	−4.0	−2.0	−0.6	3.2
2007/08	−18.5	−13.6	−8.0	−5.0	1.5
2008/09	−37.1	−28.6	−15.9	−13.2	−9.8
2009/10	34.2	39.1	41.9	45.3	51.0
2010/11	5.5	7.6	9.2	10.8	11.8

Table 6: European (excluding UK) Equities

Per cent

	9th Decile	Lower Quartile	Median	Upper Quartile	1st Decile
2001/02	−7.4	−6.8	−5.3	−4.0	−2.2
2002/03	−36.7	−35.3	−34.5	−33.3	−31.4
2003/04	31.8	33.4	35.1	36.6	38.2
2004/05	14.8	17.1	18.5	20.1	21.9
2005/06	34.3	35.3	36.0	38.1	41.1
2006/07	7.6	9.6	11.8	12.7	14.7
2007/08	−7.1	−1.9	2.1	3.0	4.3
2008/09	−37.1	−33.0	−30.8	−27.9	−23.3
2009/10	35.1	44.6	48.0	49.9	51.8
2010/11	−2.7	5.7	7.1	8.4	12.3

Table 7: Japanese Equities

Per cent

	9th Decile	Lower Quartile	Median	Upper Quartile	1st Decile
2001/02	−22.8	−21.1	−20.4	−18.1	−12.9
2002/03	−28.8	−27.4	−25.5	−25.1	−22.9
2003/04	33.0	35.8	43.8	48.0	52.6
2004/05	−6.3	−4.8	−4.2	−2.7	−1.5
2005/06	43.2	47.5	49.3	51.9	55.2
2006/07	−16.3	−12.7	−10.1	−8.3	−4.3
2007/08	−22.3	−18.6	−16.2	−15.0	−13.1
2008/09	−29.1	−21.4	−14.3	−10.6	−9.5
2009/10	24.8	27.7	29.4	32.4	38.4
2010/11	−9.4	−7.1	−3.9	−1.7	1.4

Table 8: Pacific Basin (excluding Japan) Equities

Per cent

	9th Decile	Lower Quartile	Median	Upper Quartile	1st Decile
2001/02	3.1	6.3	7.4	10.8	14.6
2002/03	−29.1	−25.8	−22.1	−19.6	−18.9
2003/04	31.8	33.5	35.4	40.2	43.6
2004/05	8.8	12.9	17.8	19.1	21.2
2005/06	29.0	33.6	35.2	38.5	43.7
2006/07	11.3	16.1	19.9	21.4	25.5
2007/08	3.1	6.1	9.1	11.5	15.5
2008/09	−29.3	−24.4	−21.9	−20.8	−17.9
2009/10	50.1	57.5	64.9	70.1	74.5
2010/11	5.0	10.9	13.3	14.4	18.9

Table 9: Overseas Bonds

Per cent

	9th Decile	Lower Quartile	Median	Upper Quartile	1st Decile
2001/02	−1.9	−0.8	0.6	2.2	3.9
2002/03	8.0	11.0	13.5	21.0	29.9
2003/04	−4.4	−3.0	−1.0	2.1	3.9
2004/05	1.9	3.2	5.4	8.3	14.3
2005/06	3.5	4.5	6.4	9.7	16.3
2006/07	−14.0	−6.0	−4.6	−2.9	2.4
2007/08	−0.5	4.5	11.7	15.2	18.5
2008/09	−21.2	−11.6	15.0	27.6	37.0
2009/10	7.8	12.7	25.1	37.8	73.4
2010/11	−0.8	4.2	4.3	9.0	11.0

Table 10: UK Bonds

Per cent

	9th Decile	Lower Quartile	Median	Upper Quartile	1st Decile
2001/02	−1.0	0.7	2.0	2.7	3.9
2002/03	10.1	11.1	12.0	12.8	13.4
2003/04	2.5	3.0	3.6	4.4	5.2
2004/05	5.3	5.7	6.1	6.4	6.9
2005/06	7.3	7.8	9.1	10.2	10.7
2006/07	−1.0	−0.5	0.3	0.9	1.4
2007/08	−3.1	−0.1	1.6	3.6	5.6
2008/09	−6.4	−3.5	0.5	2.8	7.6
2009/10	6.1	11.8	17.1	21.5	24.9
2010/11	5.2	5.8	6.2	6.7	8.1

(Continued overleaf)

Table 11: UK Index-linked Gilts   Per cent

	9th Decile	Lower Quartile	Median	Upper Quartile	1st Decile
2001/02	2.5	2.8	3.2	3.6	4.0
2002/03	10.1	10.4	10.8	11.0	11.2
2003/04	5.9	6.3	6.6	6.7	7.1
2004/05	5.4	5.6	5.7	5.9	6.4
2005/06	7.8	8.4	8.9	9.0	9.5
2006/07	2.4	2.6	2.7	3.0	3.2
2007/08	11.6	13.1	13.5	13.6	13.9
2008/09	−4.8	−2.9	−2.7	−1.6	−1.2
2009/10	9.7	10.3	10.4	11.4	12.6
2010/11	5.0	5.9	6.7	6.8	7.2

Table 12: Property   Per cent

	9th Decile	Lower Quartile	Median	Upper Quartile	1st Decile
2001/02	3.2	4.7	5.6	7.5	9.6
2002/03	6.5	8.7	9.1	11.0	12.0
2003/04	8.7	9.4	12.2	13.8	15.6
2004/05	14.8	16.7	18.6	19.9	21.2
2005/06	18.7	20.4	22.2	23.3	24.0
2006/07	12.9	14.5	16.6	19.9	21.6
2007/08	−13.2	−11.9	−10.8	−9.4	−4.2
2008/09	−35.2	−31.1	−25.2	−20.2	−11.6
2009/10	−9.8	1.8	8.8	12.9	15.0
2010/11	1.6	2.9	8.3	9.7	11.3

Notes: The figures show the range of returns in each year since 2001 obtained by funds participating in the CAPS investment performance measurement service. The most recent years' figures may be subject to later revision.

Source: BNY Mellon Asset Servicing's pension fund information service, data to 31 March 2011.

PENSION FUND ASSET DISTRIBUTION

This table shows the average distribution of pension fund assets between the major market sectors at 31 March each year between 2002 and 2011, based on proportions of overall market values. Percentages are rounded to add up to 100% for each year.

	UK Equities	Overseas Equities	Overseas Bonds	UK Bonds	Global Index-linked Gilts	Cash	Property	Other
	%	%	%	%	%	%	%	%
31.3.2002	47	26	2	15	6	2	2	–
31.3.2003	42	25	2	19	8	2	2	–
31.3.2004	40	27	1	20	8	2	2	–
31.3.2005	38	28	1	21	8	2	2	–
31.3.2006	36	29	1	22	8	2	2	–
31.3.2007	33	28	1	23	8	3	3	1
31.3.2008	27	25	2	26	11	4	3	2
31.3.2009	24	24	1	30	13	4	3	1
31.3.2010	23	27	2	27	12	4	3	2
31.3.2011	23	29	2	24	14	3	3	2

Source: BNY Mellon Asset Servicing's pension fund information service, data to 31 March 2011.

POOLED PENSION FUND PERFORMANCE

This table sets out the median returns achieved on a net-of-fees basis by the UK Pooled Pension Funds participating in the CAPS Survey over cumulative periods ending 31 March 2011.

Annualised Returns	Last 12 Months %	Last 3 Years %	Last 5 Years %	Last 10 Years %
Balanced	7.8	6.2	4.3	5.3
UK Smaller Companies	30.3	9.4	5.1	8.0
UK Equity (Standard)	10.3	5.3	3.7	4.7
Overseas	6.5	7.6	4.6	4.8
Global Equity	8.7	6.4	4.5	4.9
North America	8.9	10.4	4.3	2.1
Europe (excl. UK)	8.0	3.3	3.8	5.4
Pan-European*	–	–	–	–
Japan	–3.2	3.2	–5.4	–0.6
Pacific Basin (excl. Japan)	11.8	13.1	13.4	13.6
Emerging Markets	10.5	10.0	11.1	15.5
UK Bonds (Standard)	5.5	6.1	4.5	5.2
UK Bonds (Long Term)	6.6	6.5	3.6	5.1
International Bond	2.1	11.6	9.2	6.1
Index-linked	6.9	4.9	5.9	6.4
Cash	0.5	1.8	3.1	3.6
Property	8.4	–0.6	–0.3	6.1

Note: * Insufficient funds in this index to produce a median return at the time of publication.

Source: BNY Mellon Asset Servicing's CAPS Pooled Pension Fund Update (Quarter ended 31 March 2011).

CHANGES TO STRATEGIC ASSET ALLOCATION

	2007 (%)	2008 (%)	2009 (%)	2010 (%)
Equities	55	51	44	44
Fixed interest securities	32	33	38	39
Other	13	16	18	18

Note: Data for 2007 and 2008 cover private and 'other public sector' schemes (funded schemes, such as those of universities). 2009 and 2010 data cover the private sector only.

Source: NAPF Annual Survey, 2010.

PENSION STATISTICS

NOTES ON SOURCES USED

This section provides a snapshot of selected features of occupational pension schemes in the UK. The charts and tables on pages 19 to 23 are based on data from the following sources:

- **Occupational Pension Schemes Survey, 2010**: this survey, produced by National Statistics, covers 1,621 private and public sector schemes registered in the UK. The survey covers a range of topics, including scheme membership, DB benefits and contribution rates.

- **The NAPF Annual Survey, 2010**: the extract from this survey is based on 170 responses from NAPF fund members in the private sector.

- **The Association of Consulting Actuaries' (ACA) 2011 Pension trend survey**: this survey covers 468 employers of all sizes.

- **The Pensions Regulator's Annual Report and Accounts, 2010–2011**: summarises membership data for occupational private and public sector schemes taken from the Regulator's Score database.

- **Pension Funds and their Advisers, 2011**: an annual directory showing details of 2,700 major UK pension funds. The directory covers companies and organisations with 100 or more employees and certain smaller schemes where assets exceed £2 million.

- **The General Lifestyle Survey, 2009** (formerly known as the General Household Survey): a survey by National Statistics through field work, which started in 1971 and is normally carried out annually.

- **The Purple Book 2010, DB pensions universe risk profile**: a joint study by the Pensions Regulator and the Pension Protection Fund focusing mainly on private sector defined benefit schemes. Most of the analysis is based on a sample of almost 6,600 schemes, with much of the basic information coming from scheme returns provided to the Pensions Regulator.

It should be noted that, as some of the questions were multiple-response, percentages shown in some tables may total more than 100% and so care is needed in interpreting the figures.

Percentages throughout have been rounded.

NORMAL PENSION AGE
% Private sector schemes

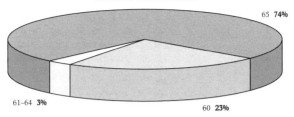

65 **74%**

61–64 **3%**

60 **23%**

Source: Based on data from the National Statistics *Occupational Pension Schemes Survey, 2010.*
            (*See note on page 18 concerning this source.*)

ACCRUAL RATES

Accrual rate used in private sector defined benefit schemes (% schemes)

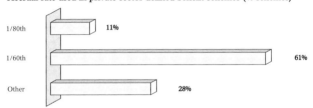

1/80th   **11%**

1/60th   **61%**

Other   **28%**

Note: 'Other' is mainly a combination of differing accrual rates depending on circumstances or member status.

Source: Based on data from the NAPF *Annual Survey, 2010.* (*See note on page 18 concerning this source.*)

CONTRIBUTION RATES

Average contributions paid into pension schemes (% total earnings)

% by benefit type	Member contributions	Employer contributions
Defined Benefit occupational schemes	6.0	21.4
Defined Contribution occupational schemes	4.5	6.9
Group Personal Pension	4.4	5.8
Stakeholder (see note)	3.8	4.3

Note: Stakeholder figures exclude nil employer contributions, which is the level for 28% of stakeholder schemes.

Source: Data from the Association of Consulting Actuaries' *2011 Pension trend survey.*
            (*See note on page 18 concerning this source.*)

PENSION SCHEME MEMBERSHIP BY BENEFIT TYPE
Private sector schemes

Status of scheme	Number of members		Number of schemes	
	DC	DB and Hybrid	DC	DB and Hybrid
Open	1,065,000	6,139,300	33,630	1,720
Closed	224,900	6,899,100	3,880	3,340
Paid up	97,700	925,600	5,060	1,760
Winding up	106,100	226,100	1,870	1,000
Total	**1,493,700**	**14,190,100**	**44,440**	**7,820**

Source: Data taken from the Pensions Regulator's Annual Report and Accounts, 2010–2011.
       (*See note on page 18 concerning this source.*)

PENSION SCHEME MEMBERSHIP BY AGE AND SEX, 2009

Scheme members in Great Britain	Percentage of employees who are members, by age group					
	18–24	25–34	35–44	45–54	55+	Total
Men full time						
Occupational pension*	30	46	57	65	59	**54**
Personal pension	4	13	24	28	29	**21**
Any pension	30	51	68	74	70	**62**
Women full time						
Occupational pension*	27	59	62	65	63	**58**
Personal pension	3	14	18	18	21	**16**
Any pension	27	62	67	70	69	**62**
Women part time						
Occupational pension*	10	42	53	51	35	**40**
Personal pension	2	6	17	13	13	**11**
Any pension	10	42	61	55	39	**44**

Note: * The data include a few people who were not sure if they were in a scheme.
Source: General Lifestyle Survey, 2009. (*See note on page 18 concerning this source.*)

THE LARGEST UK PENSION FUNDS

Pension funds estimated to be in excess of £3,000m

£ million		£ million	
34,112	BT Pension Scheme	5,931	West Yorkshire Pension Fund
30,198	Universities Superannuation Scheme Ltd	5,514	Co-operative Group Pension (Average Career Earnings) Scheme
23,569	Electricity Supply Pension Scheme	5,098	TfL Pension Fund
23,518	Lloyds TSB Group Pension Scheme No 1	4,951	E.On UK plc Electricity Supply Pension Scheme
20,400	Railways Pension Scheme	4,949	Prudential plc DB Scheme
20,250	Royal Mail Pension Plan	4,949	Marks & Spencer DB Scheme
18,805	Royal Bank of Scotland Group Pension Fund	4,810	Royal Insurance Group Pension Scheme
15,675	Barclays Bank UK Retirement Fund	4,696	Tesco plc Pension Scheme
13,042	BP plc Pension Fund	4,618	BAT DB Section
13,017	Mineworkers' Pension Scheme	4,367	The Pensions Trust
12,780	BAE Systems 2000 Pension Plan	4,282	Unilever UK Pension Fund
11,557	HSBC Bank (UK) Pension Scheme	4,237	J. Sainsbury Pension & Death Benefit Scheme
11,448	Shell Contributory Pension Fund		
11,040	National Grid UK Pension Scheme	3,962	Lancashire County Council Pension Fund
10,940	British Steel Pension Scheme		
10,445	Greater Manchester Pension Fund	3,902	Invensys Pension Scheme
10,105	AVIVA Staff Pension Scheme	3,889	Boots Pension Scheme
9,100	Strathclyde Pension Fund	3,855	BMW (UK) Holdings Ltd Operations Pension Scheme
8,277	New (British) Airways Pension Scheme	3,819	Diageo plc Pension Scheme
8,233	BBC Pension Trust	3,556	The Northern Ireland LGO Superannuation Committee
7,658	British Coal Staff Superannuation Scheme	3,270	MMC UK Pension Fund
7,499	GSK Pension Scheme	3,238	Hampshire County Council Pension Fund
7,048	Rolls-Royce Pension Fund		
7,004	HBOS plc Final Salary Pension Scheme	3,236	Zurich Financial Services DB Section
		3,183	City of Edinburgh Council Lothian Pension Fund
6,664	ICI Pension Fund		
6,479	(British) Airways Pension Scheme	3,160	Network Rail Section of the Railways Pension Scheme
6,051	IBM Pension Plan/IBM IT Solutions Pension Scheme	3,085	Essex County Council Pension Fund
6,018	West Midlands Metropolitan Authorities Pension Fund	3,067	Reed Elsevier (UK) Pension Scheme
6,000	Carlsberg UK Ltd DC Section	3,020	London Pensions Fund Authority Pension Fund

Notes: 1. Certain figures relate to the total of several funds within a group.

2. Certain figures are estimates not necessarily supplied by the fund.

Source: Based on information derived from *Pension Funds and their Advisers, 2011*, AP Information Services Ltd, a trading name of Waterlow Legal & Regulatory Ltd. (*See note on page 18 concerning this source.*)

PENSION FUNDS WITH CAPITAL VALUES OF VARIOUS SIZES, ANALYSED BY SIZE OF FUNDS

	Estimated size of fund, £ million								
	0–4.9	5–9.9	10–19.9	20–49.9	50–99.9	100–249.9	250–999.9	1,000+	Total
Number of funds	1,032	72	136	172	167	193	294	296	**2,362**
Value of funds (£ million)	149	528	2,013	5,586	12,222	32,150	150,494	1,293,457	**1,496,599**

Note: Due to rounding, figures may not add up to totals shown.
Source: *Pension Funds and their Advisers, 2011,* AP Information Services Ltd, a trading name of Waterlow Legal & Regulatory Ltd. (*See note on page 18 concerning this source.*)

PENSION FUNDS ANALYSED BY SIZE OF EMPLOYER ORGANISATION

	Number of employees per organisation								
	0–499	500–999	1,000–1,999	2,000–4,999	5,000–9,999	10,000–24,999	25,000–99,999	100,000+	Total
Number of funds	1,162	304	282	304	158	97	46	9	**2,362**

Source: *Pension Funds and their Advisers, 2011,* AP Information Services, a trading name of Waterlow Legal & Regulatory Ltd. (*See note on page 18 concerning this source.*)

SUMMARY OF INVESTMENTS BY SIZE OF PENSION FUND
(all figures are in percentages)

Type of Investment	Pension fund size, £ million								
	0–4.9	5–9.9	10–19.9	20–49.9	50–99.9	100–249.9	250–999.9	1,000+	Av.
Equities									
UK	26.6	30.3	40.7	44.7	45.5	42.0	41.5	40.8	**41.0**
Overseas	2.0	25.8	20.4	12.4	9.9	8.6	10.2	7.5	**8.2**
Fixed Interest									
UK	11.3	23.2	15.3	14.6	13.6	14.1	11.6	13.0	**12.8**
Overseas	0.0	0.4	0.9	1.4	0.6	0.8	1.1	0.9	**0.9**
Index-Linked									
Gilts	22.4	12.1	11.9	15.8	20.1	20.0	17.5	10.2	**12.5**
Property									
UK	13.3	1.2	2.8	2.3	2.3	3.0	3.2	5.4	**4.8**
Overseas	0.0	0.0	0.1	0.0	0.0	0.2	0.1	0.1	**0.1**
Cash & Deposits	1.7	3.3	4.3	3.7	2.9	2.1	1.8	3.0	**2.7**
Others	22.9	3.8	3.7	5.2	5.3	9.4	13.1	19.1	**16.9**

Note: Due to rounding, figures may not add up to 100%.
Source: *Pension Funds and their Advisers, 2011,* AP Information Services, a trading name of Waterlow Legal & Regulatory Ltd. (*See note on page 18 concerning this source.*)

OVERALL FUNDING LEVELS

	Section 179 (£bn)	Technical provisions (£bn)	Full buy-out (£bn)
Total assets	926.2	926.2	926.2
Total liabilities	887.9	1,074.4	1,359.2
Total balance	38.3	−148.2	−433.0
Total balance (for schemes in deficit)	−49.1	–	−436.5
Total balance (for schemes in surplus)	87.4	–	3.5

Note: Shows estimated figures for a total of 6,596 schemes as at 31 March 2010.
Source: *The Purple Book, DB pensions universe risk profile,* the Pensions Regulator, 2010.
 (See note on page 18 concerning this source.)

SECTION 179 FUNDING LEVELS BY SCHEME SIZE

Scheme membership	Schemes in sample	Market value of assets (£bn)	Total s179 liabilities (£bn)	Weighted average funding level (%)	Simple average funding level (%)
5–99	2,342	11.1	10.2	109	106
100–999	3,018	81.4	82.3	99	96
1,000–4,999	832	135.6	138.1	98	95
5,000–9,999	184	102.2	100.2	102	99
10,000+	220	595.9	557.2	107	104
Total	**6,596**	**926.2**	**887.9**	**104**	**100**

Note: Data as at 31 March 2010.
Source: *The Purple Book, DB pensions universe risk profile,* the Pensions Regulator, 2010.
 (See note on page 18 concerning this source.)

SECTION 179 FUNDING LEVELS BY SCHEME MATURITY

Pensions in payment as % liabilities	Schemes in sample	Market value of assets (£bn)	Total s179 liabilities (£bn)	Weighted average funding level (%)	Simple average funding level (%)
25% and less	2,698	134.8	150.3	90	92
26%–50%	2,831	513.3	501.6	102	100
51%–75%	906	255.1	218.0	117	116
76%–100%	161	23.0	18.0	128	138
Total	**6,596**	**926.2**	**887.9**	**104**	**100**

Note: Data as at 31 March 2010.
Source: *The Purple Book, DB pensions universe risk profile,* the Pensions Regulator, 2010.
 (See note on page 18 concerning this source.)

UK SOCIAL SECURITY BENEFITS AND TAX RATES

INTRODUCTION

The main Social Security benefits and tax allowances and rates are outlined in this section.

SOCIAL SECURITY BENEFIT RATES AND ELIGIBILITY RULES

This table gives the rates for 2011/2012 and 2012/2013 and sets out the main eligibility rules. Receipt of some benefits affects entitlement to other benefits. **Eligibility conditions are not necessarily comprehensive and may also be subject to change.** Further information on benefits can be found at *www.direct.gov.uk*. Information is correct as at 1 December 2011, at which date the Government had not announced certain benefit rates for 2012/2013. Spaces have been provided for these figures, which will be published at *www.pensionspocketbook.com*.

All rates are weekly unless otherwise specified

Benefit	Rates, 2011/2012	2012/2013	Eligibility
CHILDREN			
Child Benefit	Eldest child for whom benefit is payable: £20.30 Each subsequent child: £13.40 *tax free*	£20.30 £13.40	Responsible for a child who is: (i) under the age of 16 *or* (ii) aged 16–19 in full-time, but not advanced, education *or* (iii) aged 16 or 17 and registered for work or training. Usually paid to the mother.
Guardian's Allowance	Each eligible child: £14.75 *tax free*	£15.55	Must look after a child who is orphaned and be entitled to **Child Benefit** for that child. Need not be the child's legal guardian. Same rate for all children.
DISABILITY			
Disability Living Allowance	Care component: lowest: £19.55 middle: £49.30 highest: £73.60 Mobility component: lower: £19.55 higher: £51.40 *tax free*	£_____* £_____* £_____* £_____* £_____*	Under 65; *and* (i) has needed help with personal care or walking for previous 3 months and likely to need help for a further 6 months *or* (ii) is disabled and not expected to live more than 6 months. <div align="right">continued ...</div>

All rates are weekly unless otherwise specified

Benefit	Rates, 2011/2012	2012/2013	Eligibility

DISABILITY (continued)

Benefit	Rates, 2011/2012	2012/2013	Eligibility
Attendance Allowance	Lower: £49.30 Higher: £73.60 *tax free*	£_____ * £_____ *	Aged 65 or over *and* (i) has needed help with personal care for 6 months *or* (ii) is disabled and not expected to live more than 6 months.
Severe Disablement Allowance (see **Employment and Support Allowance** for new claims from 27 October 2008)	Basic rate: £62.95 Addition if age first unable to work was: Under 40 £13.80 40–49 £7.10 50–59 £5.60 *tax free*	£_____ * £_____ * £_____ * £_____ *	(i) Aged 16–64 *and* (ii) receiving allowance before April 2001, having been incapable of work for a continuous period of 196 days *and* (iii) assessed as at least 80% disabled.
Carer's Allowance	Allowance: £55.55 *(Earnings limit £100.00)* *taxable*	£_____ * (£_____ *)	(i) Caring (for 35+ hours per week) for a person receiving **Attendance Allowance**, or certain categories of **Disability Living Allowance** or **Constant Attendance Allowance** *and* (ii) aged 16 or over at date of claim.

INDUSTRIAL INJURIES & DISEASE

Benefit	Rates, 2011/2012	2012/2013	Eligibility
Industrial Injuries Disablement Benefit	100% assessment: £150.30 (person aged over 18) *tax free*	£_____ *	Disabled on or after 5 July 1948 because of accident or disease at work.
Reduced Earnings Allowance	Maximum: £60.12 *tax free*	£_____ *	(i) Accident happened or disease started before October 1990 *and* (ii) industrial injury or disease prevents return to previous regular occupation (or other work producing same income level).

All rates are weekly unless otherwise specified

Benefit	Rates, 2011/2012	2012/2013	Eligibility

INDUSTRIAL INJURIES & DISEASE (continued)

Benefit	Rates, 2011/2012	2012/2013	Eligibility
Retirement Allowance	25% of **Reduced Earnings Allowance**, subject to a maximum rate of: £15.03 *tax free*	£_____ *	Replaces **Reduced Earnings Allowance** when claimant reaches State Pension Age (SPA) and ceases employment.
Constant Attendance Allowance	Part-time rate: £30.10 Normal maximum: £60.20 Intermediate rate: £90.30 Exceptional rate: £120.40 *tax free*	£_____ * £_____ * £_____ * £_____ *	Receiving **Industrial Injuries Disablement Benefit** and needs constant care and attention.
Exceptionally Severe Disablement Allowance	Standard: £60.20 *tax free*	£_____ *	(i) Exceptionally severely disabled *and* (ii) entitled to **Constant Attendance Allowance** at one of the two higher rates *and* (iii) needs permanent attendance.

LOW INCOME

Benefit	Rates, 2011/2012	2012/2013	Eligibility
Housing Benefit	Up to full eligible rent. *tax free*		(i) Paying rent *and* (ii) capital less than £16,000 (unless qualifying for State Pension Guarantee Credit).
Income Support (from 27 October 2008 replaced by **Employment and Support Allowance** for claims for illness or disability)	Personal allowances vary with age, marital status, or dependent children. Basic rate for a single person aged 25 or over: £67.50 A couple, both aged 18 or over: £105.95 A lone parent aged 18 or over: £67.50 *tax free*	£_____ * £_____ * £_____ *	(i) Aged at least 16 but less than women's SPA *and* (ii) works less than 16 hours per week *and* (iii) joint capital less than £16,000 *and* (iv) not in receipt of **Jobseeker's Allowance**. *means tested*
Pension Credit	Single pensioner £137.35 (minimum) Couple £209.70 (minimum) *minimum after-tax income*	£_____ * £_____ *	Aged over women's SPA. Lower capital limit £10,000 (from 2 November 2009) *means tested*
Council Tax Benefit	Maximum benefit is 100% of Council Tax. *tax free*		(i) Paying Council Tax *and* (ii) capital less than £16,000 (unless qualifying for State Pension Guarantee Credit).

All rates are weekly unless otherwise specified

Benefit	Rates, 2011/2012	2012/2013	Eligibility

MATERNITY

Benefit	Rates, 2011/2012	2012/2013	Eligibility
Maternity Allowance	For up to 39 weeks: Lesser of (a) 90% of average earnings, *and* (b) £128.73. *tax free*	Lesser of (a) 90% of average earnings, *and* (b) £____*	(i) Not eligible for **Statutory Maternity Pay** *and* (ii) employed/self-employed *and* (iii) must have been employed/ self-employed for at least 26 of the 66 weeks before baby is due, and average earnings at least £30.00 per week (the Maternity Allowance Threshold).
Statutory Maternity Pay	First 6 weeks: 90% of average earnings After 6 weeks, and up to week 39: Lesser of: (a) 90% of average earnings, *and* (b) £128.73. *taxable subject to NICs*	90% of average earnings Lesser of (a) 90% of average earnings, *and* (b) £____*	(i) Employed with same employer for at least 26 weeks, 15 weeks before the baby is due *and* (ii) earning above Lower Earnings Limit.
Statutory Paternity Pay	For up to 2 weeks: Lesser of: (a) 90% of average earnings, *and* (b) £128.73. *taxable subject to NICs*	Lesser of (a) 90% of average earnings, *and* (b) £____*	As for **Statutory Maternity Pay.** For babies due after 2 April 2011, Additional Statutory Paternity Pay may be payable for up to 26 weeks where partner does not take **Statutory Maternity Pay**, etc.
Statutory Adoption Pay	For up to 39 weeks: Amount as for **Statutory Paternity Pay.** *taxable subject to NICs*	Amount as for **Statutory Paternity Pay.**	(i) Employed with same employer for at least 26 weeks before adoption agency informed matched with child *and* (ii) earning above Lower Earnings Limit.

All rates are weekly unless otherwise specified

Benefit	Rates, 2011/2012	2012/2013	Eligibility

RETIREMENT BENEFITS

Benefit	Rates, 2011/2012	2012/2013	Eligibility
Basic State Pension	Based on own or late spouse's NICs: £102.15 Based on spouse's NICs: £61.20 Over 80s pension: £61.20 Over 80s addition £0.25 *taxable*	£107.45 £64.40 £_____* £_____*	(i) Reached State Pension Age *and* (ii) NIC record sufficient. The Over 80s pension is non-contributory and subject to residence conditions. Payable to individuals who receive little/no other State pension.
Additional Pension	SERPS/State Second Pension (S2P) – *see page 34.* *taxable*		(i) Reached State Pension Age *and* (ii) paid Class 1 NICs and/or received credits.
Graduated Retirement Benefit	Per unit: 11.89p Employees may have been contracted-out and receive EPBs instead. *taxable*	_____p*	Based on NICs paid between April 1961 and April 1975.

SICKNESS

Benefit	Rates, 2011/2012	2012/2013	Eligibility
Employment and Support Allowance	**Assessment Phase:** (first 13 weeks of claim) Under 25, up to: £53.45 25 or over, up to: £67.50 **Main Phase:** (from week 14 of claim) In the Work-Related Activity Group, up to: £94.25 In the Support Group, up to: £99.85 May be contribution-based (from NI contributions) or income-related (if on low income). *taxable if contribution-based*	£_____* £_____* £_____* £_____*	Have an illness or disability that affects ability to work, and be over 16 and under State Pension Age; *and* (i) not or no longer receiving **Statutory Sick Pay** *or* (ii) self-employed or unemployed *or* (iii) have been receiving **Statutory Maternity Pay** but not gone back to work due to illness or disability. Must pass a 'Work Capability Assessment' for benefit to continue to be paid from 14th week. *continued …*

All rates are weekly unless otherwise specified

SICKNESS (continued)

Benefit	Rates, 2011/2012	2012/2013	Eligibility
Incapacity Benefit (replaced by **Employment and Support Allowance** from 31 January 2011 for new claimants; all existing claimants are expected to be transferred by Spring 2014)	**Short Term** Under State Pension Age: lower rate (up to 28 weeks): £71.10 adult dependant: £42.65 higher rate (29–52 weeks): £84.15 adult dependant: £42.65 Over State Pension Age: lower rate (up to 28 weeks): £90.45 higher rate (29–52 weeks): £94.25 adult dependant: £52.70 **Long Term** Under State Pension Age: basic rate (after 52 weeks): £94.25 adult dependant: £54.75 **Child Dependency Increases** *first child*: £8.10 *each other child*: £11.35 Age additions: incapacity began aged under 35 £13.80 aged 35–44 £5.60 **Invalidity Allowance (transitional)** lower: £5.60 middle: £7.10 higher: £13.80 *taxable (unless previously on Invalidity Benefit), except for benefits paid in first 28 weeks.*	£____ * £____ * £____ * £____ * £____ * £____ * £____ * £____ * £____ * £____ * £____ * £____ * £____ * £____ * £____ * £____ *	NIC record sufficient. First 28 weeks: (i) employees excluded from **Statutory Sick Pay** and others who meet contribution conditions *and* (ii) unable to work for at least 4 consecutive working days because of sickness or disability. From 29th week, must pass a 'Personal Capability Assessment'. Above State Pension Age, Long-Term Incapacity Benefit ceases. Child Dependency increases are payable, if before 6 April 2003, the claimant was in receipt of **Long-Term Incapacity Benefit**, **Short-Term Incapacity Benefit** at the higher rate, or **Short-Term Incapacity Benefit** at the lower rate and over State Pension Age. For existing claimants of **Invalidity Benefit** a transitional Invalidity Allowance is paid in addition. The level depends on age on the first day of incapacity.
Statutory Sick Pay	Standard rate: £81.60 (up to 28 weeks) *taxable subject to NICs*	£____ *	(i) Earnings at least equal to Lower Earnings Limit *and* (ii) has been sick for at least 4 consecutive days.

All rates are weekly unless otherwise specified

Benefit	Rates, 2011/2012	2012/2013	Eligibility

UNEMPLOYMENT

Benefit	Rates, 2011/2012	2012/2013	Eligibility
Jobseeker's Allowance	Single person aged 25 or over: £67.50 Couple both aged 18 or over: £105.95 Benefits reduced if earnings or pension over specified limits. *taxable NIC credits*	£_____* £_____*	(i) Out of work or working less than 16 hours a week *and* (ii) available for and actively seeking work *and* (iii) between 18 and State Pension Age.

WIDOW'S/WIDOWER'S BENEFITS

Benefit	Rates, 2011/2012	2012/2013	Eligibility
Widow's Pension (replaced by **Bereavement Allowance** from 9 April 2001)	Standard rate: £100.70 *Plus* State Additional pension. Lower rates where widow under age 55 on benefit becoming payable. *taxable*	£_____*	Woman widowed before 9 April 2001 and husband's NIC record sufficient, *and either:* (i) 45 or over when husband died and **Widowed Mother's Allowance** is not payable *or* (ii) 45 or over when **Widowed Mother's Allowance** ceased.
Widowed Mother's Allowance (replaced by **Widowed Parent's Allowance** from 9 April 2001)	Allowance: £100.70 Additional child allowance: *first child*: £8.10 *each other child*: £11.35 *Plus* State Additional pension. *taxable but children's allowance tax free*	£_____* £_____* £_____*	(i) Woman widowed before 9 April 2001 *and* (ii) has dependent child in respect of whom she is entitled to **Child Benefit** *and* (iii) husband's NIC record sufficient.
Bereavement Payment	Lump sum: £2,000 *tax free*	£_____*	Husband's, wife's or civil partner's NIC record sufficient or their death was work-related *and either*: (i) he or she was not entitled to **Retirement Pension** *or* (ii) claimant was under SPA when husband, wife or civil partner died.

All rates are weekly unless otherwise specified

Benefit	Rates, 2011/2012	2012/2013	Eligibility

WIDOW'S/WIDOWER'S BENEFITS (continued)

Benefit	Rates, 2011/2012	2012/2013	Eligibility
Bereavement Allowance	Standard rate: £100.70 Lower rate where widow, widower or surviving civil partner was under age 55 when benefit became payable. *taxable*	£_____*	Husband's, wife's or civil partner's NIC record sufficient or their death was work-related *and*: (i) claimant is under State Pension Age but was 45 or over when husband, wife or civil partner died *and* (ii) **Widowed Parent's Allowance** is not payable.
Widowed Parent's Allowance	Allowance: £100.70 Additional Child Allowance: *first child*: £8.10 *each other child*: £11.35 *Plus* State Additional pension. *taxable but children's allowance tax free*	£_____* £_____* £_____*	(i) Has child for whom entitled to **Child Benefit** (ii) husband's, wife's or civil partner's NIC record sufficient *and* (iii) under State Pension Age.

Note: * As at 1 December 2011 the Government had not announced many benefit rates for 2012/2013. These figures can be found at *www.pensionspocketbook.com*.

Social Fund payments are one-off or annual

Benefit	Rates	Eligibility

SOCIAL FUND

Benefit	Rates	Eligibility
'Sure Start' Maternity Grant	Lump sum: £500 Non-repayable. Paid for each baby. *tax free*	(i) Receiving **Income Support**, income-based **Jobseeker's Allowance,** income-related **Employment and Support Allowance** or certain **Tax Credits** (ii) having a baby or adopting/responsible for one not more than 12 months old *and* (iii) from 11 April 2011, no other children under 16 in family.

Social Fund payments are one-off or annual

Benefit	Rates	Eligibility

SOCIAL FUND (continued)

Benefit	Rates	Eligibility
Funeral Payments	Necessary fees, other specified expenses *and up to* £700 for any other funeral expenses. *tax free*	(i) Specified relationship with deceased *and* (ii) is in receipt of benefits listed above. certain **Tax Credits, Housing Benefit** or **Council Tax Benefit.**
Budgeting/ Crisis Loans & Community Care Grant	Varies. *tax free*	Depends on merits of case and the district Social Fund budget.
Cold Weather Payment	Payment: £25.00 for each qualifying week *tax free*	Receiving **Pension Credit** or certain other benefits during spells of very cold weather.
Winter Fuel Payment	Payment: Full rate £200.00 Reduced rate £100.00 Aged 80 or over: Full rate £300.00 *tax free*	Aged 60 or over on 5 January. (The qualifying age will rise gradually from 2010 in line with changes to the State Pension Age for women; *see page 34.*)

BASIC STATE RETIREMENT PENSIONS

From	Single person		Married couple	
	£ per week	£ per year	£ per week	£ per year
10.04.2000	67.50	3,510.00	107.90	5,610.80
09.04.2001	72.50	3,770.00	115.90	6,026.80
08.04.2002	75.50	3,926.00	120.70	6,276.40
07.04.2003	77.45	4,027.40	123.80	6,437.60
12.04.2004	79.60	4,139.20	127.25	6,617.00
11.04.2005	82.05	4,266.60	131.20	6,822.40
10.04.2006	84.25	4,381.00	134.75	7,007.00
09.04.2007	87.30	4,539.60	139.60	7,259.20
07.04.2008	90.70	4,716.40	145.05	7,542.60
06.04.2009	95.25	4,953.00	152.30	7,919.60
12.04.2010	97.65	5,077.80	156.15	8,119.80
11.04.2011	102.15	5,311.80	163.35	8,494.20
09.04.2012	107.45	5,587.40	171.85	8,936.20

Note: For Basic State pensions in years from 1948 to 1999 inclusive, see *www.pensionspocketbook.com.*

NATIONAL INSURANCE CONTRIBUTION RATES AND STATE SCHEME EARNINGS LIMITS

Tax Year	Earnings per week (£)	National Insurance Contribution Rates — Full rate — Empl-oyer (%)	Full rate — Empl-oyee (%)	Contracted-out Rebate — Earnings per week	Employer COSRS[1]/COMPS[1] (%)	Empl-oyee (%)	National Insurance Earnings Limits — LEL[2] Per Week (£)	LEL[2] Per Month (£)	UEL[2] Per Week (£)	UEL[2] Per Month (£)	State Scheme Limits — LET Per Annum (£)	UAP[1,2] Per Week (£)	UAP[1,2] Per Month (£)
2008/2009	£105.01[3]–UEL Above UEL	12.80 12.80	11.00 1.00	LEL–UEL	3.70	1.40	90.00	390	770.00	3,337	13,500	–	–
2009/2010	£110.01[3]–UEL Above UEL	12.80 12.80	11.00 1.00	LEL–UAP	3.70	1.40	95.00	412	844.00	3,656	13,900	770.00	3,337
2010/2011	£110.01[3]–UEL Above UEL	12.80 12.80	11.00 1.00	LEL–UAP	3.70	1.40	97.00	421	844.00	3,656	14,100	770.00	3,337
2011/2012	£136.01[3]–£139[3] £139.01–UEL Above UEL	13.80 13.80 13.80	0.00 12.00 2.00	LEL–UAP	3.70	1.40	102.00	442	817.00	3,540	14,400	770.00	3,337
2012/2013	£144.01[3]–£146[3] £146.01–UEL Above UEL	13.80 13.80 13.80	0.00 12.00 2.00	LEL–UAP	3.40	n/a	107.00	464	817.00	3,540	* ———	770.00	3,337

Notes:

* As at 1 December 2011 the Government had not announced many benefit rates for 2012/2013. These figures can be found at *www.pensionspocketbook.com*.

1 **COSRS:** Contracted-Out Salary Related Scheme. **COMPS:** Contracted-Out Money Purchase Scheme. **UAP:** Upper Accrual Point.

2 The National Insurance Earnings Limits and the UAP depend on the employee's earnings period. Weekly- and monthly-paid figures are shown above.

3 The Primary and Secondary Thresholds (above which, respectively, employee and employer contributions are payable) also depend on the employee's earnings period. The figures shown above (e.g. £139 for 2011/12) are for weekly-paid employees.

THE STATE PENSION SCHEMES

There are currently two tiers of state pension provision: the Basic State Pension (BSP) and the State Second Pension (S2P), which replaced the State Earnings Related Pension (SERPS) from April 2002.

State Pension Age

State Pension Age (SPA) is currently 65 for men. For women it was to be gradually increased from 60 to 65 over the ten years to April 2020. Having equalised SPA, from 2024 to 2046 it was to have gradually increased from 65 to 68.

However the Pensions Act 2011 accelerates the increase to 66. It provides for SPA to be equalised at 65 by December 2018 and then to increase to 66 by October 2020.

Basic State Pension

This is a flat-rate pension that is payable to any individual that has paid, or been credited as having paid, sufficient National Insurance contributions. Under changes made from 6 April 2010 by the Pensions Act 2007, the number of contributory years needed for a full BSP is 30 for both men and women. Individuals without a sufficient NI record receive a proportion of the full amount.

The BSP is increased in April each year. The Coalition Government announced in June 2010 that from April 2011 annual increases in the BSP will be in line with the higher of earnings increases, price increases (based on the Consumer Prices Index measure, rather than RPI) and 2.5%. However, currently the legislation only reflects the earnings link introduced by the Pensions Act 2007.

SERPS

SERPS accrued between 1978 and 2002 and is paid in addition to the BSP. It is based on a person's earnings throughout their career. When it was replaced in 2002, SERPS was targeting a pension of approximately 20% of the employee's Middle Band Earnings (i.e. earnings between the Lower and Upper Earnings Limits) at SPA.

The State Second Pension

The State Second Pension (S2P) came into effect on 6 April 2002 and is currently an earnings-related scheme like SERPS, which it replaced. Any SERPS entitlement earned up until April 2002 will remain. S2P has salary bands which build up benefits at different rates (see below). Certain non-earners (or low earners), such as those caring for the sick or disabled, also build up a S2P entitlement.

The salary bands used to calculate S2P take into account the Low Earnings Threshold (LET) and a figure which approximates to 3 × LET – 2 × Lower Earnings Limit (LEL). This figure is referred to below as the Middle Earnings Threshold (MET).

There were originally three bands:

Band 1 – LEL to LET: Target pension 40% of earnings
Band 2 – LET to MET: Target pension 10% of earnings
Band 3 – MET to UAP: Target pension 20% of earnings

From around 2030, S2P will become a flat-rate top-up to the BSP. Accrual on Band 1 will be replaced with a flat-rate accrual. Bands 2 and 3 merged from 6 April 2010 and now accrue pension at a rate of 10%; the UAP was frozen from 6 April 2009 for this purpose so that this band gradually disappears.

In April 2011, the DWP issued a Green Paper on reforming the state pension system *(see Section 31)*. Proposals include accelerating the current arrangements for moving to a flat rate S2P, or a more radical move to a single flat-rate pension.

TAX ON PENSION SCHEMES

(See Section 13 for further details)

Registered Pension Schemes

Tax Charge	Tax Rate
Lifetime allowance charge	25% if benefits taken as pension 55% if benefits taken as lump sum
Annual allowance charge	Between 0% and 50% depending on total taxable income[1]
Special annual allowance charge	Between 20% and 30%, depending on total taxable income[2]
Unauthorised payments charge	40%
Unauthorised payments surcharge	15%
Scheme sanction charge	40%, but may be reduced to as low as 15% where the unauthorised payments charge has been paid
Authorised surplus payments charge	35%
Short service refund lump sum charge[3]	20% on first £20,000 50% on balance
Charge on trivial commutation and winding-up lump sums	25% of uncrystallised rights tax free, balance taxed as the top slice of income
Special lump sum death benefits charge[4]	55%
Special ill-health lump sum charge[5]	55%

Notes:
[1] From 6 April 2011, the taxable input is treated as the individual's top slice of income and taxed as such. Before then, the taxable input was taxed at 40%.
[2] Rate for 2010/11. The taxable input is treated as the individual's top slice of income and taxed so as to restrict the relief deemed to have been received to the basic rate.
[3] These rates apply from 2010/11.
[4] This applies to pension protection, annuity protection and drawdown pension fund lump sum death benefits. The tax was 35% for deaths before 6 April 2011. From 6 April 2011, the charge also applies to certain other lump sum death benefits paid where the member was over age 75 at death.
[5] This applies to serious ill-health lump sums paid to members aged over 75.

TAX ALLOWANCES AND RATES

Tax		2011/12	2012/13
Income Tax			
Personal Allowances			
Single person[1,2]		£7,475	£8,105
Married couple where one born before 6 April 1935[3]		£7,295	£7,705
Married couple's allowance, minimum amount		£2,800	£2,960
Bands and Rates			
Starting rate for savings[4]	10%	£0–2,560	£0–2,710
Basic rate[5]	20%	£0–35,000	£0–34,370
Higher rate[5]	40%	£35,001–150,000	£34,371–150,000
Additional rate[5]	50%	over £150,000	over £150,000
Capital Gains Tax			
Exempt amount		£10,600	£10,600
Standard rate[6]		18%	__%
Higher rate[7]		28%	__%
Inheritance Tax			
Nil rate band		£325,000[8]	£_____*
Rate (above nil rate band)[9]		40%	__%
Corporation Tax		Main rate 26%	Main rate __%
Value Added Tax (VAT)			
Registration level		£73,000	£_____*
Standard rate		20%	__%
Insurance Premium Tax (IPT)			
Standard rate		6% of gross premium	__% of gross premium
Higher rate[10]		20% of gross premium	__% of gross premium

Notes:
* As at 1 December 2011 the Government had not announced many tax rates for 2012/2013. These figures can be found at *www.pensionspocketbook.com*.

[1] From 2010/11, the personal allowance is reduced by £1 for every £2 above an income of £100,000.

[2] Higher allowances apply for those aged over 65 and below an income threshold.

[3] Tax relief restricted to 10%, and amount of allowance reduces (subject to minimum amount) for income above a threshold.

[4] Applies only if non-savings income is below tis limit. (Non-savings income is taxed first, then savings income, then dividends.)

[5] The corresponding tax rates on dividends are 10%, 32.5% and 42.5%.

[6] 'Entrepreneurs' Relief' is available for gains made on certain business disposals. A flat-rate 10% tax applies, subject to a lifetime limit (increased from £2 million to £5 million from 23 June 2010, and from £5 million to £10 million on 6 April 2011).

[7] Introduced from 23 June 2010, where total income and gains exceed higher-rate Income Tax threshold.

[8] £650,000 for couples. A transfer of unused nil-rate band from a deceased spouse or civil partner may be made to the estate of their surviving spouse or civil partner who dies on or after 9 October 2007.

[9] Sliding scale of 'Taper Relief' applies on certain gifts made within seven years of death.

[10] Higher rate applies to travel insurance, breakdown insurance and insurance sold in relation to goods subject to VAT.

CONTRACTING OUT

The ability to contract out of the additional State pension was introduced alongside SERPS *(see Section 5)* in 1978.

Since 1988, it has been possible to contract out on either a salary-related (COSR) basis or a money purchase (COMP) basis. However, contracting out on a money purchase basis will be abolished from April 2012 *(see below)*. In addition, proposals for a single flat-rate state pension may involve the abolition of all contracting out, from a later date *(see Section 31)*.

Even where a scheme is no longer actively contracting out, it will need to continue to satisfy the legal requirements relating to those contracted-out rights that have already accrued.

What does contracting out involve?

When an earner is contracted out, his State additional pension (SERPS between April 1978 and April 2002; State Second Pension (S2P) thereafter – *see Section 5*) becomes subject to a contracted-out deduction in respect of his period of contracted-out service. In return, depending on the type of contracted-out scheme *(see below)*:

- the employee and employer pay reduced rates of National Insurance (NI) contributions (Contracted-out Salary-Related scheme, or COSR), *or*

- the HMRC National Insurance Contributions Office (NICO) makes payments directly to the scheme in respect of its contracted-out members (Appropriate Personal Pension, or APP), *or*

- a combination of both the above (Contracted-out Money Purchase scheme, or COMP): reduced rates of NI contributions are paid and the employer pays the level contracting-out rebates into the scheme with top-up age-related payments made to the scheme by NICO.

In order to protect contracted-out members' pensions, extra requirements and restrictions apply to such schemes. With various exceptions in relation to stakeholder schemes, NICO has responsibility for contracting-out procedures and supervision, with some aspects being handled by the HMRC Pension Schemes Services office.

Contracted-out deductions from State additional pension

Where an employee was contracted out prior to 6 April 1997, the accrual of SERPS pension up to that date is subject to a contracted-out deduction broadly equal to the guaranteed minimum pension (GMP) (or the 'notional' GMP in the case of a member of a contracted-out scheme other than a COSR).

Between April 1997 and April 2002, the contracted-out deduction for members of all types of contracted-out scheme was equal to the full SERPS pension, and so they accrued no SERPS benefit.

Following the introduction of S2P in April 2002, members of contracted-out occupational schemes continue to have a contracted-out deduction based on the SERPS level of benefit with earnings limits changed as for S2P *(see Section 5)*. A top-up pension, payable by the State, accrues to such members, equal to the amount (if any) by which the member's S2P would have exceeded the SERPS level of benefit adjusted as for S2P *(see Section 5)*. In contrast, the contracted-out deduction for members of APPs is equal to the full S2P and so they do not accrue a top-up pension from the State (except for members earning below the Low Earnings Threshold – *see Section 5*). These differences are reflected in the rebates available from April 2002 *(see page 45)*.

BASIS OF CONTRACTING OUT

Contracted-out Salary Related scheme (COSR)

Guaranteed Minimum Pensions (GMPs)
Before 6 April 1997, COSRs had to promise to pay at least a minimum pension (the GMP) to each participating employee; this reduced the employee's SERPS pension from the State and, in return, both the employer and the employee paid lower-rate NI contributions. COSRs still need to provide GMPs accrued before 6 April 1997.

These are subject to strict regulatory requirements, including revaluation for early leavers, as described in *Section 15*. Tables of revaluation rates are included *on pages 44 and 45*.

The total NI rebates for contracted-out schemes are split between employee and employer. The split has varied over time, *and components can be found on page 45*.

Legislation that allows schemes the option of converting GMPs to 'normal' scheme benefits of equal value came into effect on 6 April 2009. To use this option, trustees must have employer consent and have consulted affected members.

The Government believes that equalising occupational scheme benefits to reflect the different GMPs between men and women is necessary, and is due to provide draft guidance and regulations for consultation: *see Section 18*.

The Reference Scheme Test (RST)
From 6 April 1997, no further GMPs accrued and, in order to contract out, the scheme has to pass a 'Reference Scheme Test'.

The scheme's actuary is required to certify that the pensions provided by the scheme are 'broadly equivalent to' or 'better than' the pensions under a Reference Scheme which is specified in legislation. The test is applied 'collectively' for employees and separately for their widows, widowers or surviving civil partners. The RST is failed if benefits for more than 10% of individual employees or their survivors are not broadly equivalent to, or better than, pensions under the Reference Scheme. The RST must be carried out separately for each separate benefit scale (if relevant) within a scheme, which must satisfy the test in its own right before the members to whom it applies can be contracted out on a salary-related basis. If separate contracting-out certificates are required for individual employers participating in a scheme, then the test must be carried out separately for each employer. The main features of the Reference Scheme from 6 April 2009 are:

Pension age	65
Pension accrual rate	1/80
Pensionable salary	average qualifying earnings in the last three tax years
Qualifying earnings	90% of earnings between the Lower Earnings Limit (x52) and the Upper Accrual Point (x53)
Service	if limited to a maximum, this must not be less than 40 years
Spouse's or surviving civil partner's pension	50% of the member's pension (based on completed service for members who die before age 65)

Frequency of testing

Legislation requires the actuary to consider, at least every three years, whether there are any changes in the scheme's membership profile that might prevent the scheme from continuing to satisfy the test. A scheme's ability to pass the test must also be reconsidered whenever the actuary is informed of any changes which might affect that ability, such as:

- a change to the terms of the scheme (e.g. the definition of pensionable pay), *or*
- a significant change to the scheme's active membership profile, including remuneration patterns.

Money purchase contracting out

Abolition of money purchase contracting out

Contracting out on a money purchase basis *(as set out below)* is abolished from April 2012. Contracting-out certificates will automatically be cancelled and all affected schemes automatically contracted back in. Members who are affected must be informed of this change.

If an occupational pension scheme wishes instead to switch to contracting out on a salary-related basis, the normal requirements for a COSR *(see above)* must be met, including meeting the Reference Scheme Test.

During a three-year transitional period, existing arrangements for the payment and recovery of age-related rebates *(see below)* will continue. After April 2015, any outstanding payments will be made directly to members.

Contracted-out rights (known as 'Protected Rights' – *see below*) will cease to exist and will be treated in exactly the same way as any other money purchase benefits under the scheme. This applies to contingent spouses' rights as well as to members' rights. Some occupational pension schemes will need to change their rules to remove the Protected Rights requirements and draft regulations have been issued for consultation which propose to allow any such change to be made by resolution during the three-year transitional period.

Contracted-out Money Purchase scheme (COMP)

Occupational money purchase schemes can contract out if contributions equal to the flat-rate contracted-out rebates are paid to the scheme by the employer. Part of this is recoverable from the employee, *as discussed below.*

Prior to April 1997, COMP NI rebates were flat-rate, but since then they have been age-related. The age-related rebates, which are calculated on a unisex basis with no allowance for marital status, are based on the cost of providing the level of benefit given up and incorporate an expense allowance, but are currently capped at 7.4% of Upper Band Earnings which, from 6 April 2009, has been earnings between the Lower Earnings Limit and the Upper Accrual Point, for this purpose *(see table on page 42)*. The underlying assumptions have been revised from time to time.

The flat-rate part of the rebate (currently 3%) is paid by the employer to the trustees. Of this, 1.6% is attributed to, and may be recovered from, the employee. For members whose age-related rebate exceeds the flat-rate part, the balance is paid to the trustees in the following tax year by NICO. All rebates paid into the COMP, and any investment return on them, are known as Protected Rights and have to be used to provide benefits as set out in legislation.

Appropriate Personal Pension (APP)

Employees may take out an APP contract in order to contract out. Employers and employees continue to pay full-rate NI contributions and, following the end of the tax year, NICO then rebates part of these NI contributions by making so-called 'minimum contributions' directly into the APP. A basic rate 'tax rebate' on that part of these minimum contributions deemed to be in respect of employee NI contributions is also paid into the scheme by NICO. These payments, and any investment return on them, are Protected Rights under an APP.

Since April 1997, minimum contributions have been age-related *(see the table on page 43)*, again subject to a cap. The rebates have been revised from time to time to allow for changes in underlying assumptions. For the purpose of calculating the contracting-out rebates available from April 2010, earnings between the Lower Earnings Limit and Upper Accrual Point are divided into two bands representing different components of a member's earnings (as for S2P – *see Section 5*). Different rebate rates then apply to the portions of a member's earnings falling within each band.

Stakeholder schemes

In order to satisfy the stakeholder requirement to accept transfer payments (which may include contracted-out rights), all stakeholder pension schemes must be able to accept contracted-out rights. Most stakeholder schemes are established as personal pensions, and will be contracted out on the same basis as an APP *(see above)* and subject to the same changes when money purchase contracting-out is abolished.

Contracted-out Mixed Benefit scheme (COMB)

With effect from 6 April 1997, COSRs were permitted to retain GMP liabilities whilst contracting out on a money purchase basis for service after that date. Furthermore, from that date, two sections of a single scheme have been permitted to contract out concurrently on the two different bases.

STATE SCHEME PREMIUMS

Before 6 April 1997, contracted-out schemes were able to buy their members back into SERPS by payment of a State scheme premium in a number of circumstances, thereby extinguishing the scheme's liability to provide the member with contracted-out benefits. Only the Contributions Equivalent Premium (CEP) now remains, which COSRs may pay in respect of members with less than two years' qualifying service when either scheme membership ceases or the scheme ceases to contract out. The options for discharging Protected Rights prior to pension commencement are very limited for schemes not in wind-up.

CONTRACTING BACK IN

With the abolition of money purchase contracting out, COMPs and APPs are automatically contracted back in from 6 April 2012 *(see above)*.

In other circumstances, a contracted-out occupational scheme can decide to cease to contract out (and in some cases must do so). In order to do so the trustees or managers must notify Pension Schemes Services and will, in turn, receive a notice from them setting out the date from which the contracting-out certificate is cancelled. From this date all affected members will be contracted back in and the trustees or managers will then have two years to either discharge the rights or determine to preserve them within the scheme, in which case the scheme will need to continue to comply with the relevant requirements. (If no action is taken HMRC may issue a notice giving the scheme six months to discharge the liabilities outside the scheme.) The following methods may be used to secure the liabilities:

- transfer to another contracted-out scheme *(see Section 16)* – member consent will be required unless this is part of a bulk transfer exercise and prescribed conditions are met

- the purchase of an annuity or deferred annuity contract, *or*

- provision of benefits within the scheme that satisfy HMRC requirements.

The scheme does not need to use the same method for all members.

COMPs: AGE-RELATED REBATES

Percentage of Upper Band Earnings

Age[2]	Rebates for COMPs:[1]									
	2002–2003	2003–2004	2004–2005	2005–2006	2006–2007	2007–2008	2008–2009	2009–2010	2010–2011	2011–2012
15	2.6	2.6	2.6	2.6	2.6	3.0	3.0	3.0	3.0	3.0
16	2.6	2.6	2.6	2.6	2.6	3.0	3.0	3.0	3.0	3.0
17	2.7	2.7	2.7	2.7	2.7	3.1	3.1	3.1	3.1	3.1
18	2.7	2.7	2.7	2.7	2.7	3.2	3.2	3.2	3.2	3.2
19	2.8	2.8	2.8	2.8	2.8	3.3	3.3	3.3	3.3	3.3
20	2.8	2.8	2.8	2.8	2.8	3.4	3.4	3.4	3.4	3.4
21	2.9	2.9	2.9	2.9	2.9	3.4	3.4	3.4	3.4	3.4
22	2.9	2.9	2.9	2.9	3.0	3.5	3.5	3.5	3.5	3.5
23	3.0	3.0	3.0	3.0	3.0	3.6	3.6	3.6	3.6	3.6
24	3.1	3.1	3.1	3.1	3.1	3.7	3.7	3.7	3.7	3.7
25	3.1	3.1	3.1	3.1	3.1	3.8	3.8	3.8	3.8	3.8
26	3.2	3.2	3.2	3.2	3.2	3.9	3.9	3.9	3.9	3.9
27	3.2	3.2	3.2	3.2	3.2	4.0	4.0	4.0	4.0	4.0
28	3.3	3.3	3.3	3.3	3.3	4.1	4.1	4.1	4.1	4.1
29	3.4	3.4	3.4	3.4	3.4	4.1	4.2	4.2	4.2	4.2
30	3.4	3.4	3.4	3.4	3.4	4.2	4.3	4.3	4.3	4.3
31	3.6	3.6	3.6	3.6	3.6	4.3	4.4	4.4	4.4	4.4
32	3.6	3.6	3.6	3.6	3.6	4.5	4.5	4.5	4.5	4.5
33	3.7	3.7	3.7	3.7	3.7	4.6	4.6	4.6	4.6	4.6
34	3.8	3.8	3.8	3.8	3.8	4.7	4.7	4.7	4.7	4.7
35	3.8	3.8	3.8	3.8	3.8	4.8	4.8	4.8	4.8	4.8
36	3.9	3.9	3.9	3.9	3.9	5.0	5.0	5.0	5.0	5.0
37	4.0	4.0	4.0	4.0	4.0	5.1	5.1	5.1	5.1	5.2
38	4.1	4.1	4.1	4.1	4.1	5.3	5.3	5.3	5.3	5.3
39	4.1	4.1	4.1	4.1	4.1	5.5	5.5	5.5	5.5	5.5
40	4.3	4.2	4.2	4.2	4.2	5.6	5.6	5.6	5.6	5.6
41	4.4	4.4	4.3	4.3	4.3	5.8	5.8	5.8	5.8	5.8
42	4.6	4.5	4.4	4.4	4.4	5.9	5.9	6.0	6.0	6.0
43	4.8	4.7	4.6	4.5	4.4	6.1	6.1	6.1	6.1	6.1
44	5.0	4.9	4.8	4.7	4.6	6.3	6.3	6.3	6.3	6.3
45	5.3	5.1	5.0	4.9	4.8	6.6	6.4	6.4	6.5	6.5
46	5.5	5.4	5.3	5.1	5.0	6.9	6.7	6.6	6.6	6.6
47	6.0	5.6	5.5	5.4	5.3	7.2	7.1	6.9	6.8	6.8
48	6.8	6.1	5.7	5.6	5.5	7.4	7.4	7.2	7.1	7.0
49	7.8	6.9	6.2	5.8	5.7	7.4	7.4	7.4	7.4	7.3
50	9.0	7.9	7.1	6.4	5.9	↑	↑	↑	↑	↑
51	10.3	9.1	8.1	7.2	6.5					
52	10.5	10.5	9.3	8.2	7.4					
53	10.5	10.5	10.5	9.5	8.4					
54	10.5	10.5	10.5	10.5	9.7					
55	10.5	10.5	10.5	10.5	10.5					
56	10.5	10.5	10.5	10.5	10.5	7.4	7.4	7.4	7.4	7.4
57	10.5	10.5	10.5	10.5	10.5					
58	10.5	10.5	10.5	10.5	10.5					
59	10.5	10.5	10.1	9.7	9.3					
60	10.5	10.5	10.5	10.3	9.9					
61	10.5	10.5	10.5	10.5	10.5					
62	10.5	10.5	10.5	10.5	10.5	↓	↓	↓	↓	↓
63	10.5	10.5	10.5	10.5	10.5					

Notes: [1] Including flat-rate rebate. [2] Age on last day of preceding tax year.

Source: Aon Hewitt, compiled from government information.

APPs: AGE-RELATED REBATES

Percentage of earnings

			Rebates for APPs[1]							
	2004–2005	2005–2006	2006–2007	2007–2008	2008–2009	2009–2010	2010–2011		2011–2012	
Age[2]			Highest				Lower	Higher	Lower	Higher
15	4.2	4.2	4.2	4.7	4.7	4.7	9.4	2.35	9.4	2.35
16	4.2	4.2	4.2	4.7	4.7	4.7	9.4	2.35	9.4	2.35
17	4.2	4.2	4.2	4.8	4.8	4.8	9.6	2.4	9.6	2.4
18	4.3	4.3	4.3	4.9	4.9	4.9	9.8	2.45	9.8	2.45
19	4.3	4.3	4.3	4.9	4.9	4.9	9.8	2.45	10.0	2.5
20	4.4	4.4	4.4	5.0	5.0	5.0	10.0	2.5	10.0	2.5
21	4.4	4.4	4.4	5.1	5.1	5.1	10.2	2.55	10.2	2.55
22	4.5	4.5	4.5	5.2	5.2	5.2	10.4	2.6	10.4	2.6
23	4.5	4.5	4.5	5.2	5.2	5.2	10.4	2.6	10.4	2.6
24	4.5	4.5	4.5	5.3	5.3	5.3	10.6	2.65	10.6	2.65
25	4.6	4.6	4.6	5.4	5.4	5.4	10.8	2.7	10.8	2.7
26	4.6	4.6	4.6	5.5	5.5	5.5	11.0	2.75	11.0	2.75
27	4.7	4.7	4.7	5.5	5.5	5.6	11.2	2.8	11.2	2.8
28	4.7	4.7	4.7	5.6	5.6	5.6	11.2	2.8	11.2	2.8
29	4.8	4.8	4.8	5.7	5.7	5.7	11.4	2.85	11.4	2.85
30	4.8	4.8	4.8	5.8	5.8	5.8	11.6	2.9	11.6	2.9
31	4.9	4.9	4.9	5.9	5.9	5.9	11.8	2.95	11.8	2.95
32	4.9	4.9	4.9	6.0	6.0	6.0	12.0	3.0	12.0	3.0
33	5.0	5.0	5.0	6.0	6.0	6.0	12.2	3.05	12.2	3.05
34	5.0	5.0	5.0	6.1	6.1	6.1	12.2	3.05	12.2	3.05
35	5.1	5.1	5.1	6.3	6.3	6.3	12.6	3.15	12.6	3.15
36	5.1	5.1	5.1	6.4	6.4	6.4	12.8	3.2	12.8	3.2
37	5.1	5.2	5.2	6.5	6.6	6.6	13.2	3.3	13.2	3.3
38	5.2	5.2	5.2	6.7	6.7	6.7	13.4	3.35	13.4	3.35
39	5.2	5.2	5.3	6.8	6.8	6.8	13.6	3.4	13.8	3.45
40	5.3	5.3	5.3	7.0	7.0	7.0	14.0	3.5	14.0	3.5
41	5.3	5.3	5.4	7.1	7.1	7.1	14.2	3.55	14.2	3.55
42	5.5	5.4	5.4	7.2	7.2	7.2	14.6	3.65	14.6	3.65
43	5.7	5.6	5.5	7.4	7.4	7.4	14.8	3.7	14.8	3.7
44	5.9	5.7	5.6	↓	↓	↓	↓	↓	↓	↓
45	6.0	5.9	5.8							
46	6.2	6.1	6.0							
47	6.4	6.3	6.2							
48	6.6	6.5	6.4							
49	7.2	6.7	6.6							
50	8.0	7.3	6.8							
51	9.0	8.0	7.3							
52	10.1	9.0	8.1							
53	10.5	10.2	9.1	7.4	7.4	7.4	14.8	3.7	14.8	3.7
54	10.5	10.5	10.3							
55	10.5	10.5	10.5							
56	10.5	10.5	10.5							
57	10.5	10.5	10.5							
58	10.5	10.5	10.5							
59	10.5	10.2	9.8							
60	10.5	10.5	10.3							
61	10.5	10.5	10.5							
62	10.5	10.5	10.5							
63	10.5	10.5	10.5	↓	↓	↓	↓	↓	↓	↓

Notes: 1 For years up to 2009/10, the rebates shown applied to earnings in the highest of the three S2P earnings bands, and were multiplied by 2 and by ½ for earnings in the lowest and middle bands respectively. For 2010/11 and 2011/12 there are two earnings bands *(see page 40)* and the rebates applying to each are shown above.

2 Age on last day of preceding tax year.

Source: Aon Hewitt, compiled from government information.

FIXED RATE GMP REVALUATION FACTORS

Number of Years	8.5%	7.5%	7.0%	6.25%	4.5%	4.0%
1	1.085	1.075	1.070	1.0625	1.045	1.040
2	1.177	1.156	1.145	1.1289	1.092	1.082
3	1.277	1.242	1.225	1.1995	1.141	1.125
4	1.386	1.335	1.311	1.2744	1.193	1.170
5	1.504	1.436	1.403	1.3541	1.246	1.217
6	1.631	1.543	1.501	1.4387	1.302	1.265
7	1.770	1.659	1.606	1.5286	1.361	1.316
8	1.921	1.783	1.718	1.6242	1.422	1.369
9	2.084	1.917	1.838	1.7257	1.486	1.423
10	2.261	2.061	1.967	1.8335	1.553	1.480
11	2.453	2.216	2.105	1.9481	1.623	1.539
12	2.662	2.382	2.252	2.0699	1.696	1.601
13	2.888	2.560	2.410	2.1993	1.772	1.665
14	3.133	2.752	2.579	2.3367	1.852	1.732
15	3.400	2.959	2.759	2.4828	1.935	1.801
16	3.689	3.181	2.952	2.6379	2.022	1.873
17	4.002	3.419	3.159	2.8028	2.113	1.948
18	4.342	3.676	3.380	2.9780	2.208	2.026
19	4.712	3.951	3.617	3.1641	2.308	2.107
20	5.112	4.248	3.870	3.3619	2.412	2.191
21	5.547	4.566	4.141	3.5720	2.520	2.279
22	6.018	4.909	4.430	3.7952	2.634	2.370
23	6.530	5.277	4.741	4.0324	2.752	2.465
24	7.085	5.673	5.072	4.2844	2.876	2.563
25	7.687	6.098	5.427	4.5522	3.005	2.666
26	8.340	6.556	5.807	4.8367	3.141	2.772
27	9.049	7.047	6.214	5.1390	3.282	2.883
28	9.818	7.576	6.649	5.4602	3.430	2.999
29	10.653	8.144	7.114	5.8015	3.584	3.119
30	11.558	8.755	7.612	6.1641	3.745	3.243
31	12.541	9.412	8.145	6.5493	3.914	3.373
32	13.607	10.117	8.715	6.9587	4.090	3.508
33	14.763	10.876	9.325	7.3936	4.274	3.648
34	16.018	11.692	9.978	7.8557	4.466	3.794
35	17.380	12.569	10.677	8.3467	4.667	3.946
36	18.857	13.512	11.424	8.8683	4.877	4.104
37	20.460	14.525	12.224	9.4226	5.097	4.268
38	22.199	15.614	13.079	10.0115	5.326	4.439
39	24.086	16.785	13.995	10.6372	5.566	4.616
40	26.133	18.044	14.974	11.3021	5.816	4.801
41	28.354	19.398	16.023	12.0084	6.078	4.993
42	30.764	20.852	17.144	12.7590	6.352	5.193
43	33.379	22.416	18.344	13.5564	6.637	5.400
44	36.217	24.098	19.628	14.4037	6.936	5.617
45	39.295	25.905	21.002	15.3039	7.248	5.841
46	42.635	27.848	22.473	16.2604	7.574	6.075
47	46.259	29.936	24.046	17.2767	7.915	6.318
48	50.191	32.182	25.729	18.3565	8.271	6.571

Note: The revaluation rate of 4.0% applies for leavers on or after 6 April 2007. *The rate to be applied for leavers on or after 6 April 2012 is (at time of writing) under consultation, with 4.75% having been recommended.*

Source: Aon Hewitt.

SECTION 148 ORDERS:
REVALUATION OF EARNINGS FACTORS

Tax Year of Earnings	Tax Year of Termination								
	2011/12 (%)	2010/11 (%)	2009/10 (%)	2008/09 (%)	2007/08 (%)	2006/07 (%)	2005/06 (%)	2004/05 (%)	2003/04 (%)
1978/79	705.0	686.9	677.6	654.2	623.8	595.3	572.4	545.9	522.3
1979/80	610.5	594.5	586.3	565.7	538.8	513.7	493.5	470.1	449.2
1980/81	493.6	480.2	473.3	456.1	433.7	412.7	395.8	376.3	358.8
1981/82	397.1	385.9	380.2	365.7	347.0	329.4	315.3	298.9	284.3
1982/83	351.5	341.4	336.1	323.0	306.0	290.0	277.2	262.3	249.0
1983/84	319.2	309.8	305.0	292.8	276.9	262.1	250.2	236.4	224.1
1984/85	288.2	279.5	275.0	263.7	249.0	235.3	224.3	211.5	200.1
1985/86	264.2	256.0	251.7	241.2	227.4	214.5	204.2	192.2	181.5
1986/87	234.4	226.9	223.0	213.3	200.7	188.8	179.3	168.3	158.5
1987/88	211.3	204.3	200.7	191.7	179.9	168.9	160.1	149.8	140.7
1988/89	186.4	180.0	176.7	168.4	157.5	147.4	139.3	129.8	121.4
1989/90	158.5	152.7	149.7	142.2	132.4	123.3	115.9	107.4	99.8
1990/91	140.9	135.5	132.7	125.7	116.6	108.1	101.2	93.3	86.2
1991/92	118.8	113.9	111.4	105.0	96.7	89.0	82.8	75.6	69.2
1992/93	105.5	100.8	98.5	92.5	84.7	77.5	71.6	64.9	58.8
1993/94	95.7	91.3	89.0	83.3	75.9	69.0	63.5	57.0	51.3
1994/95	89.8	85.5	83.3	77.8	70.7	63.9	58.5	52.3	46.7
1995/96	81.8	77.7	75.6	70.3	63.5	57.0	51.9	45.9	40.5
1996/97	76.8	72.9	70.8	65.7	59.0	52.7	47.7	41.9	36.7
1997/98	68.4	64.6	62.7	57.8	51.4	45.5	40.7	35.1	30.2
1998/99	61.0	57.4	55.5	50.9	44.8	39.1	34.5	29.2	24.5
1999/00	54.5	51.1	49.3	44.8	38.9	33.5	29.1	24.0	19.5
2000/01	45.4	42.1	40.4	36.2	30.7	25.6	21.4	16.6	12.4
2001/02	39.8	36.6	35.0	31.0	25.7	20.7	16.8	12.2	8.1
2002/03	34.0	31.0	29.5	25.6	20.5	15.8	11.9	7.5	3.6
2003/04	29.4	26.5	25.0	21.2	16.3	11.7	8.1	3.8	
2004/05	24.6	21.8	20.4	16.8	12.1	7.6	4.1		
2005/06	19.7	17.0	15.6	12.2	7.6	3.4			
2006/07	15.8	13.2	11.8	8.5	4.1				
2007/08	11.2	8.7	7.4	4.2					
2008/09	6.7	4.3	3.1						
2009/10	3.5	1.2							
2010/11	2.3								

Source: Aon Hewitt, compiled from government information.

CONTRACTING-OUT REBATES

Tax Years	Employee	Employer	
	(% Upper Band Earnings)	COSR (% UBE)	COMP (See Note) (% UBE)
2002/03 to 2006/07	1.60	3.50	1.00
2007/08 to 2011/12	1.60	3.70	1.40
2012/13 to 2016/17	1.40	3.40	n/a

Note: For COMPs, in addition to the flat-rate rebates shown in the table, a further age-related payment is due from NICO. The total age-related rebate (flat-rate rebate plus age-related payment) is specified for each tax year up to 2011/12 (*see page 42*).

Source: Aon Hewitt, compiled from government information.

SCHEME DESIGN AND BENEFITS

This section gives a brief explanation of the different types of benefit commonly provided by occupational pension schemes in the UK, and some of the factors that affect the design of those benefits.

Over the past ten years or so, many employers have closed traditional final salary pension schemes because of the significant risks, and associated costs, that they have to bear. In many cases employers have replaced these with defined contribution schemes where individual members bear most of the risks. However, employers are also looking for other solutions that fall somewhere between these two extremes, retaining the risks they want to manage, whilst providing benefits which are still attractive to employees from a recruitment and retention perspective.

TYPES OF PENSION BENEFIT

Pension schemes are often classified as defined benefit (DB) or defined contribution (DC). However, many of the newer designs incorporate features of both types. Further, hybrid schemes also exist which provide different types of benefit in different circumstances. The key characteristics of the various scheme designs are covered below.

Defined Contribution

DC schemes provide benefits which depend on the amount of the contributions paid into the scheme, the investment return credited to those contributions, any expenses deducted and the financial conditions at the time benefits are converted into a future retirement income. *The types of arrangement that are based on DC are described in Section 8.* The National Employment Savings Trust (NEST), *which is discussed in Section 10*, will also provide DC benefits.

Final Salary

A traditional form of DB scheme is the final salary scheme, under which the pension paid is equal to the number of years worked, multiplied by the member's salary at or near to retirement, multiplied by a factor known as the accrual rate (commonly 1/80 or 1/60). After a career of 40 years, this would give a pension of one-half or two-thirds of the member's 'final salary'. Members can usually choose to give up some of their pension in return for a lump sum (currently tax free), although some schemes provide a lump sum as a separate benefit.

Members generally pay a fixed rate of contributions (or no contributions in some cases), with the employer funding the balance of the costs.

CARE

Career Average Revalued Earnings (CARE) schemes are DB in nature, but are a variation of the traditional final salary design. Rather than the pension at retirement being based on earnings close to retirement, it is based on the average earnings throughout the member's entire career. These earnings are usually revalued in line with some index, commonly the Retail Prices Index (RPI).

If the revaluation rate turns out to be lower than the average earnings increases received by the member (which is generally the case), then the pension at retirement will be less than for an otherwise identical final salary scheme. From an employer's perspective, this means that CARE schemes usually cost less to fund.

Cash Balance and Retirement Balance

Under these arrangements, members build up lump sum benefits on either a final salary or a CARE basis. For example, the lump sum accrual rate could be 20% of salary per annum, giving a lump sum after 40 years of 8 times either final or career average earnings. Another way of thinking of these is as a DC benefit with the investment return guaranteed at the outset. For example, the return could be defined as the increase in RPI plus 2% per annum.

Up to retirement, the scheme is considered as DB. At retirement, part of the lump sum can be taken as cash with the balance turned into pension. The conversion to pension is usually carried out by purchasing an annuity with an insurance company, in the same way as for a DC scheme. However, in some cases preferential conversion terms are offered through the scheme itself.

Hybrid schemes

There are many forms of hybrid scheme which incorporate features of the above designs. The two most common types are:

- a better of two (or more) different types of benefit, for example a DC scheme with a minimum level of benefit calculated on a DB basis, *and*

- a combination of different types of benefit, for example benefits might accrue on a final salary basis up to a certain level of earnings, but on a DC basis above that level.

Risk sharing

Each of the scheme types described above shares risks between member and sponsor to some degree. With a final salary scheme most risks, including investment and longevity, rest with the sponsor, whereas DC schemes pass most of the risks to the member. In recent years some schemes have started to incorporate alternative risk-sharing features into their benefit design. For example, longevity-adjusted schemes adjust future benefit accrual to take account of changes in longevity.

In March 2010 the DWP issued an information note on risk sharing with case studies for employers considering making changes to their DB scheme.

OTHER ISSUES AFFECTING SCHEME DESIGN

Automatic enrolment

From 2012 onwards employers will be required to automatically enrol eligible jobholders into a qualifying pension scheme and to make minimum contributions on behalf of their workers. The employer may use its own scheme, if that meets minimum quality requirements, or NEST. *This auto-enrolment regime is described in Section 9. For details on NEST see Section 10.*

Registered Pension Schemes

To obtain tax concessions, the majority of UK pension schemes are registered with HMRC. Registered schemes are subject to requirements that impact on the type and size of benefits that they can provide. *These requirements are described in Section 13. Section 14 describes arrangements outside the tax-privileged environment.*

Options after age 75

Until 5 April 2011, members of registered pension schemes were required to take lump sums, convert DC or Cash Balance funds into annuities or begin income drawdown by age 75. From 6 April 2011, most of these requirements were removed. In addition, some of the restrictions on income drawdown were removed for members with a minimum income of £20,000. *These provisions are described in Sections 8 and 13.*

Interaction with State Benefits

Many schemes are designed to target an overall level of pension at retirement, including state pensions. Schemes can also contract out of the State Second Pension (S2P), and previously SERPS. *For information on contracting out, see Section 6.* From 6 April 2012, contracting out on a money purchase basis will be abolished.

AVCs

From 6 April 1988, all occupational pension schemes had to allow members to make Additional Voluntary Contributions (AVCs). Free-standing Additional Voluntary Contributions (FSAVCs) were introduced from 26 October 1987 to allow members greater flexibility in investment choice and portability should they leave service *(see Section 8).*

With effect from 6 April 2006, the requirement for trustees to provide members with access to an AVC arrangement was removed. However, this does not stop such a facility being offered.

Pension increases in payment

The Pensions Act 1995 made it compulsory for approved occupational pension schemes to provide at least Limited Price Indexation (LPI) of pensions accrued after 5 April 1997 once in payment. However, the scope of this requirement was reduced from 6 April 2005 when the Pensions Act 2004 removed it for pensions arising from money purchase benefits coming into payment on or after that date.

For pensions that remain subject to the LPI requirement, the minimum annual increase required is the lower of the RPI increase and 5% for service between 6 April 1997 and 5 April 2005, and the lower of the RPI increase and 2.5% for service after 5 April 2005.

In July 2010, the Government announced its intention to move from using RPI to using the Consumer Prices Index (CPI) as the basis for future statutory minimum increases to pensions in payment and revaluations in deferment. Following consultation, the changes were introduced from the beginning of 2011 and much of the necessary amending legislation (including provisions to protect some schemes which retain RPI as a basis for increases) was included in the Pensions Act 2011.

Salary sacrifice

A salary sacrifice is an arrangement whereby an employee waives his entitlement to part of his salary (or bonus), in exchange for his employer paying a pension contribution of an equivalent amount.

An advantage of salary sacrifice is that savings in National Insurance contributions (NICs) can be generated. Employee contributions are paid out of salary which is subject to NICs (both employer and employee), whereas employer contributions are not.

In the past, salary sacrifice was used almost exclusively by higher earners. However the concept is now more commonplace through the growth of flexible remuneration plans, under which an employee has a flex fund which can be used to purchase selected benefits from those on offer, with the remaining money being paid like a normal salary.

Scheme modifications

Section 67 of the Pensions Act 1995, as updated by the Pensions Act 2004 with effect from 6 April 2006, sets out conditions for making 'regulated modifications' of accrued rights or entitlements to pension scheme benefits. Essentially, modifications of an occupational pension scheme are 'voidable' unless for each member or survivor:

- *either* informed consent has been given in writing by the member or survivor *or* (where permitted) the actuarial equivalence requirements, involving certification by the scheme actuary, have been met, *and*
- the trustees have formally determined to make (or have consented to) the modification and, before it takes effect, have notified the affected members and survivors.

Informed consent is always required in relation to a special category of major changes called protected modifications. Members must be given a reasonable opportunity to make representations, and the modification must take effect within a reasonable period of the consent being given.

The Pensions Regulator may make an order declaring the modification void if the requirements have not been met. It also has the power to levy fines on trustees and others exercising a power to modify a scheme, where voidable modifications have been made or the requirements specified in an order by the Regulator have not been met. The Regulator has issued a Code of Practice to help trustees comply with the legislation and to provide guidance on what the Regulator considers to be reasonable periods for the various stages of the process.

Consultation by employers

The Information and Consultation of Employees Regulations 2004 took effect on 6 April 2005. These regulations apply to businesses that employ 50 or more staff. The regulations give employees the right – in certain circumstances – to be informed and consulted about the business they work for, including:

- the prospects for employment, *and*
- substantial changes in work organisation (e.g. proposed redundancies or changes in working hours) or contractual relationships.

The requirement for employers to have an agreement to inform and consult is not automatic but can be triggered in various ways, for example by a formal request from a minimum number of members. If an employer fails to initiate negotiations for an agreement to inform and consult employees when required to do so, or when negotiations fail, 'standard provisions' apply.

In addition, from 6 April 2006, the Pensions Act 2004 introduced provisions that require employers to consult with members before they can make certain listed changes to a pension scheme. Listed changes include increasing normal pension age, closing a scheme, changing from DB to DC, ceasing or reducing DB accrual, changing what elements of pay constitute pensionable earnings or reducing an employer's contribution to a DC scheme. The Department for Work and Pensions published guidance (updated in April 2010) on the regulations, in order to help employers comply with the legislation.

Inalienability of occupational pension

With certain exceptions (e.g. where a scheme member has defrauded his employer), entitlements or rights under occupational pension schemes may not be forfeited, assigned, surrendered, subjected to a charge or lien, or set off, and an agreement to do any of these things is unenforceable. The primary legislation was amended with effect from 6 April 2005 to permit trustees to reduce future benefits to recover a previous payment made in error and from 11 August 2011 the regulations are amended to permit schemes to meet the annual allowance charge from scheme benefits *(see Section 14)*.

Cross-border activities

The Pensions Act 2004 introduced a number of provisions relating to cross-border activities under the EU Pensions Directive. A UK scheme that wishes to accept contributions from employers elsewhere in the EU (which employ members of the scheme who work elsewhere in the EU) must receive a general authorisation from the Pensions Regulator. It must also apply for and receive approval from the Regulator in respect of each EU employer. Based on information passed on about the social and labour laws of the host member state (i.e. the other EU country), the UK scheme has the responsibility for ensuring compliance, with the Regulator being able to monitor such compliance and impose sanctions for non-compliance. Where the cross-border activity is the other way round (i.e. the UK is the host state and the scheme is established elsewhere), the Regulator has the role of notifying the other country's authority of relevant UK law and monitoring compliance with it. The EU Directive requires that non-money purchase cross-border schemes are fully funded at all times. UK law interprets this as meeting the statutory funding objective introduced by the Pensions Act 2004 *(see Section 20)*. In addition, in order to be authorised, cross-border schemes must obtain annual actuarial valuations, with any deficit against the statutory funding objective being removed within 24 months of the valuation's effective date.

DEFINED CONTRIBUTION PENSION SCHEMES

Defined contribution (DC) schemes provide benefits which depend on the amount of the contributions paid into the scheme, the investment return credited to those contributions, any expenses deducted and the financial conditions at the time benefits are converted into a future retirement income. The Pensions Act 2011 amended the definition of money purchase benefits (for example in the Pension Schemes Act 1993) so that:

- a benefit other than a pension in payment is defined as money purchase if its rate or amount is calculated solely by reference to assets which 'must necessarily suffice for the purposes of its provision to or in respect of the member', *and*
- a pension in payment is defined as money purchase if it meets the above definition before it comes into payment and is then secured by an annuity contract or insurance policy made with an insurer.

At time of writing, the commencement order required to put this amendment into effect had not yet been laid.

There are various types of arrangement that may be used to provide DC benefits (also known as money purchase benefits) which are considered below. The National Employment Savings Trust (NEST) will also provide DC benefits *and is discussed in Section 10.*

TYPES OF DC PENSION SCHEME

Trust-based occupational pension scheme

Employer-sponsored occupational DC pension schemes and NEST are operated as a trust. Many occupational pension schemes are now DC and many schemes now have separate DC and DB sections. Most schemes offer additional voluntary contributions on a DC basis and many that accept transfers into the scheme will offer DC benefits in respect of the transfer payment received even if the other benefits are accruing on a DB basis.

Personal pensions and retirement annuity contracts

Personal pensions in their present form have been available since July 1988. They were introduced with the intention of extending pension choice and encouraging individuals not in occupational schemes to save for retirement. All personal pensions are DC and are provided as a contract with an insurer or other provider, rather than trust-based. Personal pensions replaced retirement annuity contracts (RACs), often referred to as s226 contracts. Those who already had RACs prior to July 1988 were allowed to continue to contribute to them. A personal pension scheme that is used for the purpose of contracting out of S2P (SERPS prior to 6 April 2002) is known as an 'Appropriate Personal Pension' (APP).

Group personal pensions

Group personal pensions (GPPs) are personal pensions arranged by an employer for the benefit of its employees. These are often seen as a low-cost (to the employer) alternative to a DC trust-based occupational pension scheme, as most administration is handled by the insurance company running the GPP and is usually included in the annual management charge deducted from the members' funds.

Self-invested personal pensions

A self-invested personal pension (SIPP) is an arrangement under a personal pension scheme which allows the member to choose the investments. As the members may select its investments, SIPPs are classed as 'investment-regulated pension schemes'. As such, SIPPs are subject to prohibitive tax charges if they invest in residential property or most tangible moveable assets.

Small self-administered schemes

Small self-administered schemes (SSAS) are a particular type of trust-based occupational pension scheme and were introduced for company controlling directors in 1973. Many of these are constituted on a DC basis. Due to the close relationship between the employer, the trustees and the members of these schemes, often all being the same people, HMRC imposed particular restrictions on SSASs. Since 6 April 2006, these restrictions have been removed and SSASs are now subject to the tax regime introduced under the Finance Act 2004. Most SSASs are 'investment-regulated pension schemes' and are, therefore, subject to prohibitive tax charges if they invest in residential property or most tangible moveable assets.

Free-standing AVC schemes

Free-standing AVC schemes (FSAVCs) are insurance contracts to which employees can contribute as an alternative to an AVC arrangement within an occupational pension scheme. Under the pre-6 April 2006 tax regime members of occupational pension schemes could only pay limited contributions (if any) to a personal pension at the same time as accruing benefits under the occupational scheme. Since 6 April 2006 these contracts are virtually indistinguishable from personal pensions and many have been closed and rolled into personal pension arrangements.

Stakeholder pensions

Stakeholder pension schemes were introduced by the Government in 2001 as a way of encouraging more private pension provision. They became available for members from 6 April 2001. Stakeholder schemes can only provide money purchase benefits. Various special requirements and restrictions apply to stakeholder schemes, including that the scheme must:

- be formally registered as a stakeholder scheme with the Pensions Regulator, *and*
- meet certain 'minimum standards', including in relation to the level of charges, flexibility of contribution payments, acceptance of transfer payments, and provision of information.

A stakeholder scheme must be contracted out, although individual members will usually be able to decide whether to be contracted out or contracted in.

Since October 2001, employers with five or more employees have had to 'designate' and provide access to a stakeholder scheme, and publicise this to those employees who are not already covered by a suitable pension scheme. For any employee who requests it, the employer must deduct contributions from the employee's remuneration and pay them within stated time limits to the designated scheme. However, there is no requirement for the employer to contribute to the scheme.

When the automatic enrolment duties are introduced *(see Section 9)* the access requirements to stakeholder schemes will be removed, although the requirements to deduct contributions and pay them to the scheme will continue for existing arrangements.

Minimum standards

With a few exceptions *(see below)*, the maximum expense charge that can be levied on a member of a stakeholder scheme is equivalent to an annual charge of 1.5% of the value of the member's fund for the first ten years of membership, reducing to 1% thereafter. However, where the member joined the scheme before 6 April 2005, the maximum is 1% throughout. No extra charges can be imposed on ceasing contributions or transferring out of the scheme. The exceptions include costs incurred in buying an annuity or administering income drawdown, stamp duty and other dealing costs incurred in buying or selling investments, market value adjustments on with-profits funds, maintenance costs on property, and costs associated with pension sharing activity or complying with an earmarking order on divorce. Costs of life assurance or waiver of contribution benefit, or financial advice, must be included within the above charge unless it is offered under a separate, optional contract with the extra charges explained.

The highest minimum contribution level which a stakeholder scheme can impose is £20 (net of basic rate tax relief), both for regular and one-off contributions.

Stakeholder schemes must accept any transfer payments from other pension schemes and, accordingly, must be contracted out.

All stakeholder schemes must produce an annual declaration confirming compliance with the various stakeholder requirements, including those relating to maximum charges. The scheme's 'reporting accountant' must give a statement as to the reasonableness of this declaration.

Investments

A stakeholder scheme must not require members to make a choice about how their money is invested. A default option must be provided, although alternative investment options can also be offered. The Government introduced a requirement from 6 April 2005 for default funds to be 'lifestyled', whereby assets in the fund are gradually moved from equities towards fixed income as retirement nears.

Subject to certain conditions, stakeholder-only with-profits funds may be offered. Money invested in deposit funds must earn a return (net of charges) of at least base rate minus 2%. Trustees or managers may not invest in collective investment schemes which contain a bid/offer spread.

BENEFITS

From 6 April 2006, all types of DC pension scheme became subject to the tax regime introduced under the Finance Act 2004.

Under the tax legislation, DC arrangements may provide the same types of benefit as other registered schemes, *which are described in Section 13*. DC schemes have greater flexibility when it comes to the form of pension benefits, which may be paid as a lifetime annuity, drawdown pension or a scheme pension. If a scheme pension is provided, the member must also have the option to purchase a lifetime annuity contract on the open market.

Drawdown pension was previously referred to in tax legislation as either unsecured pension or alternatively secured pension. Unsecured pension referred to drawdown pension paid up to age 75 (or, under transitional arrangements, age 77 for those who reached age 75 between 22 June 2010 and 5 April 2011); alternatively secured pension referred to drawdown pension paid after that age. From 6 April 2011, the previously different rules applicable to unsecured and alternatively secured pensions were harmonised, removing the distinction between the two types of drawdown.

Funds that have been designated to provide unsecured drawdown pension may be used to purchase short-term annuities or provide pension via income withdrawal.

From 6 April 2011, members who do not satisfy the minimum income requirement and are not eligible for flexible drawdown *(see below)* are subject to a limit on the maximum pension that may be drawn each year. This maximum, which is referred to as the 'basis amount', is the amount of a notional annuity that could be purchased by the designated funds using annuity tables published by the Government Actuary's Department. The basis amount must be calculated at least every three years up to age 75 and annually thereafter.

Prior to 6 April 2011, for unsecured pension, annual income could not exceed 120% of the basis amount, and for alternatively secured pension, income drawn each year had to be between 55% and 90% of the basis amount.

Flexible drawdown

From 6 April 2011, individuals who satisfy the minimum income requirement and who are not active members of a scheme are eligible for flexible drawdown. Under flexible drawdown, there is no upper limit to the amount that can be taken in any year. To satisfy the minimum income requirement, the member must have secure income above a specified level, currently set at £20,000 p.a. Secure income for this purpose includes state pensions, scheme pensions, and annuities to the extent that they are guaranteed not to decrease.

CONTRACTING OUT

Occupational money purchase schemes, personal pension schemes and stakeholder schemes may be used to contract out of S2P (SERPS prior to 6 April 2002). Prior to 1 October 2007, most SIPPs were unable to hold contracted-out benefits. *See Section 6 for details on contracting out.* Contracting out on a money purchase basis will be abolished from April 2012. Contracting-out certificates will automatically be cancelled and all affected schemes automatically contracted back in.

REGULATION OF DC SCHEMES

The Pensions Regulator (the Regulator) has a statutory responsibility for work-based DC schemes. A work-based pension scheme is any scheme that an employer makes available to employees. This includes all occupational DC schemes, any stakeholder and personal pension schemes where employees have direct payment arrangements, and it will include NEST.

The Regulator's objectives include protecting members' benefits and improving the understanding of good administration. It has issued a series of good practice guidance on the running of DC schemes for trustees and employers. This includes guidance on payment of contributions, member retirement options, communicating with members and a guide for members on investment options.

With the expected increase in DC membership following the introduction of auto-enrolment *(see Section 9)*, the Regulator initiated a consultation in January 2011 on how it can help to raise standards and achieve good outcomes for members of DC schemes. It issued an initial response to this consultation in July 2011 and indicated its intention to publish a detailed response and proposals in autumn 2011.

The Department for Work and Pensions is the government department with over-arching responsibility for most of the non-tax legislation governing pension schemes. For DC schemes it has published guidance on the default investment options offered by schemes that are used for auto-enrolment purposes. This guidance builds on one of the Investment Governance Group's *Principles for Investment Governance for DC schemes* – these principles were issued in November 2010.

The Financial Services Authority (FSA) authorises and regulates firms that operate or provide advice on personal pension schemes or on investments. It also regulates the sale and marketing of personal pension schemes. As a result, the Regulator and the FSA have joint responsibility to regulate workplace group personal pension schemes. The FSA and the Regulator have jointly published a guide on talking to employees about pensions.

The Government announced in June 2010 that the FSA is to be dismantled, and its duties are to be taken over by the Prudential Regulation Authority and the Consumer Protection and Markets Authority.

See also Section 12, The Pensions Regulatory System.

DISCLOSURE

The disclosure requirements for occupational DC schemes are discussed *in Section 17*. The requirements for other types of DC scheme are generally the same. The requirements for annual statements provided by stakeholder schemes were more detailed; however, under regulations which came into effect on 1 December 2010, schemes can adopt the alternative of providing much less detailed information (which must include the value of the member's rights at the beginning and end of the year, details of charges deducted, and a summary of contributions, tax relief and other deductions and payments), accompanied by a statement of the more detailed information that may be requested. In addition, DC schemes provided by an insurer – such as stakeholder and personal pension products – must comply with additional disclosure requirements imposed by the FSA. The DWP is undertaking a reassessment of the disclosure regulations with the aim of streamlining the provisions and this might result in more consistency between occupational DC schemes and other types of DC scheme.

AON Hewitt

Auto-enrolment. We won't let it creep up on you.

You really don't want to fall into the trap of ignoring auto-enrolment. With deadlines approaching, there is a growing realisation that implementation could be painful.

Auto-enrolment won't be significant only for payroll and pensions; it could impact your entire benefits programme. And then there are the communication, administration, data management and cost aspects to consider.

The good news is that our experienced consultants combine the latest thinking with a practical approach. Let them deliver the right solution for your auto-enrolment challenges and help you avoid being caught out by any nasty surprises.

Make auto-enrolment simple. Aon Hewitt's thinking, tools and leading-edge technology capabilities will cut out the complexity and give you the solutions you need.
To find out more, call 0800 279 5588 or email enquiries@aonhewitt.com

aonhewitt.co.uk/benefits-solutions

Aon Hewitt Limited is authorised and regulated by the Financial Services Authority. Registered in England & Wales. Registered No: 4396810. Registered Office: 8 Devonshire Square, London EC2M 4PL.

The Government first announced in 2006 that it intended to introduce a system of automatic pension scheme enrolment. The Pensions Act 2008 implemented the framework for the regime and subsequent regulations have set out the detail of the requirements. It will come into force in 2012, requiring employers (over a four-year staging period) to auto-enrol employees who satisfy earnings and age criteria into a qualifying scheme. The scheme can be the employer's or the National Employment Savings Trust (NEST), *which is described in Section 10.* This section reflects amendments set out in the Pensions Act 2011 and draft regulations published for consultation in July 2011. The earnings thresholds are expected to be confirmed in early 2012. The Pensions Regulator's site *(see Appendix 5)* sets out the latest guidance available.

AUTOMATIC ENROLMENT – EMPLOYER OBLIGATIONS

Automatic enrolment will be phased in over a four-year 'staging' period between 1 October 2012 and 1 October 2016. Larger employers (as measured by size of PAYE scheme, in some cases including pensioners) will become subject to the requirements over the first year, and smaller employers over the following three years. Each employer will have its own 'staging date'. Employers will be able to bring their staging date forward, with the largest employers allowed to select a date as early as July 2012.

From its staging date an employer will be required to automatically enrol its workers in an automatic enrolment scheme, if they are at least 22 but younger than State pension age and earn over £7,475 p.a. (in 2011/12 terms). The requirement to enrol the worker in the pension scheme will normally apply from the first day the worker becomes eligible unless the employer is operating a waiting period *(see below)* and must be completed within one month of this 'automatic enrolment date'.

Contributions will need to be deducted on the first pay day after the 'jobholder' becomes eligible, even if the pay day arises before active membership is achieved. The first month's contributions will not, however, need to be paid by the employer to the scheme until the end of the second month following the month in which the auto-enrolment date falls. This is intended to allow employers to continue to hold the money until such time as it is known whether or not the jobholder has opted out.

Opting out

An employee who must be auto-enrolled can subsequently opt out by giving notice within a one-month period, commencing with the later of the date the member received the enrolment information or on which he or she became an active member, in which case any member and employer contributions paid would be returned. The individual could usually then give notice to opt back in again.

In order to opt out, the jobholder must request an opt-out notice, generally from the scheme and not the employer. It is the employer's duty, not the scheme's, to refund to a jobholder who opts out any contributions that have been made; this will not be dependent on the employer recouping the money from the scheme.

The Pensions Regulator will have powers to issue a compliance notice to any employer who offers employees an inducement, the main purpose of which is to encourage employees to opt out of, or not join, an occupational pension scheme (including NEST) or a personal pension.

Re-enrolling

Automatic re-enrolment is required every three years (within a six-month window centred initially on the third anniversary of the employer's staging date) unless the employee has opted out within the previous twelve months. Where an employee ceases to meet the qualifying criteria but then qualifies again, he or she must be automatically re-enrolled from the date the criteria are met again.

Opting in

Workers aged 16 to 75 who are not subject to automatic enrolment (either because their earnings are below the £7,475 trigger level, or because they are outside the age range 22 to State pension age) can give notice requiring the employer to arrange for them to be enrolled in the automatic enrolment scheme. The employer then has a requirement to provide the minimum contributions or benefits on that employee's behalf (unless the employee earns below the qualifying earnings level, of £5,035 in 2006/07 values, in which case the employer must provide access to a registered pension scheme, which need not be an automatic enrolment scheme).

Waiting periods

Employers will be able to operate a waiting period, deferring the automatic enrolment date by up to three months from the staging date, the date on which an eligible worker is employed or the date that an existing worker satisfies the age and earnings conditions.

Maintaining active membership

In addition to the automatic enrolment requirements, employers must ensure that employees remain active members of a qualifying scheme, unless the employee chooses to end their membership. An employer cannot stop a scheme from qualifying, eject an employee from the qualifying scheme or force or 'induce' an employee to opt out of the scheme. Where an employer is changing its pension scheme, membership of the new scheme must commence the day after membership of the old scheme ends.

CONTRIBUTION REQUIREMENTS

When using a money purchase qualifying scheme, the contributions required are a total of 8% of qualifying earnings, with the employer paying at least 3% and the employee making up any shortfall. For NEST or personal pensions, the 'relief at source' method will provide basic rate tax relief, with the relief paid directly into the scheme and counting towards the 8%. Higher-rate tax-payers will need to claim additional relief directly from HMRC. The employer will have the authority to deduct contributions from workers' remuneration and pay them to the scheme.

For this purpose, qualifying earnings are gross earnings, including sick pay, statutory maternity pay and paternity and adoption pay, between £5,035 and £33,540 p.a. (in 2006/07 values). This qualifying earnings band will be reviewed annually, with the first review expected in January 2012.

As an alternative to using qualifying earnings, money purchase schemes can use certain alternative definitions of pensionable earnings together with the following minimum contribution tiers:

- Tier 1 – 9% total (with 4% employer) where pensionable pay is subject to a minimum of basic pay
- Tier 2 – 8% total (with 3% employer) where pensionable pay is subject to a minimum of basic pay and constitutes at least 85% of total pay, across all relevant jobholders, *or*
- Tier 3 – 7% total (with 3% employer) where all earnings are pensionable.

(For this purpose basic pay is proposed to be those elements of pay which do not vary.)

INFORMATION REQUIREMENTS

Jobholder information

When a jobholder becomes eligible, the employer must provide the scheme with specified 'jobholder information' no later than one month after the automatic enrolment date. This information may be given in advance of the automatic enrolment date. Some of the information need only be given if the scheme requests it.

Enrolment information

Specified 'enrolment information' must be provided by the employer to jobholders joining an occupational or personal pension scheme, no later than one month after the automatic enrolment date. This information may be given in advance of the automatic enrolment date.

Terms and conditions information

For workplace personal pension schemes, 'terms and conditions' information must be provided by the scheme provider to the jobholder. (This is in addition to the 'key features' to be provided under FSA legislation.)

Scheme information for existing members

Within two months of the employer's staging date, the employer must provide existing scheme members with prescribed scheme information.

Waiting period information

For schemes where a waiting period applies, the jobholder must be given specified postponement information no later than one week after the date from which the automatic enrolment was postponed.

TRANSITIONAL ARRANGEMENTS

For money purchase arrangements (including NEST), minimum contributions will be phased in over five years. This will occur in three steps:

From	Employer minimum contribution	Total minimum contribution (including tax relief)
October 2012	1%	2%
October 2016	2%	5%
October 2017	Full	Full

Higher rates will apply to 'Tier 1' certification, where pensionable pay is subject to a minimum of basic pay, but where this does not amount to at least 85% of total pay. For these Tier 1 jobholders the transitional rates are:

From	Employer minimum contribution	Total minimum contribution (including tax relief)
October 2012	2%	3%
October 2016	3%	6%
October 2017	Full	Full

Employers providing qualifying defined benefit and hybrid schemes will be able to defer automatic enrolment for existing employees until October 2016, provided jobholders can opt in during the period between the employer's staging date and October 2016. During this period, any new employees who satisfy the eligibility criteria will need to be automatically enrolled in the normal way.

EMPLOYERS PROVIDING THEIR OWN QUALIFYING SCHEMES

Unless they wish to use NEST, employers will have to provide their own automatic enrolment scheme for workers. An automatic enrolment scheme is a qualifying scheme that contains no provisions which might prevent the employer from making the required arrangements to automatically enrol, opt-in or re-enrol a jobholder and does not require the worker to express a choice or provide any information in order to remain an active member – for example, a money purchase scheme must have a default investment option.

A qualifying scheme is an occupational scheme or personal pension scheme that satisfies the quality requirement, or the alternative quality requirement, for that jobholder *(see below)*, and is registered under Finance Act 2004 or is an overseas scheme that satisfies specified requirements. Either an actuary, the scheme actuary where the scheme is required to have one, or the employer will certify whether the quality requirement is met. The certificate will normally be valid for a period of 12 months. It will be the employer's responsibility to ensure that a certificate is in place.

The quality test	Conditions to meet quality test
Money purchase schemes (occupational defined contribution schemes and group personal pensions)	*The quality requirement:* The scheme will meet the minimum contribution requirement for all relevant jobholders based on the statutory definition of qualifying earnings (earnings between £5,035 p.a. and £33,540 p.a. in 2006/07 values). *The alternative quality requirement:* For each relevant jobholder, contributions under the scheme will satisfy one or more of the three contribution tiers making up the alternative minimum contribution test *(see 'Contribution Requirements' above).* There is no requirement that all jobholders in the scheme satisfy the same test.
Contracted-out final salary schemes	Satisfies the reference scheme test by having a salary-related contracting-out certificate in force.
Contracted-in final salary schemes	Satisfies the 'test scheme standard', which requires the jobholder to be entitled to a pension at least as valuable as one paid: • at an annual rate of 1/120ths of average qualifying earnings in the last three tax years prior to exit • multiplied by number of years of pensionable service (up to a maximum of 40) • commencing at the appropriate age, currently 65, and continuing for life. The appropriate age will increase in line with future increases to state pension age, *and* • including at least the statutory minimum levels of revaluation in deferment (on the final salary basis) and of indexation in payment.
Hybrid schemes	Combination of money purchase and final salary tests; modified test scheme for cash balance and final salary lump sum schemes.
Career average schemes (CARE)	The scheme must satisfy the 'test scheme standard', as described above, including final salary revaluation in deferment.

The quality test	Conditions to meet quality test
Career average schemes (CARE) *(continued)*	(Note, however, that average salary revaluation may be adequate if other aspects such as a higher accrual rate compensate.)
	In addition, a CARE scheme cannot be a qualifying scheme unless revaluation of benefits during pensionable service is at least 2.5% (or RPI if lower) and is either guaranteed or funded for.

COMPLIANCE BY EMPLOYERS

The monitoring of employers' compliance with the automatic enrolment and contribution requirements will be a function of the Pensions Regulator. Employers will have to keep records and provide the Regulator with certain information, via a process of registration. During implementation, employers will be required to register within two months of their staging date.

It is proposed that:

(1) employers be required to keep records relating to the pension arrangements they have made, the enrolment of jobholders, opt-out and 'opt-in' notices, and the pension contributions they have made. The Regulator will use these records where needed to check that employers have undertaken enrolment and opt-out correctly, *and*

(2) occupational pension schemes and pension providers be required to keep records of enrolments and opt-outs in respect of each employer. The Regulator will use these records to confirm enrolment and payment of contributions with the pension scheme or provider, and to help identify prohibited behaviour such as employers inducing workers to opt out of pension saving.

All employers are required to re-register every three years, within one month of the automatic re-enrolment date, including providing information about the re-enrolment arrangements that have been made.

A penalty regime for employers who do not comply with the requirements will be administered by the Pensions Regulator, who will be able to issue compliance notices and unpaid contribution notices. Employers who contravene the automatic enrolment requirements may be required to take remedial action and fines may be imposed where things are not put right. In particular, workers may have to be put in the same position as if the contravention had not occurred.

A fixed penalty of £400 may be issued to employers who fail to engage with the reforms, or fail to keep records or supply information to the Pensions Regulator. Entrenched employer non-compliance may attract further penalties, rising to £10,000 per day for employers with 500 or more workers. Employers that try to screen out job applicants who might want to save in a qualifying scheme may receive a fixed fine, rising to £5,000 for employers with 250 or more workers.

Protection of employment rights

The Pensions Act 2008 includes provision to protect employees who do not opt out after automatic enrolment from suffering detrimental treatment by employers compared with those who do opt out. It includes statutory rights, building on the existing framework of employment rights, so that those individuals who wish to save should be protected from being unfairly dismissed and from other detrimental treatment (including in relation to recruitment).

STAKEHOLDER PENSIONS: ACCESS REQUIREMENTS

From October 2001, most employers have had to 'designate' a stakeholder scheme *(see Section 8 for details)*.

From 2012, the access requirements to stakeholder schemes are expected to be removed, although the requirements to deduct contributions and pay them to the scheme will continue for existing arrangements.

The automatic enrolment regime will come into force in 2012, *and is described in Section 9*. Employers will be required to auto-enrol employees into a qualifying scheme. The scheme can be the employer's own qualifying scheme *(the requirements of which are described in Section 9)* or the National Employment Savings Trust (NEST), which was formerly referred to as the Personal Accounts Scheme.

Employers will be able to auto-enrol their workers into NEST and make the required contributions to it. NEST will operate as a trust-based money purchase occupational pension scheme and will be subject to most of the legislation applying to such schemes.

A separate body, the Personal Accounts Delivery Authority (PADA), was set up to oversee the development of the Personal Accounts regime. In July 2010, PADA was wound up, and its property rights, liabilities and functions transferred to the NEST Corporation *(see below)* and the Secretary of State for Work and Pensions.

In June 2010, the Coalition Government announced a review of automatic enrolment and NEST. The review report was published in October 2010 and the Government announced that it would proceed based on the report's recommendations, which included continuing with NEST. In July 2011, a further inquiry was set up by the Work and Pensions Select Committee to consider various issues relating to NEST and automatic enrolment. This section describes how NEST will operate.

Maximum contributions

A maximum annual contribution to NEST – of £4,200 (based on 2011 earnings levels) – has been allowed for, to ensure that the scheme remains focused on low-to-moderate earners. The limit will be increased in line with average earnings to the commencement date of the scheme and subsequently each year, and is likely to be removed in 2017.

NEST will cease to accept member contributions once the annual limit is exceeded. However, it will continue to accept statutory minimum employer contributions. After the end of the tax year, any excess contributions will be refunded, without interest or investment gain. Generally, employee contributions will be refunded prior to employer contributions. There will also be a facility to offset excess contributions against contributions that are due in the following year.

Transfers

There will be a general ban on transfer payments to or from NEST. However, the scheme will accept cash transfer sums in respect of leavers with less than two years' service *(see Section 15)*. In addition, transfers out will be allowed for members who are over the Normal Minimum Pension Age (55) and members suffering from incapacity who have become entitled to benefits. This will allow members to consolidate their pension savings before an annuity purchase.

Transfers out will also be permitted to comply with a pension sharing order and NEST will accept pension credits on divorce for existing members of the scheme *(see Section 19)*.

The October 2010 report recommended that the general ban on transfers in and out be removed in 2017.

Benefits

NEST will be subject to the same rules as other registered pension schemes with regard to the payment of benefits. For example, pension income cannot be brought into payment before normal minimum pension age (55), other than in cases of ill-health, and no more than 25% of a fund can be taken as a pension commencement lump sum.

Members will be able to purchase a lifetime annuity under the open market option. NEST will also provide members with access to its Retirement Panel, which will offer a limited range of annuities from selected providers, at competitive prices, for members unwilling or unable to pursue the open market option. Each provider has given a commitment to provide annuities on pots from £1,500 upwards.

Members with NEST funds of under £2,000 will be able to take a *de minimis* lump sum. Members will also be able to convert small pension pots into cash lump sums under the trivial commutation provisions *(see Section 13)*.

Charges

Responsibility for setting the appropriate charges for NEST lies with the NEST Corporation. The Government stated that the Corporation is best placed to make decisions relating to the charging structure, the level of charges and any additional charges for particular services. In particular, trust law will provide an incentive for the Corporation to set a charging structure that is fair and to keep charges down.

The intention is that NEST will be self-financing through member charges 'in the long term' and that state support should not provide the scheme with an unfair competitive advantage.

The stated aim is to provide 'a low-cost, good value way to save'. The Pensions Commission originally suggested that an annual management charge (AMC) of 0.3% was achievable. In November 2010, the NEST Corporation confirmed that it will apply a 0.3% AMC and an additional charge on contributions going into the scheme of 1.8%, which will persist until initial setting-up costs are recovered. It is not known when the 1.8% charge will be removed.

Investment options

The NEST Corporation will be responsible for investment decisions. The NEST Order and Rules *(see below)* provide the trustee with broad powers to invest funds and require the trustee to provide a default investment fund for all members who do not make an active investment choice.

In March 2011, the Corporation published its first Statement of Investment Principles. NEST's default options will be 'target date funds' – one for each expected retirement year – and invested in a broad and diversified set of asset classes. The investment objectives for these funds include the achievement of performance in excess of inflation, using a benchmark of CPI.

Five mandates, each managed by one of three fund managers, covering equities, gilts, cash and diversified assets, will be used to build up the default funds. In addition to the default funds, NEST will provide a range of other fund choices:

- Higher Risk Fund – targeting high returns through taking more investment risk
- Lower Growth Fund – taking very little investment risk
- Ethical Fund – only investing in companies that meet ethical criteria
- Sharia Fund – only investing in companies that are compliant with Sharia principles, *and*
- Pre-retirement Fund – for members who, in NEST's early years, want to buy an annuity rather than target a cash lump sum.

Governance

NEST will be run as a trust-based occupational pension scheme:

- a trustee board – the NEST Corporation – will be the governing body, with wide-ranging powers to manage the scheme in the interests of its members, *and*
- the NEST Corporation must comply with general pensions legislation although regulations modify certain aspects of pension legislation when applied to NEST.

The trustee will take the key strategic decisions, but will delegate all executive and operational functions to a management board. The first members and their 'chair' were Government-appointed but subsequent appointments will be made by the Corporation itself. Appointments will be for no more than four years. The trustee will consult a Members' Panel on key decisions. There will also be an Employers' Panel which must be consulted when the trustee reviews the Statement of Investment Principles. It is possible that a modified version of the member-nominated directors requirements of the Pensions Act 2004 could be applied in future.

In March 2010, the NEST Order, establishing the scheme, was published together with the initial Rules of NEST. Further provisions about the scheme will be made by rules, which may only be made with the consent of the trustee. Any proposed rules must be published in draft for comment by interested persons, and the members' and employers' panels must be consulted. Rules cannot be made by the Secretary of State without trustee consent and consultation.

The main areas covered in the Order and Rules are:

- the composition and function of the members' and employers' panels

- the situations where data may be shared with the government
- trustee indemnity
- promoting awareness of the scheme
- employer and member participation in the scheme
- contributions to and refunds from the scheme
- the powers to invest scheme assets and the requirement to establish a default investment fund
- the ban on most transfers into and out of the scheme, *and*
- the types of benefit permitted.

TRUSTEES AND SCHEME GOVERNANCE

This section deals with the role of trustees within the legal framework governing pensions in the UK and with scheme governance in general. References to the legal system are to the system which in general applies in the UK. However, some differences exist under Scottish law. The existing legal framework includes trust law, tax law, social security law (in particular, specific DWP pensions legislation), financial services legislation and European Union law.

Trust law, on which private sector occupational pension provision in the UK is traditionally based, is considered in more detail below. Tax law is dealt with in *Section 13*. Various aspects of DWP pensions legislation (including provisions which transpose EU requirements into UK law) are also discussed in this and other sections. The Financial Services and Markets Act 2000 is dealt with in more detail in *Section 29*.

TRUSTS AND TRUSTEES

Trust law

The principles of trust law have mainly been established, over the years, by court precedents. However, over time some of these principles have been incorporated in legislation, for example in the Trustee Act 2000.

What is a trust?

One definition is that 'a trust is an equitable obligation binding a person (who is called a trustee) to deal with property over which he has control (which is called the trust property) for the benefit of persons (who are called the beneficiaries) of whom he may himself be one, and any of whom may enforce the obligation'.

In the case of a pension scheme, the trustees hold the pension fund assets for the benefit of the members, and their first duty is to them – not to their employer, their trade union, or any outside body. Members include not just those currently employed and paying into the scheme, but also people with deferred pensions, those who are drawing benefits and those who are potentially eligible for benefits, such as spouses and other dependants.

Why use a trust?

The vast majority of UK occupational pension schemes are set up under trust. The three main reasons why trusts have been used are:

- to provide security for the members by keeping the scheme's assets separate from those of the employer
- to ensure third-party beneficiaries, such as spouses and dependants of members, have legal rights, *and*
- (historically) to enable the scheme to be approved by the Revenue as an exempt approved scheme, and thereby qualify for valuable tax reliefs on contributions, investment income and some of the benefits paid.

Note that, whilst no longer a Revenue requirement, the Pensions Act 2004 requires funded occupational schemes to be established under irrevocable trusts and to have effective written rules specifying the benefits and the conditions on which they are payable. This reflects the requirements of the EU Pensions Directive.

Who can be a trustee?

The trustees of a scheme can be either individuals (so long as they are over 18 and not insane) or corporations, or a combination of both.

Neither the scheme actuary nor the scheme auditor can be a trustee, and certain people are automatically disqualified (e.g. undischarged bankrupts or people who have been convicted of an offence involving dishonesty). The Pensions Regulator has power to prohibit a person from acting as trustee of a particular scheme, a particular type of scheme, or schemes in general, where it is satisfied that he or she is not a fit and proper person to be a trustee. It may suspend a person from acting as a trustee where the outcome of legal proceedings is awaited. It may also appoint an independent trustee where an employer becomes insolvent or where it believes the appointment is in the best interest of the members *(see* Conflicts of interest, *below).*

The Pensions Act 1995 (as amended by the Pensions Act 2004) requires all schemes to have a minimum proportion of member-nominated trustees. Such trustees must be nominated as the result of a process involving (as a minimum) all the active and pensioner members of the scheme (or organisations representing them), and then selected as a result of a further process. The Pensions Regulator has issued a code of practice on this requirement. The minimum proportion was initially and remains one-third, but the Government has given itself the power to increase this to one-half at some time in the future.

The trust deed and rules

A scheme's definitive documentation usually has two main parts: the trust deed and the rules. The trust deed defines the powers and duties of the trustees and employer, and the duties of trustees to the members.

The rules state who is eligible to be a scheme member and cover details of the benefits promised, the areas where the trustees have discretion, the arrangements for determining the employer's contributions, and the level of members' contributions.

The trust documents govern the trustees' actions. Generally speaking, only when the deed and rules do not deal with a point is it necessary to apply the principles of trust law. However, it should be noted that Acts of Parliament can override provisions contained in trust deeds, for example the Civil Partnership Act 2004.

Scheme documentation can be altered in various ways: for example, a supplemental deed extends the definitive documentation, perhaps by introducing new powers. An amending deed changes it. Trustees may have to refer to several different documents, if amendments have not been incorporated into the main deed. It is therefore good practice to try to keep a single consolidated deed which is amended as necessary. Many trustees will now have a working copy of their rules which, whilst not a formally signed set of rules, incorporates changes into a single document.

Duties, responsibilities and rights of a trustee

The fundamental duty of a trustee is to give effect to the provisions of the trust deed. A trustee who fails to do this is in breach of trust. Other duties are many and varied, and include:

- paying out the right benefits at the right time
- keeping accurate records of members and their dependants
- keeping proper accounts, *and*
- ensuring that scheme assets are properly and prudently invested.

Under the provisions of the Employment Rights Act 1996, employee trustees (or employee directors of trustee companies) of an occupational scheme of their employer have statutory rights to time off work for the performance of their trustee duties and training, payment for this time off and rights not to suffer detriment or dismissal related principally to the performance of their trustee functions.

Legislation (for example the Pensions Acts 1995 and 2004) places a number of particular responsibilities on trustees. Exceptions apply in certain cases but, in general, these responsibilities include:

Appointment of professional advisers
The trustees must appoint an individual actuary (except for pure money purchase schemes) and an auditor (known respectively as the scheme actuary and the scheme auditor) and, where investments covered by the Financial Services and Markets Act 2000 are held, a fund manager, to carry out certain specified functions. Another actuary may also be appointed to provide actuarial advice which is not required to be given by the scheme actuary. Any person having custody of scheme assets must be appointed by the trustees, except where they are sub-custodians appointed by a main custodian or other adviser who has been specifically authorised by the trustees. A legal adviser must also be appointed by the trustees if such advice is required.

Investment of the scheme's assets
Trustees have complete power to invest scheme assets as if they were their own, subject to their duty of care, the taking of proper advice from qualified advisers, any scheme restrictions (except that any requirement for the direct or indirect consent of the employer is void) and the statutory restriction that not more than five per cent of the market value of the resources of a scheme may at any time be invested in employer-related investments. Their decision-making powers may be delegated to an external fund manager. The trustees remain responsible for any actions taken, but they are not liable for the fund manager's actions so long as they have taken steps to ensure that he has appropriate knowledge and experience, and is acting competently and in accordance with the written statement of investment principles *(see below)*.

Regulations introduced from late 2005 to comply with the EU Pensions Directive require the trustees (amongst other things) to invest predominantly in regulated markets and to ensure proper diversification.

Statement of investment principles
The trustees must prepare (and maintain) this statement, after taking advice from an experienced investment adviser and after consulting the employer (but without any requirement to agree it with the employer). Amongst other things it must cover:

- the kinds of investment to be held and the balance between them
- risk and expected return
- realisation of assets, *and*
- the trustees' policy (if any) on socially responsible investment, including the exercise of voting rights.

The statement must be reviewed at least every three years and immediately after any significant change in investment policy.

Compliance with scheme funding legislation
Scheme-specific funding was introduced under the Pensions Act 2004. Under this regime, trustees are responsible for setting the funding strategy as well as monitoring the funding level and payment of contributions. *See Section 20 for further details.*

Disclosure of pension scheme information
Under UK pensions law, scheme trustees are required to make a substantial range of information available to scheme members and others. *See Section 17 for further details.*

Compliance with the Data Protection Act 1998
For the purposes of the Data Protection Act 1998, pension scheme trustees are generally classified as data controllers. As such, they are required to ensure the adequacy of their own data security arrangements and of those who process data on their behalf; for example the scheme administrators. They are responsible for keeping the Information Commissioner up to date with details of their security measures. Trustees must obtain explicit member consent before holding or processing sensitive data, such as data relating to physical/ mental health or sexual life. They must also ensure they have suitable procedures in place for complying with requests by scheme members exercising their statutory right to see a copy of personal data held about them within 40 days.

New powers for the Information Commissioner's Office were announced on 6 April 2010. These allow it to fine data controllers, including trustees, up to £500,000 for serious breaches of the Data Protection Act. Trustees therefore need to understand how third parties use their scheme's data. They should ensure that they hold copies of all of their advisers' data security policies. Each adviser should be able to present their policy on request.

Whistle-blowing and Notifiable Events
Under the Pensions Act 2004, responsibility for reporting breaches (whistle-blowing) was extended to scheme trustees (and others). In addition, a requirement was introduced for trustees to notify the Regulator of certain events. *See Section 12 for further details.*

Scheme governance

Scheme governance encompasses the different aspects of operating a pension scheme. The Pensions Regulator continues the campaign it launched in November 2009 aimed at encouraging good governance and administration, and better management of pension scheme risks. Trustees' core responsibilities include safeguarding and investing scheme assets, monitoring funding levels, ensuring members receive the correct benefits when they fall due, and ensuring compliance with the law and the scheme's own trust deed and rules. Meeting these responsibilities requires carefully developed procedures covering aspects such as:

- the constitution of the trustee body, appointment and removal of trustees, formation of sub-committees, the process of decision taking
- skills assessment, induction, training and performance evaluation
- risk assessment and management, and internal controls *(see below)*
- dealing with conflicts of interest *(see below), and*
- relations with the sponsoring employer, exchange of information (and confidentiality agreements, where appropriate) and mutual understanding of objectives.

Internal controls
A formal requirement (imposed by the EU Pensions Directive) for schemes to establish internal controls to ensure compliance with the law and their own rules was introduced into UK law by the Pensions Act 2004. The Pensions Regulator has issued a code of practice, accompanying guidance which was updated in 2010, and a set of e-learning modules covering internal controls. The code stresses the need for trustees to set up internal controls to enable them to react to significant operational, financial, funding, regulatory and compliance risks. These controls should be proportionate, based on an assessment of the risks to which the scheme is exposed, having regard to its particular circumstances and to their likelihood of materialising and potential impact. Internal controls should be reviewed at least annually and more frequently if substantial changes take place or inadequacies are revealed. It is suggested that a statement confirming that key risks have been considered and effective controls established could be incorporated in the scheme's annual report to demonstrate good practice.

Where trustees delegate their responsibilities (e.g. to third-party administrators or investment managers and custodians), they should take care to examine the internal control assurance reports produced by their agents.

Conflicts of interest

Conflicts of interest can pose a serious risk to good governance and, as such, are subject to some very complex legal considerations. In 2008, the Pensions Regulator published guidance relating to conflicts of interest. The guidance covers five broad principles, which relate to: understanding the importance of conflicts of interest; identifying conflicts of interest; evaluation, management or avoidance of conflicts; managing adviser conflicts; and conflicts of interest policy. The principles are supported by practical guidance on matters relating to the governance of each. The Internal Controls guidance describes behaviours the Pensions Regulator expects to see in identifying and resolving conflicts of interest.

A determination by the Pensions Ombudsman in January 2009 confirmed that conflicts of interest do not invalidate trustees' decisions, so long as they are properly managed.

The Pensions Regulator has also published guidance on relations with advisers. The guidance sets out some key issues for trustees to consider in their relations with advisers and covers general issues as well as those specific to the scheme actuary, scheme auditor, legal adviser, scheme administrator, independent financial adviser and benefit consultant. The guidance also raises issues and provides hints on questions that trustees should be asking their advisers.

The importance of being able to control potential conflicts of interest was highlighted in the *Telent* case. In November 2007, Pensions Corporation bought Telent. The trustees of the Telent pension scheme asked the Pensions Regulator to intervene; it temporarily put in place three independent trustee directors with sole power over the scheme, as it was felt that a clear conflict of interest had arisen which had not been managed appropriately. In April 2008, Pensions Corporation and the Regulator came to an agreement on the future governance of the scheme – the three independent trustee directors would remain on the trustee board, comprising nine trustee directors, and measures would be put in place to identify and manage conflicts of interest on the board.

The Bribery Act 2010

This Act came into force on 1 July 2011. Trustees are exposed to some of the offences under the Act. As part of good governance, trustees should establish and maintain suitable prevention procedures. The trustees' conflicts of interest policy should also be reviewed in line with these procedures.

Defined contribution schemes and good practice guidance

In 2008, the Pensions Regulator published guidance in three specific areas relating to the regulation of defined contribution (DC) schemes. Additional information in these areas has subsequently been published and the Regulator's education drive has now extended to cover administration in DC schemes *(see below)*.

The first guide covered member retirement options. This was intended to help employers and trustees ensure that effective processes were in place and help members make retirement income decisions.

The second guide covered effective member communication and was designed to help schemes assess their communication policy. This guidance identified four events where communication is key:

- at or prior to joining a pension arrangement
- approaching retirement
- scheme design changes or changes in fund choice, *and*
- ongoing ad hoc communications through notices, the employer's intranet, etc.

The Regulator also published investment guidance. This was designed to provide individuals with basic knowledge about investment funds whilst stressing the need to obtain financial advice. The various types of guidance apply to all registered schemes that offer benefits on a DC basis (including AVCs).

In January 2011 the Regulator published a discussion paper on DC schemes, aimed to prompt discussion around how it will achieve its statutory objectives for DC schemes. The Regulator is considering how it will support the DC market and raise standards to ensure good outcomes for savers, noting that auto-enrolment is likely to create a large increase in the number of people saving in DC schemes from April 2012 onwards. Trustees need to ensure that their administrators and auditors deliver to meet the Regulator's aims.

Good scheme administration

The Pensions Regulator issued guidance in January 2009, which was updated in June 2010, on monitoring and improving (where necessary) the quality of member data. The guidance includes a framework for testing and measuring data and specific events are noted which give rise to an urgent need to review record keeping: wind-up, entry to PPF assessment, change of administrator or buy-out.

The guidance introduces a deadline of December 2012 for schemes to meet specific targets for data standards. In addition, the Regulator indicates that a failure to keep basic records would be wholly inconsistent with trustees' obligations to operate internal controls and that it can use its statutory powers against schemes in these circumstances. The Regulator now intends to take enforcement action where there is evidence of a breach of legislation.

The recommended good practice approach is continuous improvement, with regular reports of progress. After completion of any plans to improve records, the data should be measured annually as evidence that controls are continuing to operate effectively.

The education drive from the Regulator in 2011 highlights the importance of administration in enabling good member outcomes from pensions saving. As well as the risk to members' benefits, inaccurate and missing data can have serious cost implications for pension schemes. The Regulator is seeking to increase understanding amongst trustees and administrators of their accountabilities and responsibilities for achieving high standards. A number of documents have been issued to support this initiative.

Wednesbury principles

These define the process by which trustees should approach decision making in order to minimise the risk of legal challenge:

- the trustees must ask themselves the correct questions
- they must direct themselves correctly in law; in particular, they must adopt a correct construction of the trust deed and rules
- they must not arrive at a perverse decision, i.e. a decision at which no reasonable body of trustees would have arrived, *and*
- they must take into account all relevant and no irrelevant facts.

If the trustees can demonstrate that they followed this process when exercising discretionary powers, it is unlikely that their decision will be overturned by the Pensions Ombudsman or the courts. Recent Ombudsman determinations have highlighted the need for scheme minutes to include a clear record of the steps taken in reaching a decision. However, care should be taken if reasons are given, as these could be challenged.

Internal Dispute Resolution Procedure

Trustees are required to put in place, and disclose via the scheme's explanatory booklet, an internal scheme dispute resolution procedure under which scheme members may bring written complaints. This was initially set up as a two-stage procedure with an individual appointed by the trustees to rule in the first stage. If dissatisfied with the decision the complainant could then appeal to the trustees as a second stage. Schemes now have the option of replacing the two-stage procedure with a single-stage process under which all decisions are taken by the trustees. In addition the prescribed time limits were replaced by the requirement to make a decision within a reasonable period. Having exhausted the scheme's internal dispute resolution procedure, a complainant may take his complaint to the Pensions Ombudsman.

Trustee Knowledge and Understanding

The Pensions Act 2004 introduced a formal requirement for trustees to have knowledge and understanding about the law relating to pensions and trusts and the principles of funding and investment. In addition, they are required to be conversant with the scheme's trust deed and rules, statements of investment and (where applicable) funding principles and other relevant scheme documents.

The Pensions Regulator has issued a code of practice and scope guidance on these requirements. The level of knowledge and understanding expected is that necessary for the individual concerned to exercise his or her own trustee function (so more is expected of the chair of the trustee board, or a significant sub-committee). Trustees should carry out a review of their training needs at least annually and when required in response to internal and external scheme changes or new responsibilities. Records should be kept of learning activities undertaken.

Newly appointed trustees generally have a six-month period of grace before the requirements apply to them. An updated code of practice came into effect in October 2009. The code and accompanying scope documents have been restructured and extended to cover areas such as employer covenant, wind-up, buy-out and auto-enrolment. A new (much reduced) scope document for trustees of small insured DC schemes has also been published.

The Regulator maintains a web-based trustee toolkit which trustees are recommended to complete. There are also several additional modules and regular updates for specific events.

Investment governance

The Myners Principles set out guidelines for investment governance in pension schemes and cover:

- effective decision making
- clear objectives
- risk and liabilities
- performance assessment
- responsible ownership, *and*
- transparency and reporting.

The principles are voluntary with a comply or explain approach to reporting, although the Government has suggested that legislation will be introduced if pension schemes do not comply with the principles.

The Government established the Investment Governance Group to oversee the principles and provide further guidance, where necessary. In particular, the Group has published investment governance principles and best practice guidance for work-based DC pension schemes, both contract-based and trust-based. The principles are:

- clear roles and responsibilities for investment decision making and governance
- effective decision making
- appropriate investment decisions
- appropriate default strategy
- effective performance assessment, *and*
- clear and relevant communication with members.

Reporting on these principles is also on a comply or explain basis.

In July 2010 the Financial Reporting Council (FRC) published a Stewardship Code that sets out good practice to which the FRC believes institutional investors should aspire when engaging with the UK listed companies in which they invest. It is acknowledged that trustees of pension funds may not wish to become directly involved in engagement with companies in which they invest, but they are encouraged to set mandates for their investment managers that require them to act in line with the Code.

THE ROLE OF THE EMPLOYER

The employer is a party to the trust and retains certain duties and powers which may be specified in the trust deed. The employer normally carries a substantial burden of the cost of the scheme benefits, or its administration, or both, and would therefore expect to retain certain powers, especially in areas where there is a cost element, for example the power to augment benefits or to amend the scheme. The employer generally has the ultimate power to cease contributions to the scheme, which will lead to the scheme either winding up or ceasing to provide any further benefit accrual, according to the provisions of the trust deed. In normal circumstances, the employer should act in a reasonable manner to ensure that the trustees can operate the scheme satisfactorily; this includes providing information on members, paying contributions when due, and meeting any obligations imposed on them by the trust deed or by legislation.

Although the Pensions Act 2004 extended the trustees' statutory powers in relation to scheme funding, the method and assumptions, statement of funding principles, any recovery plan, and the schedule of contributions are all, generally, subject to the agreement of the employer. *See Section 20 for further details.*

The employer is also required to consult with scheme members about proposed changes to scheme rules, if these fall within prescribed categories. *See Section 7.*

THE ROLE OF THE ACTUARY

Responsibilities of the scheme actuary

The scheme actuary appointed by the trustees has a number of statutory responsibilities. These include:

- advising the trustees on various aspects of scheme funding, as required by the Pensions Act 2004 *(see Section 20)*
- producing actuarial valuations for funding purposes *(see Section 20)*
- certifying the technical provisions and schedule of contributions as required by the scheme funding legislation *(see Section 20)*
- completing required certification for contracted-out salary-related schemes *(see Section 6)*
- along with other parties who are involved in running the scheme, reporting material breaches of statutory responsibilities by the employer or trustees to the Pensions Regulator *(see Section 12)*
- advising the trustees on various matters in relation to the calculation of individual transfer values *(see Section 16), and*
- certifying bulk transfers of members without their consent *(see Section 27).*

Other actuarial advice

Most schemes require the trustees to take actuarial advice before taking decisions, on such matters as augmentations and bulk transfers, which will affect the finances of the scheme (and this is encouraged by the notifiable events framework – *see Section 12*). Actuaries also provide expert advice in benefit design and implementation, and assist both employers and trustees in ensuring that the pension provision offered to employees is both appropriate and soundly based. They also assess the pension cost to be disclosed in the company's accounts (*see Section 28*).

THE ROLE OF THE AUDITOR

Responsibilities of the scheme auditor

The statutory duties of the scheme auditor include the following:

- producing a report stating whether or not in his opinion the scheme accounts have been prepared in accordance with regulations
- producing an auditor's statement as to whether or not in his opinion the required contributions have been paid to the scheme
- if the auditor's statement is negative or qualified, giving a statement of the reasons, *and*
- along with other parties who are involved in running the scheme, reporting material breaches of statutory responsibilities by the employer or trustees to the Pensions Regulator (*see Section 12*).

THE ROLE OF THE ADMINISTRATOR

The scheme administrator has many duties. Some of these are imposed by statute and regulations. Others are set out under a contract with the trustees.

HMRC requires every registered pension scheme to appoint a Scheme Administrator to be responsible for providing information including scheme returns and event reports, accounting for tax and monitoring benefits against the lifetime allowance.

Day-to-day administrative responsibilities are very varied, ranging from organising the payment of benefits to individual beneficiaries in accordance with the scheme rules, to tasks such as organising the submission of information required by the Pensions Regulator. These may be carried out by someone other than the formal Scheme Administrator.

THE PENSIONS REGULATORY SYSTEM

The Pensions Regulator is the regulator of work-based pension schemes in the UK. This section covers its role, in particular in relation to trust-based schemes, and the roles of other bodies involved in the regulation of UK pension schemes.

THE ROLE OF THE PENSIONS REGULATOR

The Regulator was created under the Pension Act 2004, and was given wider powers than its predecessor, the Occupational Pensions Regulatory Authority (Opra), which it replaced in April 2005. The powers of the Regulator fall into three broad categories: investigating schemes, acting against avoidance and putting things right.

The Regulator has statutory objectives to protect members' benefits, to reduce the risk of calls on the Pension Protection Fund (PPF), to promote good administration and, from 2012, to maximise employers' compliance with their new duties in relation to automatic enrolment. *(See Section 9 for details.)*

In April 2011, the Regulator published its corporate plan setting out five key themes for the next three years (2011–14), which link to its statutory objectives:

- to improve governance and administration *(see Section 11)*
- to reduce risks to DB scheme members – including those in respect of scheme funding *(see Section 20)* and the transfer of risk *(see Sections 23 and 26)*
- to reduce the risks to DC scheme members *(see Section 8)*
- to prepare for automatic enrolment *(see Section 9), and*
- a commitment to be 'customer-focused and risk-based', in line with the Government principles of 'Better Regulation'.

Scheme returns

The Regulator requires all schemes to complete a regular scheme return. This provides a wide range of information about schemes, including details of membership, sponsoring employers, trustees, advisers, administration, funding and investment. These returns include the information required by the PPF to determine its annual levies *(see Section 22)*. A return is required only when the Regulator issues a 'scheme return notice'. The Regulator issues scheme return notices annually for all but the smallest schemes.

It is the trustees' legal duty to complete the scheme return online by the completion date notified on the form. The online system also allows trustees and administrators to regularly update scheme details during the year.

Codes of Practice and Guidance

The Regulator is required to publish codes of practice giving practical guidance on implementing certain parts of the legislation, and setting out the standards of conduct and practice expected. The codes are not 'law' but nevertheless would be taken into account by a court in deciding whether or not legislation had been complied with. The following codes are in effect:

- Reporting breaches of the law *(see below)*
- Notifiable events *(see below)*
- Funding defined benefits *(see Section 20)*
- Early leavers – reasonable periods *(see Section 15)*
- Reporting late payment of contributions to occupational money purchase schemes *(see below)*
- Reporting late payment of contributions to personal pensions *(see below)*
- Trustee knowledge and understanding *(see Section 11)*
- Member-nominated trustees and directors – putting in place and implementing arrangements *(see Section 11)*
- Internal controls *(see Section 11)*
- Modification of subsisting rights *(see Section 7)*
- Dispute resolution – reasonable periods *(see Section 11), and*
- Circumstances in relation to the material detriment test *(see below)*.

In addition to publishing codes of practice the Regulator has also issued regulatory guidance for trustees and employers on a number of subjects including the auto-enrolment regime, clearance, abandonment of defined benefit pension schemes, incentive exercises (in respect of the transfer or modification of defined benefits), defined contribution schemes (various guides), member record-keeping, cash equivalent transfer values, winding up and conflicts of interest.

Notifiable and reportable events

As noted above, the Regulator has issued codes of practice relating to notifiable events and reporting breaches of the law.

Trustees and/or employers are required to notify the Regulator in writing of certain 'notifiable events'. Notification is only required for schemes which are eligible for the PPF. The purpose of notification is to reduce the risk of the circumstances occurring that might lead to compensation being payable from the PPF, by providing an early warning of possible insolvency or underfunding. The events to be notified are set out below.

Notifiable events – all cases	
Trustees	A decision by the trustees or managers to grant benefits, or a right to benefits, on more favourable terms than those provided for by the scheme rules, without either seeking advice from the actuary or securing additional funding where such funding was advised by the actuary.
Employer	Any decision by the employer to take action which will, or is intended to, result in a debt which is, or may become, due to the scheme not being paid in full.

Employer (continued ...)	Ceasing to (or deciding to cease to) carry on business in the United Kingdom.
	Where applicable, receipt by the employer of advice that it is trading wrongfully, or circumstances being reached in which a director or former director of the company knows that there is no reasonable prospect that the company will avoid going into insolvent liquidation.
	The conviction of an individual for an offence involving dishonesty, if the offence was committed while the individual was a director or partner of the employer.
	Additional notifiable events
	where scheme was underfunded at last s179 valuation or there has been a reportable breach of the schedule of contributions in previous 12 months
Trustee	Any decision by the trustees or managers to take action which will, or is intended to, result in any debt (above a *de minimis* threshold) which is, or may become, due to the scheme not being paid in full.
	Making (or deciding to make) a transfer payment to, or accepting (or deciding to accept) a transfer payment from, another scheme in excess of £1,500,000 (or 5% of scheme assets if lower).
	Granting (or deciding to grant) benefits, or a right to benefits, to a member in excess of £1,500,000 (or 5% of scheme assets if lower).
Employer	Any breach by the employer of a covenant in an agreement between the employer and a bank or other institution providing banking services, other than where the bank or other institution agrees with the employer not to enforce the covenant.
	Where the employer is a company, a controlling company relinquishing, or deciding to relinquish, control of the employer company.

Separately, and not restricted to schemes eligible for the PPF, there is a duty to report significant breaches which are 'likely to be of material significance to the Regulator'. The duty to 'blow the whistle' applies to a wide range of people, including trustees, employers, scheme administrators and professional advisers. Criteria for deciding whether or not a breach is likely to be of material significance are set out in the code of practice and guidance and cover the cause and effect of the breach, the reaction to it and any wider implications.

In both cases, notification should be made in writing and where possible the standard form available from the Regulator's website should be used.

Late payments by employers

The Regulator has issued two codes of practice relating to the reporting of late payments by employers, one relating to occupational money purchase pension schemes and the other to personal pension schemes. These set out reasonable periods within which trustees/managers must report late payments of contributions to the Regulator (within ten working days of identifying that a late payment is material) and to members/employees. Late payments must be reported if the trustees/managers have reasonable cause to believe that the late payment of contributions is material. The code includes a guide to which circumstances would be considered material, such as where a contribution remains unpaid 90 days after the due date. The code for personal pensions also includes guidance on what is a reasonable period for employers to provide payment information to the managers (within 30 days of the formal request), and for managers to report to the Regulator if this information is not received (within 60 days of the formal request).

Similar requirements apply to late payments to defined benefit occupational pension schemes. These are included in the code of practice covering scheme funding *(see Section 20)*.

Acting against avoidance

The Regulator has powers to act where it believes that an employer is attempting to avoid its pension obligations (deliberately or otherwise), leaving the PPF to pick up the pension liabilities. These are referred to in the pensions industry as 'moral hazard' provisions. These provisions were extended in 2009 to cover situations, in particular 'non-insured buy-out' business models *(see Section 26)*, where the previous powers were insufficient or difficult to implement. They allow the Regulator to issue any of the following:

(a) *Contribution notices.* If the Regulator determines that a company or individual has taken action with the main purpose of avoiding an obligation to meet a debt on the employer under section 75 of the Pensions Act 1995, it may direct that those involved pay a 'contribution' to the scheme.

The Pensions Act 2008 introduced the ability for the Regulator to issue a contribution notice if the 'material detriment' test is met. This is met if, in the Regulator's opinion, 'the act, or failure to act, has been materially detrimental to the likelihood of accrued scheme benefits being received'. The Regulator has issued a code of practice and guidance relating to the test.

The Regulator issued its first contribution notice in June 2010, in connection with the 'pre-pack' administration of the sponsor of the Bonas Group Pension Scheme, against the Belgian holding company, Michel Van De Wiele. However, the original contribution notice, for over £5m, was appealed and an out-of-court settlement reached; a contribution notice for £60,000 was issued in June 2011.

(b) *Financial support directions (FSDs).* These are intended to apply in cases where corporate structures exist for legitimate business reasons but where the effect is that the 'employer' in relation to a scheme is 'insufficiently resourced' to deal with a potential section 75 obligation. Here the Regulator can require the company group to put in place 'financial support' arrangements.

The Regulator issued its first two FSDs in February 2008, both against Sea Containers Limited, in respect of two schemes belonging to its UK subsidiary. These were accepted by Sea Containers and arrangements were put in place which the Regulator has approved.

In June 2010, the Regulator determined that it would issue an FSD against a number of companies in the Nortel Group in relation to its UK pension scheme, despite rulings in the US and Canadian courts which may mean that the FSD is not enforceable in those jurisdictions. In September 2010, the Regulator determined that it would issue an FSD against six companies in the Lehman Brothers Group. Nortel and Lehman Brothers brought a joint claim in the High Court challenging the Regulator's ability to issue an FSD while they are in administration. Though the judge expressed reservations about his conclusion, he ruled that an FSD can be issued in such circumstances and that the liabilities created are payable as an expense of the administration, thereby ranking above unsecured creditors. The ruling was upheld by the Court of Appeal despite the resulting 'oddities, anomalies and inconveniences' and, at the time writing, it appears likely that the Supreme Court will also rule on the matter.

(c) *Restoration orders.* If there has been a transaction at an undervalue involving the scheme's assets, these allow the Regulator to take action to have the assets (or their equivalent value) restored to the scheme.

Companies considering corporate transactions where there is an underfunded defined benefit pension scheme can apply to the Regulator for a clearance statement. This gives assurance that the Regulator will not use its anti-avoidance powers in relation to the transaction once it is completed. The decision is binding on the Regulator unless the circumstances differ materially from what was disclosed in the clearance application.

Intervention

When the Regulator decides action must be taken to protect the security of members' benefits, there is a range of options available. These include:

- issuing an improvement notice to one or more persons
- taking action to recover unpaid contributions from the employer
- disqualifying trustees, or issuing prohibition or suspension orders to trustees

- appointing trustees, including independent trustees in certain circumstances, *and*
- imposing fines (maximum: £5,000 for individuals or £50,000 in other cases).

THE ROLE OF THE DWP

The Department for Work & Pensions (DWP) provides the 'overarching regulatory and legal framework' governing the Regulator and the PPF. It has no responsibility for the day-to-day running of the Regulator and the PPF, but expects to be informed by them of potentially significant problems.

A tripartite Memorandum of Understanding between the DWP, the Regulator and the PPF establishes the framework for cooperation between them, including discussion forums, and sets out the role and responsibilities of each body.

THE ROLE OF HMRC

Since pension benefits are often costly, employers will generally wish to take advantage of the tax reliefs that are available to schemes that meet certain criteria. This is monitored by Pension Schemes Services (PSS) within HM Revenue & Customs (HMRC). Schemes which wish to benefit from these tax reliefs must be registered *(see Section 13 for details)*.

Following registration, PSS monitors schemes to ensure that they continue to meet their requirements. Scheme administrators are required to supply HMRC with the information necessary to enable its monitoring to be effective. This includes an Event Report which must be completed annually, giving details of specified events (such as large benefit payments or payment of benefit to members with primary, enhanced or fixed protection) that have occurred during the tax year to which the report relates. They also require quarterly income tax returns to be completed and may require a copy of the audited annual accounts to be submitted.

THE PENSIONS ADVISORY SERVICE (TPAS)

TPAS (The Pensions Advisory Service) is a non-profit, independent and voluntary organisation giving free help and advice to members of the public who have problems concerning State, occupational or personal pensions. The service is available to anyone who believes he or she has pension rights: this includes working members of pension schemes, pensioners, deferred pensioners and dependants. TPAS is grant-aided by the DWP.

TPAS has no statutory powers and any decisions it reaches are subject to the agreement of the parties involved. Where no agreement can be reached, cases may be referred to the Pensions Ombudsman *(see below)*.

THE PENSIONS OMBUDSMAN

The Pensions Ombudsman's role is to investigate disputes and complaints concerning occupational and personal pension schemes. Complaints may be made by actual or potential beneficiaries against the trustees, employer or anyone involved in the administration of a scheme. The Ombudsman's jurisdiction also covers complaints made by the trustees against the employer, and vice versa, and disputes between trustees of either the same scheme or different schemes.

During an investigation, the trustees of the scheme involved, and anyone else against whom a complaint has been made, are given a chance to explain their position, and the Ombudsman can require any necessary information or documentation to be provided to him.

Unlike TPAS, the Pensions Ombudsman has statutory authority with regard to the complaints brought to him. In particular:

- he has the same powers as the court in respect of the examination and attendance of witnesses
- anyone obstructing an investigation, for example by refusing to give certain information, can be taken to court and, following representations by either or both sides, be dealt with as if he or she had been in contempt of that court, *and*
- the Ombudsman's decision, and any directions he gives, are final and binding, and are enforceable in a county court as if they were judgments of that court. An appeal can be made to the High Court on any points of law involved in the case.

The Pensions Ombudsman is able to appoint one or more Deputy Ombudsmen who have the power to carry out any of the Ombudsman's duties.

The Pensions Ombudsman works closely with the Financial Ombudsman Service in cases where their remits overlap.

LEVIES

Occupational pension schemes are generally required to pay the following levies:

- the General Levy (which also applies to personal pension schemes)
- the Fraud Compensation Levy, *and*
- the Financial Reporting Council Levy.

Schemes which are eligible for future entry into the PPF are required to pay additional levies to the PPF *(see Section 22)*.

General Levy

The General Levy covers the cost of the Pensions Regulator, the Pensions Ombudsman and any grants to support TPAS.

The current levy rates, which were last revised for 2008/09, are set out below:

Band	Number of Members:	Occupational Schemes:		Personal Pension Schemes:	
		General Levy (per member):	Min. Payment (per scheme):	General Levy (per member):	Min. Payment (per scheme):
1	2–11	–	£33	–	£14
2	12–99	£3.35	–	£1.34	–
3	100–999	£2.42	£340	£0.94	£140
4	1,000–4,999	£1.88	£2,420	£0.81	£940
5	5,000–9,999	£1.43	£9,400	£0.54	£4,050
6	10,000+	£1.00	£14,300	£0.41	£5,400

Fraud Compensation Levy

The Board of the PPF are responsible for operating the Fraud Compensation Fund *(see Section 22)*.

This is funded by a 'Fraud Compensation Levy' on all schemes eligible for this compensation at a rate determined by the PPF Board. Regulations cap the levy at 75 pence per member per year. The levy is only charged as and when needed. A levy is being raised in 2011/12 at the rate of 25 pence per member. Prior to this, levies had only been raised in 1997/98, 2004/05 and 2010/11, all at the rate of 23 pence per member.

Financial Reporting Council Levy

Since April 2006, the Board for Actuarial Standards, which is part of the Financial Reporting Council, has had responsibility for actuarial standards and regulation. The cost is met by an annual levy. For 2011/12 this is £2.9m and is collected:

- 10% from the Actuarial Profession
- 45% from life and general insurance companies, *and*
- 45% from pension schemes with 1,000 or more members (at the rate of £3.15 per 100 members).

PENSIONS TAXATION – REGISTERED PENSION SCHEMES

The taxation regime for registered pension schemes allows individuals to receive tax-advantaged benefits subject to two allowances:

- the *lifetime allowance* – an overall limit on an individual's tax-privileged retirement savings, *and*
- the *annual allowance* – a limit on an individual's retirement savings during the year.

This regime of annual and lifetime allowances for registered pension schemes first came into force on 6 April 2006 under the Finance Act 2004, and replaced the previous tax regimes for all types of pension scheme. This regime applies to all members of all arrangements in registered pension schemes. Retirement and death benefits can be provided outside a registered scheme by an 'Employer-financed Retirement Benefits Scheme' (EFRBS) – *see Section 14*.

The Finance Act 2011 has made significant changes to the regime and its operation:

- from 6 April 2011, the annual allowance was reduced to £50,000, *and*
- from 6 April 2012, the lifetime allowance will be reduced to £1.5m.

Prior to this, the lifetime and annual allowances had been increased annually. There is no commitment to increase either allowance in future years, although the legislation allows for future increases by Treasury Order.

Tax Year	Lifetime Allowance	Annual Allowance
2006/07	£1,500,000	£215,000
2007/08	£1,600,000	£225,000
2008/09	£1,650,000	£235,000
2009/10	£1,750,000	£245,000
2010/11	£1,800,000	£255,000
2011/12	£1,800,000	£50,000
2012/13	£1,500,000	£50,000

The Finance Act 2011 also made a number of changes to the authorised benefits permitted to be paid by registered schemes, including removing the requirement to annuitise members' money purchase funds by age 75. For the purpose of specifying the benefits that may be paid and testing against the above limits, the regime distinguishes between three main types of pension 'arrangement'. These are the two familiar ones, 'defined benefit' and 'money purchase', and an additional one, 'cash balance', which is expressed as a sub-category of money purchase. The type of arrangement determines how the 'pension input amount' is calculated for assessing the value of any increase in accrued rights against the annual allowance and the nature of the benefits that may be paid as authorised payments.

This section sets out the main features of the current regime, allowing for the changes made by the Finance Act 2011. At the end of this section is a brief summary of the pre-6 April 2006 regimes, parts of which are still relevant under transitional provisions.

LIFETIME ALLOWANCE CHARGE

The value of benefits must be tested against the lifetime allowance (or the part of it that remains after any previous 'crystallisations') on each occasion that benefits come into payment, or 'crystallise'. On crystallisation, up to 25% of the value of benefits crystallised (or their cost, under money purchase arrangements) within the lifetime allowance is available as a tax-free lump sum.

A single factor (for all ages) of 20:1 is used for valuing *scheme pensions (see below)* on crystallisation. The valuation of annuities provided under money purchase arrangements is based on their cost.

A lifetime allowance charge is payable if the value of the benefits being crystallised exceeds the balance of any lifetime allowance available. The rate is:

- 25% if the benefits being crystallised are taken in pension form, *or*
- 55% (equivalent to the payment of a 25% charge plus income tax at 40%) if taken as a lump sum.

If the charge is met by the administrator (and the member's benefits under the scheme are not reduced to reflect this), the tax payment is itself treated as part of the excess benefit value on which tax is calculated.

ANNUAL ALLOWANCE CHARGE

Member contributions

Member contributions of up to 100% of relevant UK earnings (or £3,600 if higher) in any one tax year attract income tax relief. Further contributions may be paid, but attract no tax relief. As well as taxable benefits in kind, 'relevant UK earnings' includes taxable income arising from share schemes and taxable redundancy payments.

Annual allowance charge

However, where the 'total pension input amount' – the aggregate of *pension input amounts (see below)* arising under schemes of which the individual is a member – exceeds the annual allowance, the individual is normally liable for a charge at their highest tax rate(s) on amounts above the annual allowance; prior to 6 April 2011, the charge was a flat-rate 40%. 'Unused annual allowance' can be carried forward for up to three years, allowing for an annual allowance charge to be reduced or not be payable.

There are exemptions from the charge in the year in which a member:

- dies
- has their benefits commuted as a *serious ill-health lump sum (see below)*, or

- becomes entitled to an ill-health pension where he/she is unlikely to be able to work in any capacity (other than to an insignificant extent) before reaching pensionable age.

These replaced a general exemption, prior to 6 April 2011, which applied in any year in which an individual's benefits under the arrangement were taken in full.

Pension input amount

Under a defined benefit or cash balance arrangement, the pension input amount for the purposes of the annual allowance is the amount of any increase in the value of the member's rights under the arrangement. This is calculated as the difference between the opening and closing values of the member's rights, with an adjustment to the opening value to allow for the increase in the Consumer Prices Index (CPI). Under a defined benefit arrangement, accrued pension is valued by multiplying the annual pension by 16; prior to 6 April 2011, a factor of 10:1 was used.

Under a money purchase arrangement (other than a cash balance arrangement), the pension input amount is the total of the contributions paid by, or in respect of, the individual. If the scheme is contracted out, flat-rate 'minimum payments' and age-related payments are excluded.

Scheme pays

Individuals facing significant charges following the reduction in the annual allowance from 6 April 2011 are generally able to require their scheme to pay the annual allowance charge on their behalf. Broadly, where a member's liability to the charge in a particular tax year exceeds £2,000, schemes are required to pay the charge and have the power to make a corresponding adjustment to the member's benefits. The legislation sets out deadlines for the scheme and the member to provide information in order to elect for the scheme to pay the charge.

Special annual allowance charge

The special annual allowance charge was introduced under the anti-forestalling measures in the Finance Act 2009. It applied for the tax years 2009/10 and 2010/11 only, pending the implementation of longer-term measures to restrict tax relief for high earners, introduced under the Finance Act 2011, *as described above*. It was levied on individuals with annual incomes in excess of £150,000 who, broadly, changed their normal pattern of regular pension contributions or the normal way in which their pension benefits accrued and had resulting pension input over £20,000. The anti-forestalling measures are set out in a summary available at *www.pensionspocketbook.com*.

OTHER TAX CHARGES

Other tax charges that may arise in particular circumstances *are discussed below*. The Finance Acts allow these charges to be varied by order. This gives the government the scope to vary them to reflect changes in the rate of income tax.

Unauthorised payments charge

If a benefit paid from a registered scheme is not *authorised (see below)* the member (or other recipient in the case of a death benefit) is liable for an unauthorised payments charge, at a rate of 40%. A 15% surcharge (resulting in an overall charge of 55%) applies if the unauthorised payment exceeds 25% of the value of the member's benefits. A payment subject to an unauthorised payments charge is, however, exempt from any further income tax charge.

Scheme sanction charge

The scheme administrator is potentially subject to a scheme sanction charge at a rate of 40% in respect of most unauthorised payments. If the member has paid an unauthorised payments charge, the scheme sanction charge is reduced by the lesser of 25% and the actual amount of the unauthorised payments charge paid.

TRANSITIONAL ARRANGEMENTS

Transitional arrangements were put in place at 6 April 2006, and subsequently at 6 April 2012, to protect benefits accrued prior to these dates, including:

- *primary protection*, whereby individuals with benefits accrued in excess of £1.5m at 5 April 2006 could register for an enhancement to their lifetime allowance
- *enhanced protection*, for individuals to have existing benefits at 5 April 2006 (whether or not already in excess of £1.5m) ring-fenced by opting out of any future 'accrual', *and*
- *fixed protection* from 6 April 2012, whereby the lifetime allowance is underpinned by £1.8m, provided no accrual is deemed to occur in any year from that date.

Transitional provisions also allow individuals to receive higher tax-free lump sums than they would otherwise under the current regime, by protecting lump sum rights at 5 April 2006.

Primary protection (6 April 2006)

This applies where total relevant pension rights in approved pension schemes as at 5 April 2006 were valued in excess of £1.5m and were registered by 5 April 2009.

The value of the accrued rights at 5 April 2006 was determined in a similar manner to values at crystallisation. However, pensions that were already in payment on 5 April 2006 were valued as 25 times the annual rate of pension in payment, to allow for the lump sum that was presumed to have been taken. If the member was taking drawdown, the maximum possible pension under the relevant drawdown provisions had to be used.

There was an overriding limit on the benefits that could be registered for protection corresponding to the maximum permitted on leaving service at 5 April 2006 under whichever of the previous tax regimes was applicable at this date.

Under primary protection, the individual is granted a personal lifetime allowance, based on the total value calculated as above, in place of the standard lifetime allowance. The personal lifetime allowance is increased annually in line with the standard lifetime allowance, but taking the latter to be at least equal to £1.8m for tax years following 5 April 2012. It is subject to adjustment if a pension debit arises as a result of a pension sharing order implemented on or after 6 April 2006.

Enhanced protection (6 April 2006)

Enhanced protection was available to all individuals with benefits in schemes that became registered pension schemes on 6 April 2006, as an alternative to primary protection. Where this applies, there are no lifetime allowance charges in respect of the individual and, prior to 6 April 2011, there were no annual allowance charges. This means that, broadly speaking:

- accrued defined benefit rights at 6 April 2006 can continue to be linked to salary (although any pre-6 April 2006 restriction due to the earnings cap will still apply), *and*
- money purchase funds accrued at 6 April 2006 can be increased by the full investment return achieved subsequently.

However, from 6 April 2011, increases in the value of defined benefit rights may be subject to annual allowance charges.

To retain enhanced protection, no further 'relevant benefit accrual' (or money purchase contributions) are permitted under any registered scheme after 5 April 2006. Registration by 5 April 2009 was required.

However, in a defined benefit arrangement, continuation of contributions or of pensionable service does not in itself count as relevant benefit accrual. Instead, for enhanced protection not to be lost, the resulting benefits must not breach the member's 'appropriate limit' at the first or a subsequent crystallisation date (or where there is a permitted transfer out of the scheme). This, in effect, means that, if the pre-6 April 2006 service benefits turn out to be lower than expected (e.g. because a reduction applies for early retirement), it may be possible to provide post-5 April 2006 service benefits without enhanced protection being lost.

As under primary protection, there was an overriding limit on the benefits that could be registered, corresponding to the maximum permitted immediately before 6 April 2006. Where enhanced protection applied, any benefits in excess of this maximum had to be surrendered (or refunded in the case of surplus AVCs).

Individuals could apply for both primary and enhanced protection – this means that if the conditions for enhanced protection are breached (and therefore this protection is lost) the individual can rely on primary protection.

Fixed protection (6 April 2012)

Fixed protection is available to all individuals with benefits in registered schemes who do not have primary or enhanced protection and who register for it before 6 April 2012. Where this applies, the tax legislation will be applied as if the individual's lifetime allowance is the greater of:

- the standard lifetime allowance, which is reduced to £1.5m from 6 April 2012, *and*
- £1.8m.

To retain fixed protection, 'benefit accrual' (or money purchase contributions) are not permitted under any registered scheme after 5 April 2012. Unlike under enhanced protection, benefit accrual under a defined benefit arrangement is tested each year rather than only when benefits are crystallised.

Protection of lump sum rights that exceed £375,000

Existing lump sum rights of more than £375,000 at 5 April 2006 are protected if the individual registered for primary or enhanced protection. If an individual with primary or enhanced protection does not have this lump sum protection, the maximum *pension commencement lump sum (see below)* is restricted to 25% of the standard lifetime allowance.

If the lump sum rights were over both £375,000 and 25% of the value of the benefits but the individual did not register, lump sum protection is available *as set out below*.

Protection of lump sum rights that exceed 25% of the value placed on total benefit rights under a scheme

Existing rights to a lump sum of more than 25% can be protected if the individual has not registered for either primary protection or enhanced protection, or their lump sum rights at 5 April 2006 were valued at less than £375,000. This is subject to the condition that all benefits under the scheme (that had not already been taken on or before 5 April 2006) are taken on the same date.

Additional protections

Further protections under the Finance Act 2004, or introduced in subsequent legislation, extend the scope for paying benefits arising under pre-6 April 2006 scheme rules without incurring unauthorised payments or lifetime allowance charges. These include:

- it is permissible to take benefits as authorised payments before *normal minimum pension age* in certain cases where such a right existed before 6 April 2006
- individuals granted a pension credit before 6 April 2006 were able to register for 'pension credit protection' which provides an enhanced lifetime allowance in a similar way to primary protection
- pensions may in some circumstances be paid to children who are over age 23 and are still in full-time education or vocational training, are suffering from serious physical or mental deterioration, or were financially dependent on the member
- benefits accrued in 'lump sum only' schemes at 5 April 2006 can be taken as tax-free lump sums on and after 6 April 2006 provided no 'relevant benefit accrual' (as for enhanced protection) has occurred, *and*
- lump sum death benefits that exceed the protected amounts under primary or enhanced protection may be protected.

Overrides during a transitional period

HMRC regulations overrode the rules of approved schemes that became registered schemes. These dealt with issues arising where existing scheme benefits were not *authorised* under the new regime, or were restricted by reference to the earnings cap, and where scheme provisions enabled benefits to be increased up to the pre-6 April 2006 'Revenue maximum'. These 'Revenue overrides' ceased on 5 April 2011, or when the scheme's rules were amended if earlier.

AUTHORISED PENSIONS PAYABLE TO MEMBER

A defined benefit arrangement may pay a member pension only in the form of a *scheme pension*, as described below.

For a money purchase arrangement, there are essentially three options as to the type of member pension that may be provided:

- a *scheme pension* as for defined benefit arrangements, provided the member had been offered an open market option
- a *lifetime annuity, or*
- a *drawdown pension*, consisting of income withdrawal and/or a short-term annuity. The rate of annual drawdown is generally subject to strict limits and referred to as *capped drawdown*. However, a member can apply for *flexible drawdown*, which removes these limits, provided they meet certain conditions *described below*.

All pensions payable from registered schemes are subject to income tax at the recipient's marginal rate and they must be paid under PAYE, where applicable.

Minimum age from which pension may be paid

Member pensions (including drawdown pension) must not commence before *normal minimum pension age*, except on ill-health retirement. Normal minimum pension age is 55; prior to 6 April 2010, it was 50. Under transitional provisions, members may be able receive an authorised pension before age 55 if such a right existed at 6 April 2006.

Scheme pension

Scheme pensions must be payable at least annually and may not be reduced from one 12-month period to the next, except in specified circumstances including the cessation of an ill-health pension, a bridging pension ceasing between ages 60 and 65, as a consequence of a pension sharing order, or where reductions are applied to all scheme pensions.

Lifetime annuity

A lifetime annuity must be payable by an insurance company, with the member having had the opportunity to select the insurance company – the 'open market option'. The annuity may be level, increasing or investment/index-linked.

Period of payment

Lifetime annuities and scheme pensions must generally be payable for life and may, additionally, carry a guarantee of up to ten years payable (to any person) in the form of continued pension instalments.

Capped drawdown

The maximum annual drawdown pension is 100% of the amount of the 'relevant annuity' that could be provided from the member's drawdown fund, where this amount is determined by reference to tables published by the Government Actuary's Department. There is no minimum level of drawdown pension.

Flexible drawdown

Flexible drawdown allows a member to gain access to the whole of their drawdown fund without an annual cap on withdrawals. To be eligible, the member must declare that the following three conditions are met:

- the member has a secure lifetime pension income, which may include state pensions, of at least £20,000 a year
- no relievable member or employer contributions have been paid to any money purchase arrangement of the member in the tax year in which the declaration is made, *and*
- at the time of the declaration, the member is not an active member of any defined benefit or cash balance arrangement.

Pension errors and arrears

The list of authorised payments was extended in 2009, with retrospective effect from 6 April 2006, to include the following payments:

- pensions paid in error or up to six months after the pensioner's death, including payments after the error is discovered, provided that all reasonable steps had been taken to prevent payment; this also applies to pension death benefits, *and*
- payment of arrears of pension from a defined benefit arrangement after the member's death; if he or she had died on or after 6 April 2006, it is required that the scheme could not reasonably have been expected to make the payment before his or her death.

These payments are taxable as pension in the tax year of payment.

AUTHORISED LUMP SUMS PAYABLE TO MEMBER

Apart from additional authorised payments prescribed under transitional provisions *(see above)*, the only lump sum benefits that may be paid to a member of a registered pension scheme are set out below.

Pension commencement lump sum

A tax-free pension commencement lump sum (PCLS) of up to 25% of the value of the benefits crystallised *(see above)* may normally be paid in connection with a member becoming entitled to a *scheme pension*, a *lifetime annuity* or *income withdrawal*. The maximum pension commencement lump sum payable is also restricted to one-quarter of the unused portion of the standard lifetime allowance.

Under regulations made in 2009, the following are also authorised payments, with retrospective effect from 6 April 2006, although not strictly PCLSs:

- a commencement lump sum based on an incorrect pension figure, annuity or scheme pension purchase price, *and*
- a commencement lump sum paid under a defined benefit arrangement, no more than a year after the scheme administrator first knew (or could reasonably have been expected to know) of the member's death, if entitlement was not established and payment could not reasonably have been expected before the member died.

Serious ill-health lump sum

Where a member is expected to live for less than one year, a serious ill-health lump sum may be paid in respect of uncrystallised benefits. Up to the available lifetime allowance, this is tax free.

Short service refund lump sum

A refund of the member's contributions (without interest) may be paid from an occupational pension scheme on leaving service, if the member has no right to preservation. The scheme administrator is liable for tax on the first £20,000 of such refunds at 20% and on the remainder at 50%. Interest may be paid in addition to the short service refund lump sum as a 'scheme administration member payment' *(see below)* and is taxed at the member's marginal tax rate.

Trivial commutation and other small lump sums

A trivial commutation lump sum is permitted only if all of a member's benefits under all pension arrangements are valued in aggregate at no more than £18,000 (or 1% of the standard lifetime allowance prior to 6 April 2012). The commutations must take place within a single 12-month window, chosen by the member, who must have reached age 60. A payment to a member that would be a trivial commutation lump sum but for the continued payment of a lifetime annuity under the same scheme is also permitted.

With effect from 1 December 2009, the range of authorised lump sum payments was significantly extended to include the following small payments, which must not exceed £2,000 and must extinguish the member's entitlement under the scheme:

- a payment from a public service or occupational pension scheme to a member who has reached the age of 60. All benefits including those in related schemes must be within the £2,000 limit
- a payment by a larger public service or occupational pension scheme (with at least 50 members) to a member who has reached the age of 60

- a payment after a 'relevant accretion', such as where a scheme passes on an unexpected additional allocation received after a member has transferred out or purchased an annuity, *and*
- a payment made by way of compensation under the Financial Services Compensation Scheme.

If the member has uncrystallised rights immediately before the lump sum is paid, 25% of the value of such rights is tax free, with the balance taxed at the member's marginal rate.

Winding-up lump sum

A winding-up lump sum, not exceeding £18,000 (or 1% of the standard lifetime allowance prior to 6 April 2012) may be paid, subject to certain conditions, to extinguish the member's entitlement to benefits under the pension scheme. If the member has uncrystallised rights immediately before the lump sum is paid, 25% of the value of such rights is tax free, with the balance taxed at the member's marginal rate.

Lifetime allowance excess lump sum

Where none of a member's lifetime allowance is available, any remaining uncrystallised benefits may be taken as a lifetime allowance excess lump sum. This may not be paid until *normal minimum pension age* (unless the member is in ill health), and is taxed at 55%.

Refund of excess contributions lump sum

Where in any tax year a member's pension contributions exceed the maximum that qualifies for tax relief (£3,600 or relevant UK earnings, if greater), a refund of the excess may be paid without giving rise to liability for income tax. Any excess contributions that had been paid net of basic rate income tax under a 'relief at source' arrangement cannot be included in the refund. A 'scheme administration member payment' *(see below)*, taxable at the member's marginal rate, may also be made in respect of interest or investment growth.

Scheme administration member payment

A scheme administration member payment is defined as 'a payment by a registered pension scheme to or in respect of... a member of the pension scheme which is made for the purposes of the administration or management of the pension scheme'. The legislation expressly states that payments of wages, salaries or fees to persons administering the scheme and payments made for the purchase of scheme assets are scheme administration payments, whereas a loan is not. A scheme administration payment may not exceed the amount that might be expected to be paid on arm's length terms.

AUTHORISED PENSIONS PAYABLE ON DEATH

A pension death benefit is a pension payable to an eligible dependant on the death of a member, other than continuing payments of member pension for a limited period under a permitted member pension. The forms of the dependant's pension that may be provided under the different types of arrangement correspond to those for members' pensions. A *dependant's scheme pension* is restricted to 100% of the member's pension (plus an adjustment for any tax-free lump sum taken) if the member was over 75 years of age at the date of death. All dependants' pensions payable from registered schemes are subject to income tax at the recipient's marginal rate and must be taxed under PAYE, where applicable.

Eligible 'dependants' are:

- a member's spouse or civil partner at date of death
- a person who was married to, or a civil partner of, the member when the member first became entitled to the pension
- a child of the member who either has not reached age 23 (extended in some circumstances under transitional provisions) or who, in the opinion of the scheme administrator, was dependent on the member at the date of the member's death because of physical or mental impairment, *and/or*
- any other person who, in the opinion of the scheme administrator, at the date of the member's death:
  - was financially dependent on the member
  - had a financial relationship of mutual dependence with the member, *or*
  - was dependent on the member because of physical or mental impairment.

AUTHORISED LUMP SUMS PAYABLE ON DEATH

The only lump sum death benefits that may be paid by a registered pension scheme are those described below (other than payments allowed for under transitional provisions – *see above*). Except where otherwise indicated, the legislation imposes no restrictions on the recipient of the benefit.

Defined benefits lump sum death benefit

On the death of a member in a defined benefit arrangement, a lump sum of unrestricted amount. This is tax free up to the amount of the member's remaining lifetime allowance if the member died before age 75. If the member died after reaching age 75, the payment is taxable at 55%.

Uncrystallised funds lump sum death benefit

On the death of a member of a money purchase arrangement, a lump sum not exceeding the amount of the uncrystallised funds, tax free up to the amount of the member's remaining lifetime allowance if the member died before age 75. If the member died after reaching age 75, the payment is taxable at 55%.

Pension/annuity protection lump sum death benefit

On the death of a member whilst in receipt of a scheme pension or lifetime annuity, a lump sum, taxable at 55%. This benefit may not exceed the amount by which the instalments paid up to the date of death fall short of the amount originally crystallised.

Drawdown pension fund lump sum death benefit

On the death of a member of a money purchase arrangement, or of a dependant, who was entitled to income withdrawal at the time of death, a lump sum, taxable at 55%.

Charity lump sum death benefit

On the death, leaving no dependants, of a member of a money purchase arrangement (or of a dependant) who was in receipt of a drawdown pension, a charity lump sum death benefit may be paid to a charity nominated by the member or dependant as appropriate. A charity lump sum death benefit may also be paid on the death of a member who has reached age 75, leaving no dependants, in respect of uncrystallised funds.

Trivial commutation lump sum death benefit/ winding-up lump sum death benefit

In specified circumstances, a lump sum, not exceeding £18,000 (or 1% of the standard lifetime allowance prior to 6 April 2012) may be paid to a dependant, taxable at his or her marginal rate.

REGISTRATION AND REPORTING TO HMRC

Registration

'Registration' of a pension scheme replaced the previous 'HMRC approval' as the process by which schemes obtain tax-advantaged status from 6 April 2006. Pension schemes that had HMRC approval prior to 6 April 2006 automatically became 'registered schemes' on 6 April 2006 unless they explicitly opted out.

Reporting

Registered pension schemes have to comply with a number of administration requirements. These include providing HMRC with quarterly returns for tax accounting purposes, reports on the occurrence of certain events and, if requested, a *Pension Scheme Return*.

OVERSEAS ASPECTS

Scheme membership

There is no restriction on non-UK-resident individuals becoming members of registered pension schemes.

The annual and lifetime allowance charges, and unauthorised payments charges, apply whether or not the individual is resident, ordinarily resident or domiciled in the UK. However, the lifetime allowance may be enhanced to allow for overseas periods of membership falling after 5 April 2006 during which contributions to the scheme are not eligible for UK tax relief.

Transfers may be accepted by registered schemes from any overseas pension schemes. The lifetime allowance may be enhanced for transfers from *recognised overseas pension schemes* (see Appendix 2, Glossary of Terms).

Transfers may be made from registered schemes to *qualifying recognised overseas pension schemes*, and count as benefit crystallisation events for lifetime allowance purposes.

Migrant member relief

Migrant member relief allows UK tax relief on contributions paid to overseas schemes where a *relevant migrant member* comes to the UK, and was a member of a qualifying tax-relieved overseas pension scheme at any time in the previous ten years. The manager of that scheme must provide HMRC with details of any relevant benefit crystallisation events that occur. Contributions and benefits accruing after A Day would normally count towards the annual and lifetime allowances, although from 2008 this excludes benefits and contributions in respect of earnings that are not subject to UK taxation.

OTHER MATTERS

Investment

There is one set of tax rules covering investments for all registered pension schemes. These allow schemes to invest in any type of investment where this is held for the purpose of the scheme, and generally exempt them from income and capital gains tax. However, other non-tax regulations do limit or prohibit certain types of investment. These rules allow 'authorised employer loans' subject to conditions. However, occupational schemes are still prevented from making such loans by the 'employer-related investment' provisions under the Pensions Act 1995 *(see Section 11)*. Investment in residential property is also allowed in certain circumstances, but not in cases where the members can direct the investment policy.

Surplus

A repayment of surplus funds to the employer is only authorised in limited circumstances and is taxed at 35%. For instance, a refund cannot reduce the assets of the scheme below the level required to buy out all members' benefits with an insurance company.

PRE-APRIL 2006 TAX REGIMES

Previous tax regimes limited benefits and/or contributions by reference to parameters such as earnings, company service and age in order for schemes to have a tax-advantaged status. Benefits outside these limits had to be provided in a separate, less tax-advantaged scheme (FURBS or UURBS – *see Section 14*).

The features of the main tax-approved regimes that existed prior to 6 April 2006 are summarised below.

Occupational pension schemes

'Revenue limits' set out maximum pensions and lump sums in three categories, according to the date the member joined the scheme ('pre-1987', '1987' and '1989'). The three categories are similar, and generally allow a member to be provided with a pension of 1/60 × final remuneration and, by commutation of this pension, a lump sum of 3/80 × final remuneration, for each year of service with the employer (up to a maximum of 40), regardless of retained benefits from previous employers' schemes or personal pensions. However, higher benefits could often be provided, with the maximum pension of $\frac{2}{3}$ × final remuneration (including retained benefits) payable after 10 or 20 years.

Ill-health and death benefits were based on a similar calculation but allowing for potential service up to the scheme's normal retirement age. Spouses' pensions were generally allowed to be up to $\frac{2}{3}$ of the member's pension, and an additional lump sum of 4 × final remuneration plus a refund of the member's own contributions could be provided on death in service. There was a limit on member contributions (including AVCs) of 15% of remuneration in any tax year.

The 1989 limits introduced the 'earnings cap' – a limit on the amount of final remuneration that could be used in calculating benefits under that regime. The 1987 limits included a monetary cap on lump sum retirement benefits but not on pension benefits.

Personal pensions and retirement annuity contracts

Personal pension schemes (and some money purchase occupational schemes) were subject to a different regime. Instead of restricting benefits, this set a maximum amount of contributions that could be paid in any tax year, which from 1989/90 onwards ranged from 17.5% of 'net relevant earnings' for those aged 35 and under to 40% for those aged 61 and over. There were no limits on the amount of pension that could be provided at retirement, although the maximum lump sum was generally limited to 25% of the member's fund.

Retirement annuity contracts were the forerunner to personal pensions, and had a similar regime, although there were lower limits on contributions.

Executive pensions

Small self-administered schemes ('SSAS') were set up to provide benefits for controlling directors and other senior employees. These generally allowed greater investment freedom, e.g. loanbacks to the employer, but were subject to stricter requirements from the Revenue in order to maintain their tax-advantaged status.

Further detail on the previous tax regimes is available at *www.pensionspocketbook.com*.

EMPLOYER-FINANCED RETIREMENT BENEFIT SCHEMES

DISGUISED REMUNERATION MEASURES

Following the introduction of a new 50% rate of income tax, the Government announced that it would introduce measures aimed at reducing the attractiveness of vehicles which are used to 'disguise remuneration and avoid, reduce or defer payment of tax'. These measures have now been introduced and are contained in the Finance Act 2011. They are expected to have a significant impact on EFRBS.

BACKGROUND

There have always been limits on the extent to which any individual can benefit from the tax advantages offered by registered (or prior to April 2006, 'approved') pension schemes. As a consequence there has for many years been a demand for top-up arrangements of one sort or another outside the 'tax-privileged' pensions savings environment.

Before April 2006, the main top-up vehicles used were Funded Unapproved Retirement Benefit Schemes (FURBS) and Unfunded Unapproved Retirement Benefit Schemes (UURBS). The tax treatment of FURBS was broadly: *taxed* on contributions on the way in, *taxed* on investment returns but *exempt* from tax on benefits paid out (TTE). There were certain tax and National Insurance advantages on contributions and investment returns, but these were progressively reduced over the years. UURBS were attractive to employers because of cash flow and National Insurance contribution (NIC) considerations. But from the employee's viewpoint, the absence of pre-funding often represented a significant risk. A compromise was the secured UURBS, a benefit promise that was unfunded but where security was given by the employer. Typically, if the employer experiences a change of control or insolvency event, this security is paid into a trust which subsequently pays a benefit to the employee.

From April 2006, FURBS and UURBS became known as Employer-Financed Retirement Benefit Schemes, or EFRBS. The taxation of funded EFRBS was changed from TTE to ETT (relief available on contributions paid in, but benefits ultimately paid out subject to tax – investment returns on the funds are taxed under both regimes). Thus the main attractions of funded EFRBS became the potential exemption from NICs and deferral of income tax. However, since corporation tax relief was also deferred until the benefits were paid, on balance funded EFRBS became unattractive and were rarely used for further contributions after April 2006. Unfunded EFRBS continued to be popular, particularly where security was available.

From April 2010 the top rate of income tax increased to 50%. At the same time, corporation tax went down, with the prospect of further reductions.

This made the tax deferral aspect of EFRBS particularly attractive. As a result, the Government announced that EFRBS would be targeted by new measures aimed at ensuring that 'disguised remuneration' provided through third parties would be no more attractive than other forms of remuneration.

TAXATION OF EFRBS

The disguised remuneration provisions contained in the Finance Act 2011 apply when a 'relevant third person' (meaning broadly someone other than the employer, connected company or employee, but including the employer or employee if they are acting as a trustee) makes provision in connection with the employee's employment. In this case, the money or assets set aside in connection with the benefit promise will be taxed (and NICs due) as employment income. Thus any new contributions paid to a funded EFRBS after 5 April 2011 will result in an income tax and NI charge on the employee (although to avoid double counting, there will be a deduction from the tax and any NI that would otherwise be due when the benefits are paid out in the future).

The disguised remuneration provisions also apply where an employer earmarks, or starts to hold, assets (or otherwise provides security) in connection with a 'relevant undertaking' to provide retirement benefits to the employee via a relevant third person (such as an insurance company or trust). As a result, except where the benefits payable from a secured unfunded EFRBS will be paid direct by the employer, any new security provided after 5 April 2011 may result in an income tax and NI charge on the employee.

Unfunded EFRBS under which there is no undertaking to provide the benefit via a third person are currently unaffected by the Finance Act 2011 provisions. However the Government has said that it will monitor changes in patterns of pension savings behaviour and will act if necessary to prevent loss of tax revenue.

The other main features of the taxation of EFRBS are as follows:

- benefits accrued under an EFRBS are not to be counted for the annual allowance or the special annual allowance, nor are they to be tested against the member's lifetime allowance when paid *(see Section 13)*

- the arrangement's investment income and capital gains are subject to tax

- lump sum and pension benefits are subject to income tax when received by the employee, *and*

- employers can deduct the costs of providing the benefits from taxable profits, but only when the benefits are paid from the scheme and chargeable to tax on the employee. (So corporation tax relief is not available until then.)

In addition, provided that the payments from the EFRBS meet specific conditions (including that the form of benefits would have been authorised if the scheme had been registered, and that employment has ceased and the member is not re-employed by the company), no NICs are payable.

However, if the EFRBS is set up so that provision of the benefits results in a reduction in the benefits payable to or in respect of the employee under a registered pension scheme, or its payment is triggered by a reduction in the benefits payable under a registered pension scheme, then corporation tax relief for the employer will generally not be available, and may be withheld in respect of contributions to the registered scheme.

UNFUNDED EFRBS AND SECURITY

The main drawback of an unfunded arrangement is its inherent lack of security. A number of ways of overcoming this drawback are considered below:

Charges over assets
The establishment of a charge over assets to provide the security for an unfunded retirement benefit promise might be considered. However, as discussed above, if this is done in conjunction with a trust (or other relevant third person) it is likely to give rise to income tax and NI charges.

Insolvency insurance
It may be possible to arrange insurance cover to pay the benefits if an employer becomes insolvent and unable to do so. Premiums paid to insure against the risk of default will be regarded as an employee benefit in kind and taxed accordingly.

Bank guarantees
Bank guarantees could be a source of external financial back-up for unfunded pensions, but are likely to be difficult to arrange and are available only for short-term cover.

ACCOUNTING

EFRBS, whether funded or unfunded, fall within the scope of FRS 17 and IAS 19 *(see Section 28)*.

DWP LEGISLATION

The Pension Schemes Act 1993, the Pensions Act 1995 and the Pensions Act 2004 are generally applicable to non-registered arrangements, although there are a large number of provisions from which such arrangements are exempt. For example, the protections against forfeiture of benefits do apply, but the scheme funding provisions do not and the disclosure requirements are limited.

Preservation and EFRBS

Preservation and transfer value rights for early leavers apply to funded EFRBS as to registered schemes. However, preservation does not apply to unfunded EFRBS unless it is explicitly written into the scheme documentation. If preservation does apply, then revaluation will also apply, and pension sharing on divorce will reflect the preserved benefit.

TAX TREATMENT OF EFRBS

A brief summary comparing the tax treatment of registered pension schemes and EFRBS is set out in this table. *Please note that this does not take account of any changes arising from the anti-avoidance measures referred to above.*

	Registered Pension Scheme	EFRBS[1]	
		Disguised Remuneration Provisions	
		do not Apply	Apply
Employer's contributions/ allocations to reserves:			
– corporation tax relief for employer	yes	no[2]	yes
– employer's NICs payable	no	no	yes
– income tax charge on employee	no[3]	no	yes
– employee's NICs payable	no	no	yes
Member's contributions:			
– income tax relief for employee	yes[3]	no	no
Investment returns/ growth in reserves:	no income tax or capital gains tax payable	income and capital gains taxable at rates applicable to trusts	income and capital gains taxable at rates applicable to trusts
Tax paid by beneficiary[4] on:			
– pension	income tax payable[5] (but no NICs)	income tax payable[5,8] (but no NICs)[6]	income tax payable[5,8,9] (but no NICs)[6]
– lump sum	tax-free (lump sum generally limited to 25%)	income tax payable[7,8] (but no NICs)[6]	income tax payable[7,8,9] (but no NICs)[6]

Notes:
1 The EFRBS is assumed to be established as an 'accumulation trust' with UK-resident trustees.
2 CT relief may generally be claimed when benefits are paid and chargeable to tax on the employee.
3 However, any 'pension input' in excess of the annual allowance or the special annual allowance may be subject to a tax charge – *see Section 13*.
4 The Finance Act 2007 amended ITEPA 2003 to include a power to make retrospective regulations extending the definition of benefits from an EFRBS that are excluded from taxation.
5 All pensions, regardless of the type of arrangement, are taxed at source via the PAYE system.
6 Provided that the payments from the EFRBS meet specific conditions, no NICs are payable.
7 The amount of the lump sum that is taxable is reduced by the amount of any contributions paid by the employee towards its provision. In addition, part of the lump sum will be tax-free if contributions, on which the employee was taxed, were paid to the FURBS before 6 April 2006; if no contributions have been made since then, the whole of the lump sum will be tax-free.
8 There is no exemption from inheritance tax for benefits payable from an EFRBS, except to the extent that they arose from contributions made to a FURBS before 6 April 2006.
9 The income tax charge will be reduced by the amount of the charge paid by the employee at the time the employer contributions were made.

LEAVING SERVICE BENEFITS

PRESERVATION

The preservation legislation provides members of an occupational pension scheme with a legal right to short service benefit (SSB) if they leave pensionable service before normal pension age (NPA). The essential principle is that an early leaver's benefits should be calculated on a consistent basis with those of a member who remains in service up to NPA.

Entitlement to SSB is dependent upon the member either having at least two years' 'qualifying service' or having transferred benefits from a personal pension into the scheme. 'Qualifying service' is the sum of all actual pensionable service under the scheme plus pensionable service in any scheme from which a transfer payment has been received. Members who do not satisfy the preservation conditions may nevertheless be granted deferred benefits if scheme rules so provide. Alternatively, the scheme may provide for them to receive a refund of their own contributions, if any, less tax and their share of any premium required to reinstate contracted-out service back into the State scheme. However, no State scheme premium can be paid in respect of protected rights, which must be preserved within the scheme (this requirement will be removed when the restrictions that apply to protected rights are abolished, from 6 April 2012). In money purchase schemes, early leavers must normally be entitled to whatever benefit derives from contributions paid by or in respect of them, and the period of two years' qualifying service before a member must be provided with this benefit is under review and may be shortened or removed.

Special provisions apply where a member is automatically enrolled before opting out under Pensions Act 2008 *(see Section 9)*.

Payment of short service benefits

Preserved benefits must normally be payable not later than the member's NPA. The preservation legislation defines NPA as the earliest age at which a member is entitled to receive benefits on retirement from the relevant employment, disregarding any special provisions for early retirement. Therefore, even if scheme rules define retirement age as 65, NPA could be earlier if members have an unqualified right to retire on an unreduced pension from an earlier age. However, until 5 April 2005, benefits need not have been paid before age 60, if scheme rules contain a specific provision to this effect. From 6 April 2005 this legislative provision was amended so that, if scheme rules so provide, benefits need not be paid before age 65.

The question of whether a scheme could have more than one NPA (for example when a member is entitled to part of his benefits from 60 and part from 65 following changes to scheme rules to comply with the *Barber* judgment) is a moot point following the 2007 Court of Appeal ruling in the case of *Cripps v TSL*.

Leavers with three months' pensionable service

From 6 April 2006, pension scheme leavers must be given the option of a transfer value (the 'cash transfer sum') in respect of accrued benefits, having completed between 3 and 24 months' pensionable service. Trustees must notify members of this option, as an alternative to a refund of contributions, if applicable, within a 'reasonable period' of leaving pensionable service. The Pension Regulator's Code of Practice defines a reasonable period as normally within three months for this purpose. If the member does not reply within a further 'reasonable period' (which must have been specified and should be at least three months, although the Regulator considers a longer period may be necessary in some circumstances) a refund of contributions may be paid by default (but not before a further month has elapsed). Where the member opts for a cash transfer sum, this must be calculated in the same way as a cash equivalent transfer value under the scheme and paid 'without unjustifiable delay' (in any event, normally within three months). Sometimes, in contracted-out schemes, the overall timetable may need to be compressed to meet the six-month deadline for payment of a Contributions Equivalent Premium.

REVALUATION

The position of early leavers from final salary occupational pension schemes improved significantly from 1986. Before then, with the exception of Guaranteed Minimum Pensions (GMPs), there was no legal requirement for preserved benefits to be increased during the period of deferment until the pension came into payment. Consequently, the purchasing power of the eventual pension could be seriously eroded by inflation. The Social Security Act 1985 introduced the requirement to increase (or 'revalue') in deferment the part of a preserved pension in excess of GMP which relates to service completed on or after 1 January 1985, for a member who left pensionable service on or after 1 January 1986. The revaluation requirement was further extended to cover the whole of the member's pension in excess of GMP for members leaving pensionable service on or after 1 January 1991. The revaluation percentage *(see table on following page)* was the *lesser* of the increase in the general level of prices and 5% per annum compound over the whole period of deferment. The Pensions Act 2008 reduced the revaluation cap for pensionable service accrued after 5 April 2009 from 5% p.a. to 2.5% p.a.

The increase in the general level of prices is based on the opinion of the Secretary of State. Prior to 2010, this assessment had reflected the Retail Prices Index (RPI). However, in July 2010 it was announced that the Consumer Prices Index (CPI) would be used to assess the increase in prices from September 2010 onwards – periods of deferment which straddle 2010 are therefore revalued with a combination of RPI and CPI.

GMPs

In addition to the revaluation requirements on the excess of the member's pension over any GMP, members of contracted-out schemes must also have their GMP revalued between leaving service and age 65 for men and age 60 for women, either:

(1)   in line with Average Earnings (Section 148 orders, *see Section 6*); *or*

(2)   by fixed rate revaluation at the following rate per annum:

- leavers after 5 April 2012 (proposed) $4\frac{3}{4}\%$
- leavers after 5 April 2007, but before 6 April 2012   4%
- leavers after 5 April 2002, but before 6 April 2007 $4\frac{1}{2}\%$
- leavers after 5 April 1997, but before 6 April 2002 $6\frac{1}{4}\%$
- leavers after 5 April 1993, but before 6 April 1997   7%
- leavers after 5 April 1988, but before 6 April 1993 $7\frac{1}{2}\%$
- leavers before 6 April 1988 $8\frac{1}{2}\%$

For leavers before 6 April 1997, schemes could choose to apply limited revaluation, which provided the lesser of Section 148 orders and 5% p.a. revaluation. A Limited Revaluation Premium was payable to the State. This option was withdrawn from 6 April 1997.

For members who left pensionable service after 31 December 1984, the revaluations on the GMP cannot be 'franked' against the excess pension over the GMP, or against revaluations on the excess. GMP accrual ceased from April 1997, but GMPs earned prior to this date continue to be revalued as above on leaving service.

Deferred Pension Revaluation Percentages

Complete years since leaving	Calendar Year of Normal Pension Age			Complete years since leaving	Calendar Year of Normal Pension Age		
	2011 (%)	2010 (%)	2009 (%)		2011 (%)	2010 (%)	2009 (%)
1	3.1	0	5.0	14	44.4	43.0	50.7
2	1.7	3.5	9.1	15	47.5	48.6	54.0
3	6.7	7.6	13.0	16	53.2	51.9	56.8
4	10.9	11.4	16.1	17	56.6	54.6	62.4
5	14.9	14.4	19.7	18	59.4	60.2	69.1
6	18.0	18.0	23.0	19	65.1	66.7	87.5
7	21.7	21.3	25.1	20	71.9	84.9	101.8
8	25.1	23.4	27.2	21	90.7	99.0	113.3
9	27.2	25.5	31.4	22	105.1	110.3	122.3
10	29.3	29.6	32.9	23	116.8	119.1	129.1
11	33.6	31.0	37.1	24	125.9	125.9	
12	35.1	35.2	42.1	25	132.9		
13	39.4	40.1	45.1				

TRANSFER VALUES

Members of registered occupational pension schemes whose pensionable service has ended have the right to the cash equivalent of all or, in particular circumstances, part of their benefits to be paid as a transfer value to another registered scheme (*see Section 16 for further details of transfer values, including: transfers of contracted-out benefits; Finance Act 2004 restrictions; and overseas transfers*).

TRANSFER VALUES

Pension scheme leavers have had the statutory right to a cash equivalent as an alternative to deferred benefits under a scheme since 1986 – *see Section 15*. Trustees are responsible for setting assumptions for the calculation of cash equivalent transfer values and may also need to consider whether it is appropriate to offer members more than the minimum required by legislation.

Individual transfers are considered in this Section; *Section 27* covers bulk transfer arrangements.

Right to a cash equivalent

Generally, members of occupational pension schemes whose pensionable service ended on or after 1 January 1986 have the right to the cash equivalent of all or, in particular circumstances, part of their benefits to be paid as a transfer value to another registered pension scheme. From 6 April 1997, this right was extended to members whose pensionable service ended before 1 January 1986. This right is normally subject to there being a period of at least one year between the termination of the member's pensionable service and NPA, although, where NPA is earlier than 60, the right arises on termination of service at any time before NPA.

Members who opt out of pension schemes without leaving their jobs also have the right to transfer at least part of their benefits. This right only entitles the member to a 'partial' cash equivalent, related to service completed on or after 6 April 1988 (when members generally first had the right to opt out).

For defined benefits transfer values there is a three-month window from the date of calculation in which the cash equivalent is guaranteed and may be taken without being subject to recalculation. There are other time limits and disclosure requirements *(see Section 17)* imposed on the process of making a transfer.

Calculation of transfer values

The trustees have responsibility for setting the basis for the calculation of transfer values. Prior to October 2008, the actuary was responsible for approving the basis.

The fundamental principle is that the initial cash equivalent transfer value (before any adjustment – *see below*) should be broadly equal to the expected cost of providing the benefit within the scheme. Trustees are required to set financial and demographic assumptions on a 'best estimate' basis, having regard to the scheme's investment strategy and having obtained advice from the actuary. (This contrasts with the scheme funding requirement to use 'prudent' assumptions.) The Regulator has issued guidance that outlines the advice on assumptions that the trustees must seek from their actuary. Nevertheless, the trustees are responsible for determining, amongst other things, the interest rate used for discounting future benefit payments and the expected longevity of members. Trustees also need to determine an appropriate allowance for member options and discretionary benefits. The Regulator's guidance makes it clear that only those options which increase the value of a member's benefits should be taken into account, although allowance can be made for the proportion of members likely to exercise such options. In deciding whether to make allowance for discretionary benefits, the guidance suggests that trustees should usually consult any person whose consent is needed, and consider past history and any allowance in scheme funding, amongst other things.

For members with defined contribution benefits, the cash equivalent transfer value is the realisable value at the date of calculation of any benefits to which the member is entitled.

Paying more or less

For underfunded defined benefit schemes, which would not have enough money to pay full transfer values for all members, the legislation permits the initial cash equivalent to be reduced in line with the extent of underfunding shown in an 'Insufficiency Report' commissioned from the actuary. The Regulator's guidance suggests that trustees should not normally make such a reduction where an employer's covenant is judged to be strong and any funding shortfall is being remedied over a reasonably short period.

The legislation also allows the trustees to pay transfer values at a level higher than best estimate. This may be appropriate if the scheme rules require it or where simpler calculations would make it cost-effective. Alternatively, the trustees may simply decide that it is appropriate to pay higher transfer values than the minimum required (perhaps following a request by, or in consultation with, the employer). Higher transfer values might encourage take-up, which, if transfer values remained below the prudent reserves required for funding the members' liabilities, could reduce a scheme's deficit (or increase its surplus). Indeed, a transfer incentive exercise may be undertaken – *see Section 23*.

Transfers of contracted-out benefit

Transfers of contracted-out benefits can be made freely between most arrangements contracted out on either the salary-related or the protected rights basis. In these cases, the nature of the contracted-out benefit may alter from GMP or 'post-97 Contracted-out Salary Related (COSR) rights' (that is, all non-AVC pension rights in the scheme accrued after 5 April 1997) to protected rights or vice versa, depending on the circumstances of the transfer. A distinction is drawn between rights earned before 6 April 1997 and those earned on or after that date. Protected rights are also separately recorded as pre-97 and post-97 protected rights. The following system of transferability has operated since April 1997:

- transfers where there are no pre-97 GMP or post-97 COSR rights, and no pre-97 or post-97 protected rights, can occur freely between salary-related or money purchase schemes, personal pensions and buy-out policies

- GMPs remain either as GMPs or become pre-97 protected rights (the basis of conversion being determined by the contracted-out status of the receiving scheme)

- pre-97 protected rights either remain as pre-97 protected rights or are replaced by GMPs based on the member's National Insurance contributions history (as determined by HMRC)
- post-97 COSR rights either remain as post-97 COSR rights or become wholly post-97 protected rights, *and*
- post-97 protected rights either remain as post-97 protected rights or become post-97 COSR rights.

However, protected rights contracting out will be abolished with effect from 6 April 2012 and all statutory restrictions on protected rights will consequently be removed from that date: *see Section 6*. Moreover, from this date, it will become possible to transfer GMPs and post-97 COSR rights to a scheme that is not contracted out, provided:

- the member consents in writing
- the transfer payment is at least equal to the cash equivalent of the member's contracted-out rights, *and*
- the member has acknowledged in writing to the transferring scheme that he has received a statement from the receiving scheme showing the benefits to be awarded in respect of the transfer payment, and he accepts that:
  - ○ the benefits in the receiving scheme may be different in form and amount to those payable by the transferring scheme, *and*
  - ○ there is no statutory requirement for the receiving scheme to provide survivors' benefits out of the transfer payment.

Disclosure and payment

Disclosure requirements, including those in respect of transfer values, are described in *Section 17*. A guaranteed cash equivalent may be accepted within the three-month 'guarantee period' without being subject to recalculation. Generally, the trustees are required to pay the transfer value within six months of the date of calculation where the cash equivalent is guaranteed and within six months of the original request where it is not (for example, where the benefits are money purchase in nature). Trustees are also required to inform members of salary-related schemes:

- that the Financial Services Authority, the Pensions Advisory Service and the Pensions Regulator provide information that may assist in their decision on whether to transfer
- of the existence of the PPF and that the scheme is eligible for it (eligible schemes only), *and*
- that it is recommended that they should take financial advice before making a decision.

Restrictions imposed by HMRC

Since 6 April 2006, the majority of restrictions on pension transfers and the benefits that could be provided in respect of them under previous tax regimes have been removed. In general, under the Finance Act 2004 tax regime, transfers of 'uncrystallised' pension rights can be made between registered pension schemes (or to deferred annuity contracts or buy-out policies) without restriction, provided that scheme rules permit. Transfers can also be made to 'qualifying recognised overseas pension schemes' *(see below)*.

The previous restrictions on partial transfers were removed by the Finance Act 2004. However, members only have a *statutory* right to a 'partial cash equivalent' in limited circumstances (e.g. on opting out *(see above)* or where contracting-out restrictions apply). Partial transfers will therefore generally be possible only where scheme rules permit.

Pensions already in payment can also be transferred, provided that scheme rules allow and certain conditions are met (e.g. the amount of the pension is not reduced except to the extent needed to meet the administrative cost of the transfer and any guarantee is no longer than that remaining before the transfer). Drawdown pension funds may be transferred to another such arrangement (which may not be used to hold any other funds).

Certain forms of transitional protection *(see Section 13)* may be lost on transfer, unless prescribed conditions are satisfied. In particular, enhanced protection (for high earners) will be lost unless the transfer is a 'permitted transfer' (requiring, *inter alia*, that the transfer is to a money purchase, but not cash balance, arrangement, or a bulk transfer that meets specified criteria).

Overseas transfers

Transfers to an overseas arrangement may only be made if that arrangement falls within the definition of a qualifying recognised overseas pension scheme *(see Appendix 2, Glossary of Terms)*. If such a transfer takes place, the scheme administrator of the recognised pension scheme must ensure that an event report detailing the transfer is submitted to HMRC. Information must also be provided to HMRC by the manager of the overseas scheme.

DISCLOSURE OF PENSION SCHEME INFORMATION

Pensions legislation including the Pension Schemes Act 1993 and the Pensions Act 1995 requires the trustees of occupational pension schemes to disclose actuarial and accounting information, as well as individual benefit details for each member. These rules override any provisions in schemes' trust documents if the two are in conflict.

Details to be disclosed differ depending on whether the benefits are of a defined benefit or defined contribution nature. One difference is that disclosures relating to defined contributions must, for members who have not yet retired, be provided automatically at least once a year, whereas disclosures relating to defined benefits need only be provided on request. Disclosure requirements also may differ for schemes with fewer than 100 members.

Information must also be disclosed to pension credit members and further disclosure requirements also arise at the time when pension sharing arrangements are being made. These are too extensive to describe in detail here, but an outline is included in *Section 19*.

The Government is expected to consult in late 2011 on changes to the existing disclosure regulations. These would consolidate the main disclosure requirements into one statutory instrument, streamlining the provisions to achieve consistency, where possible, across different types of schemes. It is also intended to extend the provisions introduced in December 2010 which allow schemes to communicate with members electronically for some disclosure requirements. The aim is to allow electronic communication for all communications between schemes and members.

The following summary sets out the main disclosure requirements for occupational schemes. Disclosure requirements for personal pension and stakeholder schemes are discussed in *Section 8*. There are also reporting requirements around the lifetime allowance and annual allowance and these are covered in *Section 13*.

SUMMARY OF DISCLOSURE REQUIREMENTS

INFORMATION	TO BE DISCLOSED TO	IN WHAT CIRCUMSTANCES	TIME LIMITS/OTHER DETAILS
Trust Deed and Rules or other documents constituting the scheme, including names and addresses of participating employers.	**Members***, **Prospective Members,** their **Spouses** and **Civil Partners.** **Beneficiaries**. Recognised independent **Trade Unions**.	**For inspection on request**, free of charge. **A copy to keep on request**; any charge must be limited to the cost incurred in copying, posting and packaging.	Within two months of the request being made. Any documentation not relevant to the rights of the particular person does not need to be disclosed.

Note: * Throughout this summary 'members' includes pension credit members, as well as pensioners and deferred pensioners.

Information	To be Disclosed to	In What Circumstances	Time Limits/Other Details
Scheme Details including an address for enquiries.	**Members*, Prospective Members,** their **Spouses** and **Civil Partners.** **Beneficiaries.** Recognised independent **Trade Unions.**	**On request**, no more than **once a year.** In addition, **new members** must receive the information **automatically within two months of joining the scheme** (expected to reduce to one month from 1 October 2012).	Within two months of the request being made. Any material change in the scheme details, and any change in the address for enquiries, must be notified to all members and beneficiaries, within three months.
Estimate of Cash Equivalent	Active members of any scheme, and deferred members of schemes providing money purchase benefits.	**On request,** no more than **once a year.**	Within three months of the request.
Statement of Entitlement to Guaranteed Cash Equivalent	Deferred and pension credit members of schemes providing final salary benefits.	**On request,** no more than **once a year.**	To be calculated within three months of the request and passed to the member within ten working days of calculation.
Statement of Prospective Transfer Credits	**Members** and **Prospective Members.**	**On request**, no more than **once a year.**	Within two months of the request.
Benefit Statements	**Members.** **Beneficiaries.**	**Automatically** when benefit is due, or changes other than as described in a previous statement. **To non-pensioner members of final salary schemes, on request,** no more than **once a year,** within two months of request. **To non-pensioner members of schemes with a money purchase element, automatically** within 12 months of the end of each scheme year in respect of money purchase benefits including Statutory Money Purchase Illustrations (SMPIs) *(see page 120).*	Where benefits become due or are changed other than as described in a previous statement within one month, or two months in cases of early retirement. Leavers must be told their rights and options within two months of the trustees being notified that the member has left service. Options under money purchase benefits are to be notified to members at least six months before normal pension age (normal benefit age for pension credit members) or earlier agreed date of retirement. Beneficiaries over age 18 must be notified of rights and options within two months of trustees being notified of death.

Information	To be Disclosed to	In What Circumstances	Time Limits/Other Details
Benefit Statements (continued)			Personal representatives of members who have died may request information, which must be provided within two months.
Summary Funding Statement	Members. Beneficiaries.	**Automatically**, annually, except where a member is entitled to only money purchase benefits. Must be issued within a **reasonable period** (generally three months) after the deadline for completion of actuarial valuation or actuarial report.	To include information on the funding and solvency positions of the scheme.
Trustees' Annual Report including: · audited accounts · latest certification of schedule of contributions · investment report.	Members, Prospective Members, their Spouses and Civil Partners. Beneficiaries. Recognised independent Trade Unions.	Reports covering the previous five years must be available: · **for inspection**, free of charge · a copy of the most recent report on request, **to keep**, free of charge · copies of earlier reports on request, **to keep**, for which any charge must be limited to the cost of copying, posting and packaging.	Within two months of the request being made. The report must be available within seven months of the end of the scheme year. The report should contain a statement that other information is available and from where it may be obtained.
Actuarial Valuation or **Report, Schedule of Contributions** or **Payment Schedule, Recovery Plan,†** **Statements of Funding Principles†** and of **Investment Principles,** and outline **Winding-Up Procedure** (if applicable)	Members, Prospective Members, their Spouses and Civil Partners. Beneficiaries. Recognised independent Trade Unions.	**For inspection**, free of charge. **A copy to keep, on request**, for which any charge must be limited to the cost of copying, posting and packaging.	Within two months of the request being made.

Note: † See Section 20.

SCHEME DETAILS

Scheme details must include:

- eligibility and conditions for membership
- the period of notice which a member must give to leave pensionable service
- whether re-entry to pensionable service is permitted and, if so, upon what conditions
- how employers' and members' normal contributions are calculated
- any arrangements made for members to pay Additional Voluntary Contributions (AVCs)
- taxation status
- contracted-out status, and whether the scheme is a contracted-out salary-related scheme (COSRS), a contracted-out money purchase scheme (COMPS), or a contracted-out mixed benefit scheme (COMBS)
- for a COMBS, any potential changes in a member's accrual of benefits as a result of the scheme being a COMBS
- for a COMPS or COMBS that is not insured, a statement describing how the value of protected rights is increased, if this is not in line with actual investment returns, and the reason why this method is used
- normal pension age
- the benefits payable, and how they are calculated, including the definition of pensionable earnings, the accrual rate and whether any are payable only on discretion
- the conditions on which benefits, including survivors' benefits, and any pension increases in excess of statutory requirements, are payable and whether any are payable only on discretion
- whether the trustees accept transfers in to the scheme
- a summary of the method of calculating transfer values
- where cash equivalents do not take into account discretionary additional benefits, a statement to this effect
- the arrangements for providing refunds, preserved benefits, and estimated or guaranteed cash equivalents for early leavers
- a statement that the scheme annual report is available on request, except for public service pension schemes
- the procedure for internal resolution of disputes and the address and job title of the contact
- the functions and addresses of the Pensions Ombudsman, The Pensions Advisory Service and the Pensions Regulator, *and*
- a statement that further information is available and an address for enquiries.

BENEFIT STATEMENTS

Active and deferred members of salary-related schemes

On request, an active member must be given:

- a statement of accrued benefits, or benefits allowing for service up to normal pension age, based on current salary, *and*
- a statement of the benefits payable if the member were to die in service within one month of the date of receipt of the information.

The trustees need not comply with a request made within a year of providing the information, so if they provide benefit statements automatically once a year there is no need to respond to one-off requests.

Leaving service rights and options must be given automatically within two months of the trustees being notified that pensionable service has ceased.

On subsequent request, a deferred member must be given a statement of the date pensionable service ceased and the amount of his/her own benefits, and any survivors' benefits, payable from normal pension age or on death.

For both active and deferred members the information must include:

- the date on which pensionable service commenced and ceased
- the accrual rate or formula for calculating the member's own benefits and any survivors' benefits
- the amount of the member's pensionable earnings (at the date pensionable service ceased for a deferred member and at the current date for an active member), *and*
- details of how any deduction from benefits (e.g. offset for State pension or any pension debit) is calculated.

Pension credit members of salary-related schemes

On request, the member must be given a statement of the amount of his/her own benefits, and any survivors' benefits, payable from normal benefit age or on death. The information must include:

- the method or formula for calculating the member's own benefits and any survivors' benefits, *and*
- details of how any deduction from benefits is calculated.

All members of money purchase schemes
(or schemes with a money purchase element)

Statements must be given automatically within 12 months of the end of each scheme year and must show, in relation to money purchase benefits:

- contributions credited to the member (before deductions) during the immediately preceding scheme year
- if the scheme was contracted out during the year, the contributions in respect of the member attributable to:

    (i)   minimum payments made by the employer
    (ii) age-related payments made to the trustees by the DWP, *and*
    (iii) the date of birth used to determine any age-related payments and a contact name and address if this is incorrect

- value of protected rights (if any) at a specified date
- value of other accrued rights (if any) at a specified date
- cash equivalents of protected rights and other accrued rights at the specified dates, if they differ from the values of these rights, *and*
- statutory money purchase illustrations (SMPIs) of projected benefits are required in addition to the above information (*see below*).

In addition, a member with money purchase benefits must be provided with an explanation of the different annuities available, his/her right to an open market option and a statement that the member should consider taking advice. This information must be provided no less than six months before the member's normal retirement date, or within seven days if a retirement date is agreed which is less than six months in the future.

TRUSTEES' ANNUAL REPORT

The report must include:

- audited accounts, including auditor's statement
- latest actuarial certificate certifying the adequacy of the schedule of contributions
- names of trustees or directors of the trust company, and the rules for changing trustees; names of the professional advisers, custodians and banks acting for the trustees, indicating any changes during the year
- a copy of the statement which any auditor or actuary of the scheme has made on resignation or removal as auditor or actuary during the year
- numbers of active, deferred and pensioner members and beneficiaries at a date during the year
- except for money purchase schemes, percentage increases made during the year to pensions and deferred pensions, in excess of those required by law – the extent to which increases were discretionary is to be stated
- except for money purchase schemes which are wholly insured, if transfer values paid during the year were not calculated in accordance with the law, an explanation as to why they have differed; if any were less than the full value of the member's preserved or pension credit benefits, an explanation as to why and when full values are likely to be available; and a statement as to whether discretionary benefits are included in the calculation and, if so, how they are assessed
- name of investment manager, and the extent to which the trustees have delegated their responsibility to him

- whether the trustees have produced a statement of investment principles and, if so, that a copy is available on request, and information on investments made other than in accordance with the statement

- except for wholly insured schemes, a statement of the trustees' policy on the custody of scheme assets

- investment report including review of performance, over the year and over a period of between three and five years, and of the scheme's assets

- details and percentage of any employer-related investment and steps taken or proposed to reduce excessive employer-related investment

- address for enquiries, *and*

- an explanation, where applicable, of why the auditor's statement about scheme contributions is negative or qualified and a statement as to how the situation has been, or is likely to be, resolved.

AUTOMATIC DISCLOSURE IN SPECIAL CIRCUMSTANCES

Trustees must disclose information automatically, rather than on request, in the following circumstances.

(a) **If any contributions are not paid by the due date,** and the trustees believe that this will be of material significance to the Pensions Regulator, members (and the Regulator) must be informed within a reasonable period (generally 30 days). The amounts and the due dates are those set out in the scheme's schedule of contributions or payment schedule.

(b) **Details of any proposed transfer without the member's consent** *(see Section 27)*, including the value of the rights being transferred, must be provided at least one month before the proposed date of the transfer.

(c) **If a scheme is being wound up** *(see Section 25)*, all members and beneficiaries (except deferred pensioners and pension credit members who cannot be traced) must be given a notice within one month of the winding-up having commenced, and at least every 12 months thereafter. These notices must report on the action being taken to determine the scheme's assets and liabilities; give an indication of when final details are likely to be known; and indicate the extent to which the value of the member's accrued benefits is likely to be reduced (where the trustees have sufficient information to state this). In addition, the first notice must state that the scheme is winding up, together with the reasons; supply a name and address for further enquiries; provide a statement where relevant that an independent trustee is required; and provide a statement to active members as to whether death in service benefits will continue to be provided.

Once the assets have been applied in accordance with the legislative requirements, members and beneficiaries (except deferred pensioners and pension credit members who cannot be traced) must be told their benefit entitlements within three months, together with details as to who is responsible for paying the benefits, and the extent to which any benefits were reduced because the assets were insufficient. In addition the trustees must make periodic progress reports covering specified information to the Pensions Regulator. (A scheme for which a Recovery Plan is in place which commences to wind up must also prepare and provide to the Regulator a 'Winding Up Procedure'.) If requested, copies must be passed to members within two months.

(d) **If a COMPS ceases to be contracted out** *(see Section 6)* with respect to one or more employments, affected members must be told within one month and certain further information must be provided within four months.

(e) **Where a refund of surplus is proposed** *(see Section 20)* to be made to the employer from a scheme that *is not winding up*, all members of the scheme must be sent a notice containing the following:

- a statement that the trustees have decided to make a payment to the employer
- the amount and date of the payment (which must be at least three months after the date of the notice)
- a statement that the trustees are satisfied that the payment is in 'the best interests of the members'
- a copy of the relevant valuation certificate, *and*
- a statement that the scheme is not subject to a freezing order.

For a scheme that *is winding up*, all members and beneficiaries must be given two written notices (the first running for at least two months and the second for at least three months) setting out the proposal and inviting representations.

(f) **Details of any independent trustee appointed on employer insolvency** *(see Section 25)* must be provided to all members and recognised independent trade unions within a reasonable period of the appointment being made. Details of the scale of fees chargeable to the scheme and of the actual fees charged by the independent trustee in the previous 12 months must be provided on request to members, recognised independent trade unions and prospective members within a reasonable period of the request.

(g) **In the appointment of member-nominated trustees or directors** *(see Section 11)*, active and pensioner members (or organisations that adequately represent them) have to be invited to participate in the nomination process, and the selection process must include some or all members of the scheme. Nominations and results of the selection process should be communicated appropriately to members.

(h) **Consultation by employers** *(see Section 7)* with members and prospective members of occupational pension and personal pension schemes is required before they can make certain 'listed changes' to the scheme. This is generally the employer's responsibility, but trustees are likely to have an interest in the process.

(i) **Modification of the accrued benefits provided by an occupational pension scheme** *(see Section 7)* requires notification to members. The Pension Regulator's Code of Practice 'Modification of subsisting rights' provides guidance on the trustees' duties and responsibilities under the various stages of the requirements, including the process for communicating with and, where necessary, obtaining the consent of, members.

EXEMPTIONS FROM DISCLOSURE

- Schemes with fewer than two members.
- Schemes providing only death-in-service benefits.
- Schemes neither established in the UK nor with a trustee resident in the UK.
- Certain public service pension schemes are not required to obtain audited accounts or an actuarial valuation, or to publish an annual report.

ELECTRONIC PROVISION OF INFORMATION

New disclosure regulations came into force on 1 December 2010 which amended the requirement to give access to scheme documentation and other information on request to allow schemes to discharge their obligations by placing the information on a website.

Subject to certain safeguards, schemes may provide information by email if they are satisfied that recipients are able to access and store or print the information. Trustees' obligations will not be met by means of email or website if the member requests otherwise in writing. If a scheme wishes to convert from paper to electronic communication, the member must be given written notification and the opportunity to opt for continued paper communication.

STATUTORY MONEY PURCHASE ILLUSTRATIONS

The legislation requires schemes under which any money purchase benefits are provided to supply members with annual illustrations of such benefits on a prescribed statutory basis, referred to as Statutory Money Purchase Illustrations (SMPIs). This legal requirement applies to any arrangement which is already required to issue annual benefit statements and covers occupational pension schemes (even those which are primarily on a defined benefit basis), free-standing and other AVCs, personal pensions, stakeholder schemes, and benefits bought out in the name of scheme trustees rather than members.

Retirement annuities and non-registered arrangements are excluded, as are members within two years of retirement and with small benefits (generally less than £5,000).

The overall aim is to provide illustrations of the amount of pension at retirement (in today's terms) on a broadly consistent basis for the different types of money purchase arrangement.

The illustrations must be prepared in accordance with the methodology and assumptions specified in detail in Technical Memorandum (TM1). Version 1.4 of TM1 has been effective since 8 February 2011. The Board for Actuarial Standards (BAS) has consulted on wide-ranging revisions to TM1 which will take effect for illustrations issued on or after 6 April 2012. The revised TM1 is due to be finalised by the end of 2011.

In particular, it must be assumed that the pension will be index-linked in payment and will generally include a 50% contingent spouse's pension (although the provider need not include this if the member is single or, in other cases, agrees to its exclusion). Any regular contributions are assumed to continue, and the member's existing contracting-out status can be assumed to continue until no later than 6 April 2012 when defined contribution contracting-out ceases.

For the period before retirement, a long-term nominal return of up to 7% p.a. is provided for under Version 1.4 of TM1. From 6 April 2012, it is proposed that the accumulation rate must be justifiable, taking account of the different asset classes in which the members' assets are invested and consistent with an assumed inflation rate of 2.5% p.a. (which is not changing). Allowance for expenses must be in accordance with FSA rules where applicable, or otherwise based on actual experience. The assumed cost of purchasing annuities at retirement will generally be based on the yield on index-linked gilts on 15 February in the previous tax year, with a 4% allowance for expenses. No allowance is to be made for mortality before retirement. After retirement, Version 1.4 requires that it must be assumed to be in line with the PMA92 (males) and PFA92 (females) tables with medium cohort mortality improvement rates (published by the Actuarial Profession) applicable to the member's year of birth. From 6 April 2012, it is proposed that unisex factors are adopted with an updated allowance for future improvements in life expectancy, with the precise details to be confirmed by the end of 2011.

Specified information about the nature of the illustration and an overview of the assumptions must be included, together with other details listed in TM1. The value of the member's current fund may (but need not) also be included, as well as further illustrations on alternative bases, but it must be made clear which of the illustrations is on the statutory basis. Since December 2010 schemes have had flexibility in the way that SMPI statements can be delivered, so that some of the information may now be provided electronically. It is hoped that this will lead to shorter, clearer and more concise statements in order to improve understanding.

The only pension resource of its kind

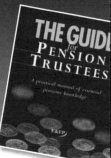

The *Guide for Pension Trustees* has been written specifically with trustees and pensions professionals in mind, in a **straightforward**, **jargon-free** style.

Recommend
Reading by

It provides you with a powerful combination of reliable, **practical** and **up-to-date** pension information and expertise all in one resource.

Subscribe today and you will receive:

- **A comprehensive** 400+page loose-leaf guide packed with pensions information.

- **Regular Updates – four supplements a year** – keeping you abreast of new developments, legislation and regulatory changes.

- **Fully searchable online resource at www.guideforpensiontrustees.com** – constantly updated with n trends & developments plus key pensions data and model documents

Essential reading for trustees and pension profession:

To subscribe visit
www.guideforpensiontrustees.com

EQUAL TREATMENT

Over several years, the UK Government has incorporated into UK statute a number of provisions mostly designed to implement the various equal treatment requirements imposed by European law. Under EU law, there are a number of equal treatment principles that are of particular relevance to UK pensions.

The first, which stems from Article 157 (originally Article 119) of the Treaty on the Functioning of the European Union ('the Treaty of Rome', as amended), requires men and women performing work of equal value to receive equal pay. Case law at the European Court of Justice (ECJ) has shown that occupational pensions (though not social security schemes) fall within the definition of pay and that the principle of equal treatment must be applied in relation to both access to, *and* benefits provided by, occupational pension schemes.

Other equal treatment principles that followed are that part-time and fixed-term workers should be treated equally to comparable full-time workers and permanent employees respectively.

Regulations on discrimination on grounds of disability, religion or belief and sexual orientation were enacted in 2003. These prevented trustees from discriminating against or harassing members and prospective members, and allowed trustees to discriminate indirectly only if they are able to justify their actions objectively. The catalyst for much of this legislation was an EU Directive on Equal Treatment, adopted in November 2000.

Legislation tackling age discrimination came into effect from 1 October 2006, with the exception of the pensions provisions, which came into force on 1 December 2006.

The Equality Act 2010 received Royal Assent on 8 April 2010, and its main provisions came into force on 1 October 2010. It has two main purposes:

- to consolidate and harmonise previous legislation on equal treatment, *and*
- to strengthen the law to support progress on equality.

The Equality Act introduced a single 'non-discrimination' rule for occupational pension schemes in respect of various 'protected characteristics', which generally prohibits indirect discrimination unless it can be justified as a proportionate means of achieving a legitimate aim. Direct discrimination in respect of age and disability can also be justified on these grounds, but indirect discrimination on the grounds of pregnancy or maternity cannot be so justified. A new deemed sex equality rule replicated and replaced previous provisions, and a new maternity equality rule was also introduced.

Further details of the principles of equal treatment, and how UK law seeks to implement them, are given below.

GENERAL PRINCIPLES OF EQUAL TREATMENT BY SEX

Equal benefits

Occupational pension schemes must provide equal benefits for men and women. In this respect, equality is only required for benefits in respect of service on or after 17 May 1990, except for claims initiated earlier.

Equal access

Men and women must have equal rights to join their employer's scheme. The exclusion of part-timers may thus constitute 'indirect' sex discrimination if the exclusion affects a much greater number of one sex than the other, *unless* the employer shows that it may be explained by objectively justified factors unrelated to sex. The right to join a scheme may be claimed in respect of service back to 8 April 1976, although time limits for bringing actions under national laws may apply *(see below)*.

Role of trustees, employers and the courts

Trustees must observe the principle of equal treatment in performing their duties. Both trustees and employers are bound to use all the means available under national laws in order to eliminate discrimination. National courts must apply the principle of Article 157 in the context of domestic laws, taking due account of the respective liabilities of employers and trustees. Article 157 may be relied on in claims against trustees as well as against employers.

APPLICATION OF PRINCIPLES OF EQUAL TREATMENT BY SEX TO OCCUPATIONAL AND STATE PENSIONS

Member contributions

The equal treatment principle of Article 157 applies to the whole benefit paid by an occupational pension scheme, and no distinction need be made between the parts derived from the employer's and from the employee's contractual contributions. However, benefits derived from members' additional voluntary contributions are not pay and so do not fall within the scope of Article 157.

Pension age and benefit accrual

Normal pension ages for men and women must not be discriminatory for benefits accrued since 17 May 1990. In respect of service from 17 May 1990 up to the date benefits are equalised (the equalisation date), the provisions applying to the less-favoured sex must be levelled up to those of the more-favoured sex, regardless of any difficulties this may cause the occupational scheme or the employer. For periods of service after the equalisation date, Article 157 does not preclude equal treatment being achieved by levelling benefits down, e.g. by raising the lower pension age. If members have a right to retire early, this right must not be discriminatory for benefits accrued since 17 May 1990.

Benefit accrual for service since 17 May 1990 must be equalised not only for scheme members but also for their dependants. For benefits not linked to length of service, e.g. lump sum benefits on death in service, equal benefits must be provided for men and women when the event triggering payment of the benefit occurs on or after 17 May 1990. Where the funds held by the trustees are insufficient, any decision on how equalisation of benefits should be achieved must be resolved on the basis of national law.

Under the provisions of the Equality Act 2010, all occupational pension schemes are deemed to have a 'sex equality rule' covering both admission of members and benefits. The rule effectively levels up any unequal terms relating to service on or after 17 May 1990.

Bridging pensions and State pension offsets

Under the Equality Act 2010 and associated regulations, unequal bridging pensions (and State pension offsets) that allow for the difference between men's and women's State pension ages are permitted. The extra pension payable to a man may not exceed the total Category A State retirement pension (i.e. basic plus additional component) payable to a woman with the earnings history of the individual in question in respect of their period of pensionable service under the scheme. Furthermore, it may be paid only between the corresponding female and male State pension ages.

On 19 April 2002, the High Court ruled in the *Shillcock* case that, for the purposes of calculating contributions and benefits, the operation of a Lower Earnings Limit (LEL) deduction from pensionable pay without pro-rating for part-timers did not constitute indirect sex discrimination and was, in any case, a reasonable method of implementing the legitimate objective of integration with state benefits and so was objectively justified.

Transfers

Schemes may, if they wish, calculate transfers out using actuarial factors which vary according to sex. The benefits to which the factors are applied are required to be equalised for service since 17 May 1990. Where a transfer value has in fact been based on unequal benefits for a period of service after 16 May 1990, the transfer value might be lower than it would have been if it had been based on equalised benefits. In such circumstances the *receiving* scheme must increase the benefits provided to those which could have been bought by the higher transfer value that should have been paid.

Actuarial factors and insurance premiums

Under current UK legislation, actuarial factors that vary according to sex may be used for commutation, early and late retirement, and surrender of pension for a dependant. Emerging pension benefits from money purchase arrangements may also be calculated using sex-dependent factors.

However, this legislation may need to be amended following the ECJ's 2011 ruling in the *Test-Achats* case *(see Section 31)* that the use of gender-based insurance premiums will be unlawful from 21 December 2012. This will affect annuities and insured benefits and other than that does not directly impact on occupational scheme benefits. However, at the time of writing, any wider indirect impact on actuarial factors used by occupational pension schemes is uncertain.

Contracting-out problems

Contracted-out schemes have particular difficulties in equalising the benefits they provide because GMPs accrued at different rates and are required to come into payment at different ages for men and women. This issue was partly addressed by regulations, originally under the Pensions Act 1995, which give contracted-out schemes some scope to provide unequal pension increases that reflect sex-related differences in the ways in which the increase in members' State pensions are calculated. While this exemption might appear to ease the position for schemes with unequal post-16 May 1990 GMPs *when pensions are in payment*, it does not address the problems associated with differences under the anti-franking legislation (primarily concerning increases in deferment). In January 2000, when the Pensions Ombudsman ruled that GMPs should be equalised for accruals since 17 May 1990, it looked as though schemes would soon be forced to address this issue. However, in February 2001, the High Court set aside the Ombudsman's ruling, principally because the judge considered the Ombudsman to have acted outside his jurisdiction. In practice, therefore, the majority of schemes are still waiting for clarification of what is required before implementing changes. In 2011, the Government indicated that it would provide draft guidance and regulations in due course.

On 6 April 2009, regulations under the Pensions Act 2007 came into effect allowing trustees to convert GMPs into 'normal' scheme benefits. However, the lack of clarity on what must be done in order to comply with equal treatment requirements prior to conversion is likely to act as a deterrent to trustees considering using this facility.

The Pension Protection Fund (PPF) has consulted on equalising compensation to allow for differences in GMPs, where schemes enter the PPF or the Financial Assistance Scheme. It confirmed in early 2011 that its preferred option is to equalise total benefits earned on or after 17 May 1990 at the higher of the level for men and women at any point in time, but at the time of writing final detail is still awaited *(see Section 22)*.

Time limits for bringing claims and backdating membership

Under equality provisions of the Pensions Act 1995, in force until August 2005, claims by members and prospective members of occupational pension schemes for unlawful unequal treatment had to be brought to industrial tribunals under the provisions of the Equal Pay Act 1970 within six months of leaving service, and backdated membership was generally limited to two years. However, the validity of these restrictions under European law (which overrides UK law) was challenged in the ECJ in the indirect sex discrimination part-timer case of *Preston v Wolverhampton*. After further legal proceedings, it was ruled that the UK's time limit of six months for bringing claims was consistent with EU law, but the two-year limit on backdating was not. Individuals may therefore claim in respect of service back to 8 April 1976.

Maternity, adoption and paternity leave

The Employment Rights Act 1996 requires *all* benefits in kind, including pension accrual, to be maintained during *statutory* ordinary maternity leave (whether paid or unpaid). The Employment Act 2002 provisions, which generally took effect from April 2003, gave similar rights to adoptive parents with the introduction of statutory adoption leave, and also introduced new requirements for continued pension accrual during statutory paternity leave and statutory parental leave. The maternity leave requirements regarding pension rights are now contained in the Equality Act 2010.

The above legislation and provisions in the Social Security Act 1989 (SSA 89) require all *paid* maternity, adoption and paternity absence to be treated as a period of normal service as far as an employer-related benefit scheme is concerned. When assessing benefits (or employer contributions to a defined contribution occupational scheme) it should be assumed that the normal pay for the job was received. However, the member is required to pay contributions based only on the remuneration actually received. For paid (but non-statutory) 'family leave' (other than maternity, adoption or paternity leave), SSA 89 only requires benefits to be based on actual (not on normal) remuneration.

Section 31 summarises the Government's plans to encourage shared parental leave. These would replace the provisions introduced in April 2011 for additional statutory paternity leave, which currently allow employed fathers to 'trade' unused statutory leave and pay with the child's mother or adopter.

State pension ages

From November 2018, State pension age is planned to be equalised at 65 for men and women and then will be increased to age 66 from October 2020. The change is being phased in for women from April 2010 to November 2018, initially by increases of one month for every two months elapsed.

EQUAL TREATMENT FOR PART-TIMERS

In 1997, the EU adopted a part-time work directive requiring member states to outlaw all discrimination against part-time workers, and not just in cases of indirect sex discrimination covered under the general 'equal pay' provisions. UK regulations implementing the directive came into force on 1 July 2000, and applied with immediate (although not retrospective) effect. Under these regulations, it is no longer possible to treat a part-timer less favourably than a 'comparable' full-timer, unless the less favourable treatment is justified on objective grounds. The regulations provide that, in determining whether or not treatment is unfavourable, a 'pro-rata' principle applies, 'unless it is inappropriate'. The extent to which it is legal to provide inferior (or no) benefits to part-timers (on grounds such as non-comparability with full-timers, 'objective justification' or inappropriateness of a pro rata principle) is only likely to become clear as case law is built up. Complaints by individuals under this legislation must generally be taken to an employment tribunal within three months of the last day on which they consider they were unfavourably treated.

EQUAL TREATMENT FOR FIXED-TERM WORKERS

UK regulations implementing the EU fixed-term worker directive came into force on 1 October 2002. Under these regulations, direct discrimination against fixed-term workers in relation to terms and conditions including pensions is prohibited, unless it is justified on objective grounds. The regulations specifically provide that less favourable treatment in relation to some contractual terms is objectively justified where the fixed-term employee's overall employment package is no less favourable than that of a comparable permanent employee. Complaints by individuals under this legislation must generally be taken to an employment tribunal within three months of the last day on which they consider they were unfavourably treated. The EU Agency Workers Directive was finalised in November 2008. UK regulations implement this directive with effect from 1 October 2011. These do not cover participation in occupational pension schemes but workers will be eligible for the auto-enrolment provisions that will apply from 2012 *(see Section 9)*.

EQUAL TREATMENT AND SEXUAL ORIENTATION

From 1 December 2003, pension schemes may not directly discriminate against members on grounds of their sexual orientation. Indirect discrimination is also unlawful, unless the practice is a 'proportionate means of achieving a legitimate aim'. However, preventing or restricting access to a benefit by reference to marital status remained lawful (*but see below*), as did discriminatory benefits in respect of service before 1 December 2003.

The Civil Partnership Act took effect from 5 December 2005. It introduced a facility for same-sex partners to register civil partnerships and thereby receive increased legal recognition. It extended the divorce pension sharing and earmarking regulations and social security legislation in line with the principle that civil partners should be treated in the same way as married people. Under the Act, contracted-out schemes have to provide the same contracted-out benefits to civil partners as to spouses for all service after 5 April 1988. In addition, subsequent legislation requires all schemes to treat civil partners in the same way as spouses for service on or after 5 December 2005.

However, a recent ECJ judgment in a German case has cast doubt on whether equality of civil partners' benefits can legitimately be restricted to service from 5 December 2005. In the *Tadao Maruko* case, the ECJ held that a registered same-sex partner should be provided with the same dependant's pension as a surviving spouse and that the pension should not be limited to pension accrual from a specific date. The UK Government has yet to comment on the implications of this case for UK legislation.

The Gender Recognition Act came into force on 4 April 2005. It is designed to give formal recognition to transsexuals who successfully register in their acquired gender.

Under the Equality Act 2010 all occupational pension schemes are deemed to have a new non-discrimination rule. This prevents trustees from discriminating against, harassing or victimising members and prospective members, on grounds of sexual orientation or gender reassignment.

EQUAL TREATMENT AND RACE, RELIGION OR BELIEF

In respect of rights that accrue from 2 December 2003, pension schemes may not directly discriminate against members on grounds of their religion or belief, and may indirectly discriminate only where the offending practice is a 'proportionate means of achieving a legitimate aim'. The anti-discrimination requirements cover admission to schemes as well as treatment once admitted. Particularly in the realm of indirect discrimination, potential issues could possibly arise for pension schemes, for example where all investment funds offered under a DC arrangement are unacceptable to members of a particular religion.

Under the Equality Act 2010 all occupational pension schemes are deemed to have a new non-discrimination rule that applies to discrimination in respect of race, religion or belief.

EQUAL TREATMENT AND DISABILITY

The Disability Discrimination Act 1995 (Pensions) Regulations 2003 took effect from 1 October 2004. From this date, any direct discrimination in relation to occupational pension schemes is unlawful, and indirect discrimination (or 'disability-related discrimination', as it is referred to in the statutory Code of Practice issued under the legislation) is only allowed if it is 'justified' by a reason that is 'both material to the circumstances of the particular case and substantial'. From 1 October 2004, trustees also became subject to the general requirement under the Act to make 'reasonable adjustments'. Although the legislation does not in general affect benefits earned before October 2004, it does extend to communications with members in relation to such rights.

Under the Equality Act 2010 all occupational pension schemes are deemed to have a non-discrimination rule that applies to discrimination in respect of disability for service from 1 October 2010. The pre-2010 justification for discrimination is replaced with the general 'proportionate means of achieving a legitimate aim' common provision for most protected characteristics. The pre-2010 duty to make adjustments is retained.

EQUAL TREATMENT AND AGE

The Employment Equality (Age) Regulations 2006 took effect from 1 October 2006. The Regulations relating to pensions were delayed and took effect from 1 December 2006. They implemented measures against age discrimination designed to satisfy the requirements of the EU Equal Treatment directive.

These Regulations were then replaced from 1 October 2010 by identical new regulations under the Equality Act 2010.

Both direct and indirect discrimination by employers and by trustees of pension schemes are prohibited, unless such a practice can be objectively justified as a 'proportionate means of achieving a legitimate aim'. There are a number of occupational pension scheme practices that are specifically exempted from being age-discriminatory. These include:

- the use of a minimum or maximum age for admission to a scheme
- the use of age-based actuarial factors in benefit calculations
- the use of a maximum period of service for benefit calculations
- limiting the payment of benefits to a minimum age
- the application of age restrictions which would be required to ensure the scheme is eligible for taxation concessions under the Finance Act 2004
- the provision of age-related employer contributions to money purchase schemes, where the aim is to provide benefits that do not vary by age of member (or to provide 'more nearly equal' benefits) in respect of each year of pensionable service, *and*
- the payment of equal contributions to money purchase schemes, irrespective of age, even though this will provide different levels of benefit to members of different ages.

Many common occupational pension scheme practices are, however, not exempt under the legislation. For example, benefit accrual may not generally cease at a fixed retirement age. In addition, there is a great deal of uncertainty concerning how much of the legislation will be interpreted, and clarification is expected to emerge only slowly as actual cases are considered by tribunals and courts.

The Equality Act 2010 retained a default retirement age of 65, but this was abolished with effect from 1 October 2011. Employers wishing to dismiss or retire an older employer will need to go through a 'fair procedure'. A compulsory retirement age will be permitted only if it can be objectively justified as a proportionate means of achieving a legitimate aim. There is an exemption, however, which allows group risk insured benefits provided by employers to cease at age 65.

Complaints by individuals under this legislation must generally be taken to an employment tribunal within three months of the last day on which they consider they were unfavourably treated.

PENSIONS AND DIVORCE

Courts are required to take benefits under pension schemes into account when considering financial provision on divorce. In many cases, this may be achieved by making a divorce settlement which distributes other marital assets in such a way as to keep pension rights intact. However, there are also two alternative approaches available for allowing one party to the divorce to benefit directly from the benefit entitlements under a pension scheme of the other party. The first alternative, earmarking, was introduced for petitions for divorce filed on or after 1 July 1996 (or 19 August 1996 in Scotland), and orders a specified portion of a scheme member's lump sum (all jurisdictions) and/or pension (England, Wales and Northern Ireland only) to be paid, instead, to his or her ex-spouse. The second alternative, pension sharing, is available where divorce proceedings began on or after 1 December 2000, and results in a 'clean break' between the divorcing parties.

Since December 2005, the provisions for pension sharing and earmarking have been extended so that they also apply when civil partnerships are dissolved. In the remainder of this Section, 'divorce' should be read to include 'dissolution of civil partnership', 'ex-spouse' to include 'ex-civil partner' etc., as the context requires.

Since 6 April 2011, legislation has allowed the sharing and earmarking of Pension Protection Fund (PPF) compensation on divorce and on dissolution of a civil partnership.

Further details of the pension sharing regime are given below.

PENSION SHARING

Provision of information

If a benefit valuation is to be included, schemes have to supply basic information within three months of the request; or within six weeks, where the member has notified them that proceedings for financial provision on divorce have commenced; or within such shorter period as may be specified in a court order. If no benefit valuation is to be included the basic information must be provided within one month. Further information must be provided within 21 days of being notified that a pension sharing order may be made, unless the prescribed information has already been supplied. Additional information requirements arise subsequently it is decided that a pension sharing order will be made.

What rights may be shared?

All rights under occupational and personal pensions and retirement annuity policies (including pensions in payment and annuities or insurance policies purchased to give effect to any such rights) may be shared. However, the regulations exclude survivors' pensions payable as a result of a previous marriage and Equivalent Pension Benefits (EPBs) where these are the only benefit under a scheme. SERPS/S2P rights are also included, but the State Graduated Scheme and the Basic State Pension are not. Since 6 April 2011, compensation payments under the PPF *(see Section 22)* may be shared on divorce.

What triggers pension sharing?

Any decision on sharing is triggered by a court order between the parties. The order is stayed until any appeals process has been completed. The order is expressed in terms of a transfer from one party to the other of a percentage of rights accrued prior to the date the order takes effect. In Scotland, these rights are restricted to those that accrued during the marriage and the transfer can alternatively be expressed as a fixed amount.

Rights to be provided to ex-spouse

The person receiving a share of his or her ex-spouse's rights usually has to be offered a transfer value in respect of those rights. Rights under unfunded schemes, including SERPS/S2P, are excluded from this requirement.

Schemes that are obliged to offer an external transfer to another suitable pension arrangement may, but do not have to, offer the ex-spouse the alternative option of a pension credit benefit within the scheme calculated on the scheme's normal transfer-in basis. Ex-spouse members of pension schemes are, essentially, treated like deferred pensioners. If the ex-spouse is also an employee member of the scheme that provides the pension credit benefit, the scheme can insist that, on taking a subsequent cash equivalent, both sets of rights are transferred.

Basis of calculation for sharing

Calculations for pension sharing are based on the scheme's current established cash equivalent basis, extended to cover cases (like pensions in payment) where a transfer value would not normally arise. There is a facility for transfer values for ex-spouses (along with other transfer values) to be reduced if the scheme is underfunded. However, the legislation provides that such a reduction is to be applied only if the ex-spouse has been offered (but has declined) the alternative of a pension credit benefit within the scheme based on the unreduced transfer value.

Pension credit benefits

Pension credit benefits, if offered under the scheme, should be determined on the incoming transfer value basis, with appropriate adjustments where added-years pensions are normally awarded and the ex-spouse is not himself or herself an active member of the scheme. Benefits are generally payable from normal benefit age but can be paid early where the member has attained normal minimum pension age or qualifies for an ill-health pension. Pension credit benefits can also be partially commuted for a pension commencement lump sum, or fully commuted in certain circumstances, in accordance with the Finance Act 2004 requirements. Except for pension credit benefits in money purchase form where the benefit had not come into payment before 6 April 2005, the regulations require LPI indexation of benefits derived from post-97 rights (other than those derived from AVCs). For this purpose, LPI is capped at

5% if the pension credit benefit was awarded before 6 April 2005, or 2.5% if awarded after 5 April 2005. Schemes are not prevented from indexing the whole of the pension credit benefit, in order to simplify administration.

Pension debits

In defined benefit schemes, the member's benefit becomes subject to a debit, designed to be of equal value to the amount transferred to the ex-spouse. For non-pensioners, this is, essentially, a negative deferred pension. Each part of the member's vested benefit entitlement immediately prior to the date the pension sharing order takes effect is reduced in the same proportion (including contracted-out benefits). Defined contribution scheme debits are the stipulated proportion of the fund value or, if applicable, of the benefit already in payment.

Contracted-out rights

Until 6 April 2009, restrictions applied to pension credit benefits derived from contracted-out rights. These were known as 'safeguarded rights'. The restrictions were removed, from that date, so these rights may now be treated in the same manner as other pension credit benefits.

Timing of implementation

Schemes generally have four months, after the date the relevant court order takes effect or (if later) receipt of all relevant divorce documentation and personal information about the divorcing parties, to implement the pension share in accordance with the option chosen by the ex-spouse or (if no valid instructions are given) in accordance with the scheme's chosen default procedure. The Pensions Regulator may (on application) extend the implementation period, in circumstances broadly similar to those which apply for the late payment of 'normal' cash equivalents.

Expense charges

Schemes are allowed to charge the divorcing parties for costs reasonably incurred in providing information for and implementing the pension share, and are usually able to insist on receiving these before they have to provide the information or implement the share. However, most charges are allowable only to the extent that they were disclosed in a Schedule of Charges at the outset, and no charge may be made for information that would be available for free under the Disclosure requirements. The trustees can require that the charges are paid in cash, with deduction from the benefits being an alternative. Only costs specifically relating to an individual divorce case can be charged, and therefore initial costs involved in setting up administrative procedures to deal with pension sharing may not be passed on.

Tax treatment

Under the tax regime introduced from 6 April 2006 *(see Section 13)*, the benefits tested against an individual's lifetime allowance are the actual benefits payable after taking account of a pension debit or credit. In most circumstances, an individual whose benefits have become subject to a debit will have scope within his or her lifetime allowance to rebuild lost rights. A divorcing member with primary protection, however, will see his or her lifetime allowance reduced to take account of a post-5 April 2006 pension debit. For a member with enhanced protection, rights lost under a defined benefit or cash balance arrangement as a result of a post-5 April 2006 pension debit could – in general – be rebuilt, although this would not be possible under a money purchase arrangement.

Under the new 'fixed protection' applying from 6 April 2012, there will be limited scope under defined benefit and cash balance arrangements to rebuild lost rights without losing protection. The value of members' rights is assessed every tax year and protection is lost if the increase over the year exceeds a certain limit, so any rebuilding would need to occur in the tax year in which the pension debit took effect.

An ex-spouse who became entitled before 6 April 2006 to a pension credit had until 5 April 2009 to register for an increased lifetime allowance, so that he or she would not lose scope to build up further tax-privileged pension rights. Similarly, individuals with primary protection would have been able to include the pension credit in the amount protected at A Day.

A pension credit received after 5 April 2006 gives rise to an increase in the personal lifetime allowance only if it arises from pension that had come into payment between 6 April 2006 and the date of the share, and the increase is registered within the required timescale. An ex-spouse with enhanced protection would lose this protection if a post-5 April 2006 pension credit paid to his or her defined benefit or cash balance arrangement caused the permitted limits to be breached. However, enhanced protection is not lost if the pension credit is paid to a money purchase arrangement which is not a cash balance arrangement, provided that this arrangement already existed at 5 April 2006.

Fixed protection will not be lost if a pension credit is paid to a money purchase arrangement which is not a cash balance arrangement, provided that the arrangement existed at 5 April 2012. If it is paid into an existing defined benefit or cash balance arrangement, fixed protection will be lost if the limit on the increase in benefits for the tax year is exceeded.

PENSION SCHEME FUNDING

ACTUARIAL VALUATIONS

Actuarial valuations are central to the process of funding defined benefit (DB) schemes. They are also used for other purposes, including accounting for pension costs *(see Section 28)*. Many different types of valuation may be called for in different circumstances. The basic principles of two of the main types, 'ongoing' and 'discontinuance' valuations, are described briefly below.

Ongoing valuation

When a DB scheme is established, the actuary's calculations of the amount of contributions to be paid have to be based on assumptions about how the scheme will evolve. However, events will invariably unfold differently from the original assumptions, and it is necessary to examine the scheme periodically to value the assets and liabilities and to revise the contribution rate.

To value the liabilities, the actuary receives individual details of the scheme's active, retired and deferred members. Data relating to changes in membership since the previous valuation may also be supplied to enable a reconciliation of the membership numbers to be carried out and to test actual experience against the assumptions of the last valuation.

Various assumptions need to be made; these are financial (e.g. the discount rate and rates of salary and pension increases) and demographic (e.g. rates of mortality, ill-health, early retirement and leaving service). The starting point for the financial assumptions is usually the yields on fixed-interest and index-linked securities available in the market at the valuation date.

Various different valuation methods are used according to the individual needs of the scheme and the employer, and to meet statutory requirements. The differences only relate to the valuation of 'active members' – those currently accruing benefits in the scheme. The method of valuing retired and deferred members is the same in all cases.

The most common method is the *Projected Unit Method*, under which the cost of providing the benefits earned in the year (or other specified period) following the valuation date allows for expected salary increases to retirement, leaving service or death, as appropriate. Valuation of past service liabilities allows for expected salary increases in the same way.

An alternative is the *Current Unit Method* in which members are assumed to leave service at the end of a specified period. This method allows for expected salary increases up to the specified date, for the cost of providing benefits earned over this period, then subsequent increases are assumed to follow the scheme rules or overriding legislation applicable to members with deferred benefits. Valuation of past service liabilities assumes all active members leave service at the valuation date.

The actuary also requires details of the assets held by the scheme. Assets are given at market value in the audited accounts, and this is the value that is used in actuarial valuations in conjunction with market-based yields for valuing liabilities. Some assets, such as insurance policies, may not have a market value, and the actuary will need to calculate a value that is consistent with the value applied to the corresponding liabilities.

Discontinuance or solvency valuation

The discontinuance or solvency valuation assesses whether the scheme's assets would be sufficient to cover the liabilities if the scheme were to be discontinued at the valuation date and no further contributions were received from the employer. The liability for active members is usually based on service to and salary at the valuation date. Future expenses should be allowed for.

This assessment can be made on various bases. However, the scheme funding legislation requires the actuary to disclose the extent to which the assets of the scheme would be sufficient, at the valuation date, to cover the liabilities assessed on an annuity buy-out basis, regardless of whether or not the scheme would be likely to secure benefits in this way if it were to discontinue. As an alternative to using the cost actually quoted by a suitable insurance company for buying out the benefits at the valuation date, the actuary may use an estimate of the buy-out cost based on the principles likely to be adopted by an insurance company. Liabilities must include a realistic allowance for expenses. Assets must be taken at market value.

SCHEME FUNDING UNDER THE PENSIONS ACT 2004

Under the 'statutory funding objective', a DB scheme is required to 'have sufficient and appropriate assets to cover its technical provisions', i.e. 'the amount required, on an actuarial calculation, to make provision for the scheme's liabilities'. Regulations require the technical provisions to be determined on a (normally 'ongoing') scheme-specific basis. There is no legal requirement for schemes to fund at a prescribed level. Each valuation must, however, include an estimate by the actuary of the solvency of the scheme, *as described above*. The trustees have ultimate responsibility for the funding decisions, but are required to take advice from the scheme actuary and – normally – to obtain the employer's agreement. However, where the trustees have power under the scheme's rules to set contribution rates without the employer's agreement, that requirement is replaced by one for consultation (although agreement should be obtained if possible). If the rules provide for the actuary to determine the contributions, the trustees and employer must still agree the contributions payable, but in addition the contributions must be certified as being no lower than the actuary would have set had he or she retained this responsibility.

Actuarial valuations are required with effective dates no more than three years apart, with additional written 'actuarial reports', covering developments since the last valuation, in each intervening year. There is a general exception from the scheme funding requirement for schemes in wind-up but, where this commenced on or after 30 December 2005, the exception is conditional upon the preparation of an annual solvency estimate by the scheme actuary (on a buy-out basis) and a winding-up procedure *(see Section 25)*.

Cross-border schemes *(see Section 7)* are subject to more onerous requirements, including a specified deadline for meeting the statutory funding objective and full actuarial valuations every 12 months.

Statement of funding principles

The trustees must have a written statement of funding principles (SFP) setting out their policy for securing that the statutory funding objective is met and recording decisions as to the basis for calculating the technical provisions and the period within which any shortfall is to be remedied. The SFP must be reviewed at each valuation and, if amended, finalised (along with the valuation report and schedule of contributions) within 15 months of the effective date of the valuation.

Calculation of technical provisions

The trustees must choose an 'accrued benefits' funding method, such as the projected unit method, for calculating the technical provisions.

It is also the trustees' responsibility (having received advice from the scheme actuary) to choose the assumptions to be adopted for the calculation of the scheme's technical provisions. The trustees should also agree the assumptions with the employer (unless there is only a requirement for consultation – *see above*).

The Pensions Regulator's code of practice on scheme funding states that trustees should set assumptions 'with a level of prudence consistent with the overall confidence they want to have that the resulting technical provisions will prove adequate to pay benefits as they fall due'. The level of prudence should take into account the employer's covenant *(see below)*. Other factors the trustees should consider include the sensitivity of the technical provisions to small changes in individual assumptions, and economic and investment market conditions.

Recovery plan

If an actuarial valuation shows that the statutory funding objective is not met, the trustees must prepare a 'recovery plan' setting out the steps to be taken (and over what period) to make up the shortfall. The trustees should aim for the shortfall to be eliminated as quickly as the employer can 'reasonably afford', taking into account his business plans and the likely impact of the additional contributions. The Regulator has stated that what is possible and reasonable will depend on the trustees' assessment of the employer's covenant. A copy of the recovery plan must be sent to the Regulator.

Schedule of contributions

The trustees must have in place a schedule of contributions setting out the rates and due dates of contributions payable to the scheme, which will normally have been agreed with the employer (unless there is only a requirement for consultation – *see above*). The schedule must be certified by the actuary as being sufficient to ensure that the funding objective will continue to be met for the next five years, or will be met by the end of the recovery plan period. In the latter case, a copy of the schedule must be sent to the Regulator. If contributions are not paid or are paid late, the trustees (and actuary or auditor, if they become aware of this) must inform the Regulator if they believe that the failure is likely to be 'of material significance'.

Intervention of the Regulator

In May 2006, the Regulator issued a statement detailing how it will regulate the funding of DB schemes. This sets out the circumstances and manner in which it may take action to intervene in a scheme where it forms the opinion that the scheme's funding plan is not compliant with the legal requirements, and outlines steps it will have expected the trustees to have taken to ensure compliance.

The Regulator has set triggers to alert it to schemes where its intervention in the funding arrangements may be warranted, which are:

(a) that the technical provisions are set below a point, commensurate with the strength of the employer and the scheme's maturity, somewhere between the level of liabilities under the PPF's 'section 179' valuation *(see Section 22)* and those under the FRS 17 (or IAS 19) accounting basis *(see Section 28), and/or*

(b) that the recovery plan exceeds ten years, is significantly 'back-end loaded' or uses inappropriate assumptions.

The Regulator has stressed that the triggers do not set a new funding standard; the trigger points are not targets, and scheme-specific circumstances will also be used to determine whether or not the funding plan is compliant: in particular the employer's strength and ability to pay off the shortfall, and the maturity of the scheme.

If a scheme does 'trigger' (or comes to the Regulator's attention by some other means) the Regulator may ask for 'readily available' information, such as management accounts, scheme valuation reports and trustee minutes, before deciding whether to intervene. The Regulator will also look specifically at the assumption for future improvements in life expectancy adopted by the scheme *(see Section 21)*.

The Regulator issued a number of other statements during the economic downturn in 2008/9 confirming that its approach is sufficiently flexible to deal with such adverse market conditions, particularly general falls in asset values and pressure on employer covenants. It commented that trustees should consider reviewing recovery plans where there is a significant change in such circumstances. For example, recovery plans lasting more than ten years or back-end loaded recovery plans may be appropriate in order not to jeopardise the financial position of the employer. However, the Regulator also said that recovery plans should not suffer to enable the employer to continue to pay dividends, and that the trustees should consider themselves as unsecured creditors and therefore take priority over shareholders.

The Regulator also has powers to intervene in cases where agreement cannot be reached between the trustees and employer or where the actuary is unable to provide the necessary confirmation. In addition, the Regulator has powers to intervene if it views the technical provisions as insufficiently prudent, even if the trustees and employer are in agreement. Possible courses of action include imposing a funding basis, modifying future accrual and freezing or winding up the scheme. However, the Regulator has stated that it aims to use its formal powers sparingly, preferring to achieve its desired outcome by more informal means.

Disclosure to members

Schemes are required to send members an annual 'summary funding statement' including information about the funding and discontinuance positions of the scheme and an explanation of any changes since the previous statement.

Employer covenant

The Regulator has stated that it is essential for the trustees to form an objective assessment of 'the employer's financial position and prospects as well as his willingness to continue to fund the scheme's benefits'. This assessment should be used to inform the trustees' decisions on both the technical provisions and any recovery plan needed. The Regulator has published guidance on 'monitoring employer support' which sets out standard practice which trustees are expected to follow in assessing and monitoring the employer's covenant.

Trustees will need to understand the employer's legal obligations and financial position. This includes any obligations to, or support available from, other employers within a corporate group, and any industry-wide factors. Trustees should place more weight on estimates of future performance than on evidence of past performance.

In order to carry out this assessment, the trustees will need to obtain information about the employer, either directly from the employer or by using commercially available services such as credit specialist advisers. Employers are generally required to provide information to trustees and their advisers to help them assess the covenant. Trustees should be prepared to accept confidentiality agreements where any information is price-sensitive. Trustees should consider using external advisers if they do not have the relevant expertise, once trustees with conflicts are excluded, to assess the information themselves.

Trustees should carry out a full covenant review before each valuation, and continue to monitor the employer's covenant between valuations. The strength of covenant can change rapidly and trustees need to be in a position to respond quickly. This may involve reviewing both funding and investment policies.

Alternative financing

A number of schemes have put in place funding mechanisms which do not involve cash being paid directly to the pension scheme. Although they generally cannot be taken into account in determining whether the statutory funding objective is met, or when estimating solvency, these arrangements can increase the strength of the employer covenant and the security of the pension scheme.

There are a number of different types of alternative financing that have been used to date, including:

- transferring company assets (e.g. property or brand names) to the scheme or to a Special Purpose Vehicle which the scheme owns fully or partially. The trustees might initially just have a right to an income stream from the assets, with final ownership to be determined at a later stage, possibly depending on the funding position of the scheme and other circumstances at that time. The Government is currently consulting on the tax treatment of such arrangements in order to avoid them benefiting from unintended tax relief.
- contingent assets, such as group company guarantees, security over assets or bank letters of credit, which pay out to the scheme if a specified event occurs, such as employer insolvency or increased employer borrowing. Certain forms of contingent asset can reduce a scheme's PPF levy *(see Section 22)*, *and*
- market instruments such as credit default swaps, which pay out if a company defaults on its corporate bond payments.

Trustees will need to take specialist advice on the suitability of a proposed alternative financing arrangement, including any particular legal issues such as employer-related investment. Ongoing advice will be needed to ensure that it continues to be available if needed and is properly enforceable.

The Regulator's guidance on monitoring employer support sets out considerations for trustees in relation to such arrangements.

Refunds of surplus

A power to repay surplus from the scheme can only be exercised by the trustees (subject to the agreement of the employer, if it was originally conferred on him) and only if it is in the members' interest and they have been notified. Furthermore, a payment of surplus from the scheme to the employer will only be permitted to the extent that the scheme's assets exceed the full buy-out cost of the accrued liabilities, as indicated by a valuation carried out under the Pensions Act 2004 funding regime or a special valuation carried out for this purpose.

LONGEVITY

Dramatic recent increases in life expectancy – particularly for men – have received much publicity, and the extra cost of paying pensions for longer has perhaps added to talk of a 'pension crisis'. Trustees of defined benefit schemes in particular need to understand the risks involved and how they can manage them. For example, trustees may be able to purchase longevity swaps to reduce longevity risk.

LONGEVITY RISK

Different types of mortality-related risk can be identified. One such risk, commonly referred to as 'mortality risk', is the risk of dying sooner than expected. 'Longevity risk' refers to the risk of living longer than expected. This is arguably more of an issue for pension schemes, given the recent increases in life expectancy and the uncertainty over how these will persist. We will concentrate on 'longevity risk' in the rest of this section.

Longevity risk has different elements. Past data may tell us fairly accurately the historic mortality rates for the general population. But for any given pension scheme there must be uncertainty over:

- how mortality rates for its members differ from those for the general population (because of factors like location, social class, diet and smoking)
- how mortality rates will change in the future – will past improvements continue? *and*
- whether there might be a 'jump' change in mortality rates in the future (e.g. caused by an epidemic or, in the other direction, a medical breakthrough).

Longevity risk can fall on different parties depending on what type of pension scheme we are considering. The risk under a traditional final salary scheme falls entirely on the trustees and the sponsoring employer (although members' future benefit accrual could be reduced if increases in life expectancy cause the scheme to become too expensive). The risk under a pure defined contribution scheme buying annuities for its pensioners falls partly on the scheme members (since they do not know how much pension their money will buy when they retire) and partly on the insurance company (since the annuity rates it sets may turn out to be wrong).

ASSUMPTIONS

To place a value on the liabilities of a defined benefit pension scheme, its trustees need to make assumptions about how long its pensioners will live. An insurance company selling annuities needs to do the same thing in order to set its annuity rates.

Mortality rates

Life expectancies are usually calculated based on mortality rates. 'Mortality rate' in this context means the assumed probability that an individual of a given age will die in the next year. The lower the mortality rates are, the longer the life expectancy is. The assumptions needed are in two parts: the rates assumed to apply for the next 12 months (the 'base tables') and how these rates are expected to change in future years. Different rates are calculated for men and women.

Base tables

There are two approaches to determining base mortality rates using data for individual scheme members. The first is to measure the scheme's actual mortality experience. This approach is limited to larger schemes because the experience needs to be of sufficient size to be statistically credible. The second approach is to use a postcode mortality model. Such models are created using a very large set of mortality experience data derived from a variety of schemes. These models relate postcodes to mortality rates by assuming similar mortality either for individuals of similar socio-economic type (typically assessed using a third-party postcode marketing database) or for individuals living in the same area (by using postcodes to determine geographic locations). These approaches may be combined in practice.

In most cases, published standard tables are used as a starting point. These are usually tables prepared by the Continuous Mortality Investigation (CMI), a research body under the aegis of the UK Actuarial Profession, based on data collated from life insurance companies or from self-administered pension schemes. The three most recent CMI tables are the '92' series and the '00' series (based respectively on life office experience from 1991 to 1994 and 1999 to 2002) and the 'S1' series (based on self-administered pension scheme experience from 2000 to 2006). The trustees and actuary may adjust the mortality rates from the standard tables to make them more appropriate for their own scheme's members (to reflect, for example, their locations and former occupations). Such adjustments may be based on an analysis of the scheme's own experience or, if this is not available or not large enough, on broad principles.

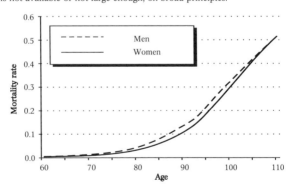

Mortality rate (probability that an individual of a given age will die in the next year)

Source: From the S1 series (pensioners, amounts), adjusted for use in 2012, allowing for default CMI_2011 projection factors and with a projected long-term improvement in mortality rates of 1.25% p.a.

Future improvements

Longevity has improved dramatically in recent years, and it is now normal to make an explicit allowance for further improvements in the future. These are of course unknown, and one way of dealing with the resulting uncertainty is to carry out calculations on two or more different sets of assumptions. By 2002, it had become clear that longevity was improving at a faster rate than had previously been assumed, with the improvements being particularly marked for the generation (or 'cohort') of pensioners born between the two World Wars. In response to this, the CMI published three sets of improvement factors for use with the '92' series of tables: the 'short', 'medium' and 'long' cohort improvement factors, allowing for the increased rates of improvement to continue until 2010, 2020 and 2040 respectively. In 2009, the CMI published the first in an annual series of models, known as 'CMI_2009', which superseded the cohort improvement factors. The CMI has since updated the model to 'CMI_2010' and 'CMI_2011', reflecting the publication of population data for 2009 and 2010 respectively.

Another possibility is to adopt a stochastic approach. This involves assigning an assumed probability distribution for future mortality rates and then carrying out a large number of simulations to assess the range of outcomes. (A similar approach is often used at present to illustrate the effect on schemes' funding levels of different rates of future investment return.)

LOOKING AHEAD

Predicting future improvements in longevity is extremely difficult, not least because of the huge uncertainties surrounding the impact that future events may have. Medical advances, changes in social behaviours (e.g. the impact of the smoking ban in enclosed public spaces in England from 1 July 2007) and increases in obesity will all have an impact.

Some experts caution against making forecasts based purely on past experience, believing instead that life expectancy will level off in the future and ultimately start to fall. Others disagree, arguing that as one disease is conquered scientists will move on to the next, and that improvements in life expectancy due to medical advances will continue at a similar rate. With research indicating that a 35-year-old non-smoker has over double the chance of living to age 80 than that of a 35-year-old smoker, the impact of further reductions in the incidence of smoking could be significant.

Such wide-ranging views make it difficult for trustees and actuaries to decide what allowance to make for future improvements in longevity. However, the Pensions Regulator's guidance on mortality assumptions for scheme-specific funding *(see Section 20)* states that, in its view, these should be chosen prudently, specifically requiring an allowance for prudence in the base table rather than necessarily in the allowance for future improvements.

MANAGING THE RISK

The requirement for 'prudence' means that trustees need to consider carefully whether they remain comfortable with the assumptions made at previous funding valuations. For many schemes, significant changes have already been made to the mortality assumptions, leading to a significant increase in the calculated value of their liabilities.

One way of reducing the longevity risk a scheme faces is by changing benefit design. This might involve changing the benefit structure, for future service, to:

- defined contribution
- cash balance, where a lump sum based on service and salary is used to purchase pension based on conversion terms that can change over time, *or*
- defined benefit, but where the normal retirement date is increased.

Purchasing annuities with an insurance company removes the longevity risk entirely, but this can be expected to be more expensive in the long term than paying pensions from the scheme itself (because the insurer will look to charge a price for taking on the risk).

Some financial institutions are now offering longevity swaps whereby each year one party pays an amount of money based on the difference (for a reference population or for the scheme itself) between the actual survivorship and what this was predicted to be. Trustees therefore receive money when fewer pensioners than expected die, and pay money to the issuer when more pensioners than expected die *(see Section 23)*.

THE PENSION PROTECTION FUND AND LEVY

The Pension Protection Fund (PPF) was formally established under the Pensions Act 2004 and commenced on 6 April 2005, with the aim, in the words of the Government, of 'guaranteeing members a specified minimum level of pension when the sponsoring employer becomes insolvent'.

The PPF covers eligible schemes where an insolvency event occurs to the employer on or after 6 April 2005. Schemes already in wind-up on that date are not covered by the PPF. The PPF is not underwritten by the Government, but is funded by levies on eligible schemes *(see below)*. A separate Financial Assistance Scheme (FAS), which is funded by the Government and managed by the PPF, provides assistance to members of schemes that went into wind-up on or after 1 January 1997 and are not eligible for the PPF *(see below)*. The Fraud Compensation Fund is also the responsibility of the PPF and covers claims from schemes that have lost assets as a result of an offence such as theft or fraud, where the employer is insolvent *(see below)*.

ADMISSION

The principle of the PPF is that it will 'assume responsibility' for 'eligible schemes' if their assets immediately before the insolvency event are insufficient to cover the 'protected liabilities' *(see below)*. 'Eligible schemes' excludes, in particular, pure money purchase schemes. 'Assuming responsibility' entails the PPF taking over the assets of the scheme and paying members the benefits provided under the 'pension compensation provisions' *(see below)*. The trustees are discharged from their obligations to pay benefits and administer the scheme.

The assessment period

During the 'assessment period', the PPF will determine whether or not the scheme is eligible. This period begins with the employer's insolvency (or, in certain circumstances, with either the trustees' application for the PPF to assume responsibility or a notification from the Pensions Regulator to the same effect). The legislation contains a lot of detail on the process for notifying insolvency events and confirming whether or not a 'scheme rescue' is possible (if, for example, the employer can continue as a going concern).

An actuarial 'entry valuation' *(see below)* on a prescribed basis has to be carried out to determine whether or not the scheme has sufficient assets to cover the 'protected liabilities' (i.e. the cost of securing the benefits provided for under the pension compensation provisions, together with any non-benefit-related liabilities and the estimated costs of wind-up). Once the PPF has approved the valuation, normally either it will proceed to assume responsibility and issue a formal 'transfer notice' to the trustees, or (if there are sufficient assets to meet the protected liabilities) the trustees must proceed with winding up. In the latter case, the trustees can make an application to the PPF for reconsideration. Where winding up takes place, this may be subject to directions made by the PPF and/or the Regulator.

During an assessment period, lots of restrictions apply. Further benefits may not accrue and further contributions may not be made. Normally, transfers out are not permitted and a wind-up cannot be started. Benefit payments must be restricted to those payable under the pension compensation provisions. The PPF can also give directions to the trustees regarding, for example, scheme investment.

The assessment period ends when the 'transfer notice' is served, or when the PPF ceases to be involved with the scheme, or if the entry valuation indicates that the scheme has sufficient assets to cover its protected liabilities, normally *(but see below)* leaving it to be wound up outside the PPF. Reasons for the PPF ceasing to be involved include a scheme rescue and a refusal to assume responsibility for the scheme because it has been set up to exploit the PPF. A transfer notice cannot be given until the assessment period has run for at least a year.

Closed schemes

Schemes that are too well funded to be taken on by the PPF but are too big to be able to find an insurer to buy out the liabilities must apply to the PPF to continue as 'closed schemes'. These closed schemes would then be subject to the same restrictions on contributions and accrual of benefits, and to directions from the PPF, that apply during an assessment period. Closed schemes are required to undertake regular valuations and, if at some point the assets have fallen below the value of the PPF liabilities, the PPF will then assume responsibility.

COMPENSATION

The admissible rules

The starting point for determining the benefits payable to members under the pension compensation provisions is the scheme's 'admissible rules'. Essentially, this means the rules as at the assessment date (i.e. the start of the assessment period), but disregarding rule changes within the previous three years that would increase the level of PPF compensation. Discretionary pension increases within the same period are also excluded to the extent that they exceed the increase in prices since the pension was last increased. Discretionary early retirement pensions that came into payment under a rule that is to be disregarded may have to cease, and the PPF can review – and, if necessary, adjust – ill-health pensions granted in the last three years.

Members' and dependants' benefits

Members over NPA at the assessment date and ill-health pensioners are entitled to 100% of the benefits under their scheme's admissible rules. Payments made by the scheme during the assessment period are offset from the PPF compensation. Members under NPA, including those already receiving pension, are entitled to 90% of accrued benefits under the admissible rules.

A future widow or widower is entitled to 50% of the pension payable to the member (unless the admissible rules had no provision for a survivor's pension).

A 'relevant partner' (of either sex, living with the member as 'man and wife') has the same entitlement. Benefits for children are payable until age 18 (or 25 in some circumstances); their amount depends on the number of children and on whether or not there is a widow, widower or relevant partner.

Provisions came into force on 6 April 2011 which enable PPF compensation to be shared on divorce or dissolution of a civil partnership, in a similar way to occupational pension scheme benefits *(see Section 19)*. The resulting pension credits are retained in the PPF and cannot be transferred elsewhere.

The compensation cap

For members whose compensation is subject to the 90% restriction, the initial rate of compensation is limited to a stipulated 'maximum permitted rate' at the date benefits come into payment. For 2011/12, a maximum pension of £29,897 p.a. at age 65 applies. The level of this 'cap' increases in line with earnings each year. The PPF has set adjustment factors to derive amounts applicable where benefits come into payment at ages above and below 65.

Revaluation and indexation

Benefits not in payment and accrued before 6 April 2009 are revalued between the assessment date and NPA (or earlier retirement) in line with CPI (RPI for periods up to 31 March 2011) up to a maximum of 5% p.a. The 5% p.a. limit is reduced to 2.5% p.a. in respect of benefits accrued from 6 April 2009.

A new provision to deal with 'non-revaluing benefits' was introduced from 1 April 2009. Under this, PPF compensation benefits are not revalued, but only where the scheme provides no revaluation to any member in any circumstances.

For deferred pensioners, revaluation between date of leaving and assessment date is based on the scheme rules.

Benefits in payment are increased annually in line with inflation up to a maximum of 2.5%. Increases apply only to benefits attributable to service from 6 April 1997. RPI was originally used as the measure of inflation but this is expected to change to CPI from 1 January 2012.

Options

Lump sum commutation, of up to 25% of benefits, is permitted using factors specified by the PPF. Early payment of benefits after age 55 (or from the later of age 50 and the 'protected' pension age, if any, that would have applied under the member's scheme) is permitted subject to actuarial reduction using factors specified by the PPF. Trivial commutation and terminal ill-health lump sums are also available in certain circumstances.

Adjustments by the PPF

Where the scheme rules are such that the appropriate compensation benefits cannot be determined in accordance with the legislation, the PPF can decide the level of compensation that will apply to members.

The PPF has received legal advice that it is required to equalise benefits to take account of differences in the way GMPs are calculated for men and women, and after lengthy consultations, it has confirmed the general approach that will be adopted. Details of the approach and timetable for implementation are still awaited. For schemes at a very advanced stage of assessment and those which have already transferred, the PPF will make the necessary changes, but other schemes will be required to make the necessary adjustments during the assessment process.

The PPF has the ability (after consultation) to adjust the rates of revaluation and increases in payment if necessary. If both of these have been reduced to zero they can recommend that the Secretary of State reduce the 90% and/or 100% levels of compensation. Such reductions would only apply in 'extreme circumstances'.

VALUATIONS

Two types of actuarial valuation are required by the PPF, each for a specific purpose – for levy calculations and to determine whether a scheme should enter the PPF.

Levy valuation

An eligible scheme must provide a 'section 179 valuation' to the PPF in order for it to determine the Pension Protection Levy payable by the scheme. These valuations must be carried out by the scheme actuary at intervals of no more than three years.

For the purposes of the valuation, assets are generally taken at the value shown in the scheme's audited accounts.

Liabilities are valued, using assumptions set out in guidance issued by the PPF, to reflect the estimated cost of buying out the benefits with an insurance company. The benefits valued are broadly those provided under the scheme's rules, but allowing for members under NPA receiving 90% (not 100%) of benefits, the compensation cap, and the PPF levels of revaluation, indexation and spouse's pension.

Entry valuation

A 'section 143 valuation' is required by the PPF to determine whether or not it should assume responsibility for a scheme that has entered an assessment period. The PPF will obtain this from the trustees, who will usually ask the scheme actuary to carry it out. It has to be obtained as soon as reasonably practicable after the insolvency event. Assets are generally taken at the value shown in the audited accounts. Liabilities are valued using assumptions set out in guidance issued by the PPF (which are similar to those for levy valuations but vary some of the demographic assumptions to reflect the circumstances of the scheme), but the actual PPF compensation benefits are taken into account rather than the broad approximations used in the section 179 valuation.

LEVIES

Schemes that are eligible for future entry to the PPF are required to pay two PPF levies. These are charged in respect of each levy year, which begins on 1 April.

Pension Protection Levy – general

The Pension Protection Levy consists of two parts: the risk-based levy (which must represent at least 80% of the total collected from all schemes) and the scheme-based levy. There are limits each year on the total estimated levy and the amount by which it can increase. These limits can only be changed by the Secretary of State following consultation and with the approval of the Treasury. Legislation allows the PPF to charge interest (at 5% above base rate) on any Pension Protection Levy that has not been paid within 28 days of the invoice date, although the PPF does have discretion to waive interest in certain circumstances.

Pension Protection Levy – 2011/12

For 2011/12, the PPF intends to collect £600 million. This is lower than in previous years to reflect the fact that the PPF expects its long-term requirement for funding to reduce as a result of future increases and revaluation on PPF benefits now being linked to CPI instead of RPI.

The risk-based levy is based on:

(a) The *assumed probability of insolvency of the employer* (or a weighted average probability for multi-employer schemes), derived by assigning the employer to 1 of 100 risk bands corresponding to failure scores calculated by Dun & Bradstreet (D&B) as at 31 March 2010. For the 2011/12 levy the PPF adopted a new table of insolvency probabilities (which were higher for all failure scores, with the increases for the best rated companies being very large).

(b) *Underfunding risk.* This is calculated as a specified percentage on the scheme's estimated PPF liabilities, the percentage depending on the funding level revealed by the levy valuation *(see above)* adjusted for market conditions at 31 March 2010. Where the funding level is 135% or lower, the underfunding risk is the difference between 136% and the funding level. A sliding scale applies for funding levels between 135% and 155%, and the underfunding risk (and hence the risk-based levy) is zero for funding levels of 155% or above.

A scaling factor (2.07 for 2011/12) equates the proposed levy estimate with the estimated risk exposure across all schemes. The risk-based levy is capped (at 0.75% of estimated PPF liabilities for 2011/12) in order to protect the weakest levy payers.

The scheme-based levy is based on a percentage of the scheme's estimated PPF liabilities – the scheme-based levy multiplier (0.0135% for 2011/12).

Pension Protection Levy – 2012/13 onwards

The PPF has set out fundamental changes to the levy calculation to apply from 2012/13. The overall intention is to make a scheme's levy more stable and predictable as it will be related to changes in the scheme's own risk profile, and less affected by the changes of other schemes (through the scaling factor) and short-term market movements.

The risk-based levy formula (including the scaling factor) will normally be fixed for three years, and will still be based on:

(a) The *assumed probability of insolvency of the employer* (or a weighted average probability for multi-employer schemes), but using the average D&B failure score over the year prior to the levy year and then assigned to 1 of 10 (rather than 100) bands.

(b) *Underfunding risk*. This is calculated as a specified percentage of the scheme's estimated PPF liabilities, but averaged over the previous five years and also adjusted to reflect the risk posed by a scheme's investment strategy in adverse market conditions (so schemes with a riskier strategy pay a higher levy). The PPF will calculate the investment risk for most schemes but schemes with liabilities of £1.5 billion or more will have to carry out their own more detailed test (and smaller schemes can choose to) which will take account of a wider range of asset classes, including derivatives.

The scheme-based levy will be used explicitly to recover any deficit within the PPF and any cross-subsidy from the cap on the risk-based levy, which will still apply to protect the weakest levy payers. At the time of writing, the PPF had announced that, subject to consultation, for 2012/13 the levy estimate would be £550 million, the scaling factor 0.89, the scheme-based multiplier 0.0085%, and the cap on the risk-based levy 0.75% of estimated PPF liabilities.

There are a number of actions that may be taken to manage a scheme's risk-based levy, including:

- *monitor the D&B failure score* – D&B scores are based on factors such as the number of directors and the promptness of paying invoices, as well as the financial position of the company, so employers may be able to take relatively simple actions to improve their scores or ensure they do not fall into a worse risk band

- *carry out the more detailed investment risk test* – schemes with liabilities of less than £1.5 billion have the option of doing this if it would reduce levies, rather than relying on the PPF's default calculations

- submitting an *out-of-cycle s179 valuation* to reflect action taken to improve the scheme's funding position

- submitting details of *deficit reduction contributions*, over and above the cost of accruing scheme benefits, made since the relevant valuation date as certified by the scheme actuary in accordance with guidance published by the PPF – this reduces the underfunding risk, *and*

- putting in place *contingent assets* (if in a standard form and legally binding) that produce cash for the scheme when an insolvency event occurs in relation to the employer – these can be in the form of a guarantee from another group company, a charge over assets of the employer, or a letter of credit, and they reduce the underfunding risk or the assumed insolvency probability, depending on the type of contingent asset.

PPF Administration Levy

This is charged to meet the costs of establishing and running the PPF (other than the cost of paying compensation). It is based on the number of member on the last day of the scheme year which ended before the beginning of the previous levy year. It is invoiced with the General Levy *(see Section 12)* and not with the Pension Protection Levy.

FINANCIAL ASSISTANCE SCHEME

The Financial Assistance Scheme (FAS) provides Government-funded support for members of underfunded pension schemes which began to be wound up between 1 January 1997 and 22 December 2008 and in limited other circumstances, where the scheme is not eligible to enter the PPF but meets other eligibility criteria.

The FAS provides a top-up to a member's benefits so that the total benefits received by the member are broadly the same as those provided by the PPF. Members who would receive higher benefits from the scheme's assets under the statutory priority order maintain that higher level of benefit.

When the FAS was set up, it did not cover all schemes described above, and was restricted to pensioners and members near retirement. The level of FAS benefits has also been increased over time, as the original benefits were much lower than those provided by the PPF.

The FAS initially provided top-up payments, after the scheme had been wound up and members' benefits had been bought out with an insurance company. (Schemes dealt with in this way are now referred to as 'FAS1' schemes.) However, with effect from 26 September 2007, schemes eligible for FAS support have been prohibited from purchasing annuities where they have not already done so. Since April 2010, the Government has started to take on the assets of these 'FAS2' schemes and make combined payments of scheme and FAS benefits to members. The PPF now manages the FAS and is aiming to wind up all FAS1 schemes by 31 March 2012 and transfer the majority of FAS2 schemes to the Government by April 2014. FAS compensation will be subject to an equalisation process in respect of GMPs, similar to that for the PPF *(see above)*.

FRAUD COMPENSATION FUND

An occupational pension scheme that has lost assets as a result of an offence (such as theft or fraud) committed after 6 April 1997 may be eligible for compensation if the employer is insolvent. The amount of any compensation payment is determined by the PPF, and is limited to the amount of any loss that cannot reasonably be recovered. Applications for compensation may be made by the trustees, administrators or scheme members.

The Fund is financed by a Fraud Compensation Levy, potentially payable by all schemes eligible for this compensation (a wider group than for the PPF). Regulations cap the levy at 75 pence per member (23 pence prior to 31 March 2011). The levy is only charged as and when needed. A levy is being raised in 2011/12 at the rate of 25 pence per member. Prior to this, levies had previously only been raised in 1997/98, 2004/05 and 2010/11, all at the rate of 23 pence per member.

Painless Pensions Administration

Achieving high quality member service within a pressurised cost environment is making pensions administration a more painful challenge for trustees and sponsoring companies.

As an award-winning provider of pensions administration, Aon Hewitt can supply the painless solution you and your members desire. Advancements in technology, streamlined processing and increasing levels of automation have pushed our service standards even higher while ensuring our costs stay competitive.

Whether you are already outsourcing or about to do so, our deep understanding of pensions and outsourcing allows us to meet the needs of members, trustees and sponsors alike.

So let us take the pain out of your pensions administration and ensure nobody gets stung.

For more information, call 01372 733829 or email enquiries@aonhewitt.com

www.aonhewitt.co.uk

Aon Hewitt Limited is authorised and regulated by the Financial Services Authority. Registered in England & Wales. Registered No: 4396810. Registered Office: 8 Devonshire Square, London EC2M 4PL.

LIABILITY MANAGEMENT EXERCISES

In recent years, employers have looked at several ways of managing defined benefit liabilities. A common theme is the reduction of risk and, in some cases, possible improvement in the financial position of the scheme for funding or accounting purposes. Some of the approaches which have been considered are outlined below.

TRANSFER INCENTIVE EXERCISES

Under transfer incentive exercises (sometimes referred to as transfer inducement exercises), members are actively encouraged to transfer their defined benefits elsewhere, through the offer of an enhancement to the standard transfer value, a direct cash payment or a combination of the two. The amount offered could be increased well above the transfer value to which individual members might normally be entitled under legislation *(see Section 16)*. The offer is normally only available for a limited period.

These exercises are typically proposed by sponsoring employers as a way of reducing exposure to investment and longevity risk. The employer might also benefit from an improvement in the scheme's funding position and/or their accounting figures. This is because the value placed on benefits for funding or accounting purposes can significantly exceed the statutory minimum transfer value, which is broadly equal to the expected cost of providing the benefit within the scheme. This means there is usually scope to pay a higher transfer value, sometimes significantly higher than the statutory minimum, whilst still remaining below the prudent reserves targeted for scheme funding. This enhanced transfer value, together with any direct cash payment, may also be attractive to some members.

The Regulator originally issued guidance on these exercises in 2007. In 2010 it issued updated guidance which sets out five principles to which employers should adhere:

- the offer should be clear, fair and not misleading
- the offer should be open and transparent
- conflicts of interest should be identified and managed appropriately
- trustees should be involved from the start of the process, *and*
- independent financial advice should be made available to members.

The guidance requires information to be tailored to members' needs and to provide a clear indication of the cost of purchasing equivalent benefits on the open market. The risks involved in accepting the offer should also be explained. In addition, the reasons for undertaking the exercise should be set out, including details of how advisers are selected and paid. Members should not be placed under pressure to accept the offer and they should be given a reasonable amount of time to make their decision.

The Regulator believes that trustees should start from the presumption that such exercises are not in members' best interests. However, the guidance acknowledges that some members' personal circumstances mean they may benefit from accepting such an offer. Generally, the employer should pay for impartial advice, tailored to each member's personal circumstances, and require members to take this advice before making a decision. The guidance includes a significant amount of information for trustees and employers to consider when undertaking one of these exercises.

PENSION INCREASE CONVERSION EXERCISES

Under a pension increase conversion exercise:

- an offer could be made to existing pensioners to exchange future (non-statutory) increases on part of their pension for a higher immediate, but non-increasing, pension, *and/or*
- a new option could be introduced for non-pensioner members to exchange the (non-statutory) increases on part of their pension when it comes into payment for a higher, fixed pension at retirement.

These exercises are also typically proposed by sponsoring employers, as a way of reducing exposure to inflation and longevity risk. Depending on the terms of the conversion, the employer might also benefit from an improvement in the scheme's funding position and/or their accounting figures. Some members may find the immediate increase to their pension more attractive than the protection against the impact of inflation provided by future increases.

There can be significant legal issues depending on the terms of the conversion *(see comments under* Scheme Modifications *in Section 7)*. Some elements of pension will need to continue to be increased to meet statutory requirements (e.g. pension relating to post-5 April 1997 service) and scheme amendment powers would also need detailed consideration. However, some of the examples reported in the press have involved cash incentives and significant reductions in value post-conversion.

The Regulator's guidance outlined above, for incentive exercises, is also applicable to pension increase conversion exercises. Although the guidance is written primarily with transfer incentives in mind, there are explicit references to pension increase conversion exercises and the same principles apply to both. As for transfer incentives, the Regulator believes that trustees should start from the presumption that pension increase conversion exercises are not in members' best interests although some members' personal circumstances mean they may benefit from accepting such an offer.

OTHER WAYS OF AMENDING LIABILITIES

There are a number of other ways in which the level or nature of liabilities can potentially be controlled or amended. Examples include:

- ceasing future accrual *(see Section 24)*

- capping future increases in pensionable salary
- commutation of small pensions, *and*
- encouraging early retirements.

INVESTMENT SOLUTIONS TO MANAGE LIABILITIES

Various forms of liability management have been developed over recent years which focus on the investment of assets to manage liability risks. Two increasingly common options, liability-driven investment (LDI) and longevity swaps, are described below.

These two options can be combined to form a 'Synthetic' or 'DIY' buy-out – significantly reducing risk by effectively replicating the effect of a buy-out or a buy-in *(see Section 26)*. This may be at a lower cost and provide more flexibility than paying a one-off insurance premium for a buy-out or buy-in.

Liability-driven investment

For many years, financial institutions – primarily investment banks and insurance companies – have provided protection against interest rate and inflation risks through the issue of 'swaps'. These require the purchaser to pay a series of cashflows (often fixed) over a period of time in return for a series of different cashflows that more closely reflect their own liabilities over that period (e.g. cashflows that increase in line with inflation).

For pension schemes, the use of these swaps is similar to investment in bonds. However, they can be structured much more flexibly to meet the estimated cashflows of a scheme, significantly reducing interest rate and inflation risks. Many pension schemes of all sizes are now making use of such strategies. However, the introduction of Consumer Price Indexation for some pension liabilities has added some complexity in this area as there is no developed market in CPI swaps.

Longevity swaps

Removing interest rate and inflation risks (e.g. by using swaps) leaves increasing longevity as the main risk remaining for a typical defined benefit pension scheme. 'Longevity swaps' can be used to reduce this risk. These allow the scheme to pay cashflows over a fixed period of time based on the expected longevity of a group of individuals, and receive cashflows over a period of time related to the actual longevity of that group. There are two main types of longevity swap for pension schemes:

(1) A *bespoke longevity swap* is based on the life expectancy of the actual members of a scheme. The provider agrees to meet the actual payments to members and the trustees pay a fixed schedule of payments to the provider. This removes the risk to the scheme from members living longer than expected. However, bespoke hedges are only available to relatively large schemes, and typically only those with a high proportion of pensioner members.

(2) An *index-based longevity swap* provides protection based on the general population rather than the scheme's membership. Therefore,

the trustees retain a risk that members' longevity is greater than that of the index population.

There have been a number of bespoke longevity transactions, mainly for larger schemes. The largest transaction to date was a swap to hedge £3 billion of pensioner liabilities in the BMW pension scheme. To date, this is the largest transaction of this kind with a UK pension scheme.

INSURANCE APPROACHES

In addition to the relatively recent innovations outlined above for managing a scheme's liabilities, insurance policies are often used to help protect the scheme from adverse death-in-service experience. Examples include:

- fully insuring the lump sum and, in some cases, the dependant's pension payable on death
- insuring higher lump sums than those specified in the rules, to contribute towards the cost of any dependant's pension payable on death, *and*
- some form of partial insurance, for example insuring benefits in excess of a predetermined limit (e.g. benefits in excess of £1 million, or benefits in relation to a specific group of employees, such as an executive group).

Due to the very competitive insurance market, advantageous terms can often be secured which, for larger schemes, can be broadly equivalent to the actual underlying death claims experience, in the long run. This can be an extremely cost-effective way to reduce risk to a pension scheme.

CEASING ACCRUAL

This section sets out the issues that employers and trustees need to consider before stopping any further benefits building up in a final salary arrangement.

In recent years, many final salary arrangements have been closed to new members, with new employees instead being offered membership of a defined contribution (DC) arrangement or a defined benefit (DB) arrangement with lower costs and/or risks to the employer (e.g. CARE or cash balance: *see Section 7*). Current employees have generally continued to build up final salary benefits with these new benefit arrangements typically applying to new joiners only.

However, it is becoming more common for employers to go further and stop final salary benefits for all their employees. This is referred to as 'ceasing accrual'. A scheme with no further benefits accruing is known as a 'frozen scheme'.

Ceasing accrual is not a simple exercise. There are a number of actions that have to be carried out by law, and others that employers may want to go through in order to maintain good employee relations. The process will require a significant amount of planning and involve a number of functions within the employer as well as other parties. Careful due diligence and good project management is important in order to identify potential issues and to set a realistic timeframe.

CONSIDERATIONS FOR EMPLOYERS

Business case

The main reason for ceasing accrual is usually to reduce the significant cost of pension benefits. However, employers may need to be able to justify the need for these cost savings to affected employees and other parties such as trade unions and the pension scheme trustees. These parties will often want to ensure that the employer has considered a range of possible options and be satisfied that ceasing accrual is a reasonable solution in the relevant circumstances. Many employers propose moving members to a DC scheme to achieve these cost savings. But it may be possible to arrive at similar cost savings by retaining a DB structure, and making a combination of changes to the benefits that are offered (e.g. moving from final salary to CARE, reducing the accrual rate, increasing member contributions etc).

Immediate financial savings may not be the only consideration. Employers may want to reduce the risk that the costs turn out to be higher than expected over the longer term. This would involve passing some or all of the risks inherent in a pension arrangement on to members.

Employers may also want to ensure that all employees are treated equally, irrespective of their length of service. If a final salary arrangement closed to new members a few years ago, the overall cost of a DC arrangement set up for new employees may have been designed to be similar to the cost of the final salary arrangement at that time. Now, because of increases in longevity and falling gilt yields, the expected cost of new benefits in the final salary arrangement is likely to be significantly higher than the cost of such a DC scheme. This means that the overall employment cost of two employees in identical jobs and on otherwise identical terms can be significantly different depending on when they joined the employer. This can lead to claims of a 'two-tier workforce'.

In proposing changes, empoyers should always bear in mind that they have a legal obligation to act in good faith in dealings with employees.

Design of future benefits

Employers will need to consider what pension benefits they will offer to members to replace their final salary benefits. If an employer has already set up a new arrangement for employees who joined after a certain date, then it may want to move all employees to this arrangement. However, the employer will want to ensure that this arrangement continues to be appropriate.

In many cases, employees are moved into a DC arrangement. However, this can be seen as moving from one extreme to the other (with the member, rather than the employer, bearing all the risks). Some employers may consider that sharing risks to some extent is a more desirable outcome.

The accounting impact of both ceasing accrual in the DB arrangement, and the new benefit structure, will need to be considered *(see Section 28)*. The savings in cash terms are unlikely to be the same as the savings in accounting terms, and in some cases there could actually be an adverse effect on the employer's profit and loss account.

There are a number of other issues in changing benefit structures, particularly if moving from final salary to DC:

- employers should consider whether the proposed new arrangement will meet the minimum requirements to avoid also having to enrol employees in the NEST scheme *(see Sections 9 and 10)*

- whether the new arrangement should be under the same trust as the final salary arrangement: there can be complex issues including implications for funding cross-subsidies, contracting out and winding up

- benefits payable on death or ill health cannot be funded in a DC arrangement in the same way that they can in a DB arrangement: advice on appropriate insurance arrangements will be needed and the costs should be considered

- final salary arrangements have more flexibility to provide extra benefits in cases of redundancy and other workforce management exercises: DC arrangements are less flexible, and employers will need to consider how to provide such benefits, particularly if these are contractual entitlements

- there are additional considerations for higher earners:
  - whether the new arrangement will provide appropriate remuneration for senior employees or whether additional benefits need to be provided through a separate arrangement (bearing in mind the disguised remuneration requirements introduced in April 2011 – *see Section 14*), *and*
  - the tax implications for those who may be affected by the reductions in the Annual Allowance from April 2011 and/or the Lifetime Allowance from April 2012 *(see Section 13)*.

Design of accrued benefits

There may also be various ways in which active members' benefits in respect of past service can be calculated. For example, depending on scheme rules, the employer may have the following options for increasing pension between date of implementation and retirement:

- statutory minimum increases in line with leaving service benefits

- increases in line with price inflation, *or*

- maintaining full salary linking.

This is an area in which legal advice is particularly important – *see below*.

If the scheme is contracted-out immediately before benefit accrual ceases, contracting-out legislation requires that a 'Protection Rule' is added to the scheme rules to ensure that any contracted-out benefits retained within the scheme (GMPs and post-1997 contracted-out rights) are protected at normal pension age and on death from being franked against benefits accrued during periods of non-contracted-out pensionable service. Separate anti-franking legislation requires GMPs to be protected at and after the age at which GMP becomes payable (65 for men and 60 for women).

Consultation and communication with employees

Ceasing accrual is a 'listed change' under the Pensions Act 2004 consultation requirements *(see Section 7)*. Employers will therefore have to carry out a 60-day consultation with affected members or their representatives and consider any representations made during the consultation before they can implement any changes. This process could take significantly longer than 60 days, particularly if member representative groups need to be set up.

Many employers will want to do more than the legal minimum, and put in place a detailed communication strategy to ensure members understand the reasons for change, the effect on their final salary benefits built up to date, and the likely benefits they will receive from the new arrangement. For many members, the headline is likely to be a significant reduction in their projected benefits at retirement. However the detailed implications will affect individual members in different ways.

In the case of a new DC arrangement, employers may wish to encourage former DB members to take more responsibility than they have in the past for ensuring their benefits will meet their needs at retirement. This is likely to involve taking decisions relating to the level of contributions paid and their investment options. Employers may want to provide a range of information to employees about this, reflecting the level of financial literacy of the workforce.

Legal issues

There are a number of areas where employers will need to take legal advice.

Members' employment contracts will need to be reviewed. This is to check how membership of the pension scheme is described. For example, some contracts give the right to membership of a final salary pension scheme. Some contracts may also contain individual pension promises.

The scheme's trust deed and rules should be consulted and may need amendment. They should be checked to ensure that the scheme does not restrict the types of amendment that can be made. If trustee consent is required for any amendment, the trustees may see this as an opportunity for negotiation *(see below)*.

One specific issue may arise if the employer wishes to break the link to final salary for accrued benefits. Case law has suggested that the wording of some trust deeds and rules may require members' benefits to be calculated by reference to their salary when they leave or retire from the employer. In such cases it would not be possible to calculate benefits using the member's salary at the date accrual ceases in the scheme. This may reduce the cost savings the employer would otherwise make.

In some cases, amending the scheme rules or members leaving the scheme as a result of ceasing accrual may trigger a wind-up *(see Section 25)* or a debt on the employer *(see Section 27)*. This could have significant financial implications, and the employer will usually want to ensure that the changes are carried out in such a way as to avoid this.

Other issues

If the current arrangement is contracted out of S2P but the new arrangement is not, the scheme employer will need to carry out the necessary actions in order to cease to contract out *(see Section 6)*. In particular, this requires the employer to give members, trustees and trade unions at least one month's notice of the intention to cease contracting out (or three months if there are trade unions involved who do not agree to a shorter period). Such a notice must include certain prescribed items of information.

There are additional considerations if the scheme has any ex-public sector workers, or if the employer might consider bidding for public sector outsourcing contracts in the future. Employers may be required to offer a certain level of DB pensions to ex-public sector workers. It is not always easy to identify ex-public sector workers, particularly if they have joined the scheme as a result of subsequent transactions between private sector companies.

CONSIDERATIONS FOR TRUSTEES

Trustees' duty

The conventionally accepted view is that trustees' primary duty is to safeguard accrued rights, and that it is the employer's role to decide the basis of pension benefits it wishes to provide to its employees for future service.

However, as well as protecting members' existing benefits, trustees will want to satisfy themselves that the employer's business case for any proposal to cease accrual is properly reasoned, the proposals are workable in practice, and that they do not breach any legal obligations. Trustees should also bear in mind that they need to consider the interests of all members of the scheme, not just the active members who will be directly affected by the ceasing of future accrual.

As noted above, if trustee consent is required in order to amend the scheme to allow the ceasing of future accrual, the trustees may use this as an opportunity for negotiation with the employer over funding, security of benefits, and even benefits themselves. The trustees may need to take legal advice, particularly where their trust deed and rules provides them with a power to veto changes to future benefits.

Safeguarding accrued rights

The issue of ceasing accrual may be raised during the valuation process *(see Section 20)*. The scheme funding regulations allow trustees to modify future accrual if it appears to them that it is not otherwise possible to obtain the employer's agreement. Alternatively, the issue may be raised by the employer during funding negotiations.

The trustees will need to consider whether a proposal to cease accrual, and the background to such a proposal, reflects a weakening in the employer's covenant – its ability and willingness to continue to fund the scheme *(see Section 20)*. This could have implications for the level of technical provisions the trustees consider necessary to safeguard accrued rights.

Even if the proposal is not made as part of the valuation process, the trustees will need to consider the effect of ceasing accrual on the funding position of the scheme *(see Section 20)*. This will include considering whether the current funding plan remains appropriate.

Trustees and employers are likely to pay closer attention to the risks remaining in the scheme, and look for ways to manage these *(see Section 23)*. This may include buying out portions of the liabilities over time *(see Section 26)*. Ceasing accrual will also require ongoing review of cashflow requirements, and the disinvestment of assets, as the proportion of the scheme's liabilities that relates to pension in payment rises.

Any changes to the adopted funding principles are likely to require a review of actuarial factors, such as commutation and early retirement terms, as well as transfer value assumptions. The employer's consent may be required to change some factors.

Benefit changes

As part of any negotiation with the employer, trustees may decide it is appropriate to suggest alternative future benefits. As the employer's proposals are likely to be aimed at cutting costs, the scope for alternative approaches may be limited. Trade unions and representations from members may also suggest approaches which partially offset the removal of members' final salary benefits.

Administration and communication

If the new pension arrangement is being set up under the same trust, the trustees will need to consider how the administration of two separate benefit structures for the same members will work, and ensure that administration systems can cope with the new benefits. Trustees will need training to understand their responsibilities and the features of the new benefits with which they are not familiar.

Trustees may want to be involved in the employer's communication process, to ensure that the employer is explaining the issues clearly and properly. Once any changes have been implemented, trustees may want to review how they communicate with members more generally.

SCHEME CLOSURE AND WIND-UP

The winding up of occupational pension schemes can raise complex legal and practical issues. The process can take several years, although legislation exists that is intended to speed it up. The trustees of a scheme that is being wound up need to understand their continuing responsibilities under the relevant provisions of the trust deed and rules, and should take legal and actuarial advice where appropriate.

Commencement of wind-up

The events that can trigger wind-up are normally set out in the scheme trust deed and rules. These can include the employer ceasing to contribute (or not being prepared to contribute at a rate the trustees consider adequate for funding the scheme), or becoming insolvent. However, the scheme rules may allow the alternative of postponing wind-up, and instead continuing to operate on a 'frozen scheme' basis with no further accrual of benefits. The trustees have an overriding power under the Pensions Act 1995 to choose to follow this route if the employer has gone into liquidation and they consider it appropriate. Continuing as a frozen scheme would be subject to neither the Pensions Regulator nor, if the employer is insolvent and a Pension Protection Fund (PPF) assessment period (*see Section 22*) has been completed, the PPF Board requiring the scheme to be wound up. During a PPF assessment period, various restrictions apply, including that benefit payments must be restricted to PPF compensation levels.

It is important for the date on which wind-up is treated as having commenced to be clearly identified and recorded. This can vary depending on the circumstances, but for most purposes can be taken as the earliest date when there are no members in pensionable service and either (i) the scheme rules provide that wind-up should commence or (ii) the power to wind up is exercised by the trustees (or by any other person or body, such as the Pensions Regulator or a court, having the authority to do so).

Winding-up procedure

Regulations effective from 24 July 2006 imposed additional requirements on trustees of underfunded occupational schemes entering wind-up. In particular, the trustees of a scheme that enters wind-up during a recovery period *(see Section 20)* must as soon as practicable prepare a 'winding-up procedure'. This procedure includes details of the action that will be taken to establish the liabilities and the method that will be used to discharge them, an indication of any accrued rights or benefits that are likely to be affected by a reduction in actuarial value, and an estimate of the amount of time that will be taken to complete these steps. The procedure must be submitted to the Pensions Regulator.

Schemes in wind-up are generally exempt from the scheme funding requirements *(see Section 20)*.

Appointment of an independent trustee and role of the Pensions Regulator

If the employer has become insolvent, the insolvency practitioner (or, if applicable, official receiver) must notify the Pensions Regulator. The Regulator then has the power to appoint an independent trustee although it does not have to do this (e.g. if one has already been appointed).

Subject to various safeguards relating to members' rights, the Regulator may modify a scheme with a view to ensuring that it is properly wound up following an application from the trustees (which must include specified information and documents). The Regulator may also order a scheme to be wound up, or give legally binding directions to trustees, administrators and others if it considers that these are necessary to speed up the process. In June 2008, the Regulator, the PPF and the Department for Work and Pensions (DWP) (on behalf of the Financial Assistance Scheme) published a joint statement saying that the important parts of a wind-up should generally be completed within a two-year period. The Regulator also maintains guidance that sets out examples of good practice in order to help schemes through the winding-up process.

Debt on the employer

Where a defined benefit scheme has insufficient assets to cover the scheme liabilities, the employer may have a legal obligation to make up the shortfall. For wind-ups starting on or after 15 February 2005, the liabilities for this purpose must be based on an estimate of the actual cost of buying out benefits and meeting the expenses of wind-up.

If the wind-up was triggered by an 'insolvency event' of the sponsoring employer, any 'debt on the employer' must be treated by the trustees as having arisen immediately before this occurred. Otherwise, the debt can be treated by the trustees as having arisen at *any* time after the commencement of wind-up and before the employer goes into liquidation.

Discharging scheme liabilities

In order to wind up a scheme, its assets must be applied to discharge its liabilities. This can be done by transfer to another occupational scheme or to personal pensions, by purchasing insurance company annuities *(see Section 26)*, by assigning existing annuity contracts to members or, in certain cases where the entitlement is small, by the payment of a 'winding-up lump sum' *(see Section 13)*.

Priority order

Because of the possibility that the assets will be insufficient to fully discharge all liabilities in this way, scheme rules normally contain a 'priority order' setting out the order in which the different liability classes (e.g. pensions already in payment, accrued pensions of active members) are to be dealt with. However, the Pensions Act 1995 introduced a statutory priority order with effect from 6 April 1997, modified by subsequent legislation, which generally overrides 'scheme-specific' priority orders. For the purpose of assigning them to appropriate priority classes, scheme liabilities are normally treated as having 'crystallised' according to their status at the date when wind-up commenced.

For wind-ups commencing on or after 6 April 2005, the statutory priority order is as follows:

(1)   benefits under certain contracts of insurance

(2)   benefits corresponding to those that would be provided if the scheme entered the PPF *(see Section 22)*

(3)   benefits from AVCs, to the extent that these are not included in the categories above

(4)   all other liabilities.

Any money purchase assets and liabilities are generally excluded from the above calculations. Such benefits would normally be expected to have priority over non-money purchase benefits, but this is dependent on the scheme rules. The classification of certain benefits as money purchase or non-money purchase has also been the subject of much legal debate; some clarification will be provided by changes (not yet in force at the time of writing) made by the Pensions Act 2011 to the legislative definition of money purchase benefits.

The liabilities set out in the statutory priority order must be valued by the scheme actuary using a specified basis. If the wind-up commenced on or after 15 February 2005, the basis used is the actual cost of securing the benefits, for example by means of an annuity buy-out. For earlier wind-ups, the basis used may differ, depending on when the wind-up commenced and whether or not the employer was insolvent.

Deficiency

Where the full buy-out debt basis *(see above)* does not apply, or such a debt cannot be collected, the assets of the scheme may be insufficient to discharge all of the scheme's liabilities. In this event, the benefits provided for the lowest priority class(es) will have to be cut back accordingly. Legislation was amended in 2009 to allow schemes in wind-up to reduce pensions already in payment, due to underfunding, without giving rise to unauthorised payments charges *(see Section 13)*.

The PPF *(see Section 22)* was established with effect from 6 April 2005. It provides some protection for eligible schemes with employers that become insolvent on or after that date. The Financial Assistance Scheme *(see Section 22)* was established to provide some support for workers who have lost pensions through underfunding in certain schemes that went into wind-up after 1996 and are not covered by the PPF.

Surplus

If a surplus of assets remains after all of the scheme liabilities have been discharged, this must also be dealt with in accordance with the scheme rules and relevant legislative requirements. As well as providing for the augmentation of benefits, either at the sole discretion of the trustees, or in consultation with (or with the consent of) the employer, there may be provision for payment of a refund to the employer. Before this can be done, a number of requirements under the Pensions Act 1995 (as amended by the 2004 Act) must be satisfied. These requirements include sending written notices to members inviting them to make representations in respect of the proposal.

Disclosure and reporting requirements

A notice must be given to members within one month of the commencement of wind-up, followed by annual progress reports. For defined benefit schemes, members must also be provided with details of the trustees' proposals for discharging liabilities before they are implemented. In all cases, once the assets have been applied to provide benefits, members must be given full details within three months.

Periodic progress reports must also be given to the Pensions Regulator. Where wind-up commenced between 1 April 2003 and 30 September 2007, the first such report had to be filed within three months of the third anniversary of commencement of wind-up. Where wind-up commences on or after 1 October 2007, the report must be filed within three months of the second anniversary of the commencement of wind-up. *(See also Section 17.)*

Scheme operation during wind-up

The process of winding up can take several years. During this period, no new members will be admitted and no further benefits will accrue. The trustees may pay provisional benefits to members on retirement, with final benefits to be confirmed when winding up is complete. From 6 April 2005, DWP legislation specifically provides for benefits paid during the winding-up period to be reduced in line with what the priority order will ultimately require *(see above)*. Trustees should also review the terms for member options and the scheme's investment strategy to ensure they remain appropriate, particularly if the employer has become insolvent. It is possible to apply to the Pensions Regulator for permission to delay paying cash equivalent transfer values.

It is important for the trustees to receive legal and actuarial advice throughout this period.

Operating as a frozen scheme

Schemes also sometimes operate as 'frozen schemes' (with no further accrual of benefits) *without* having started a winding-up process. For example, where a scheme's sponsoring employer has become insolvent but the scheme is too well funded to be taken on by the PPF *(see Section 22)*, it may be unable to purchase insurance company annuities, perhaps because it is too large. The phrase 'closed scheme' is generally used to describe a scheme that no longer permits new entrants to join but allows existing members to continue accruing future service benefits.

BUY-OUT

In *Section 25*, scheme closure and wind-up is described. It is in this context that one typically associated the concept of pensions buy-out – as a means of discharging a scheme's liabilities prior to wind-up. However, since 2007, the bulk annuity market has expanded to offer more products to ongoing schemes.

Increased competitiveness in the bulk annuity market in 2007 and 2008 led to more attractive pricing and the development of options such as partial buy-outs and 'buy-ins'. Though pricing subsequently hardened, these options remain attractive for many schemes.

These developments have arisen as a result of employers becoming increasingly sensitive to the risks associated with defined benefit schemes and the potential impact on their financial statements *(see Section 28)*. There is increasing focus on managing these risks, including interest rate, inflation and longevity risks. *Section 23 outlines options that may be alternatives to or precursors of bulk annuity exercises.*

As more schemes cease accrual *(see Section 24)*, liability transfer has become a long-term objective for many. The capacity of the bulk annuity market is a factor in the number of schemes that can transact, as it is currently a small fraction of the total liabilities in defined benefit pension schemes.

BUY-OUT OPTIONS

The following describes the main buy-out options available for pension schemes. Under the broad descriptions below there are a number of products that continue to be developed to give schemes more flexibility.

Full buy-out

In the past, full buy-out was associated with the wind-up of a pension scheme. Annuities would be purchased from an insurance company for current pensioners and deferred annuities for other members. It would represent part of what was often (and still can be) a protracted wind-up process.

The buy-out exercise itself can take a significant time, as historic issues, such as incomplete data and any inadequacies in past equalisation measures *(see Section 18)*, need to be resolved.

The liabilities are discharged from the scheme – the buy-out process results in individual annuities being purchased in members' names. This means of discharging liabilities has been associated with schemes of insolvent employers. However, solvent employers have used it to achieve a 'clean break' with their pension schemes.

Enhanced buy-out products have also been used since 2007, which expedite the full transfer of liability from the sponsoring employer. The insurer takes on additional liabilities, which may include wind-up costs, GMP equalisation and potential data changes. These are subject to an additional insurance premium. In some cases, the enhanced buy-out process has included a bulk transfer of the scheme's liabilities, or a replacement of the scheme sponsor, to aid the clean break from the original employer.

Partial buy-out

A partial buy-out allows for the discharge of some of the liabilities of a pension scheme. As with a full buy-out, annuity policies are purchased from an insurance company in the names of scheme members. They become policyholders of the insurer, ceasing to be members of the scheme. Again, this may prove to be a lengthy exercise during which issues such as incomplete data have to be resolved.

A partial buy-out may be difficult to achieve if the rules of a scheme do not give an adequate discharge of liabilities where the scheme is not winding up, and so a buy-in *(see below)* can be a more practical option.

Also, the trustees need to consider the security of all members' benefits. Buying out the liabilities of current pensioners (for example) will generally increase the security of those benefits. Trustees will need to ensure that this is not to the detriment of non-pensioners.

Buy-in

As an alternative to buy-outs, an increasing number of pension schemes have used 'buy-ins' to insure some of their liabilities. Typically, pensioner liabilities are insured as the cost relative to the value of the liabilities for scheme funding *(see Section 20)* tends to be much lower than for other members, and there are fewer operational implications.

The trustees purchase an insurance policy which is intended to match a specific part of the scheme's liabilities closely, but not necessarily exactly. For example, where there are issues with data quality or where discretionary pension increases may be given, the buy-in policy may not exactly match the scheme's liabilities.

Such transactions present fewer legal obstacles. The membership of the scheme is not affected – the individuals remain scheme members and the liability to pay their benefits remains with the scheme's trustees. The insurance policy can be regarded as an investment, which matches the corresponding liabilities more closely than alternative assets.

A buy-in may be used as a step towards full or partial buy-out at a later date.

Buy-in with additional security

Bulk annuity products are subject to the solvency and monitoring regime applicable to insurance companies, and are protected under the Financial Services Compensation Scheme *(see Section 29)*. Some larger buy-ins have included a bespoke layer of additional security, such as collateralisation, or the depositing of backing assets in a ring-fenced account which become accessible to the pension scheme in certain scenarios.

Non-insured buy-out

Alternative models have been structured that allow the transfer of pension liabilities and assets by corporate transaction, which may or may not be followed by full buy-out. For example, a company (perhaps the parent company of an insurer) may take on an organisation's pension liabilities by purchasing that organisation, retaining the pension scheme and selling on the majority of the purchased entity.

However, the Pensions Act 2008 increased the Regulator's power to appoint trustees, and to issue Contribution Notices and Financial Support Directions where there is a materially detrimental effect on the security of members' benefits *(see Section 12)*. The Government stated that the new powers were particularly aimed at non-insured buy-outs to ensure that members are protected in a changing environment without inhibiting innovation. This followed the high-profile case involving the Telent pension scheme. In November 2007, Pensions Corporation bought Telent, the sponsor of the scheme. The trustees of the scheme asked the Pensions Regulator to intervene, as it felt a clear conflict of interest had arisen which had not been managed appropriately – *see Section 11*.

This form of buy-out has not occurred subsequently, although some organisations have considered other means to transfer liabilities within the pensions (as opposed to insurance) regulatory environment, with a particular focus on their acceptability to trustees.

Synthetic buy-in

'Synthetic' or 'DIY' buy-ins can be constructed by the trustees or obtained as a bespoke product, arranged by an investment bank. These use a combination of swap contracts, including a longevity swap, to provide the same close liability matching that would be achieved with an insurance contract. This may be an attractive option for very large schemes in particular, given the substantial effort involved in constructing (and then maintaining) a portfolio of assets to closely match liabilities. *Section 23 provides further detail on this form of liability management.*

THE BUY-OUT MARKET

At the end of 2006, there were two main players in the UK pensions buy-out market, typically insuring the liabilities of schemes in wind-up or of very small schemes. This gave rise to around £1 billion of business written each year.

From 2007 to 2008, dramatic expansion in the market saw more than 30 companies offering a range of options designed to transfer pension risk. Since the downturn in markets in 2008, capital became more constrained and the growth in the market slowed. There has been some consolidation, and although activity has reduced the market has remained competitive for most types of transaction. The volume of business written has been volatile since 2007, with a perceivable trend of around £5–10 billion of business a year, which remains a small fraction of the liabilities in defined benefit schemes.

SALES, PURCHASES & CORPORATE ACTIVITY

The pension aspects of corporate sales and acquisitions require careful consideration, particularly where defined benefit schemes are involved. All parties will need to take expert legal and actuarial advice.

PRICING PENSIONS IN THE DEAL

The cost of pension provision will have a significant impact on the pricing of most deals.

Where manpower represents a material business cost and the deal is priced on the basis of future income, the purchaser should consider the future pension costs, which might be different from the equivalent costs for the vendor.

If the purchaser is taking on accrued defined benefit pension liabilities, for example by acquiring an entire pension scheme or accepting a 'bulk transfer' *(see below)*, actuarial advice will be required on the net cost to the purchaser. The net cost could be material and will need to be considered as part of pricing the offer.

The cost of any debt on the employer may also have to be allowed for *(see below)*.

ACQUISITION OF WHOLE SCHEME

If the company being acquired has its own pension scheme and this will be acquired as part of the deal, then the scheme liabilities and funding will need to be carefully examined. The current financial position on either the trustees' scheme funding valuation basis, or the accounting basis, is unlikely to be a suitable basis for pricing purposes.

The ongoing costs of benefits, and any possible changes in the trustees' funding or investment strategies as a result of the sale or of the subsequent restructuring, should be considered. These may have a substantial impact on the future profitability, and even perhaps viability, of the business.

BULK TRANSFER ARRANGEMENTS

If the transferring employees are members of the vendor's group scheme (and the scheme will be retained by the vendor), the employees may simply become deferred pensioners in the vendor's scheme but it is often desirable, in the interest of good employee relations, for a 'bulk transfer' to be arranged. The risks associated with such a transfer need to be compared against its benefits.

Under a bulk transfer, employees exchange their accrued benefits in the vendor's scheme for benefits in the purchaser's scheme and a transfer payment is made. The bulk transfer terms are a matter of commercial negotiation between the purchaser and the vendor. These will normally be set out in the 'pensions clause' of (or 'schedule' to) the legal agreement governing the transaction. This agreement may be accompanied by a side letter between the actuaries advising both parties, setting out the actuarial basis in detail. The amount transferred may not be equal to the value placed on the liabilities for pricing purposes and so there might also need to be a pricing adjustment.

As well as specifying the basis for calculating the amount of the bulk transfer payment, the pensions clause will usually also specify the terms for the benefits in the new scheme, the treatment of any excess or shortfall in the trustee transfer payment (*see* Trustee considerations, *below*), the communications, and the transfer process.

Trustee considerations

The commercially agreed bulk transfer terms will not normally be binding on the trustees of the vendor's scheme. The trustees will need to consider, having regard to their Trust Deed and Rules and the interests of *all* scheme members and beneficiaries, whether it is appropriate to pay a bulk transfer and, if so, the basis on which it should be calculated. If they decide that the payment should be calculated on a basis different to the commercial bulk transfer terms, then the shortfall or excess payment clause (if any) in the sale agreement may be triggered between the vendor and purchaser.

Similarly, the trustees of the purchaser's scheme are not obliged to accept the proposed bulk transfer payment or provide the commercially agreed level of benefits, and may seek additional funding from the purchaser before complying.

Member consent or actuarial certificate

For a bulk transfer to be paid from the vendor's scheme, *either* the transfer must be restricted to only those members who give their consent, *or* the trustees may decide that a transfer without consent is appropriate in which case they will need to obtain a certificate from their scheme actuary confirming that the past service benefits of each transferring member will be 'broadly no less favourable' after the transfer.

Where individual consents are sought, the trustees will need to ensure that members are provided with the information necessary to understand all of the options open to them and make an informed choice. Similarly, where a 'without-consent' transfer is anticipated, the members must be provided with appropriate information on the proposed transfer.

EMPLOYER COVENANT

The sale, or any subsequent transfer of assets, could have a material impact on the employer covenant provided to the scheme.

Whether or not a bulk transfer of pension assets and liabilities takes place, both the purchaser's and the vendor's scheme trustees will need to consider the impact on their employer's covenant and the subsequent impact on their scheme. They may request additional funding in mitigation and/or review the investment and funding strategies.

The impact on security can be complex and so the trustees may seek specialist covenant, legal and actuarial advice.

POTENTIAL 'DEBT ON EMPLOYER'

If the sale results in a participating employer ceasing to have any active members in the scheme, then a section 75 debt on the employer might be triggered. This might arise at the time of the sale, or at the end of a participation period, or on any subsequent restructuring. The debt can be significant and is calculated on a similar approach to that which applies on a wind-up (*see Section 25*).

The debt arises in respect of the benefits accrued whilst in service with the employer and covers both the current and the ex-employees. The debt also includes a proportion relating to any 'orphan' members. Orphan members are current or deferred pensioners with no currently participating employer. Depending on the previous corporate activity of the group, these orphan members can represent a high percentage of the total membership and therefore can substantially increase the debt for which a participating employer is liable.

The debt is payable by the participating employer involved and so can effectively fall to either the purchaser or the vendor depending on the terms of the deal. If the purchaser acquires one or more whole companies, then the debt would fall to the purchaser but the purchaser is likely to seek either a price reduction or an indemnity from the vendor. If business assets are being sold and a shell company is being retained by the vendor, and this shell ceases to have eligible active employees, then a debt effectively falls to the vendor.

There are a number of ways in which the level of a debt might be reduced. These include:

- a Scheme Apportionment Arrangement – the company and trustees can agree that some or all of the debt is reapportioned to other participating employers

- a Withdrawal Arrangement – the trustees can agree that the ceasing employer pays a lower amount, at least equal to its share of any deficit relative to technical provisions *(see Section 20)*, and that a contingent guarantor will stand behind the remaining debt

- an Approved Withdrawal Arrangement – this is similar to a Withdrawal Arrangement but Regulator approval is required and applies when the proposed immediate payment is less than the employer's share of the technical provisions deficit

- a Flexible Apportionment Arrangement – a new option expected to come into force from December 2011, allowing the company to agree with the trustees to apportion its whole pension liability to one or more other participating employers without triggering a section 75 debt, *or*

- transferring the accrued liabilities to the purchaser's scheme – this can reduce the debt, potentially down to nil, although the impact depends heavily on the terms of the transfer and the position of the vendor's scheme.

THE PENSIONS REGULATOR, MORAL HAZARD AND CLEARANCE

The 'notifiable events' framework requires the trustees of an underfunded scheme to notify the Regulator if a bulk or individual transfer payment exceeding £1.5 million (or, if lower, 5% of scheme assets) is made.

The Pensions Regulator can impact on a transaction, even if there are no notifiable events, through the 'moral hazard' provisions. These were introduced under the Pensions Act 2004 and extended in 2009. They are designed to prevent employers avoiding their obligations and give the Pensions Regulator sweeping powers, including the power to issue Contribution Notices, Financial Support Directions and Restoration Orders *(see also Section 12)*. For example, a Contribution Notice can be issued if the effect of an act, regardless of the employer's intent, is materially detrimental to the security of members' benefits. Contribution Notices may be issued in relation to a variety of events, including (but not limited to) sale or acquisition of a business, group restructuring and capital restructuring. A statutory defence prevents the Regulator acting in this way where the employer reasonably concluded that there was no material detriment and certain other conditions are met. The Regulator's powers are not limited to the current employer of the scheme.

A company or individual can avoid the risk of the Regulator later taking action by applying for clearance. Once given, clearance is binding on the Regulator unless the actual circumstances were different from those disclosed at the time.

The Regulator has issued guidance on clearance applications and this can be found at *www.thepensionsregulator.gov.uk*. The guidance includes:

- a pension scheme in deficit should be treated like any other material creditor
- the Regulator wishes to know about all events having a materially detrimental effect on a pension scheme's ability to meet liabilities, *and*
- trustees and employers should work together in relation to potentially detrimental events, communicating and sharing appropriate information.

TUPE

The TUPE requirements protect the terms and conditions relating to future benefits for employees who are transferred as part of a deal. (Accrued pension rights are also protected under preservation legislation.)

Transferring employees currently entitled to occupational scheme benefits have to be provided with pension benefits by the new employer. Where the new employer offers defined contribution benefits (including a stakeholder scheme) that employer must pay contributions that match the employee's contributions, up to a maximum of 6% of basic pay. If the new employer offers a defined benefit scheme, it must *either*:

- satisfy the Reference Scheme Test (whether or not it is contracted-out), *or*
- provide for members to be entitled to benefits of a value equal to, or more than, the sum of 6% of pensionable pay for each year of employment and the total amount of contributions paid by the member.

Transferring employees with rights to pension schemes established under contract (such as group personal pension or stakeholder arrangements) may also have their current pension rights preserved by TUPE, depending on the terms of their contracts.

In some circumstances, early retirement and redundancy terms and benefits in respect of accrued service may be preserved by TUPE requirements. Actuarial and legal advice should be taken on the issue and, in general, purchasers should seek appropriate indemnities against hidden liability.

PENSION COSTS IN COMPANY ACCOUNTS

Pension cost accounting in UK company accounts has been undergoing significant change over the last few years. International accounting standard IAS 19 has been mandatory for listed companies' consolidated group accounts since 2005. At the same time, the use of IAS 19, instead of UK standard FRS 17, became an option for individual company accounts and for the consolidated group accounts of unlisted companies. This section describes the requirements of both standards.

In June 2011, the IASB (the board responsible for international standards) published an amended IAS 19 which will apply from January 2013. The amendments, which are outlined below, include the removal of the option to defer the recognition of gains and losses. More changes will follow as the IASB and the FASB (the body responsible for US accounting standards) continue with linked projects to update and align their standards.

ACCOUNTING FOR PENSION COSTS UNDER FRS 17

Coverage

FRS 17 covers companies registered in the UK or in the Republic of Ireland, and their subsidiaries. It covers all retirement benefits (including medical care during retirement) which the employer is committed to providing, wherever they arise world-wide. Reporting entities applying the Financial Reporting Standard for Smaller Entities (FRSSE) are exempt from FRS 17, although FRSSE itself imposes requirements that are essentially a simplified version of FRS 17.

The UK Accounting Standards Board (ASB) has proposed that, with effect from 1 January 2014, entities that currently report under full UK FRS will move to reporting under the Financial Reporting Standard for Medium Sized Entities (FRSME) – unless they elect instead for full International Financial Reporting Standards (IFRS): including IAS 19 for pension arrangements. FRSME includes a slimmed-down version of IAS 19, although not as simplified as the requirements for pensions in FRSSE.

Application to Multi-employer Schemes

Where a number of companies participate in a multi-employer DB scheme, individual companies may not be able to identify 'their' assets and liabilities, or may be obliged only to contribute for benefits currently being earned. In such cases, the individual companies should account for the scheme on a cash basis (cost equals contributions paid), as in DC schemes, but must make appropriate disclosures. However, for the purposes of group accounts, multi-employer schemes are accounted for on a DB basis.

A: DEFINED CONTRIBUTION SCHEMES

Summary

For DC schemes, the charge against profits must be the amount of contributions due in respect of the accounting period.

A DC scheme is defined as one 'into which an employer pays regular contributions fixed as an amount or as a percentage of pay' without a 'legal or constructive obligation to pay further contributions if the scheme does not have sufficient assets to pay all employee benefits relating to employee service in the current and prior periods'. A scheme may be taken to be a DC scheme for the purposes of this definition, even where salary-related death-in-service benefits are provided.

Disclosure

The following disclosures should be made:

- the nature of the scheme (i.e. defined contribution; funded or unfunded)
- the pension cost charge for the period, *and*
- any outstanding or prepaid contributions at the balance sheet date.

B: DEFINED BENEFIT SCHEMES

Overview

A DB scheme is defined as a 'pension or other retirement benefit scheme other than a defined contribution scheme'. Financial statements should reflect pension assets and liabilities, measured at fair values. Retirement benefit-related operating costs, financing costs and any other changes in value of assets and scheme liabilities should be recognised in the period in which the benefit is earned or in which they arise, with no smoothing or spreading.

Benefits to Value

Benefits promised under the formal terms of the scheme must be valued. Benefits should be attributed to periods of service according to the scheme's benefit formula, except that uniform accrual should be assumed where the benefit formula is rear-end loaded.

Discretionary benefits are to be included only where the employer has a constructive obligation to provide them. Favourable early retirement terms should be reflected where there is an established practice of allowing retirement at the employee's request on these terms. No allowance should be made for future retirements at the employer's initiative.

Actuarial Assumptions and Methodology

Full actuarial valuations by a professionally qualified actuary are needed at least every three years; they should be updated to each intervening balance sheet date.

Pension scheme assets must be measured at fair value (bid price for quoted securities).

Scheme liabilities are measured using the projected unit method, which reflects the benefits the employer is committed to provide for service up to the valuation date and, where applicable, allows for projected increases to those benefits in line with pensionable earnings after the valuation date.

The expected costs of death-in-service or incapacity benefits should be charged on an insurance cost basis, to the extent they are insured. Any such benefits that are uninsured are to be charged on a projected unit method that reflects the proportion of the full benefits ultimately payable attributable to the accounting period.

The actuarial assumptions for projecting future outgoings in respect of the scheme liabilities are ultimately the responsibility of the directors (or equivalent), but should be set upon advice given by an actuary and must reflect market expectations at the valuation date, for consistency with the asset value. They should be mutually compatible and should lead to the best estimate of the future cashflows that will arise under the scheme liabilities. The projected outgoings must then be discounted. The discount rate to be used is the redemption yield at the valuation date on AA (or equivalent) rated corporate bonds of equivalent term and currency to the scheme liabilities.

Balance Sheet

Any surplus at the balance sheet date of assets over scheme liabilities calculated as above should be recognised in the balance sheet but is limited to the amount that the employer can recover through reduced employer's contributions in future and refunds which have already been agreed by the trustees at the balance sheet date.

A deficit (on the FRS basis) should be recognised as a liability to the extent of the employer's legal or constructive obligation to fund it. If the scheme rules require members' contributions to be increased to help fund a deficit, the liability should be reduced appropriately.

The net pension asset/liability shown in the balance sheet may differ from the above, due to deferred tax.

Pension Cost

The full cost of benefits, including actuarial gains and losses, is recognised in the performance statements in the accounting period in which the cost arises. The Profit and Loss account is protected from excessive volatility by the recognition of actuarial gains and losses in the Statement of Total Recognised Gains and Losses (STRGL) and the facility to vary the expected return on assets.

The different components making up the pension cost are shown in the table *on the next page*, along with definitions, details of where they should be recognised in the performance statements, and brief comments.

FRS 17: SUMMARY OF CALCULATION OF PENSION COST

Component	Where recognised	Description and Notes
Current service cost	Staff cost section of operating cost in P&L[1]	The increase in the scheme liabilities expected to arise from employees' service in the accounting period, calculated using financial assumptions based on conditions at the beginning of the period. Includes insurance cost, for the accounting period, of insured death-in-service and incapacity benefits, and a charge calculated using a projected unit method for their uninsured counterparts. Expected employees' contributions are offset from the gross cost.
+ Interest cost	Financing section of P&L	Expected increase during the period in the present value of the scheme liabilities because the benefits are one period closer to settlement.
− Expected return on assets	Combined with interest cost (above) to give a net entry in financing section of P&L	Based on actual assets held by the scheme at the beginning of the accounting period and the expected rate of return on those assets as follows: – for bonds, current redemption yields at start of period – for equities and other assets, the rate of total return expected over the long term at start of period in either case averaged over the remaining term of the related liabilities and net of scheme expenses. Appropriate allowance should be made for expected cashflows into and out of the fund during the year. May be restricted if there is an irrecoverable surplus.
+ Actuarial loss (gain)	STRGL[2]	Changes in actuarial surpluses or deficits that arise because events have not coincided with the actuarial assumptions made for the last valuation or because the actuarial assumptions have changed. An adjustment may be required where there is an irrecoverable surplus.
+ Past service cost, offset by surplus otherwise treated as irrecoverable	Staff cost section of operating cost in P&L	A past service cost (PSC) is any increase in the scheme liabilities related to employees' service in prior periods, arising in the current period as a result of the introduction of, or improvement to, retirement benefits. PSCs are required to be recognised on a straight-line basis over the period in which the additional benefits vest. Where these vest immediately, the PSC should be recognised immediately.
+ Loss (gain) on settlement/ curtailment, offset by surplus otherwise treated as irrecoverable	Staff cost section of operating cost in P&L, unless it attaches to an exceptional item immediately after operating profit in the P&L	Settlement occurs where the responsibility for, and risk attaching to, a pension obligation is irrevocably transferred to another party, e.g. by buying matching annuities or by paying a bulk transfer value. Curtailment is where defined benefit liabilities cease to accrue or current members' future service benefits are reduced, e.g. on termination of a final salary scheme and replacing it with a money purchase scheme, or due to a redundancy exercise. Losses or gains arising as a result of settlements and curtailments instigated by the employer and falling outside the scope of the actuarial assumptions are included in this component of pension cost.

Notes: [1] Profit and loss account. [2] Statement of Total Recognised Gains and Losses.
Where the surplus recognised in the balance sheet has to be restricted (as described under the heading 'Balance Sheet'), FRS 17 sets out details of

Disclosure

FRS 17's disclosure requirements have been replaced with those of IAS 19. The following disclosures are mandatory:

- a general description of the type of scheme (for example, flat-rate or final salary pension scheme, or retirement healthcare plan)
- a reconciliation of the scheme assets and liabilities to the net asset or liability recognised in the balance sheet, showing at least:
  - the present value of scheme liabilities that are wholly unfunded
  - the present value (before deducting the fair value of the scheme assets) of scheme liabilities that are wholly or partly funded
  - the fair value of any scheme assets
  - the past service cost not yet recognised in the balance sheet
  - any amounts which would, apart from the limits laid down by FRS 17, be recognised as an asset, *and*
  - the other amounts recognised in the balance sheet
- any self-investment included in the fair value of scheme assets
- reconciliations showing the movements over the period of the scheme assets and liabilities
- the total expense recognised in the profit and loss account for each of the following:
  - current service cost
  - interest cost
  - expected return on scheme assets
  - past service cost
  - any curtailment or settlement costs, *and*
  - the effect of any limit on the balance sheet asset (where recognised through the profit and loss account)
- the actual return on scheme assets
- the principal actuarial assumptions
- the amount recognised in the Statement of Total Recognised Gains and Losses, separately showing actuarial gains and losses and the effect of any limit on the balance sheet asset (where recognised outside the profit and loss account)
- cumulative gains and losses recognised outside the profit and loss account
- assets, showing the amount or percentage in each major asset category
- explanation of how expected return is derived, referring to the impact of each major asset category, but no requirement to disclose expected returns separately for each category
- five-year history of asset value, liabilities, surplus/deficit and experience gains and losses (there is no requirement to construct these retrospectively)
- expected contributions over the coming year, *and*
- explanation of any constructive obligations (e.g. to provide regular pension increases).

Where several DB schemes are involved, disclosure can be combined in the way felt to be most useful.

A Reporting Statement applies to UK companies using either FRS 17 or IAS 19, and recommends additional best practice disclosures. These are not mandatory but are intended to give a clear view of the risks and rewards arising from schemes, and are complementary to the disclosures required under those standards.

The recommended disclosures include:

- information on the relationship between the company and the scheme trustees/managers, including how the investment strategy and funding principles are determined, and any significant and unusual trustee powers
- information on and sensitivity analysis for each of the principal assumptions, including mortality
- the buy-out cost of the liabilities, if available
- information on contributions agreed with the trustees, *and*
- other information that will enable the user to evaluate risks and rewards, including on the expected rate of return of each of the major asset classes.

ACCOUNTING FOR PENSION COSTS UNDER IAS 19

Requirement to Use International Standards

Companies governed by the law of an EU Member State, whose securities are admitted to trading on a regulated market in any EU Member State, are generally required to prepare their consolidated accounts in compliance with International Accounting Standards. For the UK, this covers companies listed on AIM (Alternative Investment Market) as well as those with a full London Stock Exchange (LSE) listing.

In December 2007, the US Securities and Exchange Commission (SEC) ruled that non-US companies reporting under International Financial Reporting Standards (IFRS) would no longer have to reconcile to US accounting standards in order to obtain a listing in the USA. The SEC is continuing deliberations on whether US companies will be required to transition to IFRS – US companies would report under IFRS no earlier than 2015.

Coverage

IAS 19 covers four categories of employee benefits, with separate requirements for each:

- short-term employee benefits, such as salaries and social security contributions
- post-employment benefits, such as pensions and post-employment medical care
- other long-term employee benefits, including long-service leave *and*
- termination benefits.

Equity compensation benefits, including share options, which were previously covered by IAS 19, are now covered by IFRS 2.

Application to Multi-employer Schemes

Under IAS 19, only plans which are operated by companies which *are not under common control* are 'multi-employer' plans. If participants in a DB multi-employer plan are unable to identify separately the assets and liabilities, they can account for the plan on a cash contribution basis.

Where a DB plan is operated by a group of companies which *are under common control*, the principal sponsoring employer is required to account for the plan on a DB basis and other participating employers are allowed to use a cash contribution basis, unless there is a contractual agreement on the sharing of future pension costs, in which case each company should recognise its share of the DB cost.

A. DEFINED CONTRIBUTION SCHEMES

Overview

The treatment of DC schemes under IAS 19 is essentially the same as under FRS 17. The only disclosure required by IAS 19 is the amount of expense recognised for the period.

B. DEFINED BENEFIT SCHEMES

Overview

The most significant difference from FRS 17 is in the choice of methods that IAS 19 allows companies to use to recognise actuarial gains and losses *(see Pension Cost, below)*. There are other small differences in approach and in the information which has to be disclosed.

Benefits to Value

The benefits to be valued under IAS 19 are basically the same as those required to be valued under FRS 17, although IAS 19 is not specific about what allowance should be made for future early retirements.

Actuarial Assumptions and Methodology

IAS 19 requires assets and liabilities to be valued regularly enough that the amounts recognised in the accounts are not materially different from the amounts that would be determined from an up-to-date valuation. The involvement of a qualified actuary is encouraged but not required.

Assets must be measured at fair value. Auditors may require fair value to be taken as bid value rather than mid-market. Liabilities are measured using the projected unit method.

IAS 19 is silent on the treatment of risk benefits. We understand that most auditors expect the 'attribution method' to be used. For benefits that are not service-related, this method allocates benefits in proportion to the ratio of completed years of service to either the vesting period or, if the benefit is unvested, total projected years of service.

The actuarial assumptions are the responsibility of the directors and must be unbiased and mutually compatible, being best estimates of the variables determining the ultimate cost of the benefits. The discount rate to be used should be determined by reference to market yields at the valuation date on high quality corporate bonds of consistent term and currency. The market yields on government bonds should be used if there is no deep market in corporate bonds.

Balance Sheet

The amount recognised in the balance sheet should be calculated as:

> The present value of the DB obligation
> + Actuarial gains (or minus any losses) not yet recognised in pension cost
> − Any outstanding past service costs not yet recognised in pension cost
> − The fair value of scheme assets.

If the result is an asset, then it should be limited to the present value of:

> The available future refunds of surplus
> + The available reduction in future contributions
> + Any outstanding actuarial losses or past service costs not yet recognised in pension cost.

IFRIC 14, published by the Interpretation Committee of the IASB, addresses the impact of minimum funding requirements, the limit on an asset for a DB scheme and the interaction of these. IFRIC 14 explains that a refund or a reduction in future contributions may be considered available even if it cannot be realised at the balance sheet date. The company must have a right to any refund, without recourse to the trustees. The available reduction in future contributions must be restricted to allow for any contributions payable under any 'minimum funding requirement' that may apply. The balance sheet asset or liability must also be adjusted to reflect any irrecoverable surplus (on the accounting basis) that will be created in future by the payment of minimum contributions in respect of a past service deficit on the minimum funding basis.

Pension Cost

With the exception of actuarial gains and losses, the components of pension cost are calculated in essentially the same way as under FRS 17.

The original IAS 19 required that unrecognised actuarial gains and losses only have to be included as components of pension cost if, at the beginning of the year, they fall outside a 'corridor' equal to 10% of the greater of the present value of the DB obligation and the fair value of scheme assets. The excess outside this corridor can then be amortised over the employees' average remaining service period (or in a more stringent way if applied consistently and systematically from year to year). However, where a curtailment or settlement occurs, any associated unrecognised gains or losses will need to be recognised immediately.

On initial implementation, companies will normally recognise any opening surplus or deficit immediately, and thereafter recognise gains and losses using the 10% corridor and amortisation. Alternatively, a company can avoid the immediate recognition of the opening surplus or deficit by reconstructing IAS 19-style figures as if IAS 19 had existed since the beginning of the scheme.

Under an optional alternative approach, gains and losses are recognised in full immediately, but through a secondary performance statement called the

Statement of Recognised Income and Expense (SORIE) and not through the profit and loss account. This approach is analogous to the recognition of gains and losses through the Statement of Recognised Gains and Losses (STRGL) under FRS 17. The SORIE has now been renamed Other Comprehensive Income (OCI).

Disclosure

The disclosure requirements are the same as FRS 17 *(see page 177)* except that, to cater for the alternative approaches to recognition of gains and losses under IAS 19, the company must also disclose:

- the accounting policy for recognising gains and losses, *and*
- the amount of gains or losses in the breakdown of the expense recognised in the income statement (where relevant, i.e. where gains and losses are amortised through the income statement).

Forthcoming changes

A revised IAS 19 was issued in June 2011 and will be mandatory for reporting years ending on or after 1 January 2013. The main changes are to:

- remove the 'corridor' approach for the recognition of actuarial gains and losses – all gains and losses would be recognised immediately in OCI
- remove interest cost and expected return on plan assets, replacing them with net interest income (or expense) calculated as the discount rate applied to the net balance sheet position – this will effectively require the *expected return on assets* component of pension cost to be calculated using the discount rate instead of an expected return based on plan assets
- require administration expenses (except investment expenses) to be recognised in the profit and loss account in the year in which they occur. Investment expenses will be offset from actual investment returns and therefore from investment gains recognised in OCI
- require additional disclosures of how the entity's participation in DB plans affects the amount, timing and variability of its future cashflows, including sensitivity analysis for each significant actuarial assumption to which the entity is exposed, *and*
- treat 'other long-term employee benefits' in the same way as post-employment benefits.

RELATED PARTY DISCLOSURES (IAS 24)

Companies complying with IAS 19 also have to provide disclosure figures under IAS 24 – *Related Party Disclosures*. This Standard requires information to be disclosed for key management personnel (in aggregate) for each of the following categories:

- short-term employee benefits
- post-employment benefits
- other long-term benefits
- termination benefits *and*
- share-based payment.

IAS 24 defines key management personnel as persons having authority and responsibility for planning, directing and controlling the activities of the entity, directly or indirectly. This includes (but is not limited to) directors.

For each category, only a single figure is required. For some benefits this one figure is easy to access (for example, actual contributions paid to a DC plan). Our understanding is that, in the case of DB plans and other long-term benefit plans, the IAS 19 service cost for each relevant individual should be used rather than a proportion of the whole profit and loss charge.

DISCLOSURE OF DIRECTORS' PENSIONS

Listed company accounts are subject to disclosure requirements in relation to directors' pensions imposed by the FSA's Listing Rules in addition to those generally applicable under regulations made under the Companies Act 2006. The legislative and FSA requirements apply in addition to the requirements of IAS 24 – *Related Party Disclosures* where applicable. A summary of the legislative disclosure requirements relating to directors' pensions is given below, together with a note of the additional FSA requirements (where these differ significantly).

Unquoted company disclosures

Unquoted companies are required to make the following disclosures in the notes to their accounts:

- the aggregate value of company contributions paid or treated as paid to a pension scheme to provide money purchase benefits in respect of directors' service
- the number of directors accruing retirement benefits under money purchase schemes and the number accruing benefits under DB schemes
- except where, broadly, aggregate directors' pay and other specified emoluments fall below a specified threshold, the following must be disclosed in respect of the highest-paid director: company contributions in respect of money purchase benefits, and accrued DB pension and lump sum (both excluding benefits from AVCs) at year-end, *and*
- the aggregate amount by which directors' retirement benefits in payment exceeded the amount they were entitled to at 31 March 1997, or the date the benefits became payable, if later. This does not apply if the benefits were sufficiently funded without recourse to additional contributions and benefits were paid to all pensioner members of the scheme on the same basis.

Quoted company disclosures

For each financial year, the directors of a quoted company must produce a directors' remuneration report which must include the following pension disclosures in relation to each person who has served as a director of the company at any time during that financial year:

Money purchase schemes only
Details of company contributions paid or payable for the relevant financial year or paid in that year for another financial year.

Defined benefit schemes only

(a) Changes during the relevant financial year in accrued benefits under the scheme.

(b) Accrued benefits under the scheme as at the year-end.

(c) Transfer value of accrued rights at year-end.

(d) Transfer value of accrued rights at previous year-end.

(e) Increase in transfer value over the year [i.e. (c) – (d)] less contributions made by the director during the year.

The Companies Act 2006 regulations require transfer values to be calculated in accordance with transfer value regulations (*see Section 16*). However, the FSA's Listing Rules require calculation in accordance with actuarial guidance note GN11, even though the note is no longer effective.

To meet the FSA's requirements, the following details must also be included:

(f) The amount of the increase in accrued benefit during the year (excluding inflation), and either:

(i) the transfer value (less director's contributions) of the increase in accrued benefit net of inflation; *or*

(ii) so much of the following information as is necessary to make a reasonable assessment of the transfer value in respect of each director:

- current age
- normal retirement age
- the amount of any contributions paid or payable by the director during the period
- details of spouse's and dependants' benefits
- early retirement rights and options, expectations of pension increases after retirement (whether guaranteed or discretionary), *and*
- discretionary benefits for which allowance is made in transfer values, and any other relevant information which will significantly affect the value of the benefits.

Money purchase and defined benefit schemes

In respect of each former or current director of the company as at the year-end, the amount by which retirement benefits paid exceeded those to which the person was entitled on the later of the date the benefits first became payable and 31 March 1997. This does not apply if the benefits are sufficiently funded without recourse to additional contributions and benefits were paid to all pensioner members of the scheme on the same basis.

In addition to the disclosures required in the directors' remuneration report, the Regulations also require quoted companies to include in the notes to their accounts the disclosures *in the first two bullet points of the* 'Unquoted Company disclosures' *section above*, unless the information is capable of being readily ascertained from other information shown.

FINANCIAL SERVICES LEGISLATION AND PENSION SCHEMES

The Financial Services and Markets Act 2000 (FSMA) is the principal legislation for the regulation of the financial services market. It specifies that regulated activities, such as dealing in investments, managing investments, arranging deals in investments, offering investment advice, taking custody of investments and establishing collective investment schemes and certain pension schemes, may only be carried out as a business in the UK by persons who are either authorised or exempt. Authorisation is granted by the Financial Services Authority (FSA), which is the sole regulator of the UK financial services market, although the Pensions Regulator also has a regulatory role in respect of workplace contract-based pension arrangements.

Professional firms may be licensed by 'Designated Professional Bodies' such as the Institute of Actuaries, to carry out a limited range of 'exempt' regulated activities that are incidental to their main business without FSA authorisation. Authorised firms that are managed and controlled by suitably qualified professionals and fall within the FSA's definition of 'Authorised Professional Firms' may also be able to avail themselves of corresponding exemptions when carrying out similar non-mainstream regulated activities.

Implications for pension schemes

Pension scheme trustees and administrators are clearly concerned with investments in various ways. They may be:

- responsible for the management of the scheme's assets (whether in insurance policies or directly invested)
- involved in giving advice to scheme members and prospective members *and/or*
- involved in arranging investments for individual members, such as additional voluntary contributions and insurance company buy-outs.

Each of the above can be a 'regulated activity' requiring authorisation by the FSA, for which stringent requirements must be met, unless covered by an exemption. Establishing whether authorisation is required for a particular action can be complicated, particularly when considering relationships between trustees and individual members. The FSA has issued formal 'perimeter guidance' setting out the circumstances in which authorisation is or is not required.

Definition of investments

Under the FSMA, the definition of investments includes cash deposits (and also mortgages and general insurance contracts), shares, debentures, Government and public securities, options and futures, units in unit trust schemes and long-term insurance contracts. However, the provisions relating to managing, dealing in and advising on investments do not apply to cash deposits. Property is excluded.

Generally, a scheme member's interests under the trusts of an occupational pension scheme are not classed as investments. However, rights under a stakeholder scheme are specifically included (even if it is an occupational scheme), as are rights under a personal pension scheme (including a Self-Invested Personal Pension).

Management of investments

The FSMA specifically provides that those engaged in the activity of managing the assets of occupational pension schemes must be authorised or exempt, even if (as is the case with many trustees) they would not normally be regarded as doing so as a business. However, the Act goes on to provide that authorisation will not be required if all day-to-day decisions about the management of investments are taken on their behalf by a person who is himself authorised or exempt. Trustees are also permitted to make 'day-to-day' decisions on pooled investment products and insurance contracts, provided that they have first obtained and considered advice from an appropriate authorised person.

The Pensions Act 1995 also imposes a requirement on pension schemes for trustees to appoint a competent and experienced fund manager who has the necessary authorisation or exemption. It identifies certain matters on which trustees are required to obtain investment advice and also sets out a requirement for a written statement of investment principles to govern the investment of the scheme's assets.

The Myners principles, guidance from the Investment Governance Group and the FRC Stewardship Code set out best practice for pension scheme (and wider institutional) investment activity *(see Section 11 for further details)*. These remain voluntary, although the Government has suggested that legislation will be introduced if pension schemes do not comply with the Myners principles.

Communication with members

To reflect the requirements of the EU Distance Marketing Directive, UK legislation prevents an employee from being included in a scheme regulated by the FSA without a 'prior request'. This means that any information given to employees offering membership of a stakeholder or group personal pension arrangement will need to include a reply slip, unless consent is obtained and recorded by some other means.

However, this is expected to be amended from 2012 to allow employers to auto-enrol employees into workplace pension arrangements, including group personal pension and stakeholder schemes, as an alternative to the NEST scheme *(see Sections 9 and 10)*. Although these are regulated, contract-based schemes, the Government has received confirmation from the European Commission that this is allowed under EU law.

The FSMA also places restrictions on financial promotion, prohibiting the communication of any 'invitation or inducement to engage in investment activity', unless it is issued or approved by an authorised person. There are certain exemptions set out in secondary legislation, covering some (but not all) communications involving trustees, beneficiaries and trust settlors (generally, employers in a pension scheme context), but these are generally relevant only to occupational schemes. However, employers offering stakeholder or group personal pension arrangements to their employees can avoid the restrictions, provided certain conditions are met. These include requirements that the employer must contribute and must not receive any direct financial benefit. This exemption also applies to promotions by third-party administrators on behalf of such employers.

Ahead of auto-enrolment in 2012, the Pensions Regulator and the FSA have produced a joint guide for employers, to help build their confidence in talking to employees about pensions without breaching the rules on financial advice.

Other responsibilities of the Financial Services Authority

The FSA is the single statutory regulator under the FSMA. As part of its overall responsibility to regulate and authorise all financial businesses, unit trusts and open-ended investment companies (OEICs), and to recognise and supervise investment exchanges and clearing houses, the FSA regulates the marketing and promotion of all personal pension and stakeholder pension schemes, the authorisation of such schemes' managers, and the activities of pension scheme investment managers.

Role of the Pensions Regulator

The regulation of workplace contract-based pension schemes (such as stakeholder arrangements) is shared between the Pensions Regulator and the FSA. The two parties have produced joint guidance explaining their respective roles.

The Pensions Regulator's role includes dealing with late payment of contributions and other breaches of legislation, promoting good administration, and providing information and education. As part of this, the Regulator has published guidance on voluntary employer engagement in workplace contract-based pension schemes to support employers, as well as guidance on wider areas of good governance for defined contribution schemes. *(See Section 11 for details of the Regulator's guidance and Section 12 for more information on the Regulator itself.)*

The Financial Services Compensation Scheme (FSCS)

The FSCS is a safety net for customers of financial services firms, dealing with all financial-services-related claims. It was created under the FSMA and became operational on 1 December 2001.

The FSCS was set up to pay compensation where an FSA-authorised firm is unable, or unlikely to be able, to pay claims against it. This is generally when a firm is insolvent or has gone out of business. It covers deposit-related claims, insurance- and investment-related claims and claims related to mortgage advice and arranging.

The FSCS can also be called upon by the Government to contribute to the costs associated with the exercise of a 'stabilisation power', for example, where it intervenes to ensure the continued existence of a bank or building society, or to make payments on behalf of another compensation scheme.

Reforms to financial regulation

In response to the recent financial crisis, the coalition Government has proposed reforms to the regulation of the financial sector. They believe that the current 'tripartite' regulatory system – with the Bank of England, the FSA and the Treasury collectively responsible for financial stability – failed in a number of ways. They intend to replace the FSA, establishing a new regulatory system under which:

- a new Financial Policy Committee in the Bank of England would have primary responsibility for monitoring and responding to systemic risks
- operational responsibility for prudential regulation would be transferred from the FSA to a new subsidiary of the Bank of England, the Prudential Regulation Authority, *and*
- a new Financial Conduct Authority would regulate business to ensure conduct across financial services and markets is in the interests of all users and participants.

In June 2011 the Government published a White Paper and draft legislation, which is expected to come into force in 2013.

4 Nov 10	The Investment Governance Group published a set of six principles for Investment Governance for work-based DC schemes, outlining best practice.
10 Nov 10	The Pensions Regulator issued a statement on employer-related investments, setting out its expectations of trustees, employers and advisers.
11 Nov 10	The Government published a White Paper setting out plans for a 'Universal Credit', to replace most means-tested benefits and tax credits from 2013.
23 Nov 10	The Pensions Regulator issued updated guidance on employer departures from multi-employer DB schemes.
30 Nov 10	The Pensions Regulator published guidance on assessing, monitoring and taking action on employer covenant.
1 Dec 10	Electronic communication can be adopted as the default method of disclosing information to members.
9 Dec 10	The Pensions Regulator published revised guidance on incentive exercises.
1 Jan 11	Statutory revaluations on deferred pensions (and increases to pensions in payment if they rely on statutory provisions) linked to CPI instead of RPI.
1 Mar 11	In the *Test-Achats* case, the ECJ ruled that gender-based pricing of insurance will be illegal from 21 December 2012. This may require pension scheme trustees to review gender-based actuarial factors.
10 Mar 11	Lord Hutton published his final Independent Public Service Pensions Commission report. This recommended a new CARE scheme, with Normal Pension Age linked to State Pension Age for most public service schemes.
23 Mar 11	Chancellor George Osborne presented the 2011 Budget, including: • confirmation of plans to restrict tax relief from 6 April 2011 • acceptance of Lord Hutton's recommendations on public service pensions 'as a basis for consultation', *and* • confirmation of plans for a single, contributory, flat-rate state pension.
31 Mar 11	Regulations provide for increases to Pension Protection Fund and Financial Assistance Scheme benefits to be linked to CPI not RPI.
6 Apr 11	The Annual Allowance reduced to £50,000. The new 'scheme pays' provisions allow significant tax charges to be paid by schemes on the members' behalf from 11 August.

6 Apr 11	The requirement to annuitise DC pension funds, or commence income drawdown, before age 75 was removed. 'Flexible drawdown' introduced. Age 75 ceiling also removed from most lump sum benefits.
6 Apr 11	Increases in the Basic State Pension linked to earnings. Under a separate commitment from the Coalition Government, annual increases are also no lower than 2.5%, CPI and (in 2011 only) RPI.
6 Apr 11	Pension Protection Fund compensation became shareable on divorce.
16 May 11	The Pension Protection Fund published its final policy proposals for a new levy framework. From 2012/13 onwards, the levy formula will be fixed for three years, except in certain 'extreme' circumstances, and individual schemes' investment strategies will be allowed for via a prescribed 'stress test'.
24 May 11	The Department for Work and Pensions issued guidance to set out standards for default options in automatic enrolment DC pension schemes.
16 Jun 11	Amended IAS 19 is published, coming into force for financial years starting from 1 January 2013. Changes include the immediate recognition of all gains and losses in Other Comprehensive Income (OCI) and the replacement of interest cost and expected return on plan assets by a net interest income/(expense) item.
1 Jul 11	The Bribery Act came into force. Pension scheme trustees are exposed to some of the offences under the Act.
19 Jul 11	The Finance Act 2011 received Royal Assent, making significant changes to pensions taxation, backdated to 6 April 2011 *(see above)*, and further changes from 6 April 2012.
28 Jul 11	The Pensions Regulator published a statement to help trustees understand the importance of identifying their scheme's statutory employer and how they should do this.
1 Oct 11	The Default Retirement Age of 65 was abolished. Employers can operate a compulsory retirement age only if they can objectively justify it.
13 Oct 11	The Pensions Regulator published a statement for trustees to clarify the key differences between DB and DC schemes, and the behaviours that DC trustees should demonstrate.
25 Oct 11	The Pensions Regulator published a statement to help trustees and their advisers understand the structure of their 'hybrid' scheme.

3 Nov 11   The Pensions Act 2011 received Royal Assent. Significant changes included:

- bringing forward, to October 2020, the equalisation of the State Pension Age at 66

- some changes to help private sector schemes with RPI-based rules comply with CPI-based statutory indexation and revaluation provisions

- implementing the main recommendations of the review (published in October 2010) of auto-enrolment, *and*

- amending the definition of money purchase benefits so that these cannot generate a surplus or deficit.

28 Nov 11   The Government announced that automatic enrolment obligations will be delayed for employers with fewer than 50 employees, with details to be confirmed.

29 Nov 11   In its Autumn Statement, the Government stated that it is planning to raise the state pension age to 67 between April 2026 and April 2028.

EMERGING DEVELOPMENTS

STATE BENEFITS AND CONTRACTING OUT

The Pensions Act 2008 made the following changes to state pensions and contracting out:

- the calculation of state additional pension (SERPS and S2P) for individuals who have been contracted out and attain State Pension Age from 2020 onwards will be amended, *and*

- the abolition of all elements of protected rights at the same time as money purchase contracting out is abolished *(see below)*. Schemes will no longer be required to make special provision in relation to the protected rights of members.

Following a consultation in 2010, legislation has now been passed putting into effect the abolition of money purchase contracting out with effect from 6 April 2012 and the amendment of the 'contracted-out deduction' to survivors' SERPS benefits.

In addition, the DWP has issued draft legislation that is intended to help trustees to remove protected rights restrictions that are in their scheme rules.

HMRC is making available guidance on operational issues in a new series of bi-monthly Newsletters entitled 'countdown bulletins'.

For schemes contracted out on a DB basis, the DWP has issued draft legislation that would increase the fixed revaluation rate for GMPs from 4% to 4.75% for leavers after 5 April 2012. The DWP has also published the contracted-out rebate rates that will apply for DB schemes from April 2012 to April 2017.

In June 2010, the Coalition Government announced a review of the timing of the increase in State Pension Age to 66. Following amendment during its passage through Parliament, the Pensions Act 2011 provides that the State Pension Age will increase to 66 by October 2020, for both males and females.

In April, the DWP issued a Green Paper on:

- proposals for simplifying the state pension system to move to a flat-rate state pension

- whether the current system of means-tested state pension credits should be reformed, *and*

- the determination of the state pension age in future.

The two options for moving to a flat-rate state pension were accelerating the current arrangements for moving to a flat-rate S2P or a more radical move to a single, flat-rate benefit. The latter option would result in the end of contracting-out.

In July 2011, the DWP published a summary of the responses it had received. This does not include any Government proposals but does state that there was broad support for the single tier option for simplifying the state pension.

It also states that there was a high level of support for a mechanism to manage future increases in the State Pension Age, and that the majority of respondents considered that a periodic review would be valuable.

In November 2011 the Government stated that it is planning to raise the state pension age to 67 between April 2026 and April 2028, eight years earlier than the timescale currently set in legislation.

UNIVERSAL CREDIT

In February 2011 the Government launched the Welfare Reform Bill, which introduces the Universal Credit. This is expected to be phased in between 2013 and 2017, and will replace most means-tested benefits and tax credits for people of working age. Other, non-means-tested, benefits would remain in place.

At present some means-tested benefits are reduced pound-for-pound with increases in earnings. Under the new system it is expected that a withdrawal rate of 65% would be sufficient incentive to work for those earning below the personal tax threshold, and around 76% for basic rate taxpayers. In addition, there would be a system of disregards to enable some groups to earn varying amounts according to circumstances before the taper starts to apply. This would include half the contributions to an occupational or personal pension (as now under Income Support). Therefore, once the 2012 auto-enrolment pension reforms are fully in place *(see Section 9)*, assuming a 65% taper, each £1 that goes into the pension pot of an employee who is a basic rate taxpayer and in receipt of Universal Credit will only reduce take-home income by 34 pence after minimum employer contributions, tax relief and increased Universal Credit payment are taken into account.

EC GREEN PAPER ON PENSIONS

In July 2010, the European Commission published a Green Paper on pensions, aiming to move towards adequate, sustainable and safe European pension systems. It suggests, for discussion, the imposition of the Solvency II Life Insurance Directive principles for reserves of DB occupational pension plans. This could introduce reserving requirements considerably in excess of technical provisions under the Pensions Act 2004 scheme funding regime *(see Section 20)*. In November 2010 the Government issued its response. While the Government felt that Solvency II may offer some useful principles in the areas around governance and disclosure, it is resisting the suggestion that the capital adequacy elements be applied to pension schemes. This is on the grounds that doing so would raise funding requirements beyond those needed for financial stability and member security purposes, and would have undesirable consequences. Following the Green Paper the European Commission called for advice on a review of 23 topics relating to harmonisation of the EU-wide legislative framework for DB and DC occupational pensions, including funding, governance and disclosure. The European Insurance and Occupational Pensions Authority issued various consultations in 2011 on its draft advice although it does not make recommendations on any changes. Among the matters covered is the extent to which the legislative framework for occupational pension provision should be similar to that for other financial institutions and products, in particular the Solvency II framework for insurance.

AUTOMATIC ENROLMENT AND NEST

The Pensions Act 2008 puts in place the framework for a system of automatic pension scheme enrolment, setting out the main rules and contribution levels. The requirement to automatically enrol employees will commence in 2012. *See Section 9 for further information.* Employers without their own qualifying pension scheme, or who do not wish to use their own scheme, will be able to enrol employees in the National Employment Savings Trust. *See Section 10 for further information.*

In July 2011 the DWP launched a consultation on draft regulations for auto-enrolment. Taken together with the Pensions Act 2011 and miscellaneous draft regulations that were published earlier, this represents the last part of the legislative framework. However the picture will only be complete once the legislation has been finalised and final guidance issued.

In November 2011, the Government announced that automatic enrolment obligations will be delayed for employers with fewer than 50 employees. At the time of writing, full details of the measures, and any consequential changes for other employers, were not available.

PENSION PROTECTION FUND LEVY

On 16 May 2011 the PPF published its final proposals regarding how PPF levies will be calculated for levy years commencing from 2012/13. The proposed changes are intended to make levies more stable and predictable. *Further details are set out in Section 22.*

RESTRICTION OF TAX RELIEF

As part of the measures to restrict pensions tax relief (which include the reduction in the annual allowance to £50,000 from 6 April 2011), the lifetime allowance will be reduced to £1.8m with effect from 6 April 2012. *For more details on this, see Section 13.* Alongside this, measures have been introduced to ensure that supplementary top-up arrangements known as EFRBS are no more attractive than other forms of providing remuneration *(see Section 14)*.

The Government is also intending to restrict unintended relief given in certain asset-backed contribution arrangements. Examples include the use of a special purpose vehicle to receive employer property assets and deliver employer rental income from these assets to a pension scheme (resulting in double tax relief) and arrangements involving contingent contributions that turn out to be smaller than the amounts on which relief has been given. Options that the Government has consulted on include providing relief only when cash is received by the scheme, or the Government's favoured option of ensuring that relief given reflects the 'economic substance' of the arrangement.

PUBLIC SERVICE PENSIONS COMMISSION

The Coalition Government established an independent Public Service Pensions Commission, chaired by Lord Hutton, which is tasked with undertaking a fundamental structural review of public service pension provision. The final report was published in March 2011, and sets out recommendations on pension arrangements that are 'sustainable and affordable in the long term, fair to both the public service workforce and the taxpayer and consistent with the fiscal challenges ahead, while protecting accrued rights'. The recommendations include a new career average revalued earnings (CARE) scheme, with Normal Pension Age linked to State Pension Age for most public servants. At the Budget 2011, the Government accepted Lord Hutton's recommendations as a basis for consultation with public sector workers, unions and others and recognised that the position of the uniformed services would require particularly careful consideration. Following dissatisfaction at the proposals, the Government indicated that it would increase the proposed accrual rate and allow some protection for workers within ten years of retirement. Final details were due to be published by the end of 2011.

GMP EQUALISATION

In January 2010 the Labour Government issued a statement referring to the legislative requirements for the PPF and FAS to equalise benefits between men and women, in particular by eliminating the differences introduced by unequal GMPs accrued between 17 May 1990 and 5 April 1997.

The statement, however, went further than just PPF and FAS requirements and stated that all schemes with unequal benefits from GMPs should equalise and that the Government would be introducing legislation 'when Parliamentary time allows'. The statement also said that it is the Government's opinion that European law now requires equality even where no comparator of the opposite sex exists.

There was an outcry from industry asking for Government guidance on how equalisation should be achieved, as there are a significant number of unanswered questions. Without the answers to these questions it is uncertain how to go about equalisation in a way that would both achieve the legislative requirements and be straightforward to administer. Several legal firms have issued statements on the issue but none of these advises moving forward on the issue without Government guidance or legislation.

In March 2010, the DWP stated that it had 'no plans' to issue any government guidance on the issue, although in 2011 the Government indicated that it would provide draft guidance and regulations in due course. At the time of writing it is unclear what if any action will be required.

On 9 April 2010, the DWP issued guidance on the treatment of unequal GMPs for schemes going into the FAS, but conceded that schemes were not obliged to follow the guidance as there are alternative methods that may be equally valid.

In October 2009, the PPF issued a response to its April 2008 consultation on 'Benefit Equalisation for GMP'. The response endorses its previously stated preferred option of equalisation of total benefits earned on or after 17 May 1990 at the higher of the level for men and women at any point in time. This would apply to benefits paid before and after the assessment date. In January 2011, the PPF published a consultation setting out its proposed approach to calculating PPF compensation and FAS assistance to take account of GMP equalisation

The previously preferred method is still believed to be the most appropriate. However there are technical changes which reflect the interaction between the various branches of legislation applicable, and remove concerns that the previous proposal was too generous in some cases. The other change from the previous proposals is that it will not be necessary to show that a comparator exists – equalisation will be required in all cases. In November 2011, the PPF published details of how the approach will be implemented, and announced a pilot project.

SCOTLAND BILL

On 30 November 2010 the Scotland Bill was published, which will give the Scottish Parliament power to set its own income tax rate from 2016/17. This has potential implications for the running of pension schemes – for example, what relief to give in respect of member contributions to personal pensions and other arrangements operating under the 'relief at source' mechanism. A Technical Committee has been established by HMRC to look at impacts on pension schemes.

TEST-ACHATS

The European Court has ruled that insurance premiums based on gender will no longer be permitted. The Government view, set out in a ministerial statement in June 2011, is that the judgment only applies to 'new contracts of insurance and related financial services entered into on or after 21 December 2012'. However, in due course this will impact on many areas of insurance, including insured death benefits and annuities purchased from insurers with defined contribution pots. It is also possible that the ruling will lead to a change in UK legislation forcing trustees to revisit any gender-specific factors used in individual member calculations (for example transfer values, lump sum commutations and early or late retirements).

DEBT ON WITHDRAWAL OF AN EMPLOYER

The DWP consulted on changes to the employer debt regulations, affecting the amount payable when an employer ceases to participate in a multi-employer pension scheme. The main change was the introduction of a new 'flexible apportionment arrangement', which DWP proposed would be available from 1 October 2011 (although the government subsequently announced that this would be delayed to December 2011). This would allow all the liabilities of an employer ('Employer A') to be apportioned to one or more of the other participating employers, provided certain conditions are satisfied. Further flexibility was also proposed for periods of grace – where an employer has ceased to employ an active member for only a temporary period and the employer proposes that a debt is not triggered. Trustees would have discretion to extend the maximum period of grace from the current 12 to 36 months and employers would have 2 months, rather than 1, to make the necessary notification to trustees.

SHORT SERVICE REFUNDS

Currently there is no requirement for occupational pension schemes to preserve benefits within the scheme in respect of those members who leave within two years of joining. Such members will usually have the option of a refund of their contributions or a transfer to another pension scheme. This contrasts with the position in a personal pension (and NEST) where any funds built up in respect of a member are retained in the scheme and must be used to provide benefits in respect of that member.

With the advent of auto-enrolment and the consequent prospect of a significant increase in short-service members, this area has come into the spotlight. In January 2011, the DWP issued a call for evidence, seeking views to assist it in its review of the regulatory differences between trust-based schemes and contract-based schemes. The stated wish was to ensure that businesses are not faced with the opportunity for 'regulatory arbitrage' or with unnecessary burdens. Alongside the issue of short service refunds, the DWP requested views on the rules around trivial commutation and disclosure of information.

The Government's response published in June 2011 stated that it had not made a decision about short service refunds but that it would consult further on this area, as well as on the related areas of managing 'small pots' after auto-enrolment and improving transfers. However, the response emphasised that short service refunds are unlikely to continue in their current form for occupational defined contribution schemes. (For defined benefit schemes, changes were viewed as disproportionate.)

The independent Workplace Retirement Income Commission report of 1 August 2011 suggested that small pots could be defaulted into schemes where they can be managed efficiently, including NEST (which is currently banned from taking such transfers).

CONSULTATION ON MODERN WORKPLACES

In May 2011 the Government issued a consultation with the aim of making UK employment practices more flexible and 'family friendly' and of implementing the 2010 EU Directive on parental leave. The areas of the consultation that impact pension provision relate to parental leave. During such periods of temporary absence, any membership of a pension scheme will need to be maintained, and depending on the circumstances, benefit accrual may need to continue.

Currently benefit accrual must continue (based on a notional salary) in relation to statutory parental leave (up to 13 weeks), to mothers on paid maternity leave (up to 39 weeks) and to fathers on paid paternity leave. The latter includes ordinary paternity leave (2 weeks) and paid additional paternity leave (up to 26 weeks but effectively carved out of any unused paid maternity leave entitlement).

There is currently also the right to unpaid leave, taking the total absence to up to 1 year (maternity) or 6½ months (paternity) in addition to 13 weeks of parental leave for each parent. During this period, any membership of the scheme must be maintained.

Under the proposals, which are intended to be introduced in 2015 subject to affordability:

- paid maternity leave would be 18 weeks
- paid paternity leave would be 2 weeks
- 4 weeks of paid parental leave would be set aside for each parent
- a further 30 weeks of parental leave could be taken by either parent, of which 17 weeks would be paid, *and*
- unpaid statutory parental leave of 13 weeks per child for each parent would continue.

The effect is therefore to increase the couple's total entitlement to paid leave by four weeks, and to allow more flexibility in terms of how this leave is shared between them.

After the first year, the consultation proposes extending the right to unpaid parental leave from 13 weeks per child to 18 weeks and removing the 1-year eligibility criterion. Part of this parental leave would be transferrable from one parent to the other; part would not and so would be lost if not taken by the entitled parent. Currently the right to parental leave only applies in relation to children up to age 5, but the Government is considering extending this.

The consultation also sets out proposals to extend the right to request flexible working to all employees with a minimum 26 weeks' service.

MONEY PURCHASE BENEFITS AND LEGISLATION

The 27 July 2011 Supreme Court judgment on the winding-up of the hybrid DB/DC Imperial Home Décor scheme ruled that some benefits that the UK Government had previously regarded as non-money purchase are in fact money purchase benefits. This means that a money purchase scheme may have a deficit (or surplus) on winding up, but be outside the scope of a wide range of legislation, including legislation governing scheme funding, employer debt, the Pension Protection Fund and the Financial Assistance Scheme.

As a result the DWP inserted provision in the Pensions Act 2011 to amend the definition of money purchase benefits (for example in the Pension Schemes Act 1993) so that:

- a benefit other than a pension in payment is defined as money purchase if its rate or amount is calculated solely by reference to assets which 'must necessarily suffice for the purposes of its provision to or in respect of the member', *and*
- a pension in payment is defined as money purchase if it meets the above definition before it comes into payment and is then secured by an annuity contract or insurance policy made with an insurer.

SIGNIFICANT PENSION DATES

DISCLOSURE AND ACCOUNTING

01.11.86	Pension scheme disclosure requirements introduced.
28.09.92	Time limits for disclosure introduced.
06.04.97	New disclosure requirements introduced by Pensions Act 1995.
22.06.01	FRS 17 accounting procedures gradually introduced, starting with company accounts for years ending on or after this date.
31.12.02	New directors' remuneration reporting standards introduced.
06.04.03	Statutory money purchase illustrations (SMPIs) to be provided to pension scheme members with money purchase benefits.
01.01.05	Consolidated group accounts of companies listed and regulated in EU Member States generally required to comply with International Accounting Standards (IAS). Full implementation of FRS 17 required by UK companies not adopting IAS.
30.12.05	New requirement for trustees to provide defined benefit members with an annual summary funding statement.
06.04.07	FRS 17 disclosure requirements brought into line with those of IAS 19.
01.12.10	Pension schemes permitted to meet disclosure requirements by providing some information electronically.
01.01.13	Revised IAS 19 to apply for reporting years beginning on or after this date.

DIVORCE

01.07.96	Courts in England and Wales required to take pension rights into account when making financial provision orders on petitions for divorce filed on or after this date.
19.08.96	Courts in Scotland required to take pension rights into account when making financial provision orders on actions for divorce filed on or after this date.
01.12.00	Pension sharing provisions in force.
05.12.05	Revised forms and procedures for pension sharing and earmarking introduced.
06.04.09	Legislative restrictions on safeguarded rights abolished.
06.04.11	PPF compensation can be shared on divorce or dissolution of a civil partnership.

EQUAL TREATMENT

08.04.76	*Defrenne* judgment in ECJ established (after later clarification) the right of men and women to equal access to pension schemes.
07.11.87	Sex Discrimination Act 1986 came into force: compulsory retirement ages must be the same for men and women.
06.04.88	Protected Rights annuities must be on unisex basis.
17.05.90	*Barber* judgment (as clarified by later cases): occupational pensions are pay, and benefits in respect of service after 17.05.90 must be equal (unless claims lodged before this date).
23.06.94	Maternity and family leave provisions of Social Security Act 1989 brought into effect. Benefits during periods of paid maternity absence must continue to accrue based on notional full salary.
16.10.94	All employment rights (other than pay) to be maintained during statutory ordinary maternity leave.
02.12.96	Parts of the Disability Discrimination Act 1995 dealing with employment and the supply of services effective.
01.07.00	Discrimination against part-timers illegal under the terms of the Employment Relations Act 1999 unless objectively justified.
01.10.02	Discrimination against fixed-term workers became illegal unless objectively justified.
01.12.03	Legislation against discrimination by sexual orientation in force.
02.12.03	Legislation against discrimination by religion or belief in force.
01.10.04	Revised disability discrimination legislation in force.
05.12.05	The Civil Partnership Act 2004 came into force. Civil partners must be given the same benefits, for future service, as those who are married.
01.12.06	Legislation against discrimination by age in force.
01.04.07	Statutory maternity and adoption pay periods increased from 26 to 39 weeks.
08.04.10	The Equality Act 2010 received Royal Assent, harmonising, and in some respects extending, existing discrimination laws.
01.10.11	Default retirement age of 65 abolished.
21.12.12	Insurance premiums based on gender not permitted from this date, as a result of the *Test-Achats* ECJ judgment.

PROTECTING MEMBERS

06.04.88	Compulsory membership of occupational schemes prohibited.
7.08.90	No surplus refund to employer unless LPI given.

12.11.90	Requirement to appoint an independent trustee on employer insolvency.
02.04.91	Pensions Ombudsman in operation.
09.03.92	Self-investment restrictions effective.
29.06.92	Debt on employer on winding up of pension scheme.
06.10.96	Member-nominated trustees legislation commenced (and became fully effective from 06.04.97).
06.04.97	(i) Minimum Funding Requirement (MFR) and Statement of Investment Principles introduced.
	(ii) LPI increases became compulsory for future benefit accrual
	(iii) Appointments of scheme actuary and auditor required.
	(iv) Internal Dispute Resolution Procedures required.
	(v) Pensions Compensation Board powers commenced.
	(vi) Opra can remove or suspend trustees and impose civil penalties
03.04.00	Late payment of employees' contributions became a civil rather than a criminal offence.
29.05.00	Protection of pension rights on bankruptcy under approved pension schemes introduced.
06.04.01	Requirement for monitoring contributions to personal pensions introduced.
19.03.02	Interim MFR changes: lengthened deficit correction periods; partial abolition of annual recertification; changes to wind-up asset allocation priority calculations and debt-on-employer calculations where employer solvent.
15.03.04	For calculation effective dates from this date debt on employer increased for solvent employer scheme wind-ups beginning after 10.06.03, from MFR to full buy-out shortfall.
06.04.05	First provisions of Pensions Act 2004 came into force, including Pension Protection Fund, new Pensions Regulator and:
	(i) introduction of pension protection on transfer of employment to which TUPE regulations apply, *and*
	(ii) changes to LPI cap from 5% p.a. to 2.5% p.a. for future service Money purchase benefits exempt from LPI.
01.09.05	Financial Assistance Scheme came into operation.
02.09.05	Debt on employer when leaving multi-employer scheme increases to share of full buy-out deficiency, unless approved withdrawal arrangement put in place.
30.12.05	(i) Introduction of new scheme-specific funding requirement contained in Pensions Act 2004 replacing the MFR.
	(ii) New requirements in force for schemes operating as 'cross border' within the EEA.

| 06.04.06 | Remaining Pensions Act 2004 provisions in force, including: |

        (i)   new regulations on scheme modifications (section 67)

        (ii) new requirements for member-nominated trustees, including removal of the facility to opt out, *and*

        (iii) new requirements placed on trustees to have specific knowledge and understanding of pension issues.

| 06.04.08 | Revised debt-on-employer provisions give more flexibility in multi-employer schemes. |
| 06.04.10 | Corporate restructuring permitted without triggering an employer debt provided certain conditions are satisfied. |

STAKEHOLDER SCHEMES AND AUTO-ENROLMENT

01.10.00	Stakeholder schemes may be established.
06.04.01	Members may join stakeholder schemes.
08.10.01	Requirement for employers to provide access to stakeholder schemes.
06.04.05	Lifestyle arrangement must be made available by all stakeholder pension providers. Maximum annual management charge increased to 1.5% p.a. for the first ten years and 1% p.a. thereafter.
26.07.07	The Personal Accounts Delivery Authority (PADA) established.
05.07.10	PADA wound up and the NEST Corporation established.
01.07.12	Earliest date to which large employers can bring forward their staging date for auto-enrolment.
01.10.12	(i) Employer auto-enrolment obligations start, with employers being brought in at staging dates over a four-year period dependent on employer payroll size.

        (ii) Minimum contribution of 2% (including minimum 1% employer) of qualifying earnings where DC scheme used to meet obligations.

| 01.10.16 | Minimum contribution of 5% (including minimum 2% employer) of qualifying earnings where DC scheme used to meet auto-enrolment obligations. |
| 01.10.17 | Minimum contribution of 8% (including minimum 3% employer) of qualifying earnings where DC scheme used to meet auto-enrolment obligations. |

STATE SCHEMES AND CONTRACTING OUT

06.04.75	Benefits under Graduated Scheme cease to accrue.
06.04.78	Start of SERPS and contracting out.
01.01.85	Anti-franking introduced for leavers on or after this date.

01.11.86		Contracting-out quality test removed.
06.04.87	(i)	Contracting out via personal pension could be backdated to this date.
	(ii)	Trustees liable for CEPs/LRPs.
06.04.88	(i)	SERPS benefits reduced for individuals retiring after 2000.
	(ii)	GMP accrual rates reduced.
	(iii)	GMPs accrued after this date must receive increases of up to 3% p.a. from scheme.
	(iv)	Fixed rate GMP revaluation for future leavers reduced from 8.5% to 7.5%.
	(v)	Widowers' GMPs introduced.
	(vi)	Money purchase contracting out introduced.
	(vii)	2% incentive payments introduced.
17.05.90		Protected rights under COMPS may commence at any age between 60 and 65.
06.04.93	(i)	Fixed rate GMP revaluation for future leavers reduced to 7%.
	(ii)	2% incentive payments ceased; 1% incentive payments introduced for personal pension contributors aged 30 or over.
06.04.96		Protected rights from COMPS can be secured on winding up by means of appropriate insurance policies.
06.04.97	(i)	1% incentive payments paid to personal pension contributors aged 30 or over ceased.
	(ii)	Age-related rebates introduced for COMPS and APPS.
	(iii)	Link with SERPS broken.
	(iv)	GMP accruals cease and Reference Scheme Test introduced for COSRS.
	(v)	Limited Revaluation and State Scheme premium options (other than CEPs) removed.
	(vi)	Fixed rate GMP revaluation for future leavers reduced to 6.25%.
	(vii)	COMBS permitted.
	(viii)	Annuities purchased with post-April 1997 protected rights must in all cases have LPI, fixed 5% p.a. or full RPI increases, but need not include a widow(er)'s pension for single retirees.
01.01.01		Members' protected rights may be commuted in cases of serious ill-health.
06.04.02	(i)	State Second Pension (S2P) replaces SERPS.
	(ii)	New table of rebates effective from 2002 to 2007, with different levels of rebates applying to different tranches of earnings for personal pensions (but not occupational pensions) for the first time.

	(iii)	Fixed rate GMP revaluation for future leavers reduced to 4.5%.
	(iv)	New pre-97 protected rights annuities need not include a contingent widow(er)'s pension for retirees who are single.
	(v)	Removal of requirement for automatic periodic certification of adequacy of assets of COSRS for contracting out.

06.10.02   Inherited SERPS pension reduced from 100% to 50%, subject to age-related transitional provisions.

06.10.03   Introduction of State Pension Credits, which replace Minimum Income Guarantee.

06.04.05   Higher increases given to individuals deferring state benefits beyond state pension age, and introduction of a new lump sum option.

28.11.05   An amendment to regulations allows the bulk transfer of protected rights from one COMPS to another without the consent of the member.

06.04.07   (i)   New table of rebates effective for 2007 to 2012.
           (ii) Fixed rate GMP revaluation for future leavers reduced to 4%.

06.04.09   Trustees, with employer consent, able to convert GMPs into 'normal' scheme pensions.

06.04.10   State pension age for women starts to increase from 60 to 65, over a transitional period now due to last until December 2018.

06.04.10   Pensions Act 2007 introduces extensive changes to state pensions, including:

           (i)   reduction in the number of contributory years needed to qualify for full Basic State Pension (BSP) to 30 for both men and women, *and*

           (ii) phasing-in of reforms to S2P to make it a flat-rate top-up to BSP.

06.04.11   (i)   BSP to increase each year in line with the highest of earnings increases, price increases and 2.5%.

           (ii) First GMP increase order based on CPI rather than RPI effective.

06.04.12   (i)   Abolition of contracting out on a money purchase basis and removal of all restrictions applying to protected rights funds.

           (ii) New rebates for COSRS effective for 2012 to 2017.

           (iii) Transfers of COSRS rights to non-COSRS permitted.

December 2018   State pension age for men and women due to increase from 65 to 66 over a transitional period to October 2020.

TAXATION

06.04.70   New code approval available.

06.04.73	New code compulsory for new schemes and amended existing schemes.
05.04.80	New code for all approved schemes accepting contributions.
17.03.87	Revised limits for new members on or after this date.
06.04.87	Controls on surplus.
01.07.88	Personal pensions available.
14.03.89 & 01.06.89	1989 Revenue limits regime introduced for members joining newly established schemes on or after 14.03.89 and existing schemes on or after 01.06.89.
27.07.89	Concurrent membership of approved and unapproved schemes permissible.
30.06.95	Annuity purchase deferral and income withdrawal permitted for personal pensions.
01.01.97	Reinstatement to pension schemes permitted on special terms for those mis-sold personal pensions.
02.07.97	Tax credits on UK dividend income can no longer be claimed by pension schemes.
30.06.99	Annuity purchase deferral and income drawdown introduced for money purchase occupational schemes and buy-out contracts.
06.04.01	Changes to personal pension tax regime: (i) Contributions of up to £3,600 p.a. permitted irrespective of earnings. (ii) 'Carry forward' facility removed. (iii) 'Carry back' facility radically reduced. (iv) Contributions for risk benefits, for new entrants, limited to 10% of total contribution paid for year. (v) Concurrent membership of occupational and personal pension schemes permitted for those earning under £30,000 p.a.
11.05.01	Rate of tax on refund of surplus reduced from 40% to 35%.
06.04.06	(i) New tax regime replaces former contribution and benefit limits, permitting all individuals lifetime tax-privileged pension savings up to a standard limit. (ii) Requirement for occupational pension schemes to offer an AVC facility removed.
22.04.09	Special annual allowance charge introduced for 2009/10 and 2010/11.
01.12.09	Additional authorised payments permitted, including *de minimis* commutation payments of up to £2,000.
06.04.10	Increase in the normal minimum pension age from 50 to 55.

06.04.11	(i) Annual allowance reduced to £50,000.
	(ii) Requirement to annuitise before age 75 removed; flexible drawdown introduced.
06.04.12	Lifetime allowance reduced to £1.5 million.

TRANSFERS, PRESERVATION AND REVALUATION

06.04.75	Leavers on or after this date aged at least 26 and with 5 years' qualifying service entitled to preserved benefits.
01.01.86	(i) Statutory right to cash equivalent for leavers on or after this date. Non-GMP deferred pensions of such leavers accrued from 01.01.85 to be revalued, broadly at lower of 5% p.a. or price inflation.
	(ii) Age 26 requirement for preservation dropped.
06.04.88	Minimum period of qualifying service for entitlement to preserved benefits amended to two years, for leavers on or after this date.
01.01.91	Leavers on or after this date receive revaluations on whole non-GMP deferred pension.
9.07.94	Protected rights may be transferred to a contracted-out occupational scheme of which the individual has previously been a member.
9.03.97	Occupational pension scheme members permitted to transfer personal pension benefits into a FSAVC.
6.04.97	(i) Rights to cash equivalent extended to pre-01.01.86 leavers.
	(ii) Three-month guarantee on cash equivalent quotations for salary-related benefits introduced.
	(iii) Cash equivalents subjected to a minimum of the MFR value.
1.12.00	Investment-linked annuity allowed as an alternative to LPI increase for non-protected rights under a money purchase scheme.
4.08.03	Trustees permitted to cut back individual transfer values where scheme is underfunded.
6.04.06	Leavers with between 3 and 24 months' pensionable service entitled to a cash transfer sum as an option.
1.10.08	Transfer values to be set by trustees (on a 'best estimate' basis after taking actuarial advice).
6.04.09	Minimum revaluation of non-GMP deferred pensions accrued from this date reduced to the lower of 2.5% p.a. or price inflation.
1.01.11	First statutory revaluation order based on CPI rather than RPI effective.

UNAPPROVED BENEFITS/EFRBS

27.07.89   Membership of unapproved schemes permitted to provide benefits on top of those from approved schemes.

01.12.93   Taxation of lump sum benefits from offshore Funded Unapproved Retirement Benefit Schemes (FURBS).

06.04.98   National Insurance contributions payable on contributions to money purchase FURBS.

06.04.99   National Insurance contributions payable on contributions to final salary FURBS.

06.04.06   Special tax treatment of unapproved pension arrangements removed (subject to transitional provisions). Unapproved schemes become Employer-Financed Retirement Benefit Schemes (EFRBS).

06.04.11   New disguised remuneration provisions apply, amending the taxation of funded and certain unfunded secured EFRBS.

UK PENSIONS CASE LAW

This section lists a number of legal cases that we feel have potentially significant importance in the development and understanding of pensions. It is not intended to be an exhaustive list and the comments given are merely an indication of the case content. No reliance should be placed on these summary comments. Legal advice should always be sought for guidance as to the applicability of case law.

The year quoted below for each case usually, but not always, refers to the year of appearance in a published law report. This may be a later year than that in which the judgment was given.

TRUSTEESHIP

Re Whiteley (Court of Appeal) [1886]
The duty of a trustee is to take such care as an ordinary prudent man would take if he were minded to make investment for the benefit of other people for whom he felt bound to provide.

Learoyd v Whiteley (House of Lords) [1887]
A trustee must use ordinary care and caution and is entitled to rely upon skilled persons.

Re Skeats' Settlement (High Court) [1889]
The power of appointment of trustees is fiduciary. The person in whom the power is vested cannot appoint themselves as a trustee.

Re Hastings-Bass (Court of Appeal) [1975]
The Court may reverse a trustee decision if the effect was unintended and the trustees overlooked relevant considerations or included irrelevant considerations. However, in 2011 the Court of Appeal decided in *Pitt v Holt* that the test in *Hastings-Bass* was insufficient; a breach of fiduciary duty must be established.

Cowan v Scargill (High Court) [1984]
The duty of trustees to act in the best interests of the present and future beneficiaries of the trust is paramount. This almost certainly means best *financial* interests.

Martin v City of Edinburgh District Council (Court of Sessions, Scotland) [1989]
Whilst trustees cannot be expected to set aside completely all personal preferences and conscientiously held principles, they must exercise fair and impartial judgement on the merits of the issues before them. The investment duty of a trustee is not merely to rubber-stamp the professional advice of financial advisers.

Wilson v Law Debenture (High Court) [1995]
Courts will not compel trustees to disclose the reasons for the exercise of a discretion.

Elliott v Pensions Ombudsman (High Court) [1998]
Trustees can exercise discretion to favour certain categories of members over other categories.

Harding and Others (Trustees of Joy Manufacturing Holdings Ltd Pension and Life Assurance Scheme), petitioners (Court of Session, Inner House, Scotland) [1999]

Trustees in Scotland may not surrender the exercise of their discretion to the Court.

Edge v Pensions Ombudsman (Court of Appeal) [2000]

The main purpose of a pension scheme is not served by putting an employer out of business, nor by setting contributions or benefits at levels which deter employees from joining. Trustees are not obliged to put forward proposals on use of surplus that they do not think are fair to the employers.

When exercising discretions, trustees must give proper consideration to all relevant matters, but cannot then be criticised if they reach a decision that appears to favour one interest over others. However, any explanation given may be evaluated critically, and appropriate inferences drawn from a failure to give an explanation when called for.

Allen v TKM Group Pension Scheme (Pensions Ombudsman) [2002]

Trustees may sometimes find themselves judged to have acted with maladministration in circumstances where they would not be regarded as acting unlawfully. As a matter of good administrative practice, trustees should provide reasons for their decisions to those with a legitimate interest in the matter, and should generally make the minutes of their meetings available to scheme members.

The Ombudsman's ruling appears to contradict an established trust law principle that trustees are not obliged to reveal the reasons for their decisions when exercising discretions. An Ombudsman's ruling is, however, not a binding precedent on schemes generally and it may be that a Court would take a different view from the Ombudsman.

Lawrence Graham Trust Corporation v Trustees of Greenup and Thompson Limited Pension Scheme (Pensions Ombudsman) [2008]

The trustees made a loan to the principal employer, in breach of section 40 of the Pensions Act 1995. The Ombudsman determined that, when the employer went into liquidation, the loan had not been repaid. The trustees were guilty of breach of trust and personally liable for the outstanding amount.

Gregson v HAE Trustees (High Court) [2008]

Beneficiaries cannot bring indirect 'dog-leg' claims against directors of a corporate trustee, as this would circumvent the principle that no direct duty is owed by the directors to the beneficiaries. Although this appears to conflict with a 1997 ruling that an indirect claim could be brought, the difference seems to hinge on the specific circumstances of the case, in particular that the trustee company in the earlier case was the trustee of only one trust and had no other business interest.

Independent Trustee Services Limited v Hope (High Court) [2009]

Trustees cannot take account of the PPF in making certain decisions. Although this 'Ilford' case related specifically to the purchase of annuities to secure certain benefits, similar principles can be expected to apply in other situations.

Pitt v Holt (Court of Appeal) [2011]

To successfully reverse an action made under discretionary powers, three things must be shown: that there was a mistake, that it was a relevant mistake, and that it was serious enough to satisfy the *Ogilvie v Littleboy* test. The judgment related to private trusts, but appears to apply also to pensions.

EMPLOYERS

Re Courage Group's Pension Schemes, Ryan v Imperial Brewing (High Court) [1987]

The ability to substitute a principal employer is dependent on the purpose for which the intended substitution would be made. A rule-amending power could not be used to change the principal employer to a holding company which had no connection with the previous principal employer and whose purpose was to retain control of a surplus contributed by companies which the holding company had bought.

Imperial Group Pension Trust v Imperial Tobacco (High Court) [1991]

Pension benefits are part of the consideration received by employees for their services. The employer owes his employees a duty of good faith in relation to a pension scheme, and should not act so as to destroy or seriously damage their relationship of confidence and trust.

Hillsdown v Pensions Ombudsman (High Court) [1997]

Under the scheme, the trustees had sole power to deal with a surplus. The employer threatened to bring in employees of new employers to run down the surplus, and persuaded the trustees to agree to an amendment enabling a transfer to another scheme from which a refund to the employer could be made. The Court ruled that the amendment and transfer were for an improper purpose and ordered the refunded surplus to be returned to the scheme. It further ruled that the employer's implied obligation of trust and confidence prevented it from using a power to suspend contributions, whilst at the same time using a power to adhere further employers.

Air Jamaica v Charlton (Privy Council) [1999]

Bearing in mind the employer's obligation to exercise powers in good faith, it was difficult to see how the scheme could be amended in any significant respect once it had discontinued and wind-up was anticipated.

University of Nottingham v Eyett (High Court) [1999]

Where all the relevant information is available to the employee to make his own informed choice, the employer's implied obligation of good faith does not require it to draw the member's attention to the fact that he might have done better financially by changing the timing of his choice.

BENEFITS AND CONTRIBUTIONS

Hackwood v APS (Pensions Ombudsman) [1995]

Where trustees failed to consider the use of a power of amendment to increase benefits, this was held to be a breach of trust and maladministration. However, the employer did not breach his implied obligation of good faith by preferring his own interests, having first considered the interests of pensioners.

Barclays Bank v Holmes (High Court) [2000]

Where a defined contribution section has been added to a defined benefit scheme, the surplus in the defined benefit section may (provided that this is not contrary to the trust deed) be used to meet the defined contributions.

Merchant Navy Ratings Pension Fund Trustees v Chambers (High Court) [2001]

An amendment which allows a pensioner's benefits to be transferred without consent is not automatically prohibited. It is for the actuary to consider whether to give a 'section 67' certificate.

Royal Masonic Hospital v Pensions Ombudsman (High Court) [2001]

Unfunded pension schemes are not subject to the preservation requirements.

Hagen v ICI Chemicals and Polymers Ltd (High Court) [2001]

The Court ruled that the employer had misrepresented the position to employees, when informing them that they would receive broadly similar benefits on transfer to a new scheme following a business transfer. In fact some individuals' benefits under the new scheme were as much as 5% worse than under the old scheme.

Beckmann v Dynamco Whicheloe Macfarlane Ltd (European Court of Justice) [2002]

Benefits payable from an occupational pension scheme on redundancy, being benefits payable before normal pension age, do not fall under the exemption for occupational pension scheme rights under the TUPE legislation. The 2003 ruling in *Martin and Others v South Bank University* built on this decision, extending it to some other early retirement situations.

Aon Trust Corporation Ltd v KPMG (Court of Appeal) [2005]

The exercise of an express power in the scheme rules (to reduce benefits when the scheme was in deficit) was a power to modify the scheme, coming within the ambit of section 67 of the Pensions Act 1995. Consequently, the power could not be exercised (without member consent) if it would adversely affect accrued rights or entitlements.

The judgment also placed limitations on what could be regarded as a 'money purchase scheme'. The judge ruled that the scheme in question was no such a scheme because it provided 'average salary benefits', and hence it was subject to the funding and debt-on-the-employer legislation.

Pinsent Curtis v Capital Cranfield Trustees Ltd (Court of Appeal) [2005]

Under a scheme rule which empowered the trustees to determine 'appropriate' contributions, the trustees could seek a lump sum contribution equal to the buy-out deficit during the period for which notice had been given by the employer that he would terminate the scheme.

PNPF Trust Co Ltd v Taylor & Others (High Court) [2010]

The rules of the PNPF, an industry-wide scheme, gave the trustees the power to set contributions subject to certain conditions. The scheme funding legislation could be used to set contributions in excess of those allowable under the rules, although this would require the employer's agreement.

MG v German (Court of Appeal) [2010]

Section 91 of the Pensions Act 1995 does not prevent the bona fide compromise of disputed or doubtful entitlements or rights under an occupational pension scheme.

Prudential Staff Pensions v Prudential Assurance (High Court) [2011]

In 2006, after granting discretionary pension increases broadly in line with RPI for a number of years, the employer revised its policy by capping annual increases at 2.5%. The Court ruled that, in doing so, the employer had not breached its duty of good faith.

WINDING UP AND INSOLVENCY

Bainbridge v Quarters Trustees Ltd (High Court) [2008]

Unless they are specifically ring-fenced under the rules, money purchase assets will not be ring-fenced on wind-up. The extent to which this applies to schemes entering wind-up after 5 April 2005 is unclear.

NBPF Pension Trustees Ltd v Warnock-Smith (High Court) [2008]

Trustees may use scheme assets on wind-up to purchase insurance to protect themselves against 'run-off' liabilities and claims from overlooked beneficiaries.

MCP v Aon (High Court) [2009]

Trustees are not discharged from liabilities in a scheme wind-up despite giving notice under section 27 of the Trustee Act 1925. The case was brought against the scheme administrators, who had lost records of transferred-in members.

Houldsworth v Bridge Trustees (Court of Appeal) [2010], (Supreme Court) [2011] (commonly referred to as the *Imperial Home Décor* case)

Pensions deriving from money purchase assets but paid directly by the scheme, DC funds with notional investment returns, and money purchase benefits subject to a GMP underpin all remain money purchase benefits for the purposes of the statutory winding-up provisions (and, by implication, other areas of legislation where the same definition is used). The legislative definition of money purchase benefits has been amended, to prevent anomalies arising in future.

Nortel & Lehman Brothers v The Pensions Regulator (High Court) [2010] (affirmed, Court of Appeal [2011])

A Financial Support Direction can be issued to a company undergoing insolvency proceedings. In such cases it should be treated as an insolvency expense, ranking ahead of unsecured creditors.

Bonas UK (Upper Tribunal) [2011]

The purpose of a Contribution Notice should be to compensate the scheme for the detriment suffered, rather than to actively penalise the company.

SURPLUS AND DEFICITS

British Coal Corporation v British Coal Staff Superannuation Scheme Trustee (High Court) [1995]

An employer's liability to pay future standard contributions may be set against any scheme surplus.

National Grid Co plc v Laws (Court of Appeal) [1999]

Members have no rights in a surplus, only a reasonable expectation that any dealings with that surplus will pay a fair regard to their interests.

Wrightson Ltd v Fletcher Challenge Nominees Ltd (Privy Council) [2001]

In a balance of cost scheme, any surplus on a final dissolution is generally to be considered as resulting from past overfunding by the employer.

EQUAL TREATMENT

Defrenne v Sabena (No. 2) (European Court of Justice) [1976]

The principle of equal pay, under Article 119 (now Article 141) of the Treaty of Rome, may be relied upon by the national courts. However, this cannot be applied to claims for periods prior to 8 April 1976. (This case has been taken to indicate that *access* to pension schemes should be equal for men and women from 8 April 1976.)

Bilka-Kaufhaus GmbH v Weber von Hartz (European Court of Justice) [1986]

Where the exclusion of part-timers affected a far greater number of women than men, the equal pay requirements of the Treaty of Rome were infringed unless the employer could show that the exclusion was objectively justified.

Barber v GRE (European Court of Justice) [1990]

Benefits under a pension scheme are deferred pay and therefore subject to equal treatment between men and women.

Roberts v Birds Eye Walls (European Court of Justice) [1993]

The principle of equal treatment presupposes that men and women are in identical situations. Therefore, where a 'bridging pension' is paid only to a male member to offset the fact that a woman's State pension starts earlier, this is no direct sex discrimination. [*Note:* a later case in the ECJ, *Bestuur van het Algemeen Burgerlijk Pensioenfonds v Beune*, seemingly contradicts this conclusion, although some arguments have been advanced, distinguishing the circumstances and reconciling the results.]

Ten Oever v Stichting Bedrijfspensioenfonds voor het Glazenwassers (European Court of Justice) [1993]

A survivor's pension falls within the scope of the equal pay requirement. However, equal benefits only had to be provided in respect of benefits earned from 17 May 1990 (the date of the *Barber* judgment), unless a claim had already been started before then.

Coloroll Pension Trustees v Russell (European Court of Justice) [1994]

Equal pension benefits for men and women need only be provided for service from 17 May 1990, except where a claim had been initiated earlier. Unequal benefits must be levelled up for any service after 17 May 1990, but schemes can, in principle, change benefit structures to level down for any subsequent service after the date of change.

Additional benefits stemming from contributions paid by employees on a purely voluntary basis are not pay and therefore not subject to the same equal treatment requirements.

Preston v Wolverhampton (European Court of Justice) [2000]

Part-timers whose exclusion from membership of an occupational pension scheme amounts to indirect sex discrimination can claim retrospective membership as far back as 8 April 1976. However, national courts may impose a time limit on lodging claims after leaving service. The House of Lords later confirmed that, for the UK, this time limit is six months.

Uppingham School v Shillcock (High Court) [2002]

Offsets from pensionable salary without pro-rating for part-timers are not discriminatory where applied equally to all members. The approach adopted was in any case objectively justifiable as a reasonable method of implementing the legitimate objective of integration with the State scheme.

Allonby v Accrington & Rossendale College (European Court of Justice) [2004]

The female claimant did not have to identify a male comparator with the same employer, where the indirect sex discrimination arose from a wider 'single source'. (In this case, the single source was the entry rules to a particular statutory pension scheme.)

Bloxham v Freshfields (Employment Tribunal) [2007]

The tribunal held that the treatment suffered by Mr Bloxham when Freshfields introduced new pension arrangements was potentially discriminatory on grounds of age, but that Freshfields' actions were objectively justified as no less discriminatory means were available to them.

Foster Wheeler v Hanley (Court of Appeal) [2009]

Consent to retirement from age 60 could not be withheld from members with service in the *Barber* window (with a Normal Retirement Age of 60). For any part of the benefit due from age 65, an early retirement reduction could be applied. This was consistent with the 2007 judgment in *Cripps v TSL* in relation to the winding-up statutory priority order.

Rosenbladt v Oellerking (European Court of Justice) [2010]

A collective agreement providing for the automatic retirement of employees at age 65 constituted age discrimination, but was justified as a proportionate means of achieving legitimate aims.

Test-Achats (European Court of Justice) [2011]

From 21 December 2012, insurance premiums based on gender will not be permitted. The implications for UK occupational pension schemes are currently unclear.

ADVISERS AND PROFESSIONALS

Re George Newnes Group Pension Fund (High Court) [1969]

An actuary is an expert. If an actuary acts honestly and does not make an objective mistake, the decision is not open to challenge.

Bartlett v Barclays Trust Co Ltd (No. 1) (High Court) [1980]

A higher duty of care is expected from professional trustees.

Auty v National Coal Board (Court of Appeal) [1985]

Actuarial evidence (relating to loss of value dependent on future economic trends) can be rejected by courts on the grounds that it is based on hearsay and speculative in nature.

Re Imperial Foods Ltd Pension Scheme (High Court) [1986]

An actuarial certificate (relating to a bulk transfer payment) could not be successfully challenged in the absence of a cardinal error of principle or a mathematical error.

Re the Minworth Limited Pension Scheme, Anderson v William M Mercer (Pensions Ombudsman) [1999]

A professional trustee who had failed to give proper thought to risks associated with investment mismatching during a wind-up was 'recklessly indifferent' to the fact that it was in breach of its duties, and was therefore not entitled to be exonerated by a clause exempting trustees from liability other than arising from wilful default or fraud. In addition, the Ombudsman ruled that an actuary was inherently 'concerned with the administration' of the scheme, and so a complaint against the actuary came within his jurisdiction.

Wirral BC v Evans (Court of Appeal) [2000]

Administrators have no general duty to advise present or intending members of the scheme.

Gleave v PPF (High Court) [2008]

Insolvency practitioners cannot dispute section 75 debt claims as calculated by the scheme actuary. The companies went into administration in 2001. The insolvency practitioners had argued that the actuary had overestimated the claim, exercisable by the PPF, by using later mortality tables.

TAXATION

Hillsdown v Commissioners of Inland Revenue (High Court) [1999]

The employer had been obliged to repay a refund of surplus on which tax had been paid. The Inland Revenue had originally refused to reimburse this tax. The Court ruled that a repayment of surplus in which no beneficial interest passed was not a payment for the purposes of section 601 ICTA 1988.

JP Morgan Fleming Claverhouse Investment Trust plc and the Association of Investment Trust Companies v Commissioners of HM Revenue & Customs (European Court of Justice) [2007]

The ECJ has outlined principles for assessing whether Investment Trust Companies (ITC) should be exempt from paying VAT in respect of investment management charges. The particular question has now been referred to the UK courts to make a ruling. The NAPF and Wheels Common Investment Fund have launched a joint challenge against HMRC, on the grounds that any such exemption should also apply to pension schemes.

ERRORS AND DISPUTES

Bradstock v Nabarro Nathanson (High Court) [1996]

In negligence claims, time runs from the date when damage occurred, not from when the negligence of the advice first became known.

Armitage v Nurse (Court of Appeal) [1997]

Trustees can be indemnified under an exoneration clause, even where they have been grossly negligent, provided that they were not reckless.

Hogg Robinson v Pensions Ombudsman (High Court) [1998]

The trustees were not guilty of maladministration by refusing to extend a guarantee period where the member had had problems because of an incorrect quotation. (But the Court's implication, and the Ombudsman's subsequent determination when he revisited the case, was that the failure to produce an accurate quotation in good time was maladministration.)

Derby v Scottish Equitable (Court of Appeal) [2001]

A member who had received a substantial overpayment from a personal pension was obliged to give up the overpayment after the insurer had realised its mistake, except to the limited extent to which he had spent the money irreversibly and could claim a 'change of position'.

Steria v Hutchison (Court of Appeal) [2006]

The appeal judges ruled, against the High Court judgment, that a caveat in the booklet that it did not override the trust deed and rules was adequate to prevent an override provided it was clear and 'not tucked away in tiny print in a footnote'. However, a letter to the member that did not contain a caveat could be overriding, but was irrelevant to the outcome of the case.

Tyler v Robert Fleming Benefit Consultants and Minet Benefit Consultancy (Pensions Ombudsman) [2008]

The Ombudsman held that Minet (the former administrators) were responsible for the disappearance of data in respect of Mr Tyler. He directed Minet to put Mr Tyler in the position he would have been in had he been included in the subsequent bulk buy-out by purchasing a deferred annuity for him.

Colorcon v Huckell (High Court) [2009]

The Court granted an order for rectification of the scheme rules. Evidence showed that the rules relating to the revaluation of deferred pensioners had been amended incorrectly and contrary to the common intention of the employer and trustees.

GENERAL AND MISCELLANEOUS

Mettoy Pension Trustees v Evans (High Court) [1991]

Interpretation of pension scheme documents should be practical and purposive, rather than detailed and literal.

Nuthall v Merrill Lynch (UK) Final Salary Plan trustees (Pensions Ombudsman) [1999]

Trustees can be guilty of maladministration for unnecessary delays in transferring money to individual members' accounts, even if the payments have been made within the maximum timescales permitted by the Pensions Act 1995.

Hoover Ltd v Hetherington (High Court) [2002]

The word 'retires' signifies final withdrawal from some office, without prejudicing the individual's entitlement to work for another office or business. The Court also held that retirement from service by reason of incapacity included retirement in circumstances where the member was in fact capable of full-time work, albeit not of the kind normally undertaken by him or her.

Durant v Financial Services Authority (Court of Appeal) [2003]

Personal data is information that affects an individual's privacy. Two questions can assist in determining the nature of the information: is the information 'biographical', and who is the focus of the information? The fact that an individual's name appears in a document does not mean it will necessarily be personal data about that individual.

The Data Protection Act applies to manual data held in a 'relevant filing system'. A filing system will only be such if it is of sufficient sophistication to provide 'ready accessibility' broadly equivalent to a computerised filing system.

Bonner v NHS Pension Scheme (Pensions Ombudsman) [2004]

The scheme's inability to deal quickly with a transfer payment was maladministration. (The ruling essentially extended the duty to carry out investment transactions promptly, as seen in *Nuthall v Merrill Lynch* above, to other types of pension scheme transaction and showed that the Ombudsman expects trustees to operate without delay in all cases.)

Robins and others v Secretary of State for Work and Pensions (European Court of Justice) [2007] (commonly referred to as the Allied Steel Workers (ASW) case)

The ECJ ruled that the UK Government had not adequately protected the rights of workers in occupational schemes in the event of insolvency (in particular, an insolvency occurring in April 2003), under the 1980 European Insolvency Directive.

In a related case, shortly after the ECJ's ruling, the UK High Court found in *Bradley and others v Secretary of State* that the Government had provided misleading official information on the security of occupational pension schemes and was guilty of maladministration.

INTERNATIONAL

Introduction

The summaries below have been derived from Aon Hewitt's online eGuides. Necessarily, much detail has been omitted. For example, the 'Recent Developments' section contains a single item that we hope will be of interest. Readers interested in seeing the fully detailed eGuides should e-mail *internationalBenefits@aonhewitt.Com*.

Countries covered:

- Americas:
  - Brazil
  - Canada
  - United States of America
- Europe:
  - Notes on the European Union
  - Belgium
  - France
  - Germany
  - The Netherlands
  - Russia
  - Spain
  - Switzerland
- Asia Pacific:
  - Australia
  - China
  - India
  - Japan.

The economic indicators and social security information for selected countries on pages 218 to 223 have been obtained by Economic and Financial Publishing Ltd from the sources indicated.

ECONOMIC INDICATORS AND SOCIAL SECURITY INFORMATION FOR SELECTED COUNTRIES

Notes to the Following Table

(a)   Gradually being raised to 67 m&f by 2023 (Australia), 2025 (The Netherlands) 2026 (Italy, possibly), 2027 (Spain and USA) 2029 (Germany).

(b)   60 (m), 55 (f) for rural workers.

(c)   Flexible retirement age. Gradually being increased to 60 m&f by 2023. Increase to 67 m&f by 2026 under negotiation.

(d)   Gradually being equalised at 65 m&f by 2018, rising to 68 by 2046.

(e)   Variable depending on employee level of earnings.

(f)   Under the New Pensions System. A flat-rate National Old Age pension is also provided for poor people aged 65 and over.

(g)   Mostly funded through general taxation.

(h)   On all earnings (in some countries above a minimum amount).

(i)   Up to earnings ceiling.

(j)   • UK: Up to earnings limit, but no contributions are paid on earnings below £7,029. Employee contributes an additional 2% on earnings above the ceiling

   • USA: 6.2% on earnings up to the ceiling plus 1.45% on all earnings.

(k)   Small, flat-rate (Denmark: employer DDK2,160, employee DDK1,080).

(l)   Three times the average wage for the district, city or province.

(m)   The figure shown is the TA ceiling for contributions towards old-age benefits.

(n)   There is no earnings ceiling on contributions for those entering the social security system before 1 January 1996.

(o)   China's first national law on social insurance was adopted in October 2010 and will come into force in July 2011. It mostly unifies existing schemes.

(p)   Increasing to 34% from 1 January 2011.

State pension formula:

   A: not related to earnings

   B: related to earnings below a fixed ceiling

   C: effectively related to all earnings

   D: individual capitalisation system

Sources: *2011 World Population Data Sheet*, Population Reference Bureau; *World Development Indicators*, World Bank; *World Economic Outlook*, International Monetary Fund, September 2011; *Economic Outlook*, OECD; TradingEconomics.com; and *Social Security Programs Throughout the World: Europe 2010, Asia and the Pacific 2010* and *The Americas 2009*, US Social Security Administration and International Social Security Association, August 2010 March 2011 and March 2010.

	Australia	Belgium	Brazil	Canada	China (exc. HK/Macau)
1. Economic indicators					
Population (2011, million)	22.7	11.0	196.7	34.5	1,345.9
Percentage of population aged 15–64	67	66	68	70	74
Percentage of total population aged 65+	14	17	7	14	9
GDP (2010, local currency bn)	1,345.7	352.9	3,675.0	1,621.5	39,798.3
GDP per capita, local currency	58,005	32,480	18,851	47,449	29,738
GDP per capita, £ equivalent	37,908	28,157	6,987	30,509	2,946
Price inflation (2010, % pa)	2.8	2.3	5.0	1.8	3.3
Money market/Treasury bill rate (2011, % pa)	5.12	1.33	12.00	1.61	3.34
Government bond yield (15 September 2011, % pa)	4.27	3.9	3.97	2.11	4.07
Exchange rate (£1 as at 16 September 11)	1.5301	1.1535	2.6979	1.5552	10.0959
2. Social Security Information					
Current at	2010	2010	2009	2011	2010
State pension age	65m 64f *(a)*	65 m&f	65m 60f *(b)*	65 m&f	60m 50-60f
Contribution to State pension (employer, %)	9 *(i)*	8.86 *(h)*	20 *(i)*	4.95 *(i)*	20 *(i,o)*
Contribution to State pension (employee, %)	0 *(g)*	7.5 *(h)*	*(e)*	4.95 *(i)*	8 *(i,o)*
Earnings ceiling (local currency)	168,880	n/a	38,626.80	48,300	*(l)*
Earnings ceiling (approx £ equivalent)	110,369	n/a	14,317.60	31,057	–
Social Security pension type	A	B	C or D	A+B	A+D

Note: In some countries (notably France) the total social security contributions payable are considerably higher than the figures shown above, usually because separate contributions are levied for old-age and other social security and/or regional programmes.

	Denmark	France	Germany	Hungary	India
1. Economic indicators					
Population (2011, million)	5.6	63.3	81.8	10.0	1,241.3
Percentage of population aged 15–64	65	65	66	69	62
Percentage of population aged 65+	17	17	21	16	5
GDP (2010, local currency billion)	1,745.7	1,932.8	2,498.8	27,119.8	78,779.5
GDP per capita (2010, local currency)	313,699	29,792	30,609	2,710,636	67,279
GDP per capita (2010, current £ equivalent)	36,513	25,827	26,535	8,266	896
Price inflation (2010, % pa)	2.3	1.7	1.2	4.9	13.2
Money market/Treasury bill rate (2011, %)	1.21	1.33	1.33	5.89	8.10
Government bond yield (15 September 2011, %)	1.98	2.48	1.77	7.12	8.31
Exchange rate (£1 as at 16 September 2011)	8.5914	1.1535	1.1535	327.9268	75.0986
2. Social Security Information					
Current at	2010	2010	2010	2010	2010
State pension ages	65 m&f	60–65 m&f (c)	65 m&f (a)	62 m&f	58 m&f (f)
Contribution to State pension (employer, %)	(k)	9.9 (g,i)	9.95 (i)	24 (h)	17.61 (i)
Contribution to State pension (employee, %)	(k)	6.75 (i)	9.95 (i)	9.5 (i)	12 (i)
Earnings ceiling (local currency)	n/a	34,620 (m)	66,000	5,309,200	78,000
Earnings ceiling (approx £ equivalent)	n/a	30,013	57,216	16,190	1,039
Social Security pension type(s)	A	B	B	C	B+D

Note: In some countries (notably France) the total social security contributions payable are considerably higher than the figures shown above, usually because separate contributions are levied for old-age and other social security and/or regional programmes.

	Indonesia	Italy	Japan	Mexico	Netherlands
1. Economic indicators					
Population (2011, million)	238.2	60.8	128.1	114.8	16.7
Percentage of population aged 15–64	66	66	64	65	67
Percentage of population aged 65+	6	20	23	6	15
GDP (2010, local currency billion)	6,422,918.2	1,548.8	482,597.3	13,137.2	591.5
GDP per capita (2010, local currency)	27,623,462	25,569	3,788,643	121,054	35,583
GDP per capita (2010, current £ equivalent)	2,021	22,166	31,201	5,955	30,847
Price inflation (2010, % pa)	5.1	1.6	-0.7	4.2	0.9
Money market/Treasury bill rate (2011, %)	–	1.33	0.25	4.58	1.33
Government bond yield (15 September 2011, %)	–	5.41	1.01	6.15	2.21
Exchange rate (£1 as at 16 September 2011)	13,668.3496	1.1535	121.4263	20.3282	1.1535
2. Social Security Information					
Current at	2010	2010	2010	2009	2010
State pension ages	55 m&f	59–65 m&f (c)	65 m&f	65 m&f	65 m&f (a)
Contribution to State pension (employer, %)	4 (h)	23.81 (h)	7.852 (i)	6.9 (i)	0
Contribution to State pension (employee, %)	2 (h)	9.19 (n)	7.852 (i)	1.74 (i)	19 (i)
Earnings ceiling (local currency)	n/a	92,147	7,440,000	30,140	32,738
Earnings ceiling (approx £ equivalent)	n/a	79,883	61,272	1,483	28,381
Social Security pension type(s)	D	B+D	A+B	D	A
				(A underpin)	

Note: In some countries (notably France) the total social security contributions payable are considerably higher than the figures shown above, usually because separate contributions are levied for old-age and other social security and/or regional programmes.

	Poland	Russia	Spain	Sweden	Switzerland
1. Economic indicators					
Population (2011, million)	38.2	142.8	46.2	9.4	7.9
Percentage of population aged 15–64	71	72	68	65	68
Percentage of population aged 65+	14	13	17	18	17
GDP (2010, local currency billion)	1,412.8	44,939.2	1,062.6	3,301.1	546.2
GDP per capita (2010, local currency)	37,005	317,031	22,991	351,397	70,121
GDP per capita (2010, current £ equivalent)	7,408	6,646	19,931	33,375	50,480
Price inflation (2010, % pa)	2.6	6.9	2.0	1.9	0.7
Money market/Treasury bill rate (2011, %)	4.90	8.25	1.33	1.91	0.38
Government bond yield (15 September 2011, %)	5.68	6.0	5.16	1.80	1.01
Exchange rate (£1 as at 16 September 2011)	4.9951	47.7001	1.1535	10.5289	1.3891
2. Social Security Information					
Current at	2010	2010	2010	2010	2010
State pension ages	65m 60f	60m, 55 f	65 m&f (a)	65 m&f	65m, 64f
Contribution to State pension (employer, %)	14.26 (i)	26 (i,p)	23.6 (i)	11.91 (h)	4.2 (h)
Contribution to State pension (employee, %)	11.26 (i)	0	4.7 (i)	7 (i)	4.2 (h)
Earnings ceiling (local currency)	93,089	415,000	38,376	412,377	n/a
Earnings ceiling (approx £ equivalent)	18,636	8,700	33,269	39,166	n/a
Social Security pension type(s)	C+D	A+B+D	B	A+B+D	A

Note: In some countries (notably France) the total social security contributions payable are considerably higher than the figures shown above, usually because separate contributions are levied for old-age and other social security and/or regional programmes.

	UK	USA
1. Economic indicators		
Population (2011, million)	62.7	311.7
Percentage of population aged 15–64	67	67
Percentage of population aged 65+	16	13
GDP (2010, local currency billion)	1,453.6	14,582.4
GDP per capita (2010, local currency)	23,353	47,084
GDP per capita (2010, current £ equivalent)	23,353	29,842
Price inflation (2010, % pa)	3.3	1.6
Money market/Treasury bill rate (2011, %)	0.90	0.80
Government bond yield (15 September 2011, %)	2.26	1.92
Exchange rate (£1 as at 16 September 2011)	1	1.5778
2. Social Security Information		
Current at	2011	2011
State pension ages	65m 60f (d)	66 m&f (a)
Contribution to State pension (employer, %)	13.8 (i)	6.2 (i)
Contribution to State pension (employee, %)	12 (i)	4.2 (i)
Earnings ceiling (local currency)	42,480	106,800
Earnings ceiling (approx £ equivalent)	42,480	67,690
Social Security pension type(s)	A+B	B

Note: In some countries (notably France) the total social security contributions payable are considerably higher than the figures shown above, usually because separate contributions are levied for old-age and other social security and/or regional programmes.

AUSTRALIA

Economy and Government

Australia is a constitutional monarchy with a parliamentary government. The Queen is represented in Australia by a governor-general and six state governors.

The national (federal) Parliament consists of the Queen (through the governor-general), the House of Representatives and the Senate. The 150 members of the House of Representatives (each representing an electoral district) are elected for three-year terms. The majority party or group forms the government, selecting a prime minister and the cabinet from its ranks. The current Prime Minister is Julia Gillard of the Australian Labor Party.

Labour relations

Effective 1 July 2009, Fair Work Australia (FWA) and the Fair Work Ombudsman have subsumed or replaced much of the WorkChoices industrial relations system. FWA is responsible for facilitating collective bargaining; approving enterprise agreements; reviewing minimum wage levels and award conditions; addressing unfair dismissal claims; dealing with industrial action; and settling workplace disputes. The Fair Work Ombudsman provides advice, assistance and education to employers and employees, monitors compliance and takes legal action if necessary.

Cost of employment

The social security system is financed from general tax revenues. For workers' compensation, employers contribute varying percentages of payroll, depending on the risk category and the state.

Employment terms and conditions

FWA has updated and consolidated existing awards under new modern awards. From 1 July 2009, employers and employees, or their union representatives, may engage in enterprise-level collective bargaining within a single workplace or across multiple employers. From 1 January 2010, FWA applies the Better Off Overall Test (BOOT) to ensure that employees are better off overall in comparison to the relevant modern award. Also effective from 1 January 2010, there is no legislative provision for individual agreements. Existing Australian Workplace Agreements (AWAs) and Individual Transitional Employment Agreements (ITEAs), which were permitted until 31 December 2009, may remain in effect for up to five years. Existing workplace agreements must conform with the National Employment Standards (NES).

Social security and other required benefits

The social security system is a combination of universal and social assistance programmes financed from general tax revenues. Benefit payments and customer service are coordinated through Centrelink, which centralises the many services provided by the Departments of Family and Community Services; Education, Training, and Youth Affairs; Health and Family Services; Primary Industries and Energy; and Transport and Regional Services.

Healthcare system

Healthcare is administered at the Commonwealth (federal), state, and local levels and is delivered through a combination of public and private resources.

At the Commonwealth level, the Department of Health and Ageing is responsible for overall health policy (especially in the areas of public health, research, and information management) and is involved in the coordination of healthcare primarily through the national health insurance system known as Medicare. The Commonwealth government also maintains the Medicare fee schedules – the Medicare Benefits Schedule Book and the Schedule of Pharmaceutical Benefits for Approved Pharmacists and Medical Practitioners. Medicare Australia administers Medicare, the Pharmaceutical Benefits Scheme (the national prescription drug programme), and an immunisation programme for children, and acts as both claims payer and auditor.

Taxation of compensation and benefits

Australia has a federal tax on personal income, but no state or local income taxes. Residents are taxed on income from all foreign and domestic sources. If tax has been withheld on foreign-source income by the foreign country, a tax credit is granted equal to the lesser of Australian tax or the foreign tax. Tax on employment income is withheld at source. Non-residents are taxed on Australian-source income only. The tax year (like the fiscal year) runs from 1 July to 30 June. Tax returns based on self assessments generally must be filed by the following 31 August.

Recent developments

The federal government has accepted most of the recommendations of its superannuation review committee. The contribution rate would increase from 9% to 12%. Employers contribute to superannuation based on salaries up to a specified amount that is indexed annually on the basis of February-to-February wage figures. MySuper would replace the existing default fund. The reforms are expected to significantly reduce fees and make the processing of transactions easier and cheaper. If passed, the reforms would be implemented in 2013. Also, the government proposes to increase the cap on concessional contributions from A$25,000 to A$50,000 for individuals age 50 and over with a total superannuation balance that is below A$500,000.

BELGIUM

Economy and Government

Belgium is a constitutional monarchy with a parliamentary democracy. The current king, Albert II, is the head of state. The government is led by the prime minister (appointed by the king on the basis of majority support in the House of Representatives) and the Council of Ministers. Parliament consists of a House of Representatives with 150 members elected through a system of proportional representation and a Senate with 71 members (40 popularly elected, 31 appointed by the Regional Councils). Members of both houses stand for election every four years. The House is the dominant legislative body;

the Senate's responsibilities include oversight of constitutional revisions, treaties and relations between the linguistic communities.

Labour relations

Terms of employment and labour relations are governed by statute and through collective agreements signed at the national and inter-industry level, at the industry level, by regions or groups of companies, and at the company level. They are hierarchical – agreements signed at a lower level build on those signed at a higher level – and cumulative – they amend or add to earlier agreements. Employers must use the language of the region in which they are located for all documentation. In Brussels, which is bilingual, employers are required to communicate with an employee in his or her dominant language.

Cost of employment

The social security system is comprehensive in scope and coverage and involves substantial cost, approximately 75% of which is borne by the employer. Contributions are based on the employee's gross salary plus any bonuses and benefits in kind, with no earnings ceiling (except for workers' compensation). All employees and firms employing ten or more persons pay full social security contributions on the vacation bonus.

Employment terms and conditions

Employment law distinguishes between blue- and white-collar workers. While the classifications are ambiguous – blue-collar as 'manual' and white-collar as 'intellectual' – distinct provisions apply to each classification as regards termination procedures, probationary periods, payment intervals and non-competition agreements.

The 1978 Law on Contracts of Employment, as amended, governs contracts for blue- and white-collar workers, commercial representatives, domestic workers and students. Employment contracts may be written or verbal; however, fixed-term, part-time, temporary, replacement and student contracts must be written. In practice, almost all employment contracts are in writing.

Social security and other required benefits

Separate but closely related programmes exist for wage earners, salaried employees, the self-employed, miners and seamen. The first two programmes cover all employees in private industry and commerce, except for some company directors considered self-employed for social security purposes. Benefits for the self-employed are significantly lower than those under the other programmes. Other separately financed and administered statutory systems cover national and local government employees and railway workers.

Healthcare system

The extensive healthcare system, which covers all Belgian residents, includes hospital care, visits to doctors (both general practitioners (GPs) and specialists), dental care, pharmaceuticals and home care. The system includes both private and public elements and is highly regulated. The Ministry of Social Affairs and the Ministry of Public Health share responsibility for health insurance, hospital costs, drugs, medical practice and vaccinations. Some responsibility for public health, institutions and home care has devolved to the regional governments.

The National Institute for Sickness and Invalidity Insurance (INAMI/RIZIV) oversees health insurance. Government-approved 'mutuelle' (sickness fund) groups administer the system. All Belgians must enrol with a *mutuelle* of their choice. The *mutuelles* developed from self-funded, self-help community organisations, although now primarily funded by employee and employer (and self-employed) payroll contributions through the federal government. There are six networks of government-approved *mutuelles*, although the affiliation may not be apparent to the *mutuelle* member.

Taxation of compensation and benefits

A resident is subject to Belgian income taxes on worldwide income. An individual is resident if he or she is living in or has a 'centre of economic interest' in Belgium. Non-residents are taxed only on income produced or received in Belgium. Special rules may apply to expatriates. Income taxes are imposed at the national level. Municipalities may levy a surtax, which varies from 0% to 10%. There is no wealth tax in Belgium and the capital gains tax varies according to the type of property held and the length of time it is held. The tax year is the calendar year. Individuals must file a tax return by 30 June following the tax year.

Recent developments

The Constitutional Court has given the parliament until 8 July 2013 to harmonise the employment terms and conditions of blue- and white-collar employees, including termination of employment notice periods, waiting days for sick pay, and guaranteed pay. The date is the 20th anniversary of a State Council decision declaring that the differences between the two groups constitute discrimination.

BRAZIL

Economy and Government

Brazil is a democratic republic with a presidential government. The president serves as chief of state and head of government. The president and vice president are elected by direct popular vote for a four-year term and may be re-elected once.

Labour relations

The constitution protects employees' and employers' rights of association and prohibits government intervention in the organisation or administration of unions or employers' associations. Most employer–union negotiations occur at the industry or professional level or at the level of the enterprise. National-level negotiations between the social partners (employers, unions and government) are infrequent, generally addressing macropolitical or economic stabilisation issues.

Cost of employment

Employee social security contributions are levied on total earnings according to salary brackets, up to an earnings ceiling of R3,689.66 per month as of 1 January 2011. The employee's contribution is based on 12 months' pay only.

The employer's contribution is levied on total payroll with no ceiling. Employer contributions may vary slightly according to the nature of the business.

Employment terms and conditions

Terms of employment and labour relations are governed by the constitution and legislation. Most employment and labour laws have been consolidated in the CLT – Consolidação das Leis do Trabalho (the labour code).

Employment conditions and labour relations may also be regulated by collective agreement and individual contract. Employees may not waive rights granted to them by law. Employment contracts may be written or oral. In practice, most employment contracts are in writing.

Social security and other required benefits

The National Institute of Social Security (INSS) administers social security benefits for insured persons and their dependants, including the self-employed and foreign residents. Civil servants, military personnel, politicians and rural workers are covered by special legislation.

Social security benefits include old-age pensions, special early retirement pensions for working in a hazardous environment, survivors' pensions, long-term disability pensions, cash sickness benefits, medical care benefits, maternity leave and family allowances. Professional rehabilitation after work-related accidents is also provided under social security. Employers are responsible for prefunding severance obligations through a government-administered savings fund and must contribute to government-run training and apprenticeship programmes.

Healthcare system

The Ministry of Health is responsible for national policy, regulating the public healthcare system (Sistema Unificado de Saude, SUS), and providing technical and financial assistance to states and municipalities. State ministries of health control regional healthcare networks and provide technical and financial assistance to the municipalities. The municipalities have primary responsibility for local healthcare planning and delivery. Health councils assist the government at all three levels.

In addition to the SUS, there is a large private sector, whose growth has been stimulated by reductions in public services and the provision of employer and employee tax deductions for private health insurance. An estimated 24% of the population is covered by private health insurance or group medical plans, most of which are employer-sponsored.

Taxation of compensation and benefits

Residents are subject to a graduated federal income tax on worldwide income. An individual is considered resident if he or she has a permanent residence permit, an employment contract in Brazil (even if he or she has a temporary work visa), or lives in Brazil for more than 183 days in a 12-month period. Non-residents pay a flat withholding tax on Brazilian-source income (25% on earned income or 15% on other income). Income source is established by the location of the payer regardless of where work is performed. A resident absent from Brazil for 12 months is taxed as a non-resident.

Recent developments

The legislature is expected to review the future of the social security system. Among the issues to be addressed are an increase in the minimum retirement age; the continuation or elimination of the 'Fator Previdenciário' formula, which is based on contribution rate, contribution period, age and life expectancy; and sources of funding for the system. In related news, the Finance Ministry is expected to present a tax reform package to the Congress, which includes a provision to reduce the employer social security contribution rate from 20% to 14%.

CANADA

Economy and Government

Canada is a constitutional monarchy. The Queen is represented by a governor-general (appointed on the advice of the prime minister) who convenes and dissolves Parliament, assents to bills and exercises other executive functions. Canada is structured as a confederation of ten provinces and three territories. The federal government consists of an elected House of Commons and an appointed Senate.

Labour relations

Employment standards and human rights legislation in each of the federal, provincial and territorial jurisdictions set the minimum age for industrial employment, maximum work hours, overtime rates of pay, minimum wage rates and statutory vacations with pay. They also regulate employment practices and termination procedures, prohibit discrimination and regulate apprenticeships. Provincial and territorial legislation covers employees working within their borders, except those under federal jurisdiction (generally employees engaged in any work of an interprovincial, national or international nature). Terms of employment are also governed by collective agreements, which cannot establish terms less favourable than those provided by legislation.

Cost of employment

Retirement, death and disability benefits under the Old Age Security Act (flat-rate benefit and means-tested supplements) are financed through general revenues. In addition, there are employer and employee payroll deductions to cover the Canada Pension Plan (earnings-related benefits), employment insurance (including cash sickness and maternity), hospital/medical benefits and workers' compensation. (In Quebec, employees are covered by the Quebec Pension Plan.)

Employment terms and conditions

Full- and part-time permanent employees are not usually covered by a contract other than a collective agreement. However, it is strongly recommended that employers require all employees to enter into written employment contracts. All employees, whether or not they are party to a written employment contract, are protected under employment standards legislation at the federal, provincial or territorial level. Employment contracts are subject to all applicable employment and tax law in the contract's jurisdiction. If a self-employed person invoices for work done, he or she is treated as an agency or separate company for tax and employment law purposes and is normally liable for income tax, employment insurance, health insurance premiums and other employment costs.

Social security and other required benefits

The social security system is a combination of federal, provincial or territorial, and federal provincial programmes, which provide benefits in all the categories generally found in European social security systems. Virtually all residents are covered by social security. Foreign nationals employed in Canada and paid from a Canadian payroll may also be covered. Under specified circumstances, Canadian nationals employed outside Canada may continue to contribute to the Canada Pension Plan.

Healthcare system

Healthcare falls under provincial and territorial rather than federal control. Each province and territory administers a healthcare plan meeting criteria set out in the (federal) Canada Health Act. Healthcare represents a major expenditure and is a highly visible government concern. The ministry of health in each province or territory is responsible for negotiating the pay of health professionals, the distribution and management of hospitals and their services, setting education policies, standards and quotas for health practitioners, and funding and oversight of the agency that pays for services.

In general, provincial governments prohibit private plans from covering the services offered under the provincial plan. Supplemental plans cannot be used to purchase enhanced care for government-provided services. In June 2005, the Supreme Court of Canada ruled that individuals in Quebec have the right to obtain private health insurance for services already available under the public health care system, and in 2006 the Quebec government passed legislation allowing the purchase of private insurance for three surgical procedures (knee- and hip-replacement surgery and cataract surgery).

Taxation of compensation and benefits

Residents pay personal income tax on worldwide income. Non-residents are taxed only on Canadian-source income. Canadian income taxes are imposed by the federal government and the provincial and territorial governments. In all provinces and territories, except Quebec, provincial and territorial personal income taxes are a fixed percentage of the federal tax, collected by the federal government. Quebec assesses and collects income tax separately. Starting in 2000, the other jurisdictions delinked the provincial or territorial and federal tax calculations and moved to a separate tax on income, although individuals (other than Quebec residents) continue to file a single tax return.

Recent developments

The federal government's 2011–2012 budget includes the following inititatives related to retirement:

- new funding and minimum withdrawal rules for Individual Pension Plans

- continued efforts to bring public service compensation in line with the private sector by eliminating the accrual of severance benefits for resignation and retirement
- anti-avoidance rules for Registered Retirement Savings Plans and Registered Retirement Income Funds based on the Tax-Free Savings Account anti-avoidance rules
- amending the Canadian Human Rights Act and Canada Labor Code to prohibit federally regulated employers from setting a mandatory retirement age unless there is a bona fide occupational requirement
- allowing annual Registered Disability Savings Plan withdrawals of up to C$10,000 in taxable plan savings and a prorated amount of contributions with respect to a beneficiary with a life expectancy of five years or less, without requiring the repayment of Canada Disability Savings Grants and Canada Disability Savings Bonds paid into the plan in the preceding ten years (effective in 2011 with transitional rules applying for the first two years) *and*
- implementing the recommendations of the Task Force on Financial Literacy and appointing a Financial Literacy Leader to promote national efforts.

CHINA

Economy and Government

Formally, the government and the Communist Party are separate, complementary institutions; however, there is considerable cross-membership. Hu Jintao is currently head of state and the General Secretary of the Politburo Standing Committee of the Party. The current leadership is expected to remain in power until 2013 (two five-year terms).

Labour relations

Employment terms are mainly established by the Labour Law, which applies to all types of company. The Labour Contracts Law, effective 1 January 2008, substantially changed a number of terms of employment covered by the Labour Law. Earlier Regulations for Labour Management in Foreign-Invested Enterprises apply only to joint ventures, wholly foreign-owned enterprises and Chinese–foreign joint stock companies. Some areas of the Labour Law and the Regulations may be unclear and subject to interpretation. Local labour authorities should be consulted.

Cost of employment

Contribution rates for social security and other mandatory programmes vary according to city or province. Many cities and provinces have established contribution rates which vary from the national guidelines. City or provincial regulations supersede national guidelines.

Employment terms and conditions

From 1 January 2007, employers are required to register the following employment details at the labour and social security bureau where the business is registered: the name, legal representative, economic type and enterprise code of the employer; and the name, gender and national identification number of the employee, along with the date the contract was signed and its expiry date. Employers are required to file the required information within 30 days of hiring an employee and 7 days after termination of the employment.

Social security and other required benefits

The social security system includes pensions, housing and medical care. Each person is assigned a social security number. Social security and other mandatory programmes are financed through contributions by employers and employees which *(as mentioned above)* vary by city or province.

Healthcare system

The healthcare system has been made more complex by the move from a planned to a market economy. Between 1983 and 2003, government and social insurance expenditures fell, respectively, from 37.43% and 31.12% to 16.96% and 27.16%. Out-of-pocket expenditures have become the primary source of healthcare financing, and increased from 31.45% to 55.87% over the same period. Government expenditures have increased in recent years, accounting for 51% of total healthcare expenditures in 2006. The government is undertaking reforms to reduce the service gap between rural and urban regions and high- and low-income employees. The government also plans to establish an independent system for the production, procurement and distribution of prescription drugs and a national drug formulary. The government wants to reduce hospitals' involvement in the sale of prescription drugs in order to cut prices.

Taxation of compensation and benefits

Individual income tax rates for Chinese citizens and for foreign-national residents are the same, but different monthly allowances apply. Residence is principally based on physical presence, domicile or (in certain cases) the right to reside in China. The length of stay establishing residence is not explicitly defined; however, in practice, individuals who are in China for one full tax year or more are considered to be resident and are subject to tax on worldwide income. Temporary absences not exceeding 30 days at a time or 90 days (in aggregate) over a tax year are included in calculating the period of stay. Chinese nationals who have a domicile in China are considered resident for tax purposes. Foreign individuals resident in China for between one and five years can, with the approval of the tax authorities, be taxed only on China-sourced income. Non-residents are taxed only on China-sourced income.

Recent developments

The new Social Insurance Law, effective 1 July 2011, consolidates existing regulations and introduces several new provisions. Participants will be entitled to five types of coverage – old age pension, basic medical, unemployment, maternity and work injury insurance. Two provisions are notable. The calculation of the maternity allowance will change. Employers will be required to calculate the maternity allowance according to the average monthly pay for all employees in the previous year (currently, the employee's base pay). If there is a difference between the average monthly pay of all employees and the employee's base pay that is not covered by the Social Insurance maternity benefit, the employer must make up the difference. With regard to employees with a work-related injury, employers are required to pay for wages during the medical treatment period; monthly disability allowances for a Class 5 or 6 disability; and lump-sum disability and reemployment subsidies the employee is entitled to receive upon termination or expiration of his or her employment contract. Employers also are reminded that all foreign nationals are required to participate in Social Insurance. While this requirement was included in earlier regulations, many cities did not implement systems which allowed the participation of foreign employees.

EUROPEAN UNION

Economy and Government

The 27 Member Countries of the EU are: Austria, Belgium, Bulgaria, Cyprus, Czech Republic, Denmark, Estonia, Finland, France, Germany, Greece, Hungary, Ireland, Italy, Latvia, Lithuania, Luxembourg, Malta, Netherlands, Poland, Portugal, Romania, Slovak Republic, Slovenia, Spain, Sweden and the UK. Candidate countries include Croatia, Macedonia, Iceland, and Turkey.

The 30 countries of the EEA are the 27 Member Countries of the EU plus Iceland, Liechtenstein and Norway. The three additional countries in the EEA do not participate in the development of EU legislation and have no vote on EU matters. Also, the EEA is not a customs union and border controls with Iceland, Liechtenstein and Norway remain.

Labour relations

All EEA members, including Iceland, Liechtenstein and Norway, must observe the labour requirements of the EU, including Directive 93/104 on Working Time, and their nationals have the right of freedom of movement of employees within the EEA. The Directive applies to all public- and private-sector employees, with no exceptions for small firms, but there are numerous exceptions to the provisions for certain types of work. There are also extended transition periods for the provisions on vacation and length of the working week. The EU has also adopted directives on employee representation (works councils), information and consultation of employees.

Cost of employment

Social security benefits are provided by the programmes of each EEA Member Country. The EU itself provides no social security system. There is no obligation upon Member Countries to have a similar level of contributions or benefits under their social security programmes. However, Resolution 94/C 368/03 on EU Social Policy Objectives notes that the objectives of EU social policy include improving competitiveness, protecting workers' rights through minimum standards, convergence of social security systems rather than the imposition of uniform rules, and reinforcing dialogue among Member Countries. The United Kingdom did not agree to the Resolution, however.

Employment terms and conditions

EU directives provide the framework for national legislation on certain employment terms and conditions. EU Member Countries may pass legislation that is more favourable to employees than the terms provided by a directive.

Social security and other required benefits

The EU social security totalisation agreement now extends to the nationals and social security institutions of Iceland, Liechtenstein and Norway. The agreement allows nationals of EEA countries to combine their years of participation under the social security systems of all EEA countries to establish eligibility for benefits. Each country then pays benefits proportionate to the years of coverage under its own social security system. All EU requirements for statutory benefits are extended to Iceland, Liechtenstein and Norway, as EEA members.

In June 2010, the Council of Ministers agreed on a regulation designed to ensure that third-country nationals who are legally resident in the EU and in a cross-border situation are subject to the same rules for coordinating social security entitlements as EU citizens.

Healthcare system

Following several European Court of Justice judgments covering patient reimbursement for healthcare received in another Member Country, the long-awaited directive on cross-border care 'aims to clarify how patients can exercise their rights to cross-border health care, while at the same time providing legal certainty for Member States and health care providers'. Among the directive's major provisions:

- patients will have the right to seek healthcare within the European Union and be reimbursed up to what they would have received at home
- Member Countries will be responsible for providing healthcare in their territory, *and*
- the development of European reference networks would be facilitated, that is, specialised centres in different Member Countries. The directive also seeks to promote activities in e-health and health technology assessment.

The directive was approved on 28 February 2011. Member states will have 30 months to transpose the directive's provisions into national legislation.

Taxation of compensation and benefits

Income tax is levied by each Member Country of the EEA. The EU itself does not levy any taxes, but collects revenues from a percentage of value added taxes levied in each Member Country. There is no obligation to harmonize the income tax systems at present.

Recent developments

The European Court of Justice (ECJ) has ruled that insurance premiums based on gender will no longer be allowed from 21 December 2012. The ECJ delivered its judgment in the Belgian *Test-Achats* case. The Court broadly agrees with the earlier Opinion of the Advocate General (AG), which found that the use of insurance premiums based on gender is incompatible with the principle of equal treatment for men and women. Although the AG recommended that there should be a three-year transitional period, the judgment states that the use of gender-based premiums will be unlawful from 21 December 2012.

FRANCE

Economy and Government

France has a 'mixed' system of presidential and parliamentary government. The president is the head of state and commander in chief. He or she names the prime minister, formally presides over the cabinet (and may name members), concludes treaties, and can dissolve the parliament and call for national referenda. The prime minister is the head of government; he or she is usually the leader of the majority party in parliament and nominates cabinet members. The parliament consists of the National Assembly and the Senate. Representatives to the National Assembly are directly elected for five-year terms. Senators are elected by an electoral college and serve nine-year terms; one-third of the Senate is elected every three years. Two other institutions – the Economic and Social Council and the Constitutional Council – play important roles. The Economic and Social Council (representatives from the trade union confederations, employers' associations, social welfare groups and consumers' organisations) is consulted on long-range economic plans and various bills. The Constitutional Council reviews acts of parliament to determine their constitutionality. It consists of nine members: three are appointed by the president, three by the speaker of the National Assembly and three by the speaker of the Senate.

Labour relations

Labour relations and the terms of employment are determined by statute, case law and collective agreement. At the national level, trade union confederations and employers' associations meet to study and seek solutions for labour market problems, such as skill development and training and unemployment. Despite collaboration between the 'social partners' (government, labour and employers), workplace conflict persists. Strikes are often called during periods of corporate restructuring, especially if the unions and management cannot reach agreement on a 'job protection plan'. They are also used as a political tool – to protest governmental or EU policies.

Cost of employment

Salary *tranches* are used to determine both contributions and benefits under social security and to express premiums and costs under employer-sponsored benefit plans. The *tranches* are adjusted once a year (in January) in relation to wage and price changes.

Employment terms and conditions

In France, employees may be classified as:

- non-*cadres*: blue-collar and lower-level, white-collar employees

- *cadres*: employees who are primarily managerial or who have special academic qualifications
- *cadres assimilés*: technicians, foremen and senior white-collar employees, *and*
- *cadres supérieurs, cadres dirigeants*: executives, top management.

Employees' rights are established primarily through statute and collective agreement. However, a benefit granted repeatedly over time may become a right, unless the employer explicitly stipulates that the benefit is granted at its discretion.

Social security and other required benefits

Coverage under the social security system is mandatory for all employees in commerce, industry and public works. Pensions are payable in any country with which France has diplomatic relations. The Ministry of Employment and Social Affairs, assisted by a Secretary of State for Health, is responsible for the general supervision of the social security system. Compulsory employee and employer contributions are collected by a joint collection agency and distributed to the National Sickness Insurance Fund, the National Old Age Insurance Fund and the National Family Allowance Fund, from which benefits are paid. The government funds additional pension benefits and allowances, certain health and social services and, under certain circumstances, unemployment benefits.

Healthcare system

Membership in a health insurance fund is compulsory for any person working in France (excluding the overseas *départements* and territories), regardless of nationality, provided that an employment relationship exists and the work is paid. Dependants are covered through the employee's insurance. Coverage is now almost universal. The majority of the population is covered through CNAMTS (the programme for salaried employees).

Taxation of compensation and benefits

Residents are subject to national income tax on worldwide income. In addition to a local property tax which is levied on the occupants of all types of accommodation, taxpayers are also subject to three social taxes – the general social contribution (CSG), the social debt reimbursement (CRDS) and the social levy. Individuals who are physically present for more than 183 days a year, who have a home or primary abode in France, or whose main occupation or centre of economic activities is in France, are considered resident for tax purposes. Non-residents are subject to tax only on France-sourced income. The tax year is the calendar year. Tax returns must generally be filed by the following 1 March. Income tax is not withheld from employee pay for individuals domiciled in France. Income taxes are paid in advance (based on pre-assessments of tax liability) in two instalments equal to one-third of the total liability from the previous year or via monthly instalments. Final settlement is due in September/October or November/December, respectively, based on final assessments issued by the tax authorities.

Recent developments

The Pension Reform Law of 9 November 2010 has been enacted. The Law's provisions include:

- as of 1 July 2011, the minimum retirement age will increase from 60 by four months each year until it reaches 62 in 2018. The Law allows for some exceptions (individuals in hazardous or arduous work, with special diets, etc.)
- the retirement age for a full pension will increase from 65 to 67, regardless of the number of quarters of contributions. Effective 1 July 2016, the retirement age will increase by four months each year until it reaches 66 in 2019 and 67 in 2023
- the Law confirms the increases in the required number of contributions scheduled in the 2003 Act: to receive a full pension, insureds born in 1953 and 1954 must have 41 years and one quarter of contributions and, from 2020, the contribution requirement will be 41 years and two quarters of contributions
- individuals who entered the workforce aged 16 or 17 may continue to retire at age 60. Individuals who entered the workforce aged 14 or 15 may retire at age 58 or age 59. The retirement age for individuals with long careers will gradually increase at a rate of four months each year until it reaches age 60
- a full pension at age 65 is maintained for mothers with three children who are aged 55 or over and have interrupted their careers to care for their children. Parents who have interrupted their careers to care for disabled children will continue to receive the full pension at age 65, regardless of the number of quarters of contributions
- employers must initiate negotiations and take measures to reduce the wage gap between male and female employees or financial penalties will be introduced
- maternity benefits will be taken into account in calculating retirement pensions so that female employees are not penalised for leaving the active workforce, *and*
- employers that hire unemployed individuals over age 55 will receive assistance equal to 14% of pay.

GERMANY

Economy and Government

Germany is a parliamentary democracy with a federal system of government. It has a bicameral legislature and an independent judiciary. The president may be elected to two five-year terms, but his or her other duties are largely ceremonial; executive power is exercised by the chancellor.

The Bundestag has 622 deputies, who are elected every four years; one-half of the deputies are elected directly from single-member districts, while the remainder are elected through proportional representation. It is responsible for electing the chancellor and controls the executive branch through its power to call for a vote of no confidence. The Bundesrat (upper house or Federal Council) has 69 members who are delegates of the 16 *Länder* (state governments). Their terms vary in length. The Bundesrat represents the interests of the states at the national level.

Labour relations

Labour relations and terms of employment are determined by statutes, case law and collective bargaining. Traditionally, collective bargaining has been centralised at the industry level. During the past decade, however, some decentralisation has occurred; and the number of agreements signed at the company level has increased. Labour relations in Germany are cooperative. Employees enjoy a dual system of representation: at the industry level, they are represented by trade unions and at the company level by works councils.

Cost of employment

Annual earnings ceilings applicable in the western and eastern *Länder* for sickness, maternity and medical benefits, as well as long-term care insurance, were equalised in 2001. Two different earnings ceilings still exist for contribution to old age, survivors' and disability pensions, as well as employment promotion. As income levels become uniform, these ceiling levels also will be made uniform.

Employment terms and conditions

Employers must provide employees with specified terms of their employment within one month of the start of the employment relationship. Fixed-term contracts may not run for more than two years.

Social security and other required benefits

The social security system covers all German employees and provides old age, survivors' and long-term disability pensions, as well as unemployment insurance. Medical care (routine and long-term) and cash sickness and maternity benefits are administered through health funds. Workers' compensation is maintained through a variety of funds administered by employers' associations, or *Land* or local municipalities. When the West German social security system replaced the East German system on 1 January 1992, transitional regulations and grandfathering provisions were implemented, some of which are still in effect.

Healthcare system

The healthcare system is a hybrid of the managed care model and a centralised system in which the government can intervene. The Law to Strengthen GKV Competition (GKV Wettbewerbsstärkungsgesetz), passed in 2007, alters the traditional sole reliance on employment taxes for medical care. It creates a split-revenue system, in which insurers can charge additional contributions payable by employees, to make up any shortfall in revenue.

Taxation of compensation and benefits

Residents are taxed on worldwide income. In general, residents are defined as persons living in Germany for more than 183 days per year. Non-residents are taxed only on German-source income at a minimum rate of 25% (though executives of supervisory boards may be taxed at a higher rate). Taxable income is always assessed by calendar year. Married couples who are residents may file separately or jointly.

Recent developments

Debate over the retirement age has resumed in Germany. Under legislation passed in 2007, the retirement age is scheduled to increase from 65 to 67. The increase is gradual – one month per year beginning in 2012 and two months per year beginning in 2024 until age 67 is reached in 2029. The major union confederation DGB and members of the Social Democratic Party (SPD) oppose the scheduled increase, claiming that the labour market is not strong enough to support the participation of mature employees. The SPD proposes that the increase be postponed until 2015; however, it would keep 2029 as the date when the increase is fully implemented. Chancellor Merkel and the Christian Democrats oppose the change.

INDIA

Economy and Government

India is a federal republic with a parliamentary government. The 'union executive' consists of a president, vice president, prime minister and the council of ministers. The president serves as head of state while the prime minister serves as head of government. The president and vice president are elected to a five-year term by an electoral college that is composed of members of the national parliament and the state legislative assemblies. The president is empowered to declare a 'state of emergency' if he or she believes the country faces an external threat, and to assume control over state governments if there is a constitutional crisis in a state.

Labour relations

Labour relations and terms of employment are determined primarily by statute. National laws are applicable, except where states have passed amending acts to address local circumstances. At both the national and state levels, employers and employees must comply with omnibus acts, as well as 'sectoral' acts. The most important sectoral acts regulating the terms of employment are the Factories Act, which is a national law covering factories, and various shops and establishments acts, passed by the states and covering shops, offices and commercial establishments that are not regulated by the Factories Act. Case law and custom also play an important role in guiding labour–management relations and employment issues. The Supreme Court regularly hears appeals of decisions made by industrial tribunals; it has ruled on labour–management disputes, employee terminations, conditions of employment and wages and benefits. Custom and local practice are significant factors in the establishment of acquired rights.

Cost of employment

Contributions for old age, survivors', disability, cash sickness and maternity benefits are based on monthly basic salary plus 'dearness' allowance (cost of living) and retaining allowance (if any), (both employer and employee contributions) up to a specified ceiling. Employees whose earnings exceed the ceilings are excluded from these programmes.

Employment terms and conditions

Employment contracts can be written or oral. Typically, employers issue an 'appointment letter' that outlines the general terms and conditions of employment. A 'letter of confirmation' is sent to the employee within 30 days of hire. The contents of an appointment letter are not determined by statute except for employees covered by the Sales Promotion Employees (Conditions of Services) Act. This act requires that the job title, date of appointment, probation period, wage scale, rate of wage increases, total wages and conditions of service be delineated in the appointment letter. The Industrial Employment (Standing Orders) Act requires employers to create a written document, known as 'standing orders', that establishes the terms of employment, and provides a 'model standing orders' for any employer to use. If an employer wishes to develop its own standing orders, it must be certified by the relevant authorities, and they cannot contain terms and conditions that do not meet the standards outlined in the model document.

Social security and other required benefits

The social security system consists of programmes at the national and state levels, including compulsory savings (provident fund), pensions, and insured welfare benefits in the event of sickness, maternity, death and work-related accident or illness. Indemnities are payable by the employer upon termination of employment for any reason except just cause (with some exceptions). Employees covered by Employees' State Insurance are entitled to unemployment and medical benefits in the event of layoffs. Several states have their own unemployment programmes, which are financed from general revenue.

Healthcare system

The states are responsible for the delivery of most healthcare services. The federal (union) government responsibilities include population control, medical education, family welfare and food and drug regulation. Nationally, the Ministry of Health and Family Welfare oversees all aspects of healthcare policy and delivery through the Department of Health and Family Welfare (DHFW) and the Department of Ayurveda, Yoga and Naturopathy, Unani, Siddha and Homeopathy (AYUSH). The DHFW regulates the manufacture or import, distribution and sale of drugs and oversees medical education, training and research standards as well as numerous educational institutions. The Central Government Health Scheme (CGHS), under the DHFW, operates medical facilities for certain groups including active and retired national government employees and members of parliament. The second department (AYUSH) was created in 1995 to develop the Indian Systems of Medicine and integrate them into the general healthcare system.

Taxation of compensation and benefits

Residents are taxed on worldwide income. Non-residents are taxed on Indian source income only. A person is a resident if he or she spent at least 182 days in the previous tax year in India, or 60 days in the previous tax year plus at least 365 days in the preceding four years. However, an Indian national who leaves India to work abroad is not considered a resident unless he or she has been in India for at least 182 days in that year. Income payable for services rendered in India is considered Indian-source income, irrespective of its place of accrual or payment. Persons 'resident but not ordinarily resident' in India – someone who has not been a resident in India in nine of the ten previous years or who has not been in India a total of 730 days or more during the preceding seven years – generally do not pay tax on income earned outside India, unless it is derived from a business controlled in India. Taxable income includes wages, salaries, allowances, fees, commissions, benefits in kind, annuities or pensions, gratuities in excess of the tax-free portion, dividends, interest and discounts, rent, royalties, technical service fees and lottery or contest winnings. The tax year begins on 1 April and ends on 31 March.

Recent developments

The government may expand Employee Provident Fund (EPF) coverage to workplaces with over ten employees and increase the minimum benefit. Currently, factories and establishments with 20 or more employees must participate in the EPF. The government also indicated that it may propose legislation that would establish a minimum pension payout of INR1,000 from the EPF. To fund the increase, government or employer contributions would have to increase by 0.6% of basic pay (currently, the monthly contribution ceiling is INR6,500). The government indicated that the contribution increase may be split evenly between the government and employers. It is not known when action will be taken on these measures.

JAPAN

Economy and Government

Japan is a constitutional monarchy with a parliamentary government. The emperor serves as the symbolic head of state; the prime minister is the head of government and leads the executive branch. The prime minister is elected by the parliament or Diet and must be a member of the Diet at the time of his or her election to the executive branch. The prime minister appoints cabinet members, a majority of whom must also be members of the Diet. The Diet consists of the House of Representatives and the House of Councillors. The House of Representatives has 480 members who are elected to four-year terms. The 247 members of the House of Councillors are elected for six-year terms. Of the two houses, the House of Representatives is more powerful.

Labour relations

Employment terms are defined primarily by employers. The Labour Standards Law stipulates minimum conditions. Wages, on the other hand, are often established through the 'spring labour offensive' or *Shunto*, a system of annual industrial collective bargaining. Given Japan's recent economic difficulties, the impact of the *Shunto* on wage increases has been negligible during the past few years. Historically, labour relations have been cooperative, though recent circumstances have created some distrust between employers and workers. The 2001 Law for Promoting the Resolution of Individual Labour Disputes, aiming to facilitate the prompt resolution of labour disputes by rapid intermediation through 300 general labour consultation desks, has had somewhat limited success, however, so the 2004 Labour Tribunal Law provides a venue for the speedy resolution of labour disputes.

Cost of employment

Social security combines a universal programme providing flat-rate benefits through the National Pension Plan (NPP), with an employment-related programme providing benefits based on earnings through the Employees' Pension Insurance Plan (EPIP). Contributions to the EPIP are based on monthly covered earnings, with 30 earnings grades ranging from J¥98,000 to J¥620,000 per month and seasonal bonuses up to J¥1,500,000 per year. Contributions to the Employee Health Insurance System (EHI) are based on monthly covered earnings, with 47 earnings grades ranging from J¥58,000 to J¥1,210,000 per month and seasonal bonuses up to J¥5,400,000 per year. Contributions to unemployment insurance, workers' compensation insurance and family allowances are based on total payroll.

Employment terms and conditions

Traditionally, employment law and practices have emphasised homogeneous groups of employees, who are long-serving and receive seniority-based wages. Given this focus, employment law stipulates that employers with ten or more employees must establish a set of work rules that specify the terms of employment. These work rules generally substitute for contracts and collective agreements, even though they are not subject to negotiation.

Social security and other required benefits

The NPP provides flat-rate benefits for all residents. The EPIP provides pay-related benefits that supplement the NPP. The EPIP also provides limited flat-rate benefits. Employers and sole proprietors with five or more full-time employees, and all corporations, including employers (legal directors and auditors) and employees, must participate in the EPIP and the EHI. This includes branches and sales offices of foreign companies which are treated as incorporated businesses and representative offices which are treated as sole proprietorships. (Part-time employees must also be covered if their working hours are 75% or more of the working hours of full-time employees.) However employers with at least 1,000 employees may contract out of the EPIP under certain conditions, and employers with at least 700 employees may contract out of the EHI. Workers' compensation insurance, unemployment insurance and family allowances are provided under separate programmes.

Healthcare system

The Ministry of Health, Labour, and Welfare (MHLW) develops healthcare policy and coordinates overall health and welfare administration. In the MHLW, the Department of National Hospitals manages and administers national medical facilities including hospitals, sanatoriums and specialised medical centres. The Health Insurance Bureau handles policy planning and coordination of the health insurance systems which the MHLW oversees

The Social Insurance Agency manages and administers the various health, welfare and pension plans. While the government administers and/or coordinates health insurance coverage, healthcare providers are almost exclusively private. More than 80% of hospitals and 90% of physicians, dentists, clinics and nursing homes operate on a for-profit basis.

Taxation of compensation and benefits

Japan levies national, prefectural and municipal income taxes on individuals. Permanent residents are taxed on worldwide income. Individuals who are domiciled in Japan or who are present in Japan for one year or more are considered to be resident for tax purposes; domicile is defined as the place in which an individual's life is centred. Individuals who have been resident in Japan for fewer than five of the past ten years are considered to be non-permanent residents and are taxed only on Japanese-source income and on income received in Japan from overseas. Non-residents are taxed on income from services in Japan, even if paid overseas, at a flat 20% rate (without residents' deductions). Individuals resident in Japan for fewer than 183 days in a 12-month period are generally exempt from income tax on foreign-sourced income. The tax year is based on the calendar year. Employers are required to withhold taxes from salaries, wages and bonuses paid to resident employees. Withholding tables are adjusted for the employee's personal and family situation. Employers must make a year-end adjustment to withholding for employees (excluding employees with annual salary income of ¥20,000,000 or more) to account for any overpayment or underpayment of taxes. As a result, many employees do not need to file a tax return.

Recent developments

Effective 1 January 2012, employees may contribute to DC plans for the first time since the introduction of the DC Law in 2001. Total contributions (employer and employee) cannot exceed the prevailing contribution ceiling (J¥51,000 per employee per month if there is no concurrently funded defined benefit (DB) plan and J¥25,500 per employee per month if there is a DB plan). Employee contributions must not exceed employer contributions. The new law gives employers the ability to change DC plan rules to continue the payment of contributions until employees reach age 65 (currently age 60). The employer determines the age at which contributions cease. This change is effective within two and one-half years after the date of promulgation; the government will publish the effective date. The new law also requires DC plan sponsors to provide investment education on a continuous basis so that employees are better trained in investment. This requirement is effective 10 August 2011. Previously, plan sponsors were required to extend their 'best effort' to provide education.

THE NETHERLANDS

Economy and Government

The Netherlands is a constitutional monarchy with Queen Beatrix as the reigning head of state. Formally, the government is divided into the Crown; the legislature, represented by the States General (parliament); and the judiciary.

The States General has two houses: the Upper Chamber with 75 members and the Lower Chamber with 150 members. General elections for both chamber are held at least every four years. Members of both chambers are elected by proportional representation. Members of the Upper Chamber are elected by the members of the provincial governing bodies not more than three month after the election of the members of the provincial councils. Members of the Lower Chamber are elected directly by all Dutch nationals aged 18 and over.

Labour relations

Employment terms are determined through national labour laws, collective bargaining and individual employment contracts. Labour–management relations are cooperative. The government has a statutory obligation to consult with the Social and Economic Council (SER) over proposed changes in labou and employment laws and general decisions affecting employment. SEI functions primarily as an advisory board on macro-economic issues Additionally, the Labour Foundation (STAR), a bipartite body representin employers and unions, is a central forum for consultation and negotiation.

Cost of employment

Employers and employees pay social security contributions to two programme based on total earnings up to specified ceilings. Rates and ceilings are normally revised in January and July. Cash sickness and maternity benefits (ZW) ar funded in full by the government. There is no separate workers' compensatio programme. Benefits for work-related accidents are paid under the medica disability and survivors' benefit plans of social security. Employees contribut to the health insurance fund (ZVW) for healthcare.

Employment terms and conditions

Employment contracts are required and, unless otherwise stated, are indefinite The maximum term for a probationary period is two months if the contract i indefinite or for a fixed term exceeding two years. For fixed-term contracts tha do not exceed two years, the maximum probationary period is one month During a probationary period, the contract may be terminated without notic by either party. Only within a Collective Labour Agreement (CAO) can ther be different probation periods. If the employer terminates the employmen contract during the probation period, the employer must state the reasons fo the termination in writing, upon the employee's request.

Social security and other required benefits

The comprehensive social security system provides benefits through th National Insurance System and the Employed Persons Insurance Syster Social security programmes do not distinguish between blue- and white-colla employees. The basic National Insurance System is financed through employe contributions and provides flat-rate old age pensions and survivors' benefit family allowances and special health insurance for the entire population, a well as disability benefits for the self-employed. The Employed Person Insurance System is financed by employer and employee contributions ar provides additional health insurance for lower-paid persons, and disability, cash sickness, maternity and unemployment benefits.

Healthcare system

There is no national health service. Health insurance in the Netherlands is a three-tiered system based on a combination of private insurance companies (either independently or under contract to the government) and public entities. Prior to 2006, about 64% of the population was covered for basic healthcare services by the first tier of the system (Ziekenfondswet (ZFW)), which was compulsory for persons with income below €33,000. That portion of the population earning above the ceiling were supposed to have private health insurance, typically as a result of their employment. Due to rising national healthcare costs as well as concerns regarding equitable access to and choices for healthcare, the government passed the Health Insurance Act ((ZVW) Zorgverzekeringswet) to replace the ZFW for basic medical care and hospitalisation, effective from 1 January 2006. The second tier of insurance is the AWBZ, which covers long-term care and high-cost treatment. The AWBZ is compulsory for residents and non-residents employed in the Netherlands independent of their income. It is run by state-appointed insurers. The third tier is voluntary health insurance, which covers treatments not covered under the first two, including dental care.

Taxation of compensation and benefits

Residents are taxed on worldwide income. Non-residents are subject to tax only on Dutch-source income. Dutch tax law does not define residence, which is determined on individual circumstances such as where a person lives regularly, the length of stay in the Netherlands and the taxpayer's centre of interests. The tax year for individuals is the calendar year. Tax returns must generally be filed by 1 April of the following year. Taxes are collected via withholding or advance payment.

Recent developments

The social partners (unions, employers' associations and government) have agreed on a plan to reform the pension system. The state (AOW) pension age would increase from 65 to 66 by 2020 and to 67 by 2025. Individuals could continue to retire early; however, the AOW pension would be reduced by 6.5% for each year of early retirement. AOW pension benefits would increase by 1.6% beginning in 2013; pensions would be indexed to real earned wages.

RUSSIA

Economy and Government

The Russian Federation comprises Russia plus 21 autonomous republics and numerous other autonomous territories and regions. The president has extensive powers, nominates the highest governmental officials, including the 'chairman of the government' (prime minister) who must be approved by the legislature, and can pass decrees without consent from the legislature. Presidents are elected for four year terms and cannot serve more than two consecutive terms. The legislative body has two chambers – the State Duma (lower house) and the Federation Council (upper house). The State Duma consists of 225 members elected from single member districts and 225 members elected from party lists. The Federation Council consists of 178 members – two representatives from each of the country's regions, one from the legislative body and one from the executive body of the region.

Labour relations

An amended Russian Federation Code of Labour Laws (KZOT) came into effect in October 2006. The 2006 amendments primarily affect employment contracts, wage payment, severance and vacation pay. The Ministry of Health and Social Development's Federal Labour Inspectorate and regional and local government inspectorates have the responsibility to enforce the labour and safety laws. These inspectors have free access to all enterprises and companies to conduct inspections and have the power to levy fines for infractions.

Cost of employment

From 1 January 2010, Russia abolished the Unified Social Tax and replaced it with separate contributions to the federal Pension Fund, the Social Insurance Fund, and federal and regional Compulsory Medical Insurance Funds. Unemployment benefits are now financed through general income tax revenues.

Employment terms and conditions

All employment relationships in Russia, regardless of the location of the employee's legal employer, are subject to the Labour Code. Labour Code amendments enacted in October 2006 added specificity and broadened the definition of employer to include individual entrepreneurs and domestic employers. The Code requires that all employees have a written employment contract (a labour contract). Self-employed persons may be hired under civil law agreements, provided they are registered as entrepreneurs. Civil law agreements are regulated by the Civil Code instead of the Labour Code.

Social security and other required benefits

The administration and assets of the social security system are separated into the Pension Fund and the Social Insurance Fund. Contributions to these funds are collected locally, and the assets are managed by local officials. The Pension Fund administers the old age, survivors', and long-term disability pension plus child care allowances. The Fund is an independent body reporting to the State Duma. Cash sickness and maternity benefits, workers' compensation benefits and other social welfare benefits are paid through the Social Insurance Fund. The Fund is run by the government and guarantees benefits to all employees. A workers' compensation system, with risk-related premiums paid by employers, is managed by the Social Insurance Fund. Previously, work injuries were treated as regular death and disability (i.e. Pension Fund) events.

Healthcare system

The healthcare system is still highly inefficient and needs continued reform. The Ministry of Health and Social Development formulates federal policies and controls their execution. Below the national level the *oblast*, autonomous, or *krai* health departments govern regional healthcare. The degree of independence from the ministry varies for each regional unit. District or *rayon* health authorities have an executive role at the local level. Health insurance foundations administer medical insurance funds. Health insurance foundations have not been established in all parts of the country. The district health authorities manage the public-sector hospitals and clinics in areas without the foundations' presence.

Taxation of compensation and benefits

The Ministry of Taxes and Collections regulates tax matters and issues numerous 'instructions', 'orders' and 'letters' to expand on, clarify or reverse earlier documents, and occasionally they appear to conflict with the tax or other laws. From 1 January 2007, individuals who have been in Russia more than 183 days in a consecutive 12-month period are considered resident for tax purposes. Residents are taxable on worldwide income. Foreign nationals who are resident are taxed in the same manner as local nationals. Non-residents are taxed on income from Russian sources only; payment from offshore companies for work in Russia is counted as Russian-source income. The tax year is the calendar year. Procedures for registration with the tax authorities and filing tax returns, due dates for returns and penalties for non-compliance change frequently. Therefore, professional tax advice is necessary to ensure up-to-date information and compliance.

Recent developments

The government plans to reduce social security contributions for most businesses from 34% to 30%, except for specified small businesses that would be subject to a 20% contribution. To make up for the shortfall in social security revenues, the government would assess an additional contribution of 7% to 10% on pay exceeding RUR45,000 per month. As of 1 January 2011, the social security rate for employers increased to 34% (the rate for 'small' employers is 26%). Contributions are capped at RUR463,000 per employee. President Medvedev ordered the government to draft new legislation.

SPAIN

Economy and Government

Spain is a parliamentary monarchy; the president of the government is nominated by the monarch and subject to approval by the Congress of Deputies (lower house). The Spanish legislature is bicameral: Senators are elected in each of the provinces, and members of the Congress are elected via proportional representation. The structure of governance is semi-federal, with the powers of the national government shared with 17 'autonomous communities'. Each of these communities, or regional governments, has its own president, parliament and court system. The Basque Country and Catalonia have the strongest regional traditions, marked by their history and separate languages.

Labour relations

Employment terms and labour relations are governed by statute, national framework agreements and collective agreements. There are mechanisms at the national level and regional or provincial levels – the Economic Social Councils – to promote social dialogue among employers, trade unions, government officials and political parties. Employees have the right to affiliate with the labour union of their choice, elect union representatives and take industrial action.

Cost of employment

The social security system has been subject to several revisions in contribution rates and ceilings in recent years in an attempt to base the contributions on an amount closer to actual salary for each of the applicable wage classes (11 in all). However, the current ceilings are still too low to compensate executives effectively. All social security contributions are paid on earnings within the applicable class's wage range. Contributions are based on 12 monthly salaries (bonuses are spread *pro rata*). A minimum contribution wage base applies to each occupational group (or wage class). The maximum contribution wage base has been the same for all wage groups since 1 January 2002. The minimum wage base for the employer's workers' compensation tax is the same as for wage classes 4–11.

Employment terms and conditions

All employment contracts must be in writing. Spain has implemented the EU directive on proof of employment, which requires an employer to confirm in writing the terms and conditions of employment. There are different types of employment contract in Spain – indefinite-term contracts, temporary contracts, 'special relationship' contracts, and the partial retirement contract. The growth in type and number of temporary contracts is a consequence of government policies designed to encourage job creation. Provided there are no collective agreements to the contrary, employers may stipulate a limited trial period during which the employer or the employee may unilaterally terminate the employment contract without notice, cause or compensation.

Social security and other required benefits

The social security system is a comprehensive programme covering a significant portion of the population and providing a wide range of protection. It is based on a combination of employment-related (contributory) and universal (non-contributory) plans. The General System (*Régimen General*) is compulsory for all employees aged 16 and over, including foreign nationals working for companies that are registered in Spain. Under the *Régimen General*, there are special programmes for employees of specific industries (for example, certain types of employment in market research/public opinion firms and in the hotel and food industries). There are special systems for the self-employed, maritime workers, mining, homemakers and agricultural workers.

Healthcare system

During the 20th century, healthcare services evolved into a true system of national healthcare provision, and almost 100% of the population is covered.

all responsibility for purchasing and delivery of healthcare rests with Spain's 17 autonomous regions, aided by the National Institute of Public Health (INGS). The Ministry of Health and Consumer Affairs has overall responsibility for health policy, including establishing minimum healthcare standards and ensuring that national policies are implemented at the regional level. It has direct responsibility for public health policy, immunizations and inspection of meat and animal products imported from other countries (*sanidad exterior*), and legislation on pharmaceutical products.

Taxation of compensation and benefits

Individual income tax (IRPF – *Impuesto sobre la Renta de las Personas Físicas*) is levied by three tiers of government: the central government, the autonomous regional governments and local municipal governments. Central government taxes are administered by the Ministry of Economy and Taxation and are collected at provincial branches across the country. The laws applicable to individual taxpayers were consolidated in a new law (Ley 40/1998) effective for income and capital gains (or losses).

Recent developments

Spain's social security reform law was published in the official gazette on 2 August 2011. The major reforms to the social security system include:

- effective 1 January 2013, the statutory retirement age will gradually increase from 65 to 67 (in 2027)
- the number of contribution years for a full pension will increase from 35 to 37. However, individuals aged 65 will be permitted to retire with a full pension if they have a minimum of 38 years and 6 months of contributions
- a full pension will be calculated on the basis of the final 25 rather than 15 years' pay. The change will be implemented gradually, with the transition period beginning 1 January 2011 and ending 1 January 2022
- early retirement will be possible at age 61 if an individual has been involuntarily terminated from work and has a minimum of 33 years of contributions. For individuals retiring between age 61 and age 63 with less than 38 years and 6 months' contributions, the old age pension will be reduced by 7.5% for each year before the normal retirement age (those with 38 years and 6 months of contributions or more will have their pension reduced by 6.5% for each year)
- pension payments will increase for individuals who defer retirement until after the statutory retirement age: by 2% p.a. with 25 years' contributions, 2.75% p.a. with 25 to 37 years' contributions and 4% p.a. with more years' contributions, *and*
- individuals aged 61 to 65 who meet contribution requirements may take 'partial retirement' if their working hours have been reduced by 25% to 75%. The employer must continue to pay at least 65% of the social security contribution (currently, employers pay 100% of the contribution for employees in partial retirement).

SWITZERLAND

Economy and Government

Switzerland has a federal system of government with both parliamentary and
direct systems of democracy. The federal government (whose official name
the Helvetic Confederation) is composed of 26 cantons (20 of which are 'full'
cantons and 6 are 'half' cantons). The federal government is responsible for
matters that affect the entire country, for example foreign policy, national
defence, customs and monetary controls. The cantons implement federal law
and can pass their own legislation on local issues. Each canton has its own
parliament and government. In three half cantons, members of the federal
government are elected by assemblies of the citizens. In the other cantons
federal and cantonal government members are elected by ballot.

Labour relations

Labour relations and terms of employment are determined by the Federal
Constitution, statutes and collective agreements. The cantons are responsible
for administering federal laws and providing arbitration courts, labour courts
and appeal processes. Labour–management relations are cooperative. The
government regularly consults with union confederations and employer
associations over proposed changes in labour and employment laws.

Cost of employment

Contributions to the federal social security system are required of all employed
persons over age 17 and of residents aged 20 and older who are not part of a
direct employer–employee relationship. Widows/widowers receiving
widow's/widower's pension and spouses who do not reach normal retirement
age at the same time are required to contribute to social security during the year
prior to reaching normal retirement age. Contribution rates are applied to total
earnings, including bonuses, severance pay and income replacement benefits.
For individuals with no earned income, the contribution is based on the
individual's assets. Contributions are not required on workers' compensation
benefits, special bonuses or awards, or employer-paid insurance premiums.

Employment terms and conditions

Employment contracts may be written or oral. Contracts for special categories of
employees – apprentices, 'commercial travellers' and home workers – must be in
writing. Employment law does not specify the contents of the employment contract.
However, some provisions must be in writing to be valid (for example, non-
competition provisions). Employees' rights are established through laws and collective
agreements. However, a benefit granted repeatedly over time may become a right
unless the employer specifically states that the benefit is granted at its discretion.

Social security and other required benefits

The retirement system is based on the 'three pillars'. The federal social security
system is the first pillar, a basic universal pension financed on a pay-as-you-go basis.
Mandatory occupational pension plans under federal law (BVG/LPP) form the

second pillar and individual savings and insurance constitute the third. The federal social security system provides old-age and survivors' pensions (AHV/AVS) and long-term disability benefits (IV/AI) as well as short-term income replacement benefits (EO/APG). Workers' compensation, unemployment insurance, and family allowances are provided under separate legislation. Medical care benefits are not provided by social security.

Healthcare system

The role of the federal government is limited to matters such as control of food and drugs, control of communicable diseases, poison control, etc. Healthcare delivery is managed at the level of the 26 cantons. Each canton decides the type and scope of healthcare services to be provided to residents. Services can range from government-run hospitals (at canton- or community-level) to financial support for services provided by private facilities to purchasing services from facilities in other cantons. About half of the cost of these services is covered by the cantons through general revenues and half by patient insurance.

Taxation of compensation and benefits

Taxes are levied by federal, cantonal and municipal authorities on the worldwide income of residents, exclusive of income from foreign real estate and foreign permanent establishments. Criteria for residence, which vary for federal, cantonal and municipal tax purposes, are based on length of domicile, economic activity or ownership of property. The rates of federal tax are common to all cantons, but each canton sets its own basic tax rates and allowances for cantonal and municipal tax purposes. The cantonal and municipal taxes payable in any year are calculated by applying multiples to the basic rates. All cantons levy a wage withholding tax for foreigners who do not have a permit to stay permanently in Switzerland. Each cantonal authority is responsible for the assessment and collection not only of cantonal tax but also of federal and municipal taxes. For federal and cantonal tax purposes, the tax year is the current income year. In general, cantonal tax is payable in instalments. Federal tax bills must be settled by the end of March of the following year. The income of husband and wife is assessed jointly. Different tax tables apply to single and married persons.

Recent developments

The Federal Act on the Taxation of Employee Participation will be effective from 1 January 2013. It harmonises the tax treatment of stock option plans, which varies at the cantonal and municipal levels. Restricted stock will be taxed at 6% less than market value per year, up to a maximum of ten years. Restricted options and options from unlisted companies will be taxed at exercise; unrestricted options will be taxed at market value upon acquisition. Discounted shares will be taxed at their market value when acquired. Options received in Switzerland but exercised abroad will be subject to an 11.5% federal source tax; cantons may establish their own source tax.

UNITED STATES OF AMERICA

Economy and Government

The United States is a federal republic with powers shared by the national and state governments. The tension between the rights of states and the rights of the federal government plays a crucial role in US politics.

Labour relations

Legal mechanisms exist to impose settlements in disputes in workplaces deemed to be essential to the public good. In addition, minimum wage and maximum work hours are established by law. In general, however, the terms of employment are determined by employers or through collective bargaining. Employers are subject to extensive labour law rules. The Department of Labor is responsible for overseeing employer practices in such areas as hiring, employee benefits and overtime pay. The National Labor Relations Board oversees collective bargaining. In addition, most states also have their own labour laws, which are often different from those of the federal government.

Cost of employment

Social security benefits are financed through contributions paid by employers, employees and the self-employed under the Federal Insurance Contribution Act (FICA) and the Self-Employment Contributions Act (SECA). Employers and employees both contribute an equal percentage of pay up to an annual earnings limit (the taxable wage base).

Employment terms and conditions

The Fair Labor Standards Act (FLSA) governs maximum hours worked and overtime pay. It divides employees into two categories: 'exempt' (salaried employees including executive, professional and administrative [as defined by law]) employees and 'non-exempt' (hourly-paid) employees. The latter are covered by FLSA rules. From 23 August 2004, the determination of employees as exempt or non-exempt under the FLSA changed. Notably, the minimum salary level to qualify for the exemption from the FLSA minimum wage and overtime pay requirements increased to a minimum of US$455 per week (US$23,660 annually). For certain computer-related occupations, employees who earn at least US$27.63 per hour are eligible for the exemption even if they are not paid on a salary basis. In addition, employees must generally meet one of the duties tests to qualify for exemption.

Social security and other required benefits

There are three main programmes in the social security system: old age and survivors' insurance (OASI), disability insurance (DI) and Medicare. Sometimes they are grouped together and known as OASDHI, or old age, survivors', disability and hospital insurance. Workers' compensation and unemployment insurance are provided under separate laws. The social security system covers most employees and the self-employed. However, various classes of employee are exempt from coverage, including, for example, certain agricultural, domestic and casual workers as well as certain employees of the federal or state governments. Financing is through contributions (taxes) paid by employers, employees and the self-employed.

Healthcare system

The USA does not have a comprehensive national health insurance programme. The majority of US families rely on group health insurance plans provided by employers or on insurance that they have purchased individually.

The two existing national insurance programmes, Medicare and Medicaid, provide healthcare benefits only to certain segments of the population. Medicare, as a part of the federal social security system, provides medical benefits only for individuals aged 65 or older and for the disabled, while Medicaid helps finance medical care for people with low incomes. Medicaid is primarily funded at the federal level and administered at the state level.

Taxation of compensation and benefits

Citizens and permanent residents are subject to federal income tax on worldwide foreign and domestic income. However, tax relief may be available in the form of unilateral tax credits, double income tax treaty benefits and certain exclusions for specified foreign income. As a result, citizens and permanent residents must file annual tax returns even if they are non-resident for tax purposes for the year in question. Non-resident aliens are taxed only on certain income from sources or businesses in the USA. Most citizens and residents pay federal, state and sometimes local income taxes.

Recent developments

Health care reform continues to dominate the legislative agenda. The reform legislation, passed as two distinct acts – the Patient Protection and Affordable Care Act and the Health Care and Education Reconciliation Act – is far-reaching and complex. Some provisions have already been implemented, while the major provisions (including the state Health Insurance Exchanges, the Individual Mandate and the Employer Play or Pay Requirement) will not be effective until 1 January 2014. Highlights of key provisions include:

Grandfathered Plans

Grandfathered plans are required to:

1) cover adult children up to age 26 (prior to 2014, group health plans would be required to cover adult children only if they were not able to enrol in another employer-provided plan. Employer contributions for the cost of adult child coverage would continue to be included in gross income unless the child qualifies as a dependent for federal income tax purposes.)

2) prohibit rescissions of healthcare coverage, *and*

3) have no lifetime limits and restrictive annual limits. As of 2014, grandfathered plans will be prohibited from having annual limits on essential health benefits; pre-existing condition exclusions; and waiting periods in excess of 90 days.

Employer Mandate

In 2014, companies not offering coverage will be required to pay US$2,000 per full-time employee for all full-time employees even if one employee enrols in a health plan through the Health Insurance Exchange and receives a federal subsidy. The assessment will exclude the first 30 employees from the payment calculation. Employers offering 'unaffordable' coverage (if premiums exceeded 9.5% of family income) will be assessed US$3,000 for each full-time employee enrolled in the Exchange and in receipt of a subsidy.

Excise Tax on High-Cost Plans

In 2018, an excise tax will be assessed on high-cost plans. The threshold is scheduled to be US$10,200 for single employees and US$23,000 for families. The threshold is expected to be indexed to general inflation plus one percentage point in 2019 and to general inflation only in 2020 and beyond.

Retirees aged 55 to 64 and employees in high-risk jobs will receive a permanent adjustment in the threshold, raising it to US$11,850 for single employees and US$30,950 for families. Companies with higher health costs due to age or gender will also receive an adjustment.

Individual Mandate

Effective 1 January 2014, individuals who do not maintain insurance coverage will be subject to a penalty (either a flat dollar amount or a percentage of income). A hardship exemption would be available for individuals with income below the tax filing threshold.

Flexible Spending Arrangements (FSAs)

As of 2013, the new annual limit on FSAs will be US$2,500.

Medicare

The bill will broaden the Medicare hospital insurance tax base for high-income taxpayers; phase out the Medicare Part D coverage gap completely by 2020; and eliminate the federal income tax deduction for prescription drug expenses of Medicare beneficiaries for which the plan sponsor also receives the retiree drug subsidy under Part D.

Other developments

In other notable developments, Connecticut is the first state to require paid sick leave. Also, the 2012 federal budget includes reforms to the Pension Benefit Guaranty Corporation (PBGC). The PBGC Board would be given the authority to adjust premiums and take into account the risks that different sponsors pose to their retirees and to the PBGC.

NSIONS POCKET BOOK 2012

o you need extra copies of
e **Pensions Pocket Book**
r your colleagues?
der today and save up to 45% !

*s excellent and
v pocket-sized book
fed full with the sort
formation — facts,
res and useful lists —
sions folk constantly
d ... admirably
ight out."*

IONS TODAY

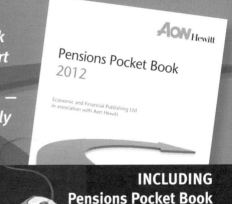

AON Hewitt

Pensions Pocket Book
2012

Economic and Financial Publishing Ltd
in association with Aon Hewitt

**INCLUDING
Pensions Pocket Book
Companion Website**

TO ORDER:
NE: www.pensionspocketbook.com/order
L: direct.order@marston.co.uk
NE: 01235 465577 with your credit card details
     01235 465556 with your credit card details

ABBREVIATIONS IN COMMON USE

AA	Annual Allowance
ABI	Association of British Insurers
ACT	Advance Corporation Tax
AEI	Average Earnings Index
APP	Appropriate Personal Pension
ARR	Age-related Rebate
ASB	Accounting Standards Board
AVCs	Additional Voluntary Contributions
AVR	Actuarial Valuation Report
AWE	Average Weekly Earnings
BAS	Board for Actuarial Standards
BCE	Benefit Crystallisation Event
BSP	Basic State Pension
CA	Certified Amount *or* Companies Act
CARE	Career Average Revalued Earnings
CEIOPS	Committee of European Insurance and Occupational Pensions Supervisors
CEP	Contributions Equivalent Premium
CETV	Cash Equivalent Transfer Value
CGT	Capital Gains Tax
CIMPS	Contracted-in Money Purchase Scheme
CMI	Continuous Mortality Investigation
COMBS	Contracted-out Mixed Benefit Scheme
COMPS	Contracted-out Money Purchase Scheme
COMPSHP	Stakeholder Contracted-out Money Purchase Scheme
CoP	Code of Practice
COSRS	Contracted-out Salary Related Scheme
CPA	Compulsory Purchase Annuity
CPF	Combined Pension Forecast
CPI	Consumer Prices Index
DB	Defined Benefit
DC	Defined Contribution
DPA	Data Protection Act
DWP	Department for Work and Pensions
ECJ	European Court of Justice
ECON	Employer's Contracting-out Number

EEA	European Economic Area
EFRBS	Employer-financed Retirement Benefit Scheme
EPB	Equivalent Pension Benefit
EPP	Executive Pension Plan
ERF	Early Retirement Factor
ETV	Enhanced Transfer Value
EU	European Union
FA	Finance Act
FAS	Financial Assistance Scheme *or*
	Financial Accounting Standard
FASB	Financial Accounting Standards Board
FCF	Fraud Compensation Fund
FRC	Financial Reporting Council
FRS	Financial Reporting Standard
FSA	Financial Services Authority
FSCS	Financial Services Compensation Scheme
FSD	Financial Support Direction
FSMA	Financial Services and Markets Act
GAD	Government Actuary's Department
GMP	Guaranteed Minimum Pension
GN	Guidance Notes
GPP	Group Personal Pension
GSIPP	Group Self-invested Personal Pension
HMRC	Her Majesty's Revenue & Customs
HMT	Her Majesty's Treasury
IAS	International Accounting Standard
IASB/IASC	International Accounting Standards Board/Committee
ICTA	Income & Corporation Taxes Act
IDR/IDRP	Internal Dispute Resolution (Procedure)
IFRS	International Financial Reporting Standard
IGG	Investment Governance Group
IHT	Inheritance Tax
ISA	Individual Savings Account
ITEPA	Income Tax (Earnings and Pensions) Act
JWG	Occupational Pension Schemes Joint Working Group
LDI	Liability-Driven Investment
LEL	Lower Earnings Limit
LET	Low Earnings Threshold
LPI	Limited Price Indexation

LRF	Late Retirement Factor
LTA	Lifetime Allowance
MIR	Minimum Income Requirement
MND	Member-nominated Director
MNT	Member-nominated Trustee
MPP	Maximum Permitted Pension
NAPF	National Association of Pension Funds
NEST	National Employment Savings Trust
NI	National Insurance
NICO	National Insurance Contributions Office
NMPA	Normal Minimum Pension Age
NPA/NPD	Normal Pension Age/Normal Pension Date
NRA/NRD	Normal Retirement Age/Normal Retirement Date
OEIC	Open-ended Investment Company
OMO	Open Market Option
ONS	Office for National Statistics
OPS	Occupational Pension Scheme
OPSI	Office of Public Sector Information
PA	Pensions Act
PAYE	Pay As You Earn
PAYG	Pay As You Go
PCLS	Pension Commencement Lump Sum
PIP	Pension Input Period
PLA	Purchased Life Annuity *or* Personal Lifetime Allowance
PMI	Pensions Management Institute
PPF	Pension Protection Fund
PPP/PPS	Personal Pension Plan/Scheme
PR	Protected Rights
PRAG	Pensions Research Accountants Group
PSA	Pension Schemes Act
PUP	Paid-up Pension
QROPS	Qualifying Recognised Overseas Pension Scheme
RAC	Retirement Annuity Contract
RPI	Retail Prices Index
RPSM	Registered Pension Schemes Manual
RST	Reference Scheme Test
S2P	State Second Pension
SAA	Special Annual Allowance
SAAC	Special Annual Allowance Charge

SCON	Scheme Contracted-out Number
SERPS	State Earnings-related Pension Scheme
SFO	Statutory Funding Objective
SFP	Statement of Funding Principles
SFS	Summary Funding Statement
SHP	Stakeholder Pension
SI	Statutory Instrument
SIP	Statement of Investment Principles
SIPP	Self-invested Personal Pension
SLA	Standard Lifetime Allowance
SMPI	Statutory Money Purchase Illustration
SoC	Schedule of Contributions
SORP	Statement of Recommended Practice
SPA	State Pension Age
SRI	Socially Responsible Investment
SSA	Social Security Act
SSAS	Small Self-administered Scheme
SSB	Short Service Benefit
SSPA	Social Security Pensions Act
STRGL	Statement of Total Recognised Gains and Losses
TAS	Technical Actuarial Standard
TKU	Trustee Knowledge and Understanding
TPAS	The Pensions Advisory Service
TPR	The Pensions Regulator
TUPE	Transfer of Undertakings (Protection of Employment) Regulations
TV	Transfer Value
UAP	Upper Accrual Point
UEL	Upper Earnings Limit
WGMP	Widow's/Widower's Guaranteed Minimum Pension
WR&PA	Welfare Reform and Pensions Act

Source: Aon Hewitt.

GLOSSARY OF TERMS

Bold Text:	Cross references that it is felt might improve the understanding of the term concerned.
Italicised Text:	Terms which, whilst not forming part of the basic definition, provide the reader with additional guidance.

DEFINITIONS

The definitions in this Glossary are current at the time of going to print.

A DAY   6 April 2006, when the FA 2004 tax regime came into force.

ACCRUAL RATE   The rate at which rights build up for each year of **pensionable service** in a **DB scheme**.

ACCRUED BENEFITS   The benefits for service up to a given point in time, whether **vested rights** or not. They may be calculated in relation to current earnings or projected earnings.

*Allowance may also be made for **revaluation** and/or **pension increases** required by the scheme rules or legislation.*

ACCRUED RIGHTS   The benefits to which a member is entitled, as of right, under an **occupational pension scheme**. These include **accrued benefits**. Depending on the context, accrued rights for an **active member** can be based on benefits as if the member had left service or could include a right to have benefits linked to future salary changes.

*The term is given various specific definitions in PSA 1993 for the purposes of **preservation**, **contracting out** and in the Disclosure Regulations. It is also given a specific meaning in PA 1995, e.g. in relation to scheme amendments.*

ACTIVE MEMBER   A member of an **occupational pension scheme** who is at present accruing benefits under that scheme in respect of current service.

ACTUARIAL EQUIVALENCE   A test of actuarial value which compares benefits immediately before and after a modification. For the test to be satisfied, the total value of the member's subsisting rights immediately after the modification must be no less than the value of those rights immediately before the modification. This term is used in connection with **section 67** of PA 1995.

ACTUARIAL GAINS AND LOSSES   Used in pension cost accounting to mean changes in actuarial deficits or surpluses that arise because

(a) events have not coincided with the actuarial assumptions made for the last valuation (experience gains and losses) *or*

(b) the actuarial assumptions have changed.

ACTUARIAL REDUCTION   A reduction made to a member's **accrued benefits** in order to offset any additional cost arising from their payment in advance of the **normal pension date**.

ACTUARIAL REPORT   A written report, prepared and signed by the **scheme actuary**, on the developments affecting the scheme's **technical provisions** since the last **actuarial valuation** was prepared.

ACTUARIAL VALUATION

(1) Commonly refers to an investigation by an actuary into the ability of a **DB scheme** to meet its liabilities. This is usually to assess the **funding level** and a recommended contribution rate based on comparing the value of the assets and the actuarial liability.

(2) Under PA 2004, specifically refers to a written report, prepared and signed by the **scheme actuary**, valuing the scheme's assets and calculating its **technical provisions**.

ADDED YEARS   The provision of extra benefits by reference to an additional period of **pensionable service** in a **DB scheme**, arising from the receipt of a **transfer payment**, the paying of **AVCs** or by way of **augmentation**.

ADDITIONAL VOLUNTARY CONTRIBUTIONS (AVCs)

Contributions over and above a member's normal contributions if any, which the member elects to pay to an **occupational pension scheme** in order to secure additional benefits.

ADMINISTRATOR

(1) The person or persons notified to HMRC as being responsible for the management of a pension scheme.

(2) The person who is responsible for the day-to-day administration of the pension scheme.

(3) A type of insolvency practitioner in relation to companies under the Insolvency Act 1986.

AGE-RELATED REBATE   Payments made by NICO to a contracted-out occupational **money purchase scheme**, or an appropriate personal pension scheme, for members who have **contracted out**. These increase with the age of the member.

Contracting out *on a money purchase basis is being abolished from 6 April 2012.*

AMORTISATION

(1) The spreading of an actuarial surplus or deficiency over an appropriate period.

(2) An accountancy term for the reduction in the value of an asset, such as leasehold property, caused by the passage of time. If the cause is not solely related to time, the corresponding term is depreciation.

ANNUAL ALLOWANCE The maximum amount of pension saving that can be built up in any one tax year before liability to an **annual allowance charge**.

ANNUAL ALLOWANCE CHARGE The tax charge levied on an individual who is a member of one or more **registered pension schemes** in respect of the amount by which the **total pension input amount** for a tax year exceeds the **annual allowance**.

ANNUAL REPORT The means by which the **trustees** of an **occupational pension scheme** communicate financial and other information about the scheme to the members, the employer and other interested parties.

The term is used to describe the specific information that is required to be made available by trustees in relation to each scheme year under the Disclosure Regulations. Subject to certain exemptions, this must include a copy of the audited accounts and other information specified, including an investment report. The detailed content of the audited accounts is described in the Pension Scheme **SORP**.

Trustees often publish a simplified annual report for members containing the above material suitably summarised.

ANNUITY A series of payments, which may be subject to increase, made at stated intervals until a particular event occurs. This event is most commonly the end of a specified period or the death of the person receiving the annuity.

An annuity may take one of a number of different forms including **compulsory purchase annuity**, *deferred annuity,* **purchased life annuity** *and reversionary annuity.*

ANTI-FRANKING REQUIREMENTS The requirements which ban the process whereby statutory increases in **GMP** e.g. between termination of **contracted-out** employment and **state pensionable age** are offset against other scheme benefits, rather than being added to a member's total benefits.

The requirements are covered in Chapter III of Part IV PSA 199

ARRANGEMENT   Under FA 2004, a contractual or trust-based arrangement made by or on behalf of a member of a pension scheme under that scheme. A member may have more than one arrangement under a scheme.

ASSESSMENT PERIOD   The period of time when a scheme is being assessed to determine whether the **Pension Protection Fund** can assume responsibility for it.

ASSET ALLOCATION STRATEGY   The splitting of the assets of a pension scheme between the various **asset classes** such as equities, bonds and cash. This will primarily reflect the long-term needs of the fund, the 'strategic view', but may be adjusted to favour particular asset classes or markets which look attractive in the short term, the 'tactical view'.

ASSET AND LIABILITY MATCHING   A process of selecting assets which are likely to generate proceeds broadly equal to the cashflow needed to meet the liabilities as they occur under different economic scenarios.

An example of this would be the matching of a level pension with fixed interest securities.

ASSET AND LIABILITY MODELLING   A technique used to test the effect of different economic scenarios on the assets and liabilities of an **occupational pension scheme**, the inter-relationship between them, the **funding level** and the contribution rates.

ASSET CLASS   A collective term for investments of a similar type. The main asset classes are equities (shares), bonds, cash and property.

ATTAINED AGE METHOD   A funding method in which the actuarial liability makes allowance for projected earnings. The contribution rate is that necessary to cover the cost of all benefits which will accrue to existing members after the valuation date by reference to total earnings throughout their future working lifetimes projected to the dates on which benefits become payable.

AUGMENTATION   The provision of additional benefits in respect of particular members of an **occupational pension scheme**, normally where the cost is borne by the scheme and/or employer.

AUTHORISED PAYMENT   A payment made by a **registered pension scheme** to an employer or member which is permitted under the provisions of FA 2004.

AUTOMATIC ENROLMENT   The process whereby employers must automatically enrol workers that meet specified eligibility conditions into a **qualifying pension scheme**. Workers will have the option to opt out. Employers without a qualifying scheme may use the **NEST**.

BASIC PENSION   The flat-rate (not earnings-related) state pension paid to all who have met the minimum NI contribution requirements. The amount paid is increased if the recipient is married and a spouse or widow(er) may claim on the record of his/her spouse.

BENEFICIARY   A person entitled to benefit under a pension scheme or who will become entitled on the happening of a specific event.

BENEFIT CRYSTALLISATION EVENT   One of eleven events defined in FA 2004 that triggers a test of benefits 'crystallising' at that point against the individual's available **lifetime allowance**.

BRIDGING PENSION   An additional pension paid from a scheme between retirement and **state pensionable age**, which is usually replaced by the state pension payable from that age.

BULK TRANSFER   The transfer of a group of members from one **occupational pension scheme** to another, sometimes with a **transfer payment** that is enhanced in comparison with an individual's **cash equivalent**.

BUY-IN   The purchase by **trustees** of an **occupational pension scheme** of an insurance policy in the name of the trustees. This remains an asset of the trustees.

BUY-OUT   The purchase by **trustees** of an **occupational pension scheme** of an insurance policy in the name of a member or other **beneficiary**, in lieu of entitlement to benefit from the scheme following termination of the member's **pensionable service**.

CAPPED DRAWDOWN   A form of **income withdrawal**. The maximum income is capped at the level of an equivalent single life level annuity that could be provided from the drawdown fund. The cap is checked at the outset and periodically after that. There is no minimum level of drawdown pension.

CASH EQUIVALENT   The amount which a member of a pension scheme may, under section 94 PSA 1993, require to be applied as a **transfer payment**.

CASH TRANSFER SUM   The amount that a leaver with between 3 and 24 months' **pensionable service** may require to be applied as a **transfer payment**, as an alternative to a refund of contributions.

CODES OF PRACTICE   **The Pensions Regulator** issues various codes of practice providing practical guidance on compliance with the requirements of PA 2004.

COMBINED PENSION FORECASTS A statement issued by the current pension arrangement to the member showing the combined benefits at retirement that the member may receive from the pension scheme and the state.

COMMUTATION The forgoing of a part or all of the pension payable from retirement for an immediate lump sum benefit.

COMPULSORY PURCHASE ANNUITY An **annuity** which must be purchased on retirement for a member of an insured pension scheme.

CONTRACTED OUT/CONTRACTED IN A pension scheme is contracted out where it provides benefits (**GMPs**, **protected rights** or **section 9(2B) rights**) in place of **SERPS** or **S2P** and has been given a **contracting-out certificate** or appropriate scheme certificate by HMRC. Members are contracted out if they are in employment which is contracted out by reference to an **occupational pension scheme** or have elected to contract out via an appropriate personal pension scheme.

A pension scheme is commonly called contracted in where it is not contracted out, i.e. it provides benefits in addition to S2P. The term 'contracted in' is not referred to in legislation.

Contracting out *of S2P on a money purchase basis is being abolished from 6 April 2012.*

CONTRACTED-OUT REBATE The amount by which the employer's and the employee's NI contributions are reduced or rebated in respect of employees who are **contracted out** by virtue of their membership of an appropriate personal pension scheme or an **occupational pension scheme**.

The contracted-out rebate consists of a flat-rate rebate and (for contracted-out **money purchase schemes** *and appropriate personal pension schemes) an* **age-related rebate**.

CONTRACTING-OUT CERTIFICATE The certificate issued by HMRC, in respect of an **occupational pension scheme** which satisfies the conditions for **contracting out**, confirming that the employees in the employments named in the certificate are to be treated as being in contracted-out employment.

CONTROLLING DIRECTOR A director who, on his own or with associates, owns or controls 20% or more of the ordinary shares of the employing company.

CROSS-BORDER SCHEME If a UK scheme has members working in another EU member state, who are not **seconded employees**, the scheme is operating as a cross-border scheme. Such schemes require regulatory approval to accept contributions in respect of cross-border operations and are subject to additional regulations for example in relation to the **statutory funding objective**.

DEFERRED MEMBER/PENSIONER   A member entitled to **preserved benefits**.

DEFINED BENEFIT SCHEME (DB Scheme)   A scheme where the scheme rules define the benefits independently of the contributions payable, and benefits are not directly related to the investments of the scheme. The scheme may be funded or unfunded.

DEFINED CONTRIBUTION SCHEME (DC Scheme)   A scheme which determines the individual member's benefits by reference to contributions paid into the scheme in respect of that member, usually increased by an amount based on the investment return on those contributions. Sometimes referred to as a **money purchase scheme**.

DEPENDANT   For HMRC purposes, a person who was married to, civil partner of, financially dependent on the member or dependent on the member because of physical or mental impairment at the date of the member's death is a dependant of the member.

A child of the member is a dependant of the member if the child has not reached the age of 23, or has reached age 23 and, in the opinion of the scheme **administrator**, was at the date of the member's death dependent on the member because of physical or mental impairment.

DISCLOSURE

(1) A requirement introduced by PSA 1993 (formerly SSPA 1975) and strengthened by PA 1995 for pension schemes to disclose information about the scheme and benefits to interested parties

(2) Rules introduced by regulatory bodies to disclose product and commission information to the purchasers of life assurance and insured pension products.

DISCONTINUANCE   The cessation of the liability of the sponsoring employer to pay contributions to a pension scheme.

DISCRETIONARY INCREASE   An increase to a pension in payment or to a **preserved benefit** arising on a discretionary basis, i.e. other than from a system of **escalation** or **indexation**. Such an increase may be of a regular or an ad hoc nature.

ELIGIBLE JOBHOLDER   For the purposes of **automatic enrolment** this means a **jobholder** who is at least age 22, has not reached **state pensionable age** and is in receipt of earnings above the income tax personal allowance. Eligible jobholders must be auto-enrolled into the employer's **qualifying pension scheme** or **NEST** within a month of becoming eligible and the employer must contribute towards it.

EMPLOYER COVENANT   The employer's legal obligation, willingness and ability to fund its pension scheme now and in the future.

EMPLOYER-FINANCED RETIREMENT BENEFIT SCHEME

A scheme which is neither a **registered pension scheme** nor a section 615(3) scheme.

ENHANCED LIFETIME ALLOWANCE   This is where the **standard lifetime allowance** has been increased as a result of **primary protection**, or **pension credits**, or transfers from overseas schemes or where the member has not always been a relevant UK individual. This results in a **personal lifetime allowance**.

ENHANCED PROTECTION   A form of protection from the **lifetime allowance charge** that was available for all members who registered for it under the FA 2004 tax regime, regardless of the amount of their benefits pre-**A Day**.

ENTITLED WORKER   For the purposes of **automatic enrolment**, this means a worker who ordinarily works in Great Britain, is aged at least 16 and under 75 and is in receipt of earnings below the lower limit for **qualifying earnings**. Entitled workers are entitled to join a pension scheme but it need not be a **qualifying pension scheme** and the employer is not obliged to contribute.

ESCALATION   A system whereby pensions in payment and/or **preserved benefits** are automatically increased at regular intervals and at a fixed percentage rate. The percentage may be restricted to the increase in a specified index.

EXPRESSION OF WISH   A means by which a member can indicate a preference as to who should receive any lump sum death benefit.

The choice is not binding on the **trustees**, *and, as a result, inheritance tax is normally avoided.*

FINAL PENSIONABLE EARNINGS/PAY/SALARY   The pensionable earnings on which the benefits are calculated in a **DB scheme**. The earnings may be based on the average over a number of consecutive years prior to retirement, death or leaving **pensionable service**.

FINANCIAL ASSISTANCE SCHEME   A scheme introduced by the government to help workers who have lost pension rights through company insolvency but do not qualify for the **Pension Protection Fund**.

FIXED RATE REVALUATION   A method used by a COSRS to revalue **GMP** between termination of **contracted-out** employment and age 65 (men), 60 (women) as one of the alternatives to applying **section 148 orders**.

The rate is reviewed periodically.

FIXED PROTECTION   A form of protection from the **lifetime allowance charge** available to individuals with benefits in **registered pension schemes**, who do not have **enhanced** or **primary protection**, provided they register for it before 6 April 2012 and do not accrue further benefits. It is intended for those adversely affected by the reduction in the **lifetime allowance** to £1.5 million from 6 April 2012.

FLEXIBLE DRAWDOWN   A form of **income withdrawal** available to individuals who meet the **minimum income requirement**. Individuals who satisfy certain criteria can take unlimited amounts as income and are not subject to **capped drawdown**.

FLEXIBLE RETIREMENT   The option available from 6 April 2006 under FA 2004 to take benefits in stages – the member can also remain in employment with the same employer.

FRAUD COMPENSATION FUND   Replaced the Pensions Compensation Scheme, with effect from 6 April 2005. Payments can be made from the fund in cases where the assets of a scheme have been reduced since 6 April 1997 as a result of an offence involving dishonesty, including an intent to defraud.

FRS 17 – RETIREMENT BENEFITS   FRS 17 is mainly concerned with **DB schemes**, but applies to all retirement benefits as well as pensions, for example medical care in retirement. Exemptions exist for smaller entities.

It requires the scheme assets and liabilities to be valued on a 'fair value' basis and the resulting surplus (or deficit) to be recognised as an asset (or liability) in the balance sheet of the reporting company. The components in the change in the net asset or liability over time are disclosed in its profit and loss account, with the exception of **actuarial gains and losses**, which are recognised in the **statement of total recognised gains and losses**.

FRS 17 requires extensive disclosures in the company's accounts.

FUNDING LEVEL   The relationship at a specified date between the value of the assets and the actuarial liability. Normally expressed as a percentage.

*The funding level may be calculated separately in respect of different categories of liability, e.g. pensions in payment and **AVCs**.*

GUARANTEED MINIMUM PENSION (GMP)   The minimum pension which an **occupational pension scheme** must provide as one of the conditions of **contracting out** for pre-6 April 1997 service (unless it was contracted out through the provision of **protected rights**).

HYBRID ARRANGEMENT   Under FA 2004, an **arrangement** where only one type of benefit will ultimately be provided, but the type of benefit that will be provided is not known in advance because it will depend on certain circumstances at the point benefits are drawn.

HYBRID SCHEME

(1) An **occupational pension scheme** in which the benefit is calculated as the better of two alternatives, for example on a final salary and a money purchase basis.

(2) An occupational pension scheme which offers both defined benefit and defined contribution benefits.

INCOME WITHDRAWAL   An alternative to buying a **lifetime annuity**. It allows a member of a **money purchase arrangement** to draw an income from their pension fund while the fund remains invested.

INDEPENDENT TRUSTEE   An independent trustee must be registered and an 'independent person in relation to the scheme'. This requirement will be satisfied if he or she has no interests in the assets of the employer or scheme and is not connected with the employer, insolvency practitioner or official receiver.

INDEXATION

(1) A system whereby pensions in payment and/or **preserved benefits** are automatically increased at regular intervals by reference to a specified index of prices or earnings.

(2) An investment strategy designed to produce a rate of return in line with a particular index, either by replicating the constituents or by sufficient sampling to give a proxy.

INTERNAL DISPUTE RESOLUTION PROCEDURE (IDRP)

Occupational pension schemes (subject to exceptions) are required by section 50 PA 1995 to have a procedure to deal with disputes between **trustees** on the one hand and members and **beneficiaries** on the other hand.

JOBHOLDER   For the purposes of **automatic enrolment** this means a worker who ordinarily works in Great Britain, is aged at least 16 and under 75 and to whom **qualifying earnings** are payable.

LEVY

(1) The general levy meets the expenditure of the **Pension Ombudsman**, the **Pensions Regulator** and grants made by the Pensions Regulator (e.g. to TPAS). It is payable by registrable **occupational pension schemes** and **personal pension schemes**.

(2) The Fraud Compensation Levy is payable by occupational pension schemes to fund the **Fraud Compensation Fund**.

(3) Schemes that are eligible for future entry to the **PPF** pay a Pension Protection Levy to the PPF which is based on a **section 179 valuation**. A PPF Administration Levy and a PPF Ombudsman Levy are also payable.

LIFESTYLING   An **asset allocation strategy** used mainly in **DC scheme** whereby a member's investments are adjusted depending on age and term to retirement. Typically assets are switched from equities into bonds and cash as retirement approaches.

LIFETIME ALLOWANCE   The lifetime allowance is an overall ceiling on the amount of tax-privileged savings that any one individual can draw. The exact figure will be the same as the **standard lifetime allowance** for the tax year concerned, or a multiple of this figure where certain circumstances apply.

LIFETIME ALLOWANCE CHARGE   The tax charge levied on excess funds, following a **benefit crystallisation event**, for any individual with a benefit value more than their **lifetime allowance** (unless they have **enhanced protection**).

LIFETIME ANNUITY   Under FA 2004, an **annuity** contract purchased from an insurance company of the member's choosing that provides the member with an income for life.

LIMITED PRICE INDEXATION (LPI)   The requirement under PA 1995 to increase pensions in payment under an **occupational pension scheme** (excluding **AVCs** and money purchase benefits) by a minimum amount. The minimum is in line with price inflation or, if lower, 5% p.a. for benefits accrued between 6 April 1997 and 5 April 2005 and 2.5% p.a. for benefits accrued after 5 April 2005.

LIMITED REVALUATION   A method used by COSRS to revalue **GMP** by the lower of 5% per annum and **section 148 orders**, between termination of **contracted-out** employment and age 65 (men), 60 (women). It was withdrawn from 6 April 1997.

LOWER EARNINGS LIMIT (LEL)   The minimum amount (historically approximately equivalent to the single person's **basic pension**) which must be earned in any period in order for an individual to accrue state pension benefits.

MINIMUM CONTRIBUTIONS Contributions payable to an appropriate scheme by NICO in respect of a member who has elected to contract out. The contributions consist of the **age-related rebate** and, where payment is to an APPS or APPSHP, basic rate tax relief on the employee's share of the rebate.

Contracting out on a money purchase basis is being abolished from 6 April 2012. There will be transitional arrangements for minimum contributions.

MINIMUM INCOME REQUIREMENT (MIR) The level of secure lifetime income that is required to qualify for **flexible drawdown**. The intention is that individuals must demonstrate a sufficient level of income to prevent them exhausting their savings and falling back on the state. Only certain sources of income – such as **annuities**, **scheme pensions** and state pensions – count towards the MIR. The Treasury will review this limit at least every five years.

MINIMUM PAYMENTS The minimum amount which an employer must pay into a contracted-out money purchase scheme. This minimum amount consists of the flat-rate rebate of NI contributions in respect of employees who are **contracted out**.

Contracting out on a money purchase basis is being abolished from 6 April 2012.

MONEY PURCHASE ARRANGEMENT Under FA 2004, this is an **arrangement** under which the member is entitled to money purchase benefits. A cash balance arrangement is one type of money purchase arrangement.

MONEY PURCHASE SCHEME A **DC scheme** where the benefit is provided from contributions to the scheme, increased by the amount of investment return on those contributions.

NATIONAL EMPLOYMENT SAVINGS TRUST (NEST) A multi-employer **DC scheme**, established by the government, which will be used by some employers to meet the **automatic enrolment** requirement.

NET PAY ARRANGEMENT The procedure whereby contributions to an **occupational pension scheme** are deducted from the member's pay before tax is calculated under PAYE, giving immediate tax relief at the highest applicable rate.

NON-ELIGIBLE JOBHOLDER A **jobholder** who is not an **eligible jobholder**. A non-eligible jobholder is not eligible for **auto-enrolment** but can opt in, in which case the employer will need to contribute in the same way as for eligible jobholders.

NORMAL MINIMUM PENSION AGE   The earliest age, currently 55, at which a member is allowed to draw benefits from a **registered pension scheme**, other than in ill health. Prior to 6 April 2010 normal minimum pension age was 50. There are transitional provisions allowing members to protect existing rights at **A Day** to receive their benefits from an earlier age.

NORMAL PENSION AGE (NPA)

(1) Commonly the age by reference to which the **normal pension date** is determined.

(2) The statutory definition (relevant for **preservation** and **contracting-out** purposes) is generally the earliest age at which a member is entitled to receive benefits (other than **GMP**) on his/her retirement from employment to which the scheme relates, ignoring any special provisions as to early retirement on grounds of ill health or otherwise (section 180 PSA 1993). This is commonly interpreted to mean the earliest age at which a member has the right to take benefits without reduction.

This may be different from definition (1) above or **normal retirement age**.

NORMAL PENSION DATE (NPD)   The date at which a member of a pension scheme normally becomes entitled to receive his/her retirement benefits.

NORMAL RETIREMENT AGE (NRA)

(1) For employment purposes the age at which the employees holding a particular position normally retire from service.

This is often (but not always) the same as **normal pension age** *or definition (2) below.*

(2) The age of a member of an **occupational pension scheme** at the **normal retirement date** as specified in the scheme rules.

NORMAL RETIREMENT DATE (NRD)   The date (usually the date of reaching a particular age) specified in the rules of an **occupational pension scheme** at which a member would normally retire.

NOTIFIABLE EVENTS   Certain specified events to be automatically notified to the **Pensions Regulator** under section 69 of PA 2004.

OCCUPATIONAL PENSION SCHEME   A scheme organised by an employer or on behalf of a group of employers to provide pensions and/or other benefits for or in respect of one or more employees on leaving service or on death or on retirement. An occupational pension scheme can be registered with the **Pensions Regulator** as a **stakeholder pension scheme** if the necessary conditions are met.

The statutory definitions are in section 1 PSA 1993 and section 150 FA 2004.

OPEN MARKET OPTION The option to apply the proceeds of an insurance or investment contract to buy an **annuity** at a current market rate from the same or another insurance company.

OVERSEAS PENSION SCHEME A pension scheme established outside the UK for local residents of that country or employees of an international organisation, which is subject to local pension scheme and taxation regulations.

PARTICIPATING EMPLOYER An employer, some or all of whose employees have the right to become members of an **occupational pension scheme**.

Usually applied where more than one employer participates in a single scheme.

PAYMENT SCHEDULE A schedule, required under section 87 PA 1995 for **money purchase occupational pension schemes**, specifying contribution rates to be paid and the due dates for such payments.

PENSION COMMENCEMENT LUMP SUM Under FA 2004, the term for the tax-free cash sum that may be paid to a member on taking pension benefits.

PENSION CREDIT

(1) The amount of benefit rights that an ex-spouse of a scheme member becomes entitled to following a **pension sharing order**.

(2) An income-related (means-tested) benefit that boosts a pensioner's state pension to ensure they have a minimum level of income.

PENSION DEBIT The amount of benefit rights given up by a scheme member when a **pension sharing order** is made in respect of that member.

PENSION GUARANTEE An arrangement whereby, on the early death of a pensioner, the pension scheme pays a further sum or sums to meet a guaranteed total.

This total may be established by relation to, for instance, a multiple of the annual rate of pension or the accumulated contributions of the late member.

PENSION INCREASE   An increase to a pension in payment.

> *Such an increase may arise as a result of* **escalation** *or* **indexation** *or may be a* **discretionary increase**.

PENSION INPUT AMOUNT   The amount of contributions paid and increases in value of a member's benefits for **annual allowance** purposes.

PENSION INPUT PERIOD   A period of no more than 12 months over which the **pension input amount** for an **arrangement** is measured.

PENSION PROTECTION FUND (PPF)   A fund set up under PA 2004 to provide benefits to members of **DB schemes** that **wind up** due to the employer's insolvency with insufficient assets to pay benefits.

PENSION SCHEMES REGISTRY   The register of **occupational pension schemes** and **personal pension schemes**, maintained by the **Pensions Regulator**.

> *The registry enables members to trace schemes with which they have lost touch and collects the* **levy**.

PENSION SHARING ORDER   An order made in accordance with the provisions of Chapter I of Part IV of WR&PA 1999 which make provision for the pension rights of a scheme member to be split on divorce.

PENSION TAX RELIEF AT SOURCE   The procedure whereby member contributions are paid net of basic rate tax and the scheme **administrator** claims the tax from HMRC. Any higher rate tax is claimed under self assessment.

PENSIONABLE SERVICE   The period of service which is taken into account in calculating benefits.

> *PSA 1993 gives the term a statutory definition for the purpose of the* **preservation**, **revaluation** *and* **transfer payment** *requirements of the Act. PA 1995 gives a further statutory definition.*

PENSIONS OMBUDSMAN   The Pensions Ombudsman deals with disputes about entitlement and complaints of maladministration from members of **occupational pension schemes** and **personal pension schemes**. The Ombudsman's role also includes investigating complaints or disputes between **trustees** of occupational pension schemes and employers, and between trustees of different occupational pension schemes or between trustees of the same scheme.

PENSIONS REGULATOR, THE (The Regulator, TPR)   An independent body set up under PA 2004 to regulate **occupational pension schemes** from 6 April 2005. Its role is to protect members of occupational pension schemes, to promote good administration of schemes, and to reduce the risk of situations arising 'that may give rise to a claim on the **Pension Protection Fund**'. It has the power to impose orders and fines on **trustees** and employers.

PERSONAL LIFETIME ALLOWANCE   The **lifetime allowance** applicable to individuals who have registered for **primary protection**. This would be higher than the **standard lifetime allowance** and is indexed in line with changes in the standard lifetime allowance.

See also **enhanced lifetime allowance**.

PERSONAL PENSION SCHEME   A scheme provided by an insurance company (or another financial institution) to enable individuals to save for a private retirement income.

A personal pension scheme can be registered with the **Pensions Regulator** as a **stakeholder pension scheme** if the necessary conditions are met.

The statutory definition is in section 1 PSA 1993.

PRESERVATION   The granting by a scheme of **preserved benefits** to a member leaving **pensionable service** before **normal pension age** under an **occupational pension scheme**, in particular in accordance with minimum requirements specified by PSA 1993.

PRESERVED BENEFITS   Benefits arising on an individual ceasing to be an **active member** of an **occupational pension scheme**, payable at a later date.

PRIMARY PROTECTION   A mechanism by which individuals could register pre-**A Day** rights of more than £1.5m and obtain an increased **personal lifetime allowance**.

PRINCIPAL EMPLOYER   Commonly used in scheme documentation for the particular **participating employer** in which is vested special powers or duties in relation to such matters as the appointment of the **trustees**, amendments and **winding up**. Usually this will be the employer which established the scheme or its successor in business.

PRIORITY RULE   The provisions contained within the scheme documentation setting out the order of precedence of liabilities to be followed if the scheme is wound up.

Section 73 PA 1995 introduced an overriding statutory order of priorities, which was amended by PA 2004 with effect from 6 April 2005.

PROJECTED UNIT METHOD   A funding method in which the actuarial liability makes allowance for projected earnings. The contribution rate is that necessary to cover the cost of all benefits which will accrue in the control period following the valuation date by reference to earnings projected to the dates on which the benefits become payable.

Also known as the projected unit credit method.

PROSPECTIVE MEMBER   An individual, not currently a member of the pension scheme of his/her employer, who is either entitled to join or will become eligible to join in the future by virtue of continuing in employment with the employer.

PROTECTED RIGHTS   The benefits from a scheme **contracted out** on a money purchase basis deriving from at least the **minimum contributions** or **minimum payments**, which are provided in a specified form as a necessary condition of contracting out.

*Protected rights will be abolished from 6 April 2012, when contracting out of **S2P** on a money purchase basis is abolished.*

PUBLIC SECTOR PENSION SCHEME   An **occupational pension scheme** for employees of central or local government, a nationalised industry or other statutory body.

PUBLIC SECTOR TRANSFER ARRANGEMENTS   The arrangements of the **transfer club** to which certain schemes, mainly in the public sector, belong.

PURCHASED LIFE ANNUITY   An **annuity** purchased privately by an individual. In accordance with section 717 of Income Tax (Trading and Other Income) Act 2005, instalments of the annuity are subject to tax in part only.

QUALIFYING EARNINGS   The band of gross annual earnings between limits set each year on which contributions for the purposes of **automatic enrolment** are calculated. Qualifying earnings include a worker's salary, wages, overtime, bonuses and commission, as well as statutory sick, maternity, paternity and adoption pay.

Information on the current limits can be found in Section 9. The automatic enrolment legislation assumes that the lower limit for qualifying earnings is below the income tax personal allowance.

QUALIFYING PENSION SCHEME   For the purposes of **automatic enrolment** this means any **occupational** or **personal pension scheme** sponsored by the employer that meets statutory minimum criteria.

QUALIFYING RECOGNISED OVERSEAS PENSION SCHEME   A **recognised overseas pension scheme** where the scheme manager has advised HMRC of its status and undertaken to provide HMRC with certain information.

QUALIFYING SERVICE   The term defined in section 71(7) PSA 1993 denoting the service to be taken into account to entitle the member to short service benefit. The current condition is for at least two years' qualifying service.

RECOGNISED OVERSEAS PENSION SCHEME   Under FA 2004, an **overseas pension scheme** which is established and recognised in a prescribed country and satisfies all prescribed requirements.

RECOGNISED TRANSFER   Under FA 2004, a transfer representing a member's **accrued rights** under a **registered pension scheme** to another registered pension scheme (or, in certain circumstances, to an insurance company) or a **qualifying recognised overseas pension scheme**.

RECOVERY PLAN   If an **actuarial valuation** shows that the **statutory funding objective** is not met, the **trustees** will have to prepare a 'recovery plan' setting out the steps to be taken (and over what period) to make up the shortfall.

REFERENCE SCHEME TEST   The comparison of the benefits provided by a COSR with those under the reference scheme to ensure that they are at least equal, as required under section 12B PSA 1993.

The **scheme actuary** *must certify that the scheme complies with the reference scheme test.*

REGISTERED PENSION SCHEME   A pension scheme is a registered pension scheme at any time when, either through having applied for registration and having been registered by HMRC, or through acquiring registered status by virtue of being an approved scheme on 5 April 2006, it is registered under Chapter 2 of Part 4 of FA 2004.

RESTRICTED EMPLOYER-RELATED INVESTMENT   The restriction under section 40 PA 1995 and investment regulations of employer-related investment to 5% of scheme assets.

RETIREMENT ANNUITY   An **annuity** contract between an insurance company or friendly society and a self-employed individual or a person not in pensionable employment, which was established before 1 July 1988.

REVALUATION
(1)   Application, particularly to **preserved benefits**, of **indexation** or **escalation** or the awarding of **discretionary increases**. PSA 1993 imposes a minimum level of revaluation in the calculation of **GMP** and of preserved benefits other than GMP.
(2)   An accounting term for the revision of the carrying value of an asset, usually having regard to its market value.

SALARY SACRIFICE An agreement between the employer and employee whereby the employee forgoes part of his/her future earnings in return for a corresponding contribution by the employer to a pension scheme.

This is not the same as an **AVC**.

SCHEDULE OF CONTRIBUTIONS A schedule specifying the contribution rates and payment dates (normally) agreed between the employer and the **trustees** and certified by the **scheme actuary** as being adequate to satisfy the **statutory funding objective**.

Required for most **DB schemes** *under section 227 PA 2004.*

SCHEME ACTUARY The named actuary appointed by the **trustees** or managers of an **occupational pension scheme** under section 47 PA 1995.

SCHEME ADMINISTRATION MEMBER PAYMENT Under FA 2004, payments made by a **registered pension scheme** to a member, or in respect of a member, for the purposes of administration or management of the scheme.

SCHEME AUDITOR The auditor appointed by the **trustees** or managers of an **occupational pension scheme** under section 47 PA 1995.

SCHEME PAYS Where a member's pension savings exceed the **annual allowance** for the tax year and the **annual allowance charge** is more than £2,000, the scheme can be obliged to pay all or part of the charge on the member's behalf and reduce the member's benefit entitlement accordingly.

SCHEME PENSION Under FA 2004, a pension entitlement provided to a member of a **registered pension scheme**, which is an absolute right to a lifetime pension payable by the scheme.

SCHEME RETURN A form submitted to the **Pensions Regulator** by schemes containing information that it will use to make sure the information it holds on the register of pension schemes is accurate, calculate **levies** due from pension schemes and regulate pension schemes. The information collected is also used by the **Pension Protection Fund**. Schemes with five or more members must complete an annual scheme return.

SECONDED EMPLOYEE For the purposes of the legislation on **cross border schemes**, this is an employee who is sent, by a UK employer, to work overseas for a limited period in another EU member state, is still working under the control of the UK employer and, at the end of that period, intends to return to resume work for that employer in the UK or to retire.

SECTION 9(2B) RIGHTS Rights to benefits (other than benefits from AVCs) under an **occupational pension scheme** which is **contracted out** on a salary-related basis by virtue of section 9(2B) PSA 1993 and which are attributable to contracted-out employment after 5 April 1997.

Section 9(2B) rights are benefits payable under the scheme, not just the minimum level of benefits required under the **reference scheme test***.*

SECTION 32 POLICY Used widely to describe an insurance policy used for **buy-out** purposes.

This term came into use as a result of section 32 FA 1981, which gave prominence to the possibility of effecting such policies.

SECTION 32A POLICY A policy which under section 32A PSA 1993 enables **protected rights** to be bought out on the **winding-up** of a **contracted-out money purchase scheme**.

SECTION 67 Section 67 of PA 1995 requires that **trustees** obtain members' consents, or a certificate from an actuary, before making any modification to an **occupational pension scheme** which would or might affect members' entitlements or **accrued rights** in respect of service before the modification.

SECTION 75 DEBT A debt due to a pension scheme under PA 1995 from a sponsoring employer if that employer becomes insolvent, or the scheme starts to **wind up**, when the scheme is underfunded.

SECTION 143 VALUATION A written valuation of a scheme's assets and liabilities for the purposes of enabling the **Pension Protection Fund** to determine whether it must assume responsibility for a scheme.

SECTION 148 ORDERS Orders issued each year in accordance with section 148 Social Security Administration Act 1992 specifying the rates of increase to be applied to the earnings factors on which **S2P** and **GMP**s are based.

This **revaluation** *is based on the increase in national average earnings. Formerly known as section 21 orders.*

SECTION 179 VALUATION A written valuation of a scheme's assets and liabilities, prepared and signed by the **scheme actuary**, for the purposes of enabling **Pension Protection Fund levies** to be calculated.

SELF-ADMINISTERED SCHEME An **occupational pension scheme** where the assets are invested, other than wholly by payment of insurance premiums, by the **trustees**, an in-house investment manager or an external investment manager.

...continued

Although on the face of it the term self-administered should refer to the method of administering contributions and benefits, in practice the term has become solely related to the way in which the investments are managed.

SELF INVESTMENT   The investment of the assets of an **occupational pension scheme** in employer-related investments.

A 5% limit is imposed on employer-related investments by PA 1995 (with certain exemptions).

SERIOUS ILL HEALTH COMMUTATION   Full **commutation** of benefits if a member's life expectancy is less than 12 months.

SHORT SERVICE REFUND LUMP SUM   A refund of contributions available to employees who have stopped accruing benefits under the scheme and have less than two years' **qualifying service**.

SHORT-TERM ANNUITY   Under FA 2004, an **annuity** contract purchased from a member's drawdown pension fund held under a **money purchase arrangement** that provides that member with pension income for a term of no more than five years.

SOCIALLY RESPONSIBLE INVESTMENT (SRI)   Investment strategies or restrictions that take account of the social, environmental or other impacts that a company's activities can have on individuals and the environment.

*Pension funds are required to disclose in their **Statement of Investment Principles** the extent to which they take these factors into account.*

SPECIAL ANNUAL ALLOWANCE (SAA)   The maximum amount of pension savings that could be built up in the 2009/10 and 2010/11 tax years before liability to a **special annual allowance charge**.

SPECIAL ANNUAL ALLOWANCE CHARGE (SAAC)   The tax charge levied on members with income exceeding £130,000 (£150,000 prior to 9 December 2009) in 2009/10 or 2010/11 only and **pension input** exceeding the **special annual allowance** in the relevant year.

STAGING   The process of introducing **automatic enrolment** at monthly stages on allocated dates between 2012 and 2016.

STAGING DATE   This is the first date from which an employer must comply with its **automatic enrolment** duties. It will depend on the employer's size (as measured by the number in its PAYE scheme on 1 April 2012). An employer will have a single staging date; where it operates multiple PAYE schemes, the staging date will be determined by the largest one.

STAKEHOLDER PENSION SCHEME A **DC scheme** able to accept contributions from 6 April 2001. A scheme, which in addition to being registered with HMRC, must satisfy the CAT standards necessary to be registered with the **Pensions Regulator** as a stakeholder scheme.

Employers who do not come within one of the employer exemptions must offer their relevant employees access to a stakeholder pension scheme.

STANDARD LIFETIME ALLOWANCE The maximum amount of tax relievable pension savings that can be built up by an individual who has not registered for **primary protection** or **enhanced protection**.

STATE EARNINGS-RELATED PENSION SCHEME (SERPS)

The additional pension provisions of the state pension scheme. This was replaced by the **State Second Pension (S2P)** from 6 April 2002.

STATE PENSIONABLE AGE (SPA) The age from which pensions are normally payable by the state pension scheme as defined in Schedule 4 PA 1995.

STATE SECOND PENSION (S2P) The state pension scheme introduced with effect from 6 April 2002 to replace **SERPS** and to enhance the **basic pension**.

STATEMENT OF FUNDING PRINCIPLES Statement by the **trustees** setting out their policy for securing that the **statutory funding objective** is met and recording the decisions as to the basis for calculating the scheme's **technical provisions** and the period within which any shortfall is to be remedied.

STATEMENT OF INVESTMENT PRINCIPLES (SIP) A written statement of principles governing decisions about investment for an **occupational pension scheme**, which **trustees** are required to prepare and maintain. Trustees must have regard to advice from a suitably qualified person and consult with the employer.

STATEMENT OF RECOMMENDED PRACTICE (SORP) Guidance on best accounting practice for the presentation of financial information prepared by the particular industry to which the SORP relates.

STATEMENT OF TOTAL RECOGNISED GAINS AND LOSSES (STRGL)
One of the four primary statements in the company financial statements, together with the profit and loss account, balance sheet and statement of cash flows. The statement shows the components as well as the total of realised gains and losses, where these have been earned but not recognised. Where a gain is both earned and recognised it will be disclosed in the profit and loss account.

...continued

Under **FRS 17**, **actuarial gains and losses** are disclosed in the STRGL and not in the profit and loss account.

STATUTORY EMPLOYER   In a **DB scheme**, the employer legally responsible for meeting the **statutory funding objective**, paying any **section 75 debt** and triggering entry to the **PPF**.

STATUTORY FUNDING OBJECTIVE   The requirement that a **DB scheme** 'must have sufficient and appropriate assets to cover its **technical provisions**'.

SUMMARY FUNDING STATEMENT   A summary of the scheme's funding position. It must be issued to all scheme members and **beneficiaries** (annually except for small schemes) and is their primary source of information on funding matters. Its content is prescribed by regulations.

TECHNICAL PROVISIONS   Under the scheme funding provisions of PA 2004, the amount required on an actuarial calculation to make provision for the scheme's liabilities.

TOTAL PENSION INPUT AMOUNT   The aggregate of the **pension input amounts** for a period in respect of each **arrangement** relating to an individual under **registered pension schemes** of which the individual is a member.

TRANSFER CLUB   A group of employers and **occupational pension schemes** which has agreed to a common basis of **transfer payments**

TRANSFER PAYMENT   A payment made from a pension scheme to another pension scheme, or to purchase a **buy-out** policy, in lieu of benefits which have accrued to the member or members concerned to enable the receiving arrangement to provide alternative benefits.

The transfer payment may be made in accordance with the scheme rules or in exercise of a member's statutory rights under PSA 1993. See also **cash equivalent**

TRIVIAL PENSION   A pension which is so small that it can be fully exchanged for cash (**commuted**).

TRUST   A legal concept whereby property is held by one or more persons (the **trustees**) for the benefit of others (the **beneficiaries** for the purposes specified by the trust instrument. The trustees may also be beneficiaries.

TRUST DEED   A legal document, executed in the form of a deed, which establishes, regulates or amends a **trust**.

TRUSTEE   An individual or company appointed to carry out the purposes of a **trust** in accordance with the provisions of the **trust deed** (or other documents by which a trust is created and governed) and general principles of trust law.

TRUSTEE REPORT   A report by the **trustees** describing various aspects of an **occupational pension scheme**. It may form part of the **annual report**.

UPPER ACCRUAL POINT (UAP)   The maximum amount of earnings on which **S2P** and **contracted-out rebates** are based. It replaced the **UEL** for this purpose from 6 April 2009.

UPPER BAND EARNINGS   Earnings between the **lower earnings limit** and the **upper accrual point**.

UPPER EARNINGS LIMIT (UEL)   The upper limit to earnings on which full-rate NI contributions are payable by employees. NI contributions are payable by employees at a lower rate on earnings above this limit.

VESTED RIGHTS

(a)   For **active members**, benefits to which they would unconditionally be entitled on leaving the scheme

(b)   for **deferred pensioners**, their **preserved benefits**, *and*

(c)   for pensioners, pensions to which they are entitled including where appropriate the related benefits for spouses or other **dependants**.

WHISTLE-BLOWING   The statutory duty imposed on **trustees**, employers, **administrators** and advisers by section 70 PA 2004 to advise the **Pensions Regulator** as soon as practicable in writing if they have reasonable cause to believe there is a material problem with an **occupational pension scheme**.

WINDING UP   The process of terminating an **occupational pension scheme** (or less commonly a **personal pension scheme**), usually by applying the assets to the purchase of immediate **annuities** and deferred annuities for the **beneficiaries**, or by transferring the assets and liabilities to another pension scheme, in accordance with the scheme documentation or statute (section 74 PA 1995).

WITH-PROFITS POLICY   An insurance policy under which a share of the surpluses disclosed by **actuarial valuations** of the insurance company's life and pensions business is payable in addition to the guaranteed benefits or in reduction of future premiums.

Many of the definitions used in this Glossary of Terms originate from *Pensions Terminology – A Glossary for Pension Schemes, Revised and Updated, Seventh Edition 2007*, published by The Pensions Management Institute, whose kind permission to reproduce here is gratefully acknowledged. The Eighth Edition of *Pensions Terminology* is now available from the PMI.

COMPOUND INTEREST TABLES

How to use the compound interest tables to generate additional factors:

Present value of a payment of one unit due in n years' time	$$v^n = \frac{1}{(1+i)^n}$$
Present value of an annuity of one unit per annum payable annually in arrears for n years	$$a_{\overline{n}\rceil} = \frac{1-v^n}{i}$$
Present value of an annuity of one unit per annum payable annually in advance for n years	$$\ddot{a}_{\overline{n}\rceil} = \frac{1-v^n}{d}$$
Present value of an annuity of one unit per annum payable continuously for n years	$$\bar{a}_{\overline{n}\rceil} = \frac{1-v^n}{\delta}$$
Present value of an annuity of one unit per annum payable in two half-yearly instalments in arrears for n years	$$a_{\overline{n}\rceil}^{(2)} = \frac{i}{i^{(2)}}\, a_{\overline{n}\rceil}$$
Present value of an annuity of one unit per annum payable in four quarterly instalments in arrears for n years	$$a_{\overline{n}\rceil}^{(4)} = \frac{i}{i^{(4)}}\, a_{\overline{n}\rceil}$$
Present value of an annuity of one unit per annum payable in twelve monthly instalments in arrears for n years	$$a_{\overline{n}\rceil}^{(12)} = \frac{i}{i^{(12)}}\, a_{\overline{n}\rceil}$$
Accumulated value after n years of an annuity of one unit payable annually in arrears	$$s_{\overline{n}\rceil} = \frac{(1+i)^n - 1}{i}$$

ccumulated value after n years of a single unit payment $[(1+i)^n]$

n	i=1%	i=2%	i=3%	i=4%	i=5%
1	1.010000	1.020000	1.030000	1.040000	1.050000
2	1.020100	1.040400	1.060900	1.081600	1.102500
3	1.030301	1.061208	1.092727	1.124864	1.157625
4	1.040604	1.082432	1.125509	1.169859	1.215506
5	1.051010	1.104081	1.159274	1.216653	1.276282
6	1.061520	1.126162	1.194052	1.265319	1.340096
7	1.072135	1.148686	1.229874	1.315932	1.407100
8	1.082857	1.171659	1.266770	1.368569	1.477455
9	1.093685	1.195093	1.304773	1.423312	1.551328
10	1.104622	1.218994	1.343916	1.480244	1.628895
11	1.115668	1.243374	1.384234	1.539454	1.710339
12	1.126825	1.268242	1.425761	1.601032	1.795856
13	1.138093	1.293607	1.468534	1.665074	1.885649
14	1.149474	1.319479	1.512590	1.731676	1.979932
15	1.160969	1.345868	1.557967	1.800944	2.078928
16	1.172579	1.372786	1.604706	1.872981	2.182875
17	1.184304	1.400241	1.652848	1.947900	2.292018
18	1.196147	1.428246	1.702433	2.025817	2.406619
19	1.208100	1.456811	1.753506	2.106849	2.526950
20	1.220190	1.485947	1.806111	2.191123	2.653298
21	1.232392	1.515666	1.860295	2.278768	2.785963
22	1.244716	1.545980	1.916103	2.369919	2.925261
23	1.257163	1.576899	1.973587	2.464716	3.071524
24	1.269735	1.608437	2.032794	2.563304	3.225100
25	1.282432	1.640606	2.093778	2.665836	3.386355
26	1.295256	1.673418	2.156591	2.772470	3.555673
27	1.308209	1.706886	2.221289	2.883369	3.733456
28	1.321291	1.741024	2.287928	2.998703	3.920129
29	1.334504	1.775845	2.356566	3.118651	4.116136
30	1.347849	1.811362	2.427262	3.243398	4.321942
31	1.361327	1.847589	2.500080	3.373133	4.538039
32	1.374941	1.884541	2.575083	3.508059	4.764941
33	1.388690	1.922231	2.652335	3.648381	5.003189
34	1.402577	1.960676	2.731905	3.794316	5.253348
35	1.416603	1.999890	2.813862	3.946089	5.516015
36	1.430769	2.039887	2.898278	4.103933	5.791816
37	1.445076	2.080685	2.985227	4.268090	6.081497
38	1.459527	2.122299	3.074783	4.438813	6.385477
39	1.474123	2.164745	3.167027	4.616366	6.704751
40	1.488864	2.208040	3.262038	4.801021	7.039989

	i=1%	i=2%	i=3%	i=4%	i=5%
d	0.009901	0.019608	0.029126	0.038462	0.047619
$i^{(2)}$	0.009975	0.019901	0.029778	0.039608	0.049390
$i^{(4)}$	0.009963	0.019852	0.029668	0.039414	0.049089
$i^{(12)}$	0.009954	0.019819	0.029595	0.039285	0.048889
δ	0.009950	0.019803	0.029559	0.039221	0.048790

te: For GMP fixed rate revaluation factors *see page 44.*

Accumulated value after n years of a single unit payment $[(1+i)^n]$

n	i=6%	i=7%	i=8%	i=9%	i=10%
1	1.060000	1.070000	1.080000	1.090000	1.100000
2	1.123600	1.144900	1.166400	1.188100	1.210000
3	1.191016	1.225043	1.259712	1.295029	1.331000
4	1.262477	1.310796	1.360489	1.411582	1.464100
5	1.338226	1.402552	1.469328	1.538624	1.610510
6	1.418519	1.500730	1.586874	1.677100	1.771561
7	1.503630	1.605781	1.713824	1.828039	1.948717
8	1.593848	1.718186	1.850930	1.992563	2.143589
9	1.689479	1.838459	1.999005	2.171893	2.357948
10	1.790848	1.967151	2.158925	2.367364	2.593742
11	1.898299	2.104852	2.331639	2.580426	2.853117
12	2.012196	2.252192	2.518170	2.812665	3.138428
13	2.132928	2.409845	2.719624	3.065805	3.452271
14	2.260904	2.578534	2.937194	3.341727	3.797498
15	2.396558	2.759032	3.172169	3.642482	4.177248
16	2.540352	2.952164	3.425943	3.970306	4.594973
17	2.692773	3.158815	3.700018	4.327633	5.054470
18	2.854339	3.379932	3.996019	4.717120	5.559917
19	3.025660	3.616528	4.315701	5.141661	6.115909
20	3.207135	3.869684	4.660957	5.604411	6.727500
21	3.399564	4.140562	5.033834	6.108808	7.400250
22	3.603537	4.430402	5.436540	6.658600	8.140275
23	3.819750	4.740530	5.871464	7.257874	8.954302
24	4.048935	5.072367	6.341181	7.911083	9.849733
25	4.291871	5.427433	6.848475	8.623081	10.834706
26	4.549383	5.807353	7.396353	9.399158	11.918177
27	4.822346	6.213868	7.988061	10.245082	13.109994
28	5.111687	6.648838	8.627106	11.167140	14.420994
29	5.418388	7.114257	9.317275	12.172182	15.863093
30	5.743491	7.612255	10.062657	13.267678	17.449402
31	6.088101	8.145113	10.867669	14.461770	19.194342
32	6.453387	8.715271	11.737083	15.763329	21.113777
33	6.840550	9.325340	12.676050	17.182028	23.225154
34	7.251025	9.978114	13.690134	18.728411	25.547670
35	7.686087	10.676581	14.785344	20.413968	28.102437
36	8.147252	11.423942	15.968172	22.251225	30.912681
37	8.636087	12.223618	17.245626	24.253835	34.003949
38	9.154252	13.079271	18.625276	26.436680	37.404343
39	9.703507	13.994820	20.115298	28.815982	41.144778
40	10.285718	14.974458	21.724521	31.409420	45.259256

	i=6%	i=7%	i=8%	i=9%	i=10%
d	0.056604	0.065421	0.074074	0.082569	0.090909
$i^{(2)}$	0.059126	0.068816	0.078461	0.088061	0.097618
$i^{(4)}$	0.058695	0.068234	0.077706	0.087113	0.096455
$i^{(12)}$	0.058411	0.067850	0.077208	0.086488	0.095690
δ	0.058269	0.067659	0.076961	0.086178	0.095310

Note: For GMP fixed rate revaluation factors *see page 44.*

ANNUITY FACTORS

MALE LIFE ANNUITIES ON S1PMA (Year of Use=2011) TABLE

With future improvements in life expectancy based on the CMI_2011 Core Projections for males with a long-term rate of improvement of 1.25% p.a.

Exact age:	50	55	60	65	70	75
Interest						
0%	36.797	31.787	26.946	22.325	17.725	13.593
1%	30.311	26.792	23.228	19.666	15.955	12.484
2%	25.406	22.901	20.245	17.472	14.453	11.518
3%	21.638	19.830	17.826	15.645	13.169	10.672
4%	18.698	17.373	15.844	14.112	12.065	9.927
5%	16.369	15.385	14.204	12.814	11.109	9.268
6%	14.498	13.757	12.834	11.708	10.277	8.682
7%	12.975	12.409	11.679	10.759	9.549	8.159
8%	11.719	11.281	10.698	9.938	8.908	7.691
9%	10.672	10.328	9.856	9.224	8.341	7.270
10%	9.789	9.515	9.130	8.599	7.837	6.890

Note: The columns represent the present value of a life annuity of one unit per year payable continuously to a male from the exact age given subject to the mortality experience of the S1PMA table, adjusted for use in 2011, allowing for future improvements in life expectancy based on the CMI_2011 Core Projections for males with a long-term rate of improvement of 1.25% p.a. and valued at the rates of interest shown.

FEMALE LIFE ANNUITIES ON S1PFA (Year of Use=2011) TABLE

With future improvements in life expectancy based on the CMI_2011 Core Projections for females with a long-term rate of improvement of 1.25% p.a.

Exact age:	50	55	60	65	70	75
Interest						
0%	39.102	34.215	29.388	24.558	19.792	15.330
1%	31.876	28.545	25.084	21.441	17.668	13.978
2%	26.479	24.180	21.671	18.894	15.882	12.809
3%	22.380	20.772	18.933	16.795	14.370	11.793
4%	19.215	18.076	16.712	15.050	13.081	10.905
5%	16.732	15.914	14.891	13.586	11.974	10.126
6%	14.755	14.160	13.384	12.348	11.018	9.439
7%	13.157	12.718	12.123	11.294	10.188	8.830
8%	11.849	11.521	11.059	10.389	9.462	8.287
9%	10.765	10.516	10.154	9.607	8.825	7.803
10%	9.855	9.664	9.377	8.926	8.261	7.368

Note: The columns represent the present value of a life annuity of one unit per year payable continuously to a female from the exact age given subject to the mortality experience of the S1PFA table, adjusted for use in 2011, allowing for future improvements in life expectancy based on the CMI_2011 Core Projections for females with a long-term rate of improvement of 1.25% p.a. and valued at the rates of interest shown.

Accounting Standards Board	*www.frc.org.uk/asb*
Association of British Insurers	*www.abi.org.uk*
Association of Consulting Actuaries	*www.aca.org.uk*
Association of Member-Directed Pension Schemes	*www.ampsonline.co.uk*
Association of Pension Lawyers	*www.apl.org.uk*
Board of Actuarial Standards	*www.frc.org.uk/bas*
Companies House Executive Agency	*ww.companieshouse.gov.uk*
Chartered Insurance Institute	*www.cii.co.uk*
Department for Work and Pensions	*www.dwp.gov.uk*
DirectGov	*www.direct.gov.uk*
Equality and Human Rights Commission	*www.equalityhumanrights.com*
Faculty/Institute of Actuaries	*www.actuaries.org.uk*
Financial Ombudsman Service	*www.financial-ombudsman.org.uk*
Financial Services Authority	*www.fsa.gov.uk*
Financial Services Compensation Scheme	*www.fscs.org.uk*
Government Actuary's Department	*www.gad.gov.uk*
HM Revenue & Customs	*www.hmrc.gov.uk*
HM Treasury	*www.hm-treasury.gov.uk*
Information Commissioner's Office	*www.ico.gov.uk*
Law Society	*www.lawsociety.org.uk*
National Association of Pension Funds	*www.napf.co.uk*
National Employment Savings Trust	*www.nestpensions.org.uk*
Office for National Statistics	*www.statistics.gov.uk*
Office of Public Sector Information	*www.opsi.gov.uk*
Pension Protection Fund	*www.pensionprotectionfund.org.uk*
PPF Ombudsman	*www.ppfo.org.uk*
Pensions Management Institute	*www.pensions-pmi.org.uk*
Pensions Ombudsman	*www.pensions-ombudsman.org.uk*
Pensions Regulator	*www.thepensionsregulator.gov.uk*
Pensions Research Advisory Group	*www.prag.org.uk*
Society of Pension Consultants	*www.spc.uk.com*
TPAS The Pensions Advisory Service	*www.pensionsadvisoryservice.org.uk*